FILM NOIR AND THE SPACES OF MODERNITY

FILM NOIR AND THE SPACES OF MODERNITY

EDWARD DIMENDBERG

HARVARD UNIVERSITY PRESS

Cambridge, Massachusetts, and London, England

2004

Library of Congress Cataloging-in-Publication Data
Dimendberg, Edward.
    Film noir and the spaces of modernity / Edward Dimendberg.
      p. cm.
    Includes bibliographical references and index.
    ISBN 0-674-01314-X (alk. paper) — ISBN 0-674-01346-8 (pbk. : alk.paper)
    1. Film noir—United States—History and criticism.   I. Title.
PN1995.9.F54D56 2004
791.43'6552—dc22   2003068815

FOR LYNNE

ACKNOWLEDGMENTS

Writing this book over the course of more than a decade has incurred many debts, and it is a pleasure to recall them, even as I find myself missing those who contributed much to its gestation but are no longer alive to read it. For their friendship, intellectual exchange, and moral support, I am grateful to Alexander Alberro, Stan Allen, Nora Alter, David Anfam, Emily Apter, Douglas Armato, Clark Arnwine, Ingrid Bachmann, Richard Becherer, Matthew Biro, Iain Boyd Whyte, Michelle Bonnice, Oliver Botar, Christine Boyer, Bill Brown, Giuliana Bruno, Brian Carter, John Cartwright, Edward Casey, Beatriz Colomina, Margaret Crawford, Dana Cuff, Martina Dase, Michael Dear, Fred Dewey, Elizabeth Diller, John Divola, Wolf Donner, Stephanie Emerson, Philip Ethington, Anne Friedberg, David Frisby, John Ganim, Michael Geyer, Sylvie Gilbert, Maria Gough, Ardath Grant, Ellen Grimes, Billie Harris, K. Michael Hays, Thomas Hines, Greg Hise, Stanley Holwitz, David James, Kent Jones, William Jordy, John Kaliski, Leandro Katz, Norman Klein, Elizabeth Knoll, Sanford Kwinter, James Lastra, Sylvia Lavin, Robert Levit, Andrew Light, Akira Lippit, Dianne Macleod, Amy Mandelker, Roland Marchand, Anna McCarthy, Thomas McDonough, Detlef Mertins, Kent Minoturn, Aamir Mufti, Mary Murrell, Dietrich Neumann, Joan Ockman, Richard Peña, Marjorie Perloff, Alessandra Ponte, Leah Pressman, Eric Rentschler, Howard Rodman, Michael Rogin, Jonathan Rosenbaum, David Rothenberg, Wolfgang Schivelbusch, Ricardo Scofidio, Allan Sekula,

Robert Somol, Sally Stein, Sharon Sterne, Will Straw, Georges Teyssot, William Uricchio, Horst Wegener, Garrett White, Mark Wigley, and Lorraine Wild.

A more congenial environment for interdisciplinary scholarship than the University of Michigan is difficult for me to imagine, and my ability to complete this book was bolstered by the unflagging support and perspicacious advice of many colleagues. For shaping the Department of Germanic Languages and Literatures at Michigan into a cosmopolitan center of contemporary German Studies, its Chair, Frederick Amrine, whose friendship and support I cherish, enjoys my deepest gratitude. Caroline Constant, Robert Fishman, Daniel Herwitz, Andrei Markovits, Scott Spector, and Gaylyn Studlar shared their acute reactions to my work and helped me to refine my argument. Scott Olin prepared the book's digital images. Philip Hallman has facilitated my access to films. I also am grateful to the students in my classes at Michigan, the Southern California Institute of Architecture, and the UCLA Department of Architecture and Urban Design, who provided an early audience for my thoughts on film noir.

Many friends read this book in manuscript, and even when I did not follow their advice I always gained from it. Robert Bruegmann, Martin Jay, Ulrich Keller, Vanessa Schwartz, Edward Turk, and Anthony Vidler generously took time away from their own writing to serve as keen interlocutors. Dana Polan shared his enthusiasm for film noir and encouraged me with sharp insights from the earliest stages of my efforts. Anton Kaes, fellow traveler in the "slime of history" and a masterful integrator of film history with cultural history, challenged me and provided an invaluable roadmap. Annette Michelson published an early excerpt from the manuscript in *October*, and her rigorous investigations of film and modernity long have inspired my work and provided it with a model. Richard Sieburth urged me to listen to the sounds of film noir and to those of my own prose. At the University of California, Santa Cruz, Hayden White was a generous and supportive mentor. Richard Terdiman has long been an acute reader of my work and a true comrade. Thanks as well to Victor Burgin, David Hoy, Teresa de Lauretis, and Stephen Heath. While at Santa Cruz, I was fortunate to know and learn from Reyner Banham.

Much of this book was completed in Los Angeles, where the opportunity to meet with and interview four distinguished practitioners of film noir, John Alton, A. I. Bezzerides, Abraham Polonsky, and Malvin Wald, was a privilege. Research at the Huntington Library in San Marino was greatly facilitated by Jennifer Watts. Steve Ricci and Robert Rosen enabled me to view many rare films at the UCLA Film and Television Archive. Additional research was conducted at the UCLA Young Research Library Department of Special Collections, the Los Angeles Community Redevelopment Agency, the Los Angeles Public Library, and the Margaret Herrick Library of the Academy of Motion Picture Arts and Sciences. Ned Comstock of the USC Cinema and Television Library kindly answered my questions and provided many leads. Farther afield from Los Angeles, the Library of the Museum of Modern Art in New York, the Avery Art and Architecture Library at Columbia University, and the Harry Ransom Humanities Research Library at the University of Texas, Austin, also provided research assistance and access to materials. Terry Geesken and Mary Corliss of the Film Stills Library of the Museum of Modern Art helped me to obtain many of the book's images.

In 1999 I occupied the Craig Francis Cullinan Chair at the Rice School of Architecture, and I am grateful to Dean Lars Lerup for his friendship and for the opportunity to present early versions of several chapters in a series of public lectures. The final writing of the manuscript took place while I was a visiting scholar at the Canadian Centre for Architecture in Montreal. For their hospitality and practical assistance, I thank Phyllis Lambert, Nicholas Olsberg, Gerald Beasley, Wendy Owens, and former staff members Mélanie Dugas, Réjean Legault, Manon Gosselin, and Maria Antonella Pellizari. Invitations to present my work-in-progress at Princeton University, New York University's Deutsches Haus, Iowa State University, Cleveland State University, the University of Florida, the University of California, Riverside, and at conferences organized by the Getty Research Institute, the University of Chicago, University College Dublin, and the University of Quebec in Montreal allowed the book's ideas to develop and to obtain a public hearing. Financial support for my research was provided by a postdoctoral fellowship from the J. Paul Getty Trust, a grant from the Graham Foundation for Advanced Studies in the Fine Arts, and a residential fellowship at the University of California Humanities Research Institute. At Michigan, I received a research fellowship from the Horace H. Rackham School of Graduate Studies and a publication subvention from the Office of the Vice President for Research.

At Harvard University Press, Alison Kent first expressed interest in this book, and after her departure I found a skilled and sympathetic editor in Lindsay Waters. Thomas Wheatland and Maria Ascher expertly assisted me throughout all stages of the publication process. Thanks to Ann Hawthorne for brilliantly and sensitively editing the manuscript. Three senior film scholars helped tremendously as I neared completion. Tom Gunning and James Naremore magnanimously evaluated my project for the Press, and I appreciate their critical engagement as well as their numerous comments and suggestions from which the book has benefited. Miriam Hansen has championed this study far longer than I can remember, and her friendship and scholarly example were seldom far from my thoughts as I worked on it.

My mother, Anita Dimendberg, my sister, Deborah November, and my brother-in-law, Michael November, shared their love and encouragement while I worked on this project. So did Helen and Nathaniel Wisch. Lynne Berman has given me more than words can express. She enriches my perceptions, makes me laugh, and provides the love, companionship, and fun that make our life together the best of all possible worlds.

Excerpts from Chapter 2 were published in *Philosophy and Geography* (1997) under the title "Henri Lefebvre on Abstract Space"; earlier versions of Chapter 4 appeared in *October* (1995) under the title "The Will to Motorization: Cinema, Highways, and Modernity" and in *Wide Angle* (1998) under the title "From Berlin to Bunker Hill: Cinema, Urban Space, Late Modernity, and Film Noir in Fritz Lang's and Joseph Losey's *M*." An excerpt from Chapter 5 was published under the title "City of Fear: Defensive Dispersal and the End of Film Noir" in *Any* (1997). I thank the editors of these journals for their permission to use this material in revised form. The epigraph to the book is taken from the translation in Walter Benjamin, *The Arcades Project*, trans. Howard Eiland and Kevin McLauqulin (Cambridge, Mass.: Harvard University Press, 1999), 437.

CONTENTS

Which of us, in his moments of ambition, has not dreamed of the miracle of a poetic prose, musical, without rhythm and without rhyme, supple enough and rugged enough to adapt itself to the lyrical impulses of the soul, the undulations of reverie, the jibes of conscience? / It was, above all, out of my exploration of huge cities, out of the medley of their innumerable interrelations, that this haunting ideal was born.

—**Charles Baudelaire,** *Paris Spleen*

INTRODUCTION

I cannot remember the precise moment when film noir entered my awareness. Yet this blockage of memory may well have been an empathic response to the films I viewed and the first gesture toward writing this book. Preoccupied as film noir remains with traumas of unrecoverable time and space, the inability to dwell comfortably either in the present or the past, I also have been unable to remember and just as unable to forget, touched by a body of films that today still colors my memories and experiences of urban space. Growing up in New York City during the 1960s, I encountered residues of a vanished world, a receding horizon of the postwar culture of the 1940s and 1950s that I later would come to recognize in the films noir I viewed as a teenager.

Antiquated subway cars that remained in service with twisted straps and rattan seats battered and worn down by generations of riders. A decaying Pennsylvania Station that would soon undergo destruction and redevelopment. Harlem neighborhoods awaiting transformation by urban renewal projects. Abandoned lots and industrial sites along the Hudson River waterfront, forgotten by urban planners and time alike. And a frequently shabby metropolis, epitomized by Times Square, that seemed at odds with the modernism promoted as high culture in 1960s America. The early twentieth-century avant-garde art that I first encountered through visits as a child to the Museum of Modern Art seemed far removed from the dec-

Billboard advertisement in New York City for opening of *The Killers* (Robert Siodmak, 1946). Courtesy of Mark Hellinger Collection, Cinema and Television Library, University of Southern California.

ades that immediately preceded my birth as well as the years of student protests and the Vietnam War that I later watched on television.

In the 1990s I examined film noir's representations of postwar American cities and landmarks, places that in many cases had disappeared by the 1970s and 1980s. Yet many of them, such as the Bradbury Building in Los Angeles, were then resurfacing in the nostalgic salvage operations of postmodernism, the very cultural force that legitimated scholarship on film noir.[1] While many historians emphasized the continuity between earlier European cinema and American films noir, I was drawn to ponder the latter's incommensurability with both previous and subsequent cultural moments. How could film noir illuminate the late-modern spaces of the 1940s and 1950s to which it provided unique access? What lessons might its spatial representations offer in the present?

One clue presented itself in the writing of the German philosopher Ernst Bloch. Toward the end of the Weimar Republic he sought to understand how Hitler and the National Socialists capitalized upon the nostalgia for older cultural forms and relations of production experienced by social groups such as the peasantry. Bloch was struck by how their way of life remained largely premodern and existed as a "nonsynchronous" element among the faster-moving currents of the twentieth century.[2] He argued that "history is no entity advancing along a single line, in which capitalism for instance, as the final stage, has resolved all the previous ones; but is a *polyrhythmic and multi-spatial entity, with enough unmastered and as yet by no means revealed and resolved corners.*"[3] Bloch's understanding of the nonsynchronous as a temporal and spatial category prepares the way for comprehending film noir as an amalgam of diverse historical and cultural elements, a "polyrhythmic and multi-spatial entity," in his phrase, or a work of *bricolage* in that famously advanced by Claude Lévi-Strauss. Invoking the past while anxiously imagining the future, films noir reveal multiple spatialities, no less than multiple temporalities. Yet their older ideological remnants are scarcely the precapitalist customs and objects that Bloch discussed in the context of a German nation whose political and social conflicts would soon explode upon the world stage more vividly than any possible film.[4]

Instead, the nonsynchronous character of film noir is best apprehended as a tension between a residual American culture and urbanism of the 1920s and 1930s and its liquidation by the technological and social innovations accompanying World War II, as well as the simultaneous dissolution of this new social compact of the 1940s and 1950s by the society emerging in the 1960s, in which the simulacra and spectacles of contemporary postmodern culture are clearly visible in retrospect. Describing the industrial city of Ludwigshafen in 1928, Bloch captured a milieu that strikingly prefigures the later spatial and cultural ambience of this cinema: "Here there is the most genuine hollow space of capitalism: this dirt, this raw and dead-tired proletariat, craftily paid, craftily placed on the conveyor belt, this project-making of ice-cold masters, this profit-business without remnants of legends and clichés, this shoddy-bold cinema glamour in the sad streets. This is what it now looks like in the German soul, a proletarian-capitalist mixed reality without a mask."[5]

Viewed from the position of the modernizing postwar era, let alone the twenty-first century, the universe of film noir, with its harassed working-class protagonists, petty criminals, seedy gambling joints, ramshackle urban neighborhoods, and threatening skyscrapers, seems akin to a modern vision of purgatory. Yet like the glint of utopia Bloch discerned in Ludwigshafen by dint of its unsentimental illumination of capitalist rationality, film noir also evokes what he hopefully characterized as a "genuine hollow space of capitalism" deployed "without a mask."

It conveys a palpable fascination for a transitional period in American society whose seemingly transparent social structure—a world in which power relations could still be traced with relative ease by a morally irreproachable detective figure—would shortly vanish. Eclipsed by the dispersal of space in the suburbs and the geographic ubiquity and impersonality of the large corporation and the more opaque social and economic relations developing in its wake, the dark cities of film noir nonetheless retain a firm hold upon the contemporary imagination.

More than half a century after the term *film noir* first surfaced in France, its definition might seem obvious. According to standard histories, it consists in a body of American films—estimations of its size vary from several dozen titles to nearly five hundred—produced between 1940 and the late 1950s. French critics, unable to view American films during the Occupation, were struck in the postwar moment by the despairing mood in 1944 releases such as *Double Indemnity* (Billy Wilder) and *Murder, My Sweet* (Edward Dmytryk) and popularized the term in a series of articles published in 1946. Early examples of film noir include *The Stranger on the Third Floor* (Boris Ingster, 1940), *The Maltese Falcon* (John Huston, 1941), *Phantom Lady* (Robert Siodmak, 1944), *Detour* (Edgar G. Ulmer, 1945), *Scarlet Street* (Fritz Lang, 1946), *The Big Sleep* (Howard Hawks, 1946), and *Gilda*

(Charles Vidor, 1946), although the narrative techniques of *Citizen Kane* (Orson Welles, 1941) suggest it as a key progenitor of the cycle. Later contributions include *Out of the Past* (Jacques Tourneur, 1947), *T-Men* (Anthony Mann, 1948), *The Asphalt Jungle* (John Huston, 1950), *In a Lonely Place* (Nicholas Ray, 1950), and *The Big Combo* (Joseph H. Lewis, 1955).

The fact that only during the 1970s did Hollywood employ the notion of film noir as a marketing tag for films earlier labeled as "melodramas," "thrillers," or even "psychological chiller-dillers" is well known.[6] Similarly, the story of French critics encountering previously inaccessible Hollywood productions during the postwar years and their canonization of directors and films has become a staple of film history and subsequent film production.[7] And the formal and narrative conventions of film noir—"low-key" lighting rich in shadows, voice-over narrators, crime story narratives, violent protagonists, and femmes fatales—are today indelibly associated with the film cycle. Yet consider the following description from French film critic Nino Frank's 1946 essay "The Crime Adventure Story: A New Kind of Detective Film," a founding statement of film noir criticism:

> And so these "dark" films, these films noirs, no longer have anything in common with the ordinary run of detective movies . . . The step forward is a big one; after films like these, the characters of ordinary detective films will seem puppets. Today's spectator is sensitive to nothing more than this impression of real life, of lived experience, and—why not?—of certain disagreeable realities that do in truth exist, whose repression never served any purpose; the struggle of life is no invention of our own time.[8]

Distinguishing film noir from the older detective film, its protagonist "nothing more than a thinking machine," Frank locates a key trait of the new cinema in the sensitivity of its spectator to the "impression of real life, of lived experience [*empreinte de la vie, du 'vécu'*]." A few sentences later he comments upon the conspicuous narrator in many films noir and notes that this device "allows the narration to be fragmented and transitions to be dispensed with quickly, while making for a greater impression of lived experience."[9]

The expression "lived experience" recurs throughout Frank's essay, characterizing film spectator and film form alike. By evoking a concern with temporality and spatiality associated with the earlier vitalist philosophies of Henri Bergson, the later thought of Eugène Minkowski, and the existential phenomenology of Jean-Paul Sartre, it decisively locates film noir in the crux of the twentieth-century sociocultural transformations registered by these thinkers.[10] More than simply a quest for enhanced realism, the high cultural premium associated with greater access to lived experience alludes to the modernity of film noir.[11] Its fragmented narration remains well attuned to the violently fragmented spaces and times of the late-modern world.

Today, when every shopping mall delivers the superficial accoutrements of urban civilization and the Internet promises to decrease the significance of spatial concentration, the period from 1940 to 1959, within which the Hollywood film noir can be conveniently located, adumbrates the height of late modernity and its distinctive spatiality. The historical coincidence of film noir with the eclipse of the concentrated "centripetal" urban space in the American metropolis constitutes one key strand of this dynamic. New modalities of dispersed "centrifugal space" constitute the other.[12]

To be sure, cities have not disappeared, their tangibility and vibrant polyphony a welcome counterpoint to the immateriality of electronic communication today omnipresent in our lives. Nor has film noir faded from view; scarcely a week passes without the latest neo-noir film release or book publication trumpeting its continued vitality.[13] New studies of directors, stylistic analyses of specific films, historical surveys, canonical registers, and feminist, psychoanalytic, sociocritical, and political interpretations of films noir have appeared with regularity over the past thirty years, spurred by the growth of cinema studies as an academic discipline during the 1970s.[14]

Yet just as the postwar shopping center radically transformed urban centrality, no longer fixed in a single "Main Street" but now dispersed in many locations (some of which are not streets at all), the contemporary cult of film noir suggests a hunger for an experience of cinema noticeably absent from the current media landscape. In an age of the multiplex, big-budget special-effects extravaganzas, and the competing attractions of cyberspace, the fascination that films noir of the 1940s and 1950s still hold for cinephiles conveys a profound nostalgia. But for what object? No less, perhaps, than an experience of space and time, an "image of the city," in Kevin Lynch's phrase, rendered fragile by the passage of the twentieth century and unsatisfiable by the continued transformation of cities into centers of consumption and images of desirable "lifestyles."[15]

Nostalgia and longing for older urban forms combined with a fear of new alienating urban realities pervade film noir. The loss of public space, the homogenization of everyday life, the intensification of surveillance, and the eradication of older neighborhoods by urban renewal and redevelopment projects are seldom absent from these films. Thus, it is hardly surprising that the movement of protagonists from urban center to periphery is a pervasive spatial trope. Unlike the contemporaneous conquests of the big sky and the open frontier by characters in the film genre of the western, the protagonists in film noir appear cursed by an inability to dwell comfortably anywhere.[16]

Robert Ryan's egress from the violent metropolis into the snowy wilderness in *On Dangerous Ground* (Nicholas Ray, 1952) and Sterling Hayden's return to his Kentucky farm in *The Asphalt Jungle* (John Huston, 1950) are but two typical attempts by film noir protagonists to flee from the ravages of a disenchanted urban world. Enticing as features of the metropolis remain to many characters in these films, seldom do their narratives conclude on a hopeful note about life in the metropolis or the rural alternative. Yet such spatial representations persisted in the film cycle throughout the 1940s and 1950s. Their consistent ability to attract film spectators, confirmed by more than forty years of remakes and revivals, reflects their satisfaction of complex cultural needs.

Pervasive cinematic and spatial figures such as aerial or long-shot skyline views of the metropolis, crowd sequences filmed from ground level, postwar homecomings to the city, and escapes from the urban center underscore the ideological significance of spatiality in the film noir cycle.[17] To articulate what its films do not and could not say, the silences and unspoken desires through which their spatial meanings take shape, is to grasp their import to American culture of the 1940s and 1950s.[18] By refusing sharp distinctions between figure and ground, content and context, the analysis of spatial relations in the film noir cycle may help to redefine it as an object of inquiry and to profile features overlooked by the genre or mise-en-scène criticism through which film noir has commonly been studied.

The tradition of urban geography forcefully developed by Henri Lefebvre, especially in his book *The Production of Space*, performs a key role in this endeavor.[19] Lefebvre's understanding of layered spatialities (a striking spatialization of Ernst Bloch's notion of the nonsynchronous) and his emphasis on the predominance of abstract space in contemporary societies provide a sophisticated and nuanced theory with which to analyze the late modernity of film noir and its differences from earlier modernisms.

Cultural historians increasingly have recognized the contradictory character of the 1940s and 1950s, one in which extraordinary American prosperity and supremacy on the international stage coexisted with domestic cultural responses ranging from euphoric celebration to anxiety and fear.[20] From Abstract Expressionism to beat culture to film noir, postwar culture in the United States possessed an often somber underside that contrasts markedly with the allegedly optimistic public face of the period. Rather than an autonomous or sui generis worldview, a freefloating existential angst, some of the anxiety during this period can be understood as a cultural reaction to rapid and unprecedented changes in the built environment, whose aging centers were now displaced by an array of modern constructions.

By the end of World War II, large expanses of Dresden, Rotterdam, Warsaw, and Berlin lay in ruins, while American cities such as New York and Los Angeles possessed deteriorating infrastructures as a result of years of depression and military conflict.[21] If the challenges confronting urban planners in 1945 entailed "sweeping away the rubble of war and securing control over this spatial flux" that was the American city, the social, psychological, and cultural repercussions of this "war at home" remain impossible to underestimate.[22] From the new interstate highways, to the popularization of television, to the excision of old neighborhoods through urban renewal programs, the impact upon everyday life was profound. Perceptions of time and space, bodily rhythms, and experiences of speed, distance, and density were destroyed and remade no less palpably than the metropolitan fabric.

The anxieties and phantasms of the past continued to inhabit this new postwar American spatiality, proving less vanquished than simply relocated in the period's most representative spatial constructions: the freeway, the suburban house, the glass office tower, the public housing project, the superblock, and the shopping center.[23] The rapid popularization of these forms after 1939 suggests a fundamental break from earlier spatialities of the early twentieth century, let alone the nineteenth. While these transformations of the built environment are not without precursors, their concurrent manifestation during the span of twenty years was striking and unprecedented.

Few commentators neglect the significance of the city in films noir, generally explaining the metropolis as a transplantation from crime fiction, a visual motif, a determinant of ambience or mood, or an element of narrative causality, and seldom deviating from the explication of visible detail.[24] More rarely do they travel to the extracinematic precincts of geography, city planning, architectural theory, and urban and cultural history. Though frequently analyzed in relation to political conflicts of postwar America, film noir has often been studied in isolation from the geographic dynamics of the period. Treating the city as expression of some underlying myth, theme, or vision has tended to stifle the study of spatiality in film noir as a historical *content* as significant as its more commonly studied formal and narrative features.[25]

To recover occluded controversies and spaces, sometimes omitted from conventional histories, but often simply neglected and forgotten, in the encounter between the film noir cycle and the built environment of the United States during the period from 1939 to 1959 is a goal of this book.[26] In several instances, such as the Bunker Hill neighborhood in Los Angeles, these places and the alternate futures they once seemed to promise were physically obliterated, a spatial disfiguration that solicits comparison to the campaigns of destruction accompanying World War II. More than fifty years since the commencement of the urban renewal program associated with passage of the Federal Housing Act of 1949, its massive deployment of resources and social dislocations propose a closer affinity to the practice of war than many at the time might have allowed. Cultural historian Warren Susman understands film noir and much American postwar culture as the return of repressed violent instinctual energies during an era of peace and abundance.[27] This wise assessment provides a basis for interpreting the post-1939 built environment within the cultural dynamic of "expenditure" and loss.[28]

Arising at a moment of unprecedented architectural destruction, the representations of the built environment in the film noir cycle reintroduce forgotten fragments of the city into consciousness. Functioning akin to the fortuitous blow that allows the main character in *Street of Chance* (Jack Hively, 1942) to regain his past, cinematic representations of the city in film noir provide an *aide-mémoire* for an American culture whose spatial environment was undergoing rapid transformation. Analogous to Haussmann's nineteenth-century reconstruction of Paris that Walter Benjamin and Richard Terdiman analyze in their discussions of Baudelaire, these post-1939 mutations in the built environment of the American city also entailed a "massive disruption of traditional forms of memory" and the attendant experiences of loss and displacement that produce a sense of being in exile at home.[29]

Following the insight of Maurice Halbwachs that "individuals always use social frameworks when they remember," we might well approach film noir as a social memory bank that provides a means for the film spectator to remember disappearing urban forms.[30] As Halbwachs notes in his distinction between remembrance and general history:

> General history starts only when tradition ends and social memory is fading or breaking up. So long as remembrance continues to exist, it is useless to set it down in writing or otherwise fix it in memory. Likewise the need to write the history of a period, a society, or even a person is only aroused when the subject is already too distant in the past to allow for the testimony of those who preserve some remembrance of it.[31]

To remember, as Terdiman argues, is already "to be separated" and to occupy a state where "history becomes conceivable as the continual creation of new absences" accompanying the breakdown of organic tradition and social patterns of remembrance.[32] Here we might reflect upon the multivalence of the film noir cycle and its irreducibility to a single tendency. Its spatial representations alternately confirm and transcend the alienation and the sense of separation, the exhilaration and the sense of promise, experienced by the inhabitant of the post-1939 American city.

Reading the spatial histories of the period 1939–1959 through films, crime fictions, photographs, and documents will, I hope, enable a *frisson* of historical difference, an experience of the distance that separates earlier moments from a present suddenly revealed as merely one outcome among many contingent possibilities. "History," as Siegfried Kracauer trenchantly observed, "resembles photography in that it is, among other things, a means of alienation."[33]

To explore the relationships produced by transposing the three-dimensional lived space of the built environment to the two-dimensional viewed (and three-dimensional auditory) space of the movie screen is also integral to the study of spatiality in film noir. At once a mode of textuality and a mode of cultural representation, the film noir cycle reveals practices of representing and inhabiting space and suggests how culture itself can be understood as a mode of representational and spatial practice.[34] Whether considering the prevalence of aerial views throughout film noir or the very darkness of its images which acquire a proto-three-dimensional quality and envelop the spectator in a darkened theater, issues of spatial form and the translation between forms also demand attention.

Until recently, film noir scholarship remained trapped in a quagmire of attempts to define its object of study. In what now appear as dryly academic (if not quasi-theological) debates, scholars argued whether film noir was a genre, a tone, a mood, a style, or a moment in film history. Yet space cannot be comfortably assimilated to any of these categories and suggests both their limitations and the possibility of a new optic through which to approach film noir. In this study I refer to the film noir cycle, a locution first introduced by Raymond Borde and Etienne Chaumeton, and by which I understand a historically circumscribed group of films sharing common industrial practices, stylistic features, narrative consistencies, and spatial representations. Yet no single level of analysis can satisfactorily define film noir in its complexity, regardless of how one designates it. The reality, as James Naremore recognizes, is that "nothing links together all the things described as noir—not the theme of crime, not a cinematographic technique, not even a resistance to Aristotelian narratives or happy endings. Little wonder that no writer has been able to find the category's necessary and sufficient characteristics and that many generalizations in the critical literature are open to question."[35]

Relinquishing the search for the abiding essence of film noir yields other benefits, however. It directs attention to the negotiation between creators, shared conventions, and social practices manifested in all cultural production.[36] With few significant exceptions, cinema historians have been slow to incorporate these insights.[37] To approach film noir as process and product of such negotiations provides a strategy for reading cinema and the built environment as mutually implicated in the construction of common spatial fantasies and anxieties. It recognizes that film noir can be both a symptom and a catalyst of spatial transformations. By articulating a "space of representation," in the phrase of Lefebvre, film noir simultaneously registers and inflects the psychic and cultural manifestations of late modernity.

Although the claims that have been advanced concerning the alleged subversive relation of film noir to the norms of the classical Hollywood cinema deserve to be met with skepticism, its fundamental divergence from other American film types of the 1940s and 1950s seems incontrovertible.[38] For in an age when technicolor and widescreen traded upon considerable prestige, the black-and-white film noir, especially its B variant, occupied a marginal status, the product of a film aesthetic that would soon disappear in striking parallelism with the disappearance by the early 1960s of many earlier landmarks of urban space.[39]

A beneficiary of innovations that permitted greater location cinematography, film noir revealed spatialities also evident in other forms of postwar culture, including photography, pulp fiction, and modernist painting and sculpture.[40] As the last mass-cultural instance of the linkage between black-and-white photography and the metropolis that functioned over a century from Atget to Weegee to Gary Winogrand as a privileged vehicle for registering the vicissitudes of urban modernity, film noir needs to be grasped not simply as a body of films but as a set of representational conventions and spatial tropes, including the systematic elision of color from the representation of urban actuality.

Commentators have disputed the reception of films noir, locating audience reactions to them along a continuum ranging from benign enjoyment to intense anxiety.[41] Were spatial representations in the film noir cycle understood by spectators in the 1940s and 1950s as nostalgic representations or as cultural and social indictments? To study film noir as a repository of possible meanings and associations that circulated widely in American culture of the 1940s and 1950s is to concede that such meanings may not have been universally accessible to all its members. While this stress upon spatiality is only one possible reading, an interpretive "making meaning," in the words of David Bordwell, it remains crucial to an explanation of the modernity of the film cycle.[42]

Frequently adapted from crime stories set in the metropolis, film noir possesses a "pulp" literary infrastructure that also explains its abiding concern with the city, even when a film appears to be set in a location different from that of its fictional antecedent.[43] Writers such as Raymond Chandler, Cornell Woolrich, and W. R. Burnett endowed their fictions with an awareness of the experiential dimension of urban life whose manifestation in the film noir cycle remains palpable.

While much attention has been paid to these literary antecedents, the specifically modernist genealogy of characteristic metropolitan spatial representations in the film cycle has been slighted. Whether one thinks of location cinematography on deserted city streets, glittering illuminated skylines, or urban perspectives filmed from unusual angles, these spaces and images can be unpacked to reveal latent social anxieties and aspirations that connect film noir with cinema and the visual arts, as well as with the rapid technological changes of the twentieth century.

It is possible to watch the opening Wall Street sequence of *Force of Evil* (Abraham Polonsky, 1948) and to imagine its overhead abstracting view of pedestrians as indebted to the photographic aesthetics of László Moholy-Nagy, if not Alvin Langdon Coburn. But unlike Karl Struss's famous photographs of the Brooklyn Bridge or the diagonally composed architectural photographs of Alexander Rodchenko from the 1920s, film noir deployed representational strategies of avant-garde photography or modernist painting in the service of an aesthetic transfiguration *without* social transcendence. The metropolis portrayed in the film noir cycle seldom appears defamiliarized or re-enchanted, a space of genuinely enhanced freedom and possibility. Instead, it hyperbolically presents the contrasts and rhythms of the city (including music and sound) as elements of a highly ra-

Frame enlargement from *Force of Evil* (Abraham Polonsky, 1948).

tionalized and alienating system of exploitative drudgery permitting few possibilities of escape.

No longer romanticized as a fantasy domain of speed, dynamic machine production, new perspectives on quotidian realities, or technological precision, as in the early modernist projects of the Futurists or Le Corbusier, the post-1939 American city was rendered by many artists, social critics, and filmmakers as a coldhearted and treacherous mechanism more likely to provoke fear than awe. Recalling earlier demonizations of the city associated with nineteenth-century American or European literature, if not German expressionism, the less affirmative late-modernist representations in film noir depicted the city as a menacing environment.[44] Yet if for earlier modernists the factory and its system of mechanized production were emblematic of the new social order, for many late modernists this mechanization was now evident on the level of the entire society, now experienced as a nightmare of spatial regimentation, consumer manipulation, and corporate economic control.

After 1939 the danger increasingly addressed by cultural and intellectual practitioners as diverse as Billy Wilder and Lewis Mumford was not the moral dissolution that the metropolis could induce in its inhabitants but rather the potential loss of individual identity and the growing power of a technological society organized by new spatial forms and the mass media.[45]

Unlike the spatially segregated and classbound society presented in *Metropolis* (Fritz Lang, 1927), the late modernity in film noir is defined by the influence of consumer culture, television, and a built environment dominated by a homogenized and homogenizing abstract space.

A painting by Edward Hopper, an artist whose work exercised some influence upon the visual style of film noir, provides a suggestive point of reference.[46] Departing from the more hopeful resonances of his canvases of the 1920s and 1930s, with their luminosity and promise of new beginnings, in 1946 Edward Hopper produced *Approaching a City*, of which he offered this account: "I've always been interested in approaching a big city by train; and I can't exactly describe the sensations. But they're entirely human and perhaps have nothing to do with esthetics. There is a certain fear and anxiety, and a great visual interest in the things that one sees coming into the city."[47]

Taking train travel and a New York City railroad tunnel as its literal inspiration, Hopper's painting juxtaposes different modalities of urban

Edward Hopper, *Approaching a City* (1946), oil on canvas, 27 ⅛ × 36 in. Acquired 1947, The Phillips Collection, Washington, D.C.

space. Devoid of any human figures, the single largest surface in Hopper's canvas is a concrete wall, counterposed to a series of generic buildings whose functions remain unclear, with the distinction between industrial and residential structures blurred. On the left side, their windows become increasingly homogeneous as the viewer gazes toward the open mouth of the dark tunnel. Nowhere does the image convey a sense of being in the center of the metropolis.

Presenting the railroad as its compositional center, a transportation technology challenged by the postwar automobile boom, Hopper's painting invokes the nonsynchronous. It suggests how impersonal edifices, a familiar New York locale, and the train (invisible apart from its spatial traces) congeal in the representation of an uncertain postwar moment that centers upon a void. The emptiness of the tunnel elicits the fear and promise of entering the urban realm described by Hopper and pervasive in the film noir cycle.

Writing contemporaneously with the creation of Hopper's painting, cinematographer John Alton, known for his work on many films noir, observed that "the well-known *Main Street* of the small town so familiar to all is fast disappearing," a victim of changes in urban morphology that challenged the supremacy of urban centrality.[48] Through its stress upon the activity of arriving in the metropolis and the experience of liminality that this provokes, *Approaching a City* alludes to a shift in experience of the urban center, here evoked by its absence. The increasingly prevalent mode of centrifugal space that appears to be "neither city nor country," in the phrase of urban planner Hans Blumenfeld, bestows the experience of entering the older concentrated metropolis with a unique charge whose modalities in the film noir cycle range from fear to fascination to nostalgia.[49]

Writing a few years later about New York's Stuyvesant Town housing project, Mumford voiced similar anxieties about uniform urban architecture:

There is now, within New York City's city limits, a good handful of housing projects in various stages of completion . . . Yet almost all these projects are solemn reminders of how different the postwar world is from what most people hoped it would be . . .

When I first inspected Stuyvesant Town, a year ago, the development seemed to me an unrelieved nightmare. Though the buildings are not a continuous unit, they present to the beholder an unbroken facade of brick, thirteen stories high, absolutely uniform in every detail, mechanically conceived and mechanically executed, with the word "control" implicit in every aspect of the design. This, I said to myself, is the architecture of the Police State, embodying all the vices of regimentation one associates with state control at its unimaginative worst. But the entrepreneurs of this enterprise are not commissars; they are the presidents and directors of a great life-insurance company, and they have performed this feat of regimentation in the name of free enterprise and individual initiative.[50]

By describing this postwar building as a nightmare of architectural monotony Mumford cleverly turns the prevalent Cold War criticism of the Soviet Union and standardized construction to bear upon America. His suggestion that American capitalism and economic prosperity were not synonymous with the best of all possible worlds also found cinematic expression at the time. Mumford himself narrated *The City* (Ralph Steiner and Willard Van Dyke, 1939), a cinematic excoriation of the polluted and mechanized metropolis that resonates with much American culture of late modernity. One need only think of the urban decrepitude in *The Crooked Way* (Robert Florey, 1949) or *The Window* (Ted Tetzlaff, 1949) as paradigmatic examples of similar metropolitan squalor in film noir.

Located chronologically between the early modernist 1920s cinematic avant-gardes (Dadaism, Surrealism, Expressionism, Soviet montage practice) and the post-1959 experimentation of the New American cinema and the international new waves, film noir poses the challenge of defining modernism within the classical Hollywood cinema. At once an instance of narrative film originating within an industrial mode of production that simultaneously created westerns and musicals, film noir cannot be assimilated comfortably to either the modernist avant-garde or the formal language of postwar film industry.

Instead, it is best characterized as an instance of late modernism, a cinematic practice thoroughly industrial yet finely attuned to both the realities of earlier modernisms and the post-1939 built environment and media culture. Perhaps the approach most helpful to grasping its liminality is

suggested by the work of film theorist Siegfried Kracauer in his 1960 book
Theory of Film: The Redemption of Physical Reality. Its insight into what Miriam Hansen calls "the gaps and fissures in the filmic text that allow for
contingency and indeterminacy" persuasively explains the formal and historical identity of film noir.[51]

Evoking Nino Frank's 1946 essay on film noir as well as the work of
Walter Benjamin, Kracauer identifies the metropolis as a quintessential
cinematic space, in which an enhanced receptivity to "life" becomes possible.[52] He links film form with urban form and the cinema of late modernism with spatial modernity in an exemplary manner. Far more than other
film analysts, Kracauer directs attention to features operating "below" the
paradigm of the classical Hollywood filmmaking, calling into question its
accuracy and universality as an account of narrative cinema.[53] The instances of stasis and digression, the breakdowns and gaps Kracauer identifies throughout *Theory of Film*, often involve spatial representations and
establish a bridge between film noir and the postwar built environment.

From architect Joseph Hudnut to historian Paul Zucker to the paintings
of Hopper, the newly emerging metropolis of the 1940s and 1950s appeared to many contemporary observers increasingly bereft of its former
glories, a site of social and technological alienation, the domain of the
older "invisible city" now increasingly overtaken by expanding rings of
centerless suburbs. This new form of settlement, with the city center gutted by urban renewal and surrounded by highways and tract homes on its
periphery—must be understood as a historical content of the film noir
cycle.

This spatial infrastructure presents itself in two discrete but interrelated
modes. Centripetal and centrifugal space, tendencies toward concentration and dispersal, recur and often overlap throughout film noir. Far from
existing as mutually exclusive options, both manifest themselves in the
post-1939 built environment as instances of a dynamic tendency toward
the construction of centers that Lefebvre understands as intrinsic to space
itself.[54] Whether we think of the debates around the destruction of down-
towns, or the enthusiastic reception of superhighways or live television
news coverage, the need for grasping the new cultural aspirations and anxieties connected to experiences of the center and the periphery remains
essential to understanding the 1940s and 1950s.

Historian Mike Davis has explored how literary and cinematic expressions engage the local historical and social conditions of Los Angeles, yet the Californian subset of film noir is but a key chapter of its more expansive treatment of late modernity, a process of reconfiguring place and identity that exceeds a single geographic locus.[55] Although many films noir are set in New York or Los Angeles, the film cycle needs to be understood as probing into these particular spatial histories as well as the more general processes of modernization.

Commencing in 1939, the year of the New York World's Fair, the completion of Rockefeller Center, Ralph Steiner and Willard van Dyke's *The City*, and the publication of *The Big Sleep* by Raymond Chandler, the time frame of this book concludes in 1959, the year of the Nixon-Khrushchev kitchen debate in a model suburban home, Robert Wise's *Odds against Tomorrow*, Irving Lerner's posturban *City of Fear*, and the death of Raymond Chandler. By 1960 the original film noir cycle disappears, a victim of changes in personnel and industrial structures in the American cinema.

Yet its waning also should be understood in relation to transformations in the concentrated "centripetal" American metropolis that provided the physical and narrative infrastructure for the film cycle prior to its rebirth in the 1970s in postmodern culture.[56] To the extent that such films presuppose a different mode of production from the original film noir cycle as well as a vastly different set of spatial and cultural referents, they remain distinct from the films of the 1940s and 1950s and constitute a separate topic of study.

The first chapter considers key representations of centripetal space in a series of New York City films noir that aspire to represent the city in its actuality through synoptic views of the metropolis. It centers upon *The Naked City* (Jules Dassin, 1948) in relation to the work of the photographer Weegee and contemporaneous urban transformations. Chapter 2 defines centripetal space in relation to key episodes in nineteenth- and twentieth-century urbanism and relevant cinematic analogues. It also introduces the analytical spatial concepts developed by Lefebvre.

Chapter 3 investigates the connection between centripetal space and modernism with reference to spatial passage, the walk through the metropolis that has become a signature of modernity. Using the theoretical armature developed by Kracauer in *Theory of Film: The Redemption of Physi-*

cal Reality, it analyzes *Killer's Kiss* (Stanley Kubrick, 1955) in the context of the destruction of Pennsylvania Station and treats cinematic representations of the Los Angeles neighborhood of Bunker Hill in relation to postwar discourses of urban renewal.

The final two chapters consider centrifugal space, exemplified by decentralized urban development schemes, interstate highways, the discourse of traffic planning, and the growing imbrication of space with the mass media. Chapter 4 examines highway discourses and *Plunder Road* (Hubert Cornfield, 1957) as paradigmatic of the new emphasis upon time in this spatial mode. The final chapter examines a range of films noir that reveal the dynamics of centrifugal space and the mass media. It relates the end of the film cycle to transformations in the character of the built environment and reads *The Big Carnival* (Billy Wilder, 1951) and other films in relation to the tensions that permeate centrifugal space and signal the transformation of the centripetal metropolis.

NAKED CITIES

It's fast becoming a rule that if a studio isn't making a picture with the name of a city in a title the studio isn't adhering to the call of the times. At least half a dozen pictures currently are in production with such titles, and a number of others either have recently been completed or are about to take off.

—*Daily Variety*, May 4, 1944

Cutting from an exterior shot of an illuminated New York City subway train barreling through a dark tunnel to an interior view of riders pressed together in close proximity, *Pickup on South Street* (Samuel Fuller, 1953) begins with a mass of urban bodies occupying centripetal space. Through a montage sequence of gazes exchanged between federal agent Zara (Willis B. Bouchey) and police captain Dan Tiger (Murvyn Vye), who are following a woman called Candy (Jean Peters) suspected of transmitting military secrets to Communists, the film underscores the balance between noticing and disregarding other people required by urban life.[1]

The arrival of pickpocket Skip McCoy (Richard Widmark) in the train car underscores this studious indifference among the passengers. Standing close to Candy, he steals the wallet from inside her purse unbeknownst to any of the passengers but the two law enforcement officials. As they follow her out of the subway, the camera captures these figures crossing the street in a crane shot, switching scales from a close-up to an extreme long shot so as to place not merely the criminal suspect but now the entire city under surveillance. Following Candy into the lobby of an office building and watching her make a telephone call, the two agents continue to observe their suspect without attracting her attention, beneficiaries of the customary distance between citydwellers.

In his celebrated writings on the metropolis Georg Simmel argues that socialization in the modern city entails learning to ignore other people and developing a calculated indifference to the bodies with which one shares public transportation and the street.[2] Yet passage through the spaces of urban modernity also involves noticing people, including the "stranger" whose presence in an anomalous setting momentarily punctures the anonymity that structures the social world.[3] Walter Benjamin emphasized the significance of the outsider in the literature of detection and the role of the urban masses in shielding an asocial person from discovery.[4] From the French *physiologie* and its descriptions of particular social types (such as the flaneur and the *badaud*) to the physiognomic profiling of individual criminals associated with Bertillonage, the activity of surveillance required equal scrutiny of the collective, the crowd, as a space for the malfeasant to evade the law.[5]

Common to the surveillance of individual and group alike are the classification and location of bodies in the urban realm, whose anthropomorphic features culminate in the metaphor of the city as body contemporaneous with the nineteenth-century visual technologies of surveillance and the surgical urbanism of Baron Haussmann.[6] Gazed upon and surveyed during the process of criminal investigation, the metropolis appears an interstitial supplement to detection, surveyed no less than its wrongdoers and criminals. Investigating this "naked city" as well as its inhabitants, the film noir cycle also explores an urban "body" that emerges as the product of intersecting cultural, cinematic, and technological discourses.

A century after the rise of surveillance discourses in the middle of the nineteenth century, the persistence of the urban stranger as a figure in twentieth-century metropolitan narratives is conveyed by the following 1946 account of the Grand Central Station Restaurant and Oyster Bar and the gaze of its manager:

At present George carries on in that temporary post of acting assistant manager.

Location filming on Lower East Side of New York during production of *The Naked City* (Jules Dassin, 1948). Courtesy of Film Stills Collection, Museum of Modern Art, New York.

At present, too, he is the eagle eye. He's the fellow, that is to say, who every minute sees all that's going on—and sees that nobody slips out without paying his check. It's a tribute to his watchfulness, perhaps, that those who do escape average, from one year's end to the other, two each day; and two a day, out of the immense number of customers served, is considered an irreducible minimum.

Even so, that isn't the end of the story; for George has a reputation for uncanny skill in recognizing the cheaters when they come back . . . There was an ever so slight display of hands. There was a quick, subtle shrug. And in the accents of a diplomat George, who now stood before us, conceded: "Well, I have a trick memory."

But it's more than a memory; it's a good memory plus a quite astonishing ability to visualize a face from somebody else's description of it . . .

This is because the great bulk of customers are old-timers; people who come here every day and occupy the same seats in the same order. The waiters prize these regular customers, and lay themselves out to attract as many as possible; and their sitting down and getting up imparts to the day's work a kind of rhythm—which is broken each time a stranger sits down. So the stranger makes a greater impression upon the waiter than he quite realizes; and the waiter—perhaps thinking of the "regular" whom the stranger displaces—notices more about the stranger than the average person would think possible . . .

The absent-minded regular is not a man to be watched, however; and Old Eagle-Eye Jacques concentrates on the deliberate cheats— chiefly the fellow who eats at different counters a light meal and a large meal, and who tries to get out, and sometimes does get out, by paying the smaller check. In the usual, routine way, Eagle-Eye gets the waiter's description of that fellow; and, having succeeded once, the fellow almost invariably comes back, though it may be as much as two years later. But even after two years, Eagle-Eye remembers him, the story goes; and this time watches him closely, and catches him red-handed, and reaches into his little box and fishes out that other check now two years overdue.[7]

This remarkable vignette offers many insights into what one might call "metropolitan specularity" in centripetal space. Situated centrally in the city, the restaurant serves a homogeneous group of customers whose daily routines involve lunch there, often in the very same seat day after day. Regularity and habit characterize their spatial behavior, as well as that of the waiters who serve them and whose daily working rhythm is constituted by recognition of familiar faces in the crowd of diners. Determining that

someone "doesn't belong" somewhere presupposes the routine surveillance of a space and the detection of "strangers" far more precise (and perhaps more common) than one might imagine.

The "eagle eye" of the manager, a metaphorical overview of the environment transposed from a rural to an urban setting, allows him to recognize customers from the waiters' descriptions and to apprehend them in
the act of cheating on their bills. By recognizing strangers, the restaurant workers function within the city as human pistons in a social machine,
a veritable Panopticon for the surveillance and confirmation of identities. Their sophisticated observations give one pause before accepting the
Simmelian account of urban reserve as the sine qua non of metropolitan
life. Keen observation skills imply an aptitude for physiognomic description and spatial memory, the opposite of Simmel's understanding of urban
distance. They require an effortless translation between visual and verbal
signs evident in the scrutiny of photographs of pickpockets by federal
agent Zara in *Pickup on South Street*, as well as the actual practices of the
New York City Police Department.[8] Detection and discovery of the criminal were alive and well in New York.[9]

These surveillance regimes presupposed the immense human traffic of
the centripetal metropolis, for which reason the literature of detection also
emerges concurrently with the modern nineteenth-century metropolis
and its architectural typologies of railroad stations, department stores, and
commercial buildings. Spatial itineraries within a setting such as Grand
Central Station provide the foundation for surveillance in their stories,
and frequently involve the inability of a criminal protagonist to shed a routine and to step out of the institutions of daily life. Alternately agent
and medium, subject and object, the city teeming with its population is
both seer and seen, an indispensable catalyst of narrative development, for
which reason it is often regarded almost as if it were a character participating in the action.[10]

Analyzing centripetal urban space in the film cycle entails confronting a
changing set of scales, from the decrepit room in a boardinghouse, to an
office building, a street, a neighborhood, or an entire skyline. Film noir
adds characteristic twentieth-century spaces such as the skyscraper, the
jazz nightclub, the magazine or newspaper office, the bus terminal, the
diner, the automobile, the traffic-congested street, and the highway to the

narrative forms of the nineteenth century. Beginning on the micro level of the evidentiary trace and moving to the larger frames of architecture and the city, the interplay of bodily detection and metropolitan representation pervades film noir. Just as the criminal body possesses specific identifying features, so does the metropolis, although these can signify a generic rather than an individual identity in the film cycle. Many films noir are recognizably set in a specific city (whether that of the studio backlot or an actual location), others less so, and some cannot be spatially identified at all. This variance suggests a scale of "urban specificity" that can be applied to construct a typology of its urban representations.

Linking the fragment of evidence to the urban space in which it is found, Benjamin notes: "The original social content of the detective story was the obliteration of the individual's traces in the big-city crowd."[11] Traces can be understood as the objects of surveillance practices—material records, photographs, or verbal reports documenting a person's routine in centripetal space.[12] They may range from a clue (a fingerprint, an article of clothing, a cigarette stub) indicating a criminal's identity or whereabouts to the electronic traces left on answering machines, phonographs, or dictaphones. As indexical signs of a citydweller's passage through familiar streets, a place of employment, shops, or entertainment establishments, traces mimic the recording activity of photography and film. Both a reflection of particular characteristics of a city and a spatial practice itself, they can serve as a catalyst for a crime, a clue to the identity of a perpetrator, and a motive for disappearance and evasion.

Many commentators have noted that the literature of detection emerging in the nineteenth century overlaps with the invention of visual technologies such as the kaleidoscope, the stereoscope, and photography itself. It also coincides with significant innovations in surveillance practices such as Jeremy Bentham's 1843 plan of the Panopticon, the introduction of fingerprinting in 1860 by Sir William Herschel (a British administrator in Bengal), the appearance in 1876 of criminologist Cesare Lombroso's book *Criminal Man* with its Darwinian theory of criminal types, Alphonse Bertillon's 1884 photographic division and system of narrative description of physiognomic features, and Edward Henry's 1896 Dactyloscopy system of fingerprint classification.[13] While the confluence of these technologies with the emergence of photography has often been noted, their specific effect on the character of urban space has been less discussed.[14] As Christoph Asendorf observes,

> The decomposition of people into individual features through Bertillonage and Dactyloscopy follows the general scanning of urban space since the beginning of the nineteenth century. The course leads from segmentation of space to the dissection of body, finally to the detail, the fingerprint. As the field of observation becomes ever smaller, its statements become increasingly exact. The reduction of the surface of the body to a detail presents no obstacle to the techniques of identification. Its provisional outcome is the analysis of molecules and the transformation of what remains invisible to the eye into an enlarged visible image.[15]

Police identification technologies divide the body of the criminal subject into progressively smaller distinctive features (facial characteristics, fingerprints, and today DNA sequences) through which it becomes parcelized, surveyed, and "screened" in ever more diminutive and precise fragments for investigation.[16] Similarly, the homogeneous space of the crime is separated into a trail of metonymic details that leads to the body of the absent perpetrator.[17] Historians of visual culture have recognized a similar conception of discrete temporal instants in the work of Eadweard James Muybridge, Etienne-Jules Marey, and the birth of cinema, yet the imbrication of modernity within a comparable process of spatial fragmentation (well captured by Lefebvre's notion of abstract space) is no less pronounced.[18]

From the destruction of insalubrious and politically dangerous *quartiers* by Haussmann, to the reduced and Taylorized spaces of the Dwelling for Subsistence Living *(Wohnung für das Existenzminimum)*, to the dismemberment of individual blocks and buildings by urban renewal programs, the general trend toward spatial segmentation within the modern metropolis is unmistakable. Culminating in the ubiquitous influence of the grid upon the superblocks, shopping malls, and tract houses inserted into the postwar American landscape, this decomposition can operate upon the smallest fragments of the building site or block up to the scale of the city itself. Similarly, the practice of criminological identification entails both the reconstruction of identity according to general criteria and a division of the body into its individuating features.[19] Bertillon's methods entailed generalizable descriptions as well as individual measurements and an individualized photograph. As Allan Sekula notes, in the nineteenth-century practice of urban surveillance "photography came to establish and delimit the terrain of the *other*, to define both the *generalized look*—the typology— and the *contingent instance* of deviance and social pathology."[20]

A suggestive case in point is the representation of Los Angeles in *The Street with No Name* (William Keighley, 1948). Originally intended as a sequel to *The House on 92nd Street* (Henry Hathaway, 1945) to be made by that film's director, it reveals a semidocumentary style similar to that of the earlier film, a consequence of its shooting schedule, which reportedly covered only three days in the studio out of a total of sixty-five days spent filming.[21] The film commences with a shot of the seal of the FBI followed by a series of long shots of the exterior of its headquarters in Washington, D.C., succeeded by a statement that "wherever possible it was photographed in the original locale and played by the actual FBI personnel involved."

It next presents a message from J. Edgar Hoover, then director of the FBI, on a teletype machine: "The street on which crime flourishes is the

Frame enlargement of segmentation of criminal activity zones from *The Street with No Name* (William Keighley, 1948).

street extending across America. It is the street with no name. Organized gangsterism is once again returning." Yet despite the film's emulation of a documentary mode, emphasized by the stentorian voice of its narrator, it curiously refrains from acknowledging Los Angeles as its setting. Depicting many recognizable landmarks of the city, most notably the Main Street "Skid Row" district, the film refers only to "Center City," a designation that it retains with such assiduity that when FBI agent Gene Cordell (Mark Stevens) arrives on a bus, the imaginary municipality is listed as the final destination on its front hood.

The film's disavowal of Los Angeles (already hinted at by its title) and the representation of this metropolis as the space of a generalized criminal threat, a "center city" for illicit activity, is undercut by the dissection of urban space in an early scene. As the FBI agents confer in their office, they analyze the whereabouts and spatial routine of a suspect on a city map. Divided up into zones A, B, and C, the activities of the suspect are localized within one of these sectors marked on the map by a circle, within which the agents have fragmented his spatial routine into a series of movements between the hotel where he lives on Dock Street and the poolhalls and gymnasium where he spends his time.[22] Yet the emphasis upon Main Street as the site of the film's early action conveys the close connection between criminality and urban blight, as if to metonymically fuse this neighborhood with the city as a whole.

A similar concern with spatial division is evident in *He Walked by Night* (Alfred Werker, 1948). Its opening credits are superimposed upon a map of Los Angeles into which pins have been inserted to mark the location of crime scenes. Next, a montage sequence of long shots of Los Angeles (the basin, a business district, Union Station, a view from atop Bunker Hill, another view of the basin, and a beach) is accompanied by a voice-over narration. Although the narrator describes Los Angeles as "the fastest growing city in the nation. It's been called a bunch of suburbs in search of a city," the acknowledgment of a centrifugal geographic tendency is quickly defused by the conclusion of the sequence with a view of Los Angeles City Hall and the headquarters of the police department, recognizable centers of law and order.

Here the police communications bureau is shown in operation, and we watch its staff members relay telephone reports of crime incidents to spa-

Frame enlargement of crime-suspect facial identification technique
from *He Walked by Night* (Alfred Werker, 1948).

tially dispersed patrol cars. The clearest linkage between spatial fragmentation and the city occurs when the police construct a composite portrait
of the killer's face using a technique that combines the physiognomic de-
tailing of Bertillonage with a projection of lantern slides. Crime victims
from various parts of the city each contribute a fragment of his facial description, and the resulting facsimile is later shown to a group of letter car-
riers, one of whom recognizes the criminal as a customer on his route. The
police conduct surveillance on his block and eventually apprehend the
killer after a vigorous pursuit through the Los Angeles sewer system.

What after Sekula I call the "generalized look" of urban space of film
noir is understood to encompass both the appearance of the metropolis
and the act of gazing upon it. Yet if the screening and surveillance of the
criminal body in the nineteenth century led to its recording and analysis
by the institutions of power, in what sense is this true of urban space in
twentieth-century film noir? Is it possible to assimilate its metropolitan
representations to nineteenth-century systems of surveillance and analysis
such as photography, Bertillonage, or the Panopticon? Which tropes and
images in film noir reveal the late-modern "generalized look" of and at the
city? And how should one understand the power relations that such an image and gaze imply?

Phantom Lady (Robert Siodmak, 1944) provides numerous suggestions about the twentieth-century urban trace and its culture of metropolitan specularity. The film narrates the story of Scott Henderson (Alan Curtis), framed for the murder of his wife by his best friend, Jack Marlow (Franchot Tone). While in jail, Henderson is assisted in the attempt to prove his innocence by his devoted secretary, Carol Richman (Ella Raines). She eventually locates the one person who can exonerate Henderson, a mysterious phantom lady. Once this vital witness is located, Marlow unsuccessfully attempts to murder Richman and jumps to his death to avoid capture by the police. Henderson and Richman then begin their lives together.

The film proposes one ideological strand of the film noir cycle as consisting in an incessant struggle between perceptual indifference and engaged cognition, forgetfulness and remembrance, that confirms the understandings of metropolitan experience advanced by Simmel and Benjamin. Something of this tension is suggested in the first image of the film, a close-up of the exotic hat worn by the elusive female protagonist Ann Terry (Fay Helm). Filmed from behind, the shot conveys the point of view not of any character but of the camera as a third-person narrator. At once a significant clue, a trace, the hat also functions as a metonymic fragment allowing the body to be located in urban space. Suggesting the gaze a city-dweller would focus upon a conspicuous sartorial detail encountered in a public place, the hat comes to signify its missing owner as the sole person who can prove a man innocent of murder, the seer but here also the object of surveillance, the seen.

With the arrival a few seconds later of Scott Henderson through the glass door of Anselmo's Bar, the film introduces its central narrative concerns and devices. Although Henderson converses with Terry and attends the theater with her, her identity is not revealed until late in the narrative. In a curious way the two remain strangers despite contact with each other, thus underscoring the distance between their superficial exchange and an actual encounter with the subjectivity of another person. From Terry's quick self-inspection in her compact, to the bartender's reflection in the mirror behind him, to his final stare as the couple departs, this scene prefigures the profusion of mirrors and gazes that recurs throughout *Phantom Lady*. It opposes these moments of specularity to the less duplicitous social relationships based on friendship and romantic love.

"Did you ever walk down Broadway and watch the people's faces? It's fun," Henderson asks Terry in the taxi cab while commenting upon its driver, "There's a typical New York face for you." Riding through Times Square, their journey to the theater seems to oppose this world of ordinary physiognomies to the specter of a metropolis in which only the stars of screen and stage emblazoned upon the marquees possess fixed and recognizable identities. A world in which calculated indifference prevails and the stranger evades notice is proposed as an anomalous horror. Later observed by the star of the review, Estela Monteiro (Aurora), and the drummer, Cliff March (Elisa Cook Jr.), Terry breaks through the habitual layer of urban disinterest. The fact that she and Monteiro wear identical hats leads Henderson to exclaim of the latter, "Just look at her face. She could murder you."

Despite Monteiro's subsequent disavowal that "I don't look at my audience," characters in *Phantom Lady* frequently exchange glances. After Henderson has been accused of murdering his wife, his secretary, Carol "Kansas" Richmond, returns to Anselmo's to stare down the bartender (Andrew Tombes Jr.). She later eyes March during the performance, and he returns her glance with an erotically inviting smile. Each scene involves acknowledging strangers and confronting them visually, a direct interdiction of the distance that Simmel understands to define urban sociality. Such moments underscore the disparity between an active acknowledgment of the other and the mere sharing of urban space, while nonetheless revealing the fundamentally tenuous nature of the social exchange that the gaze promotes. They evoke the gaze at an attractive woman who vanishes in the urban crowd sketched by Charles Baudelaire in his poem "A une passante" and its ethos of romantic loss.

In keeping with these moments that seem to define urban life as a conflict between overstimulation or isolation, the film underscores anonymity as the general condition of the metropolis. Thus, in the scene in which Henderson and Terry return to Anselmo's after the theater, the bar is filmed in an elaborate crane shot that dissolves into the exterior of Henderson's residence and then into the nameplate on the front door of his apartment. The opposition between gazes attributed to individual characters and the anonymous gaze of the camera becomes conspicuous through this sequence. As if to underscore the distinction between recognizing subjectivity and surveying space, the film repeatedly opposes these modes of looking, an engagement with another person or the scrutiny of places, as the two halves of metropolitan experience.

Paradigmatic of such an anonymous space presented not as the point of view of any character, but as the third-person view of the camera, is the overhead street shot in which Richmond follows the bartender after he leaves Anselmo's. Filmed in a mobile crane shot, the characters are joined only by a newspaper vendor and two pedestrians who cross the frame, conveying the autonomy of the metropolis as a realm capable of functioning with minimal human interaction. This overhead presentation of the studio-constructed street proposes the surveillance of urban space as the intersection point of the city with the cinematic apparatus. Though not presented as a specific place, it suggests that *any* place in the city is potentially surveyable.

The latent transformability of a street corner into a site of observation, the city (and the cinema) as a machine for making space visible, is conveyed in the ensuing subway sequence. Terry and the bartender wait together in eerie silence on the elevated platform, itself an anomalous remnant of an earlier New York transit system.[23] A rear projection sequence of a crowd appears when they arrive at their destination, as if to underscore their lack of connection to other people. After the bartender is run over by a car, the camera lingers upon his hat lying in the gutter, another individuating detail now revealed as insignificant. Such moments in which traces of individual subjectivity disappear within the mechanism of an urban technological system confirm Jean-Paul Sartre's assertion that "when the American puts a nickel into the slot in the tram or in the underground, he feels just like everyone else. Not like an anonymous unit, but like a man who has divested himself of his individuality and raised himself to the impersonality of the Universal."[24]

The sharing of identity with "everyone else" in the metropolis contrasts markedly with the earlier individuating function of photography and nineteenth-century surveillance techniques wielded by the police and their representatives. Though similarly grounded in urban space, the experience described by Sartre of functioning as an anonymous other within the metropolis elicits a new set of cultural responses to the perceived loss of individuality. It entails a new array of technologies and strategies of power, a different regime of visibility in which the film noir cycle is as socially implicated as were nineteenth-century criminological discourses in their re-spective social and specular order.

Mirrors occupy a privileged role in *Phantom Lady* as spaces in which in-dividual identity is alternately focused and dispersed, congealed and shat-tered. While Richmond stares at the bartender, the crowd in Anselmo's is visible in the bar's room-length mirror, the separate identity of its individ-ual members temporarily fused into a unity. A moment later, the bartender drops a glass upon noticing Richmond as his multiplied reflection elon-gates behind him. When Richmond later joins March in the jazz cellar, her vibrating image in the mirror seems pushed to the breaking point by the erotic beat of the music.[25] Henderson's friend Marlow later collapses in Monteiro's dressing room before a mirror that reflects his image in trip-licate.

After Richmond locates Terry in her Long Island estate, she enters her bedroom a second time and finds the disturbed woman combing her hair in front of a mirror. Terry gives the visitor the hat she has duplicated, ac-knowledging that "You want to wear it for him" and thereby confirming the status of the hat as a crucial armature of a female identity defined by the mirror and the male gaze, an identity already sketched in Woolrich's novel: "It was only in the foyer—at a full-length glass out in the foyer—that she finally put her hat on again. And at once she came alive, she was something, somebody again. It was wonderful, he reflected, what that hat could do to her. It was like turning on the current in a glass chandelier."[26]

Terry attempts to explain Monteiro's rage to Henderson: "It's no use expecting a man to understand. Steal my jewelry, steal the gold-fillings from my teeth, but don't steal my hat."[27] Within this specular regime, Henderson's murdered wife appears as the other phantom lady of the film, visible only as a portrait in his living room or an off-screen corpse pre-sented only to the husband and the male detectives.[28] Yet this gendered identity can quickly recede within the metropolis as an amalgam of the identities of "everyone." When asked to describe the phantom lady with whom he attended the theater, Henderson replies in Woolrich's novel: "That she'd been to high school. That she was city-bred. She talked like we all do here. Pure metropolitan. About as colorless as boiled water."[29]

Although the other characters in the film refer to "Carol" or "Miss Richmond," Henderson calls his secretary "Kansas," as if to underscore her identity as distinct from the metropolis, an identity later confirmed by the reproach of Detective Burgess, "Why don't you go home to Kansas?" Henderson and Marlow, the innocent man and his best friend who frames him, share an antipathy toward the existing city. Speaking with admiration of her boss, Richmond observes, "He had such plans to build model cities. Sunlight in every room. Children's play yards everywhere for everyone." Yet Marlow rejects this optimistic vision of the planned future and its utopia of architectural transparency. "I never liked cities. Noise, dirt, and the people in them. They hate me because I'm different from them," he states in a triumphant self-proclamation as urban stranger.

Both descriptions point to the actual city and the anxiety it causes protagonists in *Phantom Lady*, a fear that its space has become insubstantial. Henderson drives with the police officers through a metropolis portrayed by Woolrich as possessing "the dream-like glide of unreal buildings and unreal streets moving backward past them, like shadows on glass." Upon finding that no one will corroborate his innocence, he implores the detectives: "I'm frightened; take me back to the detention-pen, will you? Please, fellows, take me back. I want walls around me, that you can feel with your hands. Thick, solid, that you can't budge!" A similar account of the urban social world as a void that necessitates refuge in a sheltering internal space is present in Woolrich's account of the bartender's growing anxiety as Richmond stares at him:

> Symptoms that he had never noted in himself before, and would not have recognized by their clinical name of agoraphobia, began to assail him with increasing urgency; a longing to take cover, to seek refuge back within the locker-room, even a desire to squat down below the level of the bar-top where she could no longer see him readily. He mopped his brow furtively once or twice and fought them off. His eyes began to seek the clock overhead with increasing frequency, the clock that they had once told him a man's life depended on.[30]

If the gaze and the mirror provoke entrapment in socially defined identities and the empty spaces of the city elicit an anonymous identity, the numerous windows throughout the film never promote an equitable specular exchange. Their transparent openness never yields to spaces that are less threatening and more secure. In the courtroom where Henderson is being tried, the window displays an indifferent city of tall buildings framed by a cornice inhabited by pigeons. Cutting from March's room and a neon sign on the street visible through its window to the jail cell in which a beam of light highlights the condemned Henderson, the film compares the drummer's dingy flat to a site of incarceration. Light does not alter the material or spiritual condition of either man but seems instead to produce virulent shadows.

Filmed through the window of a delicatessen after she escapes from March's apartment, Richmond's dash across an empty street further suggests the limitations of spatial permeability to control fear. This opacity of the seemingly transparent is later confirmed in the scene in which Marlow is visible through the window of the country store from which he pretends to telephone Detective Burgess. Marlow appears to be making the call, at least when viewed from Richmond's position in the automobile. Yet the third-person view of the camera, accessible only to the spectator, reveals that he is feigning a conversation. The duplicitous character of transparency in this scene, its nonidentity with truth, is later confirmed by the lavish windows of the killer Marlow's modern-furnished apartment and his final jump through the glass to his death.

Asking Richmond to turn out the light in his already semidarkened apartment strewn with shadows across its walls because "it hurts my eyes, it chokes me," Marlow embodies the prototypical film noir protagonist. His predilection for darkness and an urban space impervious to the gaze of surveillance and its fragmentation of space coincides with his hatred of the city. At once a rejection of the modernist utopia of transparency, stripped of any utopian prospect and revealed as potentially malevolent, the articulation of such a space that is neither too insubstantial nor too constricting, neither too anonymous nor too visible, pervades the film noir cycle. Its openness to the surveillant gaze constitutes a key background condition for the emergence of the trope of the naked city.

AERIAL AND MILITARY GAZES

In 1944, the year in which *Phantom Lady* appeared, the Kodak Company sponsored an advertising campaign in the motion picture trade journal *Variety*. These spots saluted the ubiquity of photography and cinema in the American war effort, a point reiterated in numerous articles and editorials appearing in the publication.[31] On January 14 an ad captioned "On Target" was devoted to the superiority of the Kodak optical systems for fire control. Declaring the alleged preeminence of German lensmaking skill to be a myth, the text extolled the virtues of its sponsor's products in a manner that seamlessly fused corporate self-promotion, technological advances in optics, and patriotism. At the heart of its bluster were the twin claims for the enhancement of human vision and the concomitant improvement of military performance facilitated by the company's output:

> For America's bombsights—which have shown our enemies the bitter meaning of "high altitude precision bombing"—most of "the optics" are made by Kodak.

Kodak advertisment published in *Variety*, January 14, 1944.

For our Army and Navy, Kodak also makes 29 of the most complex types of optical systems for fire control—the sighting of guns—including the famous height finder for anti-aircraft . . .

Effective fire power—hits, not "tries"—is the result of sighting through a series of lenses . . . an optical system . . . which locates, magnifies, and "ranges on" the target.[32]

Expressed in a montage of official photographs provided by the U.S. Army Air Forces, the destruction of an enemy cruiser is rendered in a series of three images that commences with falling bombs and concludes with drifting bubbles emanating from the location of the obliterated ship. Powerfully confirming Paul Virilio's description of the battlefield as a range of perception, the ability to see becomes synonymous with the ability to destroy.[33] "Serving Human Progress through Photography," in the final grandiloquent words of the advertisement, the eradication of a military adversary is presented as both a moral and a technological triumph for all of humanity, a victory of corporate and governmental cooperation. Only a small appeal for war bonds at the bottom of the page and its reminder of defeat at Corregidor acknowledges the pain and suffering of the combatants. Photographed from high altitude, the conduct of war appears identical with the operation of machines, their efficient operation an unmistakable confirmation of progress, with the fear of their breakdown, an anxiety hinted at by the confident bravado of the advertisement, nowhere directly articulated.

The belief in technological omnipotence soon manifested itself in the postwar procedural film such as *The House on 92nd Street* (Henry Hathaway, 1945), which took as its theme the real-life efforts of the FBI to crack a German spy ring that was smuggling military secrets to Germany during the war. Here x-ray mirrors and surveillance cinematography waged a no less ferocious battle against crime and political subversion on the domestic front. In the words of the narrator, "For war is thought. And thought is information. And he who knows most strikes hardest." Depicted as an endless series of rows of filing cabinets maintained by female clerks, the FBI in the film simultaneously accumulates both verbal and visual information. The *House on 92nd Street* includes actual surreptitious surveillance films made of German agents on American soil and notes that wherever possible scenes were filmed in the actual localities depicted, as if to endow its newsreel style of depicting landmarks such as Bowling Green and Columbus Circle with the cachet of military surveillance footage.

Technological prowess was emphasized repeatedly in other Kodak ads from 1944. The K-24 aerial reconnaissance camera "runs its own show" and produced images with a minimum of human intervention. Its self-sufficiency motivated the slogan that Kodak famously employed to market cameras in the postwar era: "You press the button . . . it does the rest."[34] Cinema also featured prominently in the promotional campaign, not merely as a means of recording "essential information of immediate tactical, technical, or strategic value," but also because "these first-hand motion pictures have tremendous morale value when released for public showing."[35] Or, as Arthur Mayer noted in 1944, "General Marshall recently said that the Second World War has seen the development of two new weapons: the airplane and the motion picture."[36] Complementing the function of recording military operations for tactical or civilian purposes, the entertainment value of Hollywood film for military personnel received equal praise.[37] In the words of another ad:

> When the boys are months and miles from home, a movie's more than a show. It's a window into a life they left behind. Here are the longed-for city streets; their beloved villages and farms; their ways and their people—their America. "Movies tonight" are a godsend to Service men and women; one of the most deeply appreciated gifts the home folks can send.
>
> The sending, of course, is done by you of "the movies." Hundreds of current features go to fighting craft and fighting men in every theater of the war. There's home in every reel. And it would do your heart good to see the boy's eyes light up when word gets around that it's "movies tonight."[38]

Formulated as a second-person encomium to workers in the motion picture industry, the text praises cinema's ability to conjure the urban streets and the rural farms which signify home.[39] Providing "a window into a life they left behind" for military personnel, Hollywood functioned as the architect of nostalgia.[40] It receives thanks for its role in the war effort, perhaps the ultimate objective of the Kodak campaign. Both the film industry (the "'you' of 'the movies'") and the spaces of the home front are endowed with a permanence that suggests they are fixed and changeless entities, despite the profound transformations that both in fact were undergoing.

This constellation underscores the relation between the ubiquity of the city as a topos in Hollywood cinema of the early 1940s and the destined audience of these films, members of the armed forces. The omnipresence of the metropolis as a trope in film noir is here prefigured by an emphasis upon the social utility of urban representations, their ideological value in portraying home and community that might also explain the pervasive appeal of the city to the Hollywood cinema of 1944 conveyed in the epigraph to this chapter.

Recurrent violence proposes itself as another link between the motion pictures produced during wartime combat and the spatial representations in the film noir cycle. Brutal newsreels of military conflicts such as the 1943 battle with the Japanese at Tarawa conveyed an intensity that led one commentator to claim that "nothing like this had ever hit our public screens." Training films such as *Baptism of Fire* employed a voice-over narrator (soon to become a trademark feature of film noir) to reassure the soldier approaching combat for the first time. In *Kill or Be Killed* combatants are instructed that "jungle law is the law of the battlefield. Gouging and maiming make up the rules." In one still from the film, a cold-eyed fighter (resembling the weary film noir protagonist Robert Mitchum) exemplifies the ideal hard comportment of the warrior.[41] By the time newsreel footage of German atrocities was screened in movie houses, *Variety* noted that few spectators felt compelled to walk out during their presentation.[42]

Prefiguring the postwar tendency of film productions to collaborate with law enforcement agencies, a Hollywood screenwriter was sent to parachute school in preparation for his work on a documentary titled *These Are the Paratroopers*.[43] Documentary films produced by the Office of War Information for exhibition in foreign countries utilized nonprofessional actors and extensive location photography as well as the lightweight newsreel cameras. More than fifty-two such films had been completed by 1944, directed in some cases by figures such as Irving Lerner earlier active in the radical documentary movement of the 1930s and later associated with film

noir. The domestic audience for these productions was said to be fifty million. Frequently set in an urban milieu, films such as *A Place to Live* (Irving
Lerner, 1939) and *The Town* (Josef von Sternberg, 1947) further illustrate
the persistence of the town and city in the documentary cinema engen-
dered by the war. They lend credence to Mayer's 1944 prediction that
what filmmakers "have seen in the past few years will surely be evidenced
in more realistic backgrounds and more topical themes than big-budget
pictures have ever before known."[44]

If depictions of the city as familiar and reassuring heartened soldiers at
war, their subsequent transformation into menacing sites of danger and
surveillance in film noir raises the problem of accounting for the prevalence of both types of representations in the American cinema of the
1940s. One suggestive hint is provided by sociologist Alfred Schutz in his
1946 essay "The Homecomer":

> To a certain extent, each homecomer has tasted the magic fruit of
> strangeness, be it sweet or bitter. Even amid the overwhelming long-
> ing for home there remains the wish to transplant into the old pattern
> something of the novel goals, of the newly discovered means to real-
> ize them, of the skills and experiences acquired abroad. We cannot be
> astonished, therefore, that a United States War Department Survey
> of June, 1944 [according to *Time*, June 12, 1944] showed that 40 per
> cent of the discharged veterans being sent back to civilian life through
> eastern "separation centers" did not want their old jobs back and did
> not want even to return to their old communities. On the Pacific
> Coast the percentage was even greater.[45]

Such a passage evokes the deep ambivalence toward the idea of home
experienced after savoring "the magic fruit of strangeness," if not the very
mobility and rootlessness conveyed by films noir with veterans such as *Act
of Violence* (Fred Zinnemann, 1949). Yet it also poses the question of how
to understand the continuities between film personnel active in the armed
forces motion picture units and their subsequent work in the Hollywood
studio system. How might *they* have responded to the urban environment of post-1945 America? These issues find an apposite referent in *The
Naked City* (Jules Dassin, 1948). Its insistence upon apprehending an un-

mediated urban and architectural reality inflects many 1940s films noir and the discourses of observation, detection, and surveillance present in the film cycle.

Consider the opening aerial cinematography sequence of *The Naked City*. In three shots lasting under two minutes, Manhattan Island is first approached from its southern tip. Wall Street and the Battery Park area become prominently visible in the bottom half of the frame. This dissolves into the next shot, which commences slightly south of the Empire State Building and concludes below Central Park. A final shot moves southward along the west side of the island. The overall shape of the trajectory is circular, suggesting the loop of a reconnaissance flight in which a single territory (or target) is observed from multiple positions. Accompanied by the sound of airplane engines and producer Mark Hellinger's voice-over narration, the metropolis is introduced by means of aviation technology that is heard but never seen. The military newsreel connotations of the sequence are obvious, perhaps an echo of the narrator's brief stint as a war correspondent during which he participated in a bombing run in the Pacific theater.[46]

Filmed from an oblique rather than a vertical perspective, the skyscrapers and buildings of Manhattan never congeal into total abstraction. It is

Frame enlargement of New York skyline from *The Naked City* (Jules Dassin, 1948).

always possible to ascertain the approximate location of the aerial cinematographers with respect to Manhattan's urban geography. Despite high-
lighting the geometric grid, the orthogonal forms of individual buildings,
and the shadowy trenches of long avenues, New York is rendered realisti-
cally in the tradition of a pictorial landscape, complete with a horizon line
and the heroic connotations of romantic narrative.[47] Through a depth that
pulls the spectator forward into the image but constantly introduces new
details from its sides into its center, these shots recall the tradition of panoramic representation associated with earlier aerial urban photography.
They suggest the famous kite photographs taken by George R. Lawrence
after the San Francisco earthquake in 1906 that similarly extend into the
distance.[48] Like Lawrence's images, the aerial sequence that commences
The Naked City provides an overwhelming quantity of visual information
whose totality is more significant than any component.

Yet here its significance involves not a recording of the destruction so
evident in the San Francisco photographs, but its complete opposite, the
absence of any devastation to New York. The sheer fact of the city's survival intact at the conclusion of the war is silently celebrated in this sequence. As if confirming the melancholy analysis of technological progress
formulated by Theodor Adorno and Max Horkheimer in their *Dialectic of
Enlightenment* (1946), the device in which "you press the button . . . it does
the rest" that once proved heartening now generates anxiety. As E. B.
White noted in his book *Here Is New York* (1949):

> The subtlest change in New York is something that people don't
> speak much about but that is in everyone's mind. The city, for the first
> time in its long history, is destructible. A single flight of planes no
> bigger than a wedge of geese can quickly end this island fantasy, burn
> the towers, crumble the bridges, turn the underground passages into
> lethal chambers, cremate the millions. The intimation of mortality is
> part of New York now: in the sound of jets overhead, in the black
> headlines of the latest edition.
>
> All dwellers in cities must live with the stubborn fact of annihila-
> tion; in New York the fact is somewhat more concentrated because of
> the concentration of the city itself, and because, of all targets, New
> York has a certain clear priority. In the mind of whatever perverted

George R. Lawrence, "San Francisco in Ruins after 1906 Earthquake." Library of Congress.

dreamer might loose the lightning, New York must hold a steady, ir-
resistible charm.[49]

New York's concentration provides both reassurance and a desirable target for violent attack. Discussing the planned construction of the United
Nations, White presents the building and the surrounding city as a spatially manifested *Aufhebung* of the conflicting temporalities of destruction
and preservation:

> This race—this race between the destroying planes and the struggling
> Parliament of Man—it sticks in all of our heads. The city at last per-
> fectly illustrates both the universal dilemma and the general solution,
> this riddle in steel and stone is at once the perfect target and the per-
> fect demonstration of nonviolence, of racial brotherhood, this lofty
> target scraping the skies and meeting the destroying planes halfway,
> home of all people and all nations, capital of everything, housing the
> deliberations by which the planes are to be stayed and their errand
> forestalled.[50]

Its jacket emblazoned with an aerial photograph of Manhattan taken by
the Fairchild Aerial Surveys, *Here Is New York* celebrates the vitality and
survival of the city even while it broods over its future. This image recalls a
sequence near the beginning of *The Best Years of Our Lives* (William Wyler,
1946) in which three servicemen return to their small American city after
completing a tour of duty. Flying over the American landscape in a military transport plane, they comment upon the automobiles, highways, and
countryside that they view through the plane's windshield. At once a confirmation of the country's changed postwar geography, the scene visually
corroborates its escape from destruction.

Although the impulse to photograph from an elevated vantage point
touched many photographers throughout the nineteenth century, aerial
and elevated photographs of the city experienced a vogue in the 1940s
work of figures such as Andreas Feininger and Arthur Haug.[51] Unlike the
earlier elevated views of Alvin Langdon Coburn, László Moholy-Nagy,
or Berenice Abbott, these photographs rendered the city in sharp photo-
journalistic detail rather than in the idioms of romantic lyricism or mod-

Jacket of E. B. White, *Here Is New York* (New York:
Harper and Brothers, 1949).

ernist abstraction.[52] Frequently conveying large spatial expanses such as
Manhattan Island or the highway system around the Triboro Bridge, such
photographs often adopted similar viewpoints. Their repetition of standard views proposes them as a kind of photodocumentary cliché, an image
of the city instantly recognizable by everyone.

Contemporaneously with the aerial cinematography in *The Naked City*,
companies such as Fairchild promoted their services to urban planners,
thus underscoring the connection between the technological progress facilitated by the war and its utility to filmmakers and city builders alike.
From highway construction to metropolitan renewal projects, aerial surveys facilitated the massive spatial reconfigurations of the postwar period,
utilizing the advances realized during the war.[53] "The photomap, showing
as it does every cultural detail, has no substitute where large-scale con-

demnation and routing problems through metropolitan areas are encountered."[54] If aerial photography once again served human progress, in the language of the Kodak advertisement, it did so now by aiding the planning and regularization of civilian space. Through the reorganization of spatial fragments, now on the scale of the urban region, the construction of freeways and the implementation of redevelopment schemes dramatically transformed the postwar American landscape. These macro images of the metropolis formed "a planning nucleus around which improvements, extensions and other projects having to do with modern city administration are conceived and executed" and anticipated the aerial surveillance and helicopter patrols that metropolitan police departments would later employ in their regulation of urban space.[55]

Decisively appropriating the airplane and the motion picture, the war effort had an equally pronounced impact upon filmic representations of the city. Unlike earlier cinematic and literary depictions, for which the appeal of the aerial perspectives over Manhattan was largely picturesque, these postwar representations appear inextricably bound up with social planning and control, if not the violent threat alluded to by White.[56] Borrowing from the ideas of Michel Foucault and Paul Virilio, the practices of aerial photography and cinematography can easily be related to the operations of power in modern societies.[57] They exemplify the broad shift toward the regulation of spatial territories that these thinkers identified with the arrival of modernity, especially the logics of mobilization and command employed in modern warfare.[58] From law enforcement observation of neighborhoods to the use of satellite images to plan the future location of shopping centers, the aerial view of urban space facilitated its oversight, management, and planning, thus suggesting a new sense of the city and its "truth."

SERIALITY AND HUMANISM

What might it mean to encounter the metropolis unadorned, stripped of secrets and pretenses? Naked. In its very promise to expose the bare truth, the catachresis "naked city" evokes a Gordian knot of language, desire, and visual mastery whose overdetermined character belies any claim to expose an unmediated urban reality. How could so evocative a term and its promised divulgence of once-secret knowledge not heed a particular agenda, even if one only faintly grasped? Exploring the nexus of the 1945 book *The Naked City* by the photographer Weegee and the 1948 film noir of the same title brings into focus the technological, rhetorical, spectatorial, and narrative strategies each employs to represent the city in a direct and unexpurgated manner.

The first image in Weegee's book shows the Manhattan skyline punctured by a bolt of lightning, a clever pun on the photographer's practice of never shooting any image without flash, and an uncharacteristic framing of the city in extreme long shot.[59] Here the city is presented as simultaneously source and recipient of vital energy. At once a proxy for the urban masses to whose scopophilic desires he caters, Weegee is similarly capable of transforming gawking spectators into subjects, rendering them as both the origin of the city's violent dynamism and its observers. He prophetically dedicates *The Naked City* "to you, the people of New York," and thus introduces the second-person mode of address that positions the reader as a partner in a dialogue.

Title page from Weegee, *The Naked City* (New York: Essential Books, 1945). Copyright © Weegee / International Center of Photography / Getty Images.

Simultaneously participant in and observer of the urban spectacle, Weegee introduced a modern form of self-consciousness into the medium of urban photography. In his photographs we watch spectators watching themselves being photographed. Yet their conscious awareness of his presence complicates the potential voyeurism in many such images, suggesting them instead as the product of a pact—perhaps even an emotional bond— between photographer and the urban crowd. For the figure of the photographer himself probably elicited as much attention as the disasters he chronicled. This quality of his work, its pretense to speak the city, distinguishes it from that of Berenice Abbott or Paul Strand, photographers who sought to remain invisible in the metropolis they recorded.

Born Usher Fellig in 1899 to a Jewish family near the city of Lemberg in what was then Austrian Galicia and today belongs to the Ukraine, Weegee arrived in New York in 1910, living with his family on the Lower East Side.[60] In 1914 he left home, sleeping in Pennsylvania Station, in flophouses, and on the benches of Bryant Park and supporting himself through odd jobs. Around 1921 he landed a job in the darkroom of the *New York Times*, drying prints for the newspaper and its syndication service. His proficiency with a squeegee is one explanation for the origin of his name; his resemblance to a devilish figure emblazoned on the then-popular Ouija board is another. His alleged telepathic gifts, forever trumpeted by the photographer, which made him a kind of human Ouija board, is a third. In 1927 Weegee was hired as a darkroom printer for the Acme News Service, which provided photographs and news stories to papers across the country. He began to accompany photographers on the night shift, and by the early 1930s he was moonlighting as a news photographer, selling photographs of fires, late-night arrests, and auto accidents to Acme and other agencies.

Well before the earliest films noir of the 1940s and the deep-focus cinematography of *Citizen Kane*, Weegee had perfected the techniques applied in his news photography from 1935 to 1945.[61] Working with a Speed Graphic 4-by-5-inch camera, he exposed his images with flash illumination at a speed of 1/200 second and an aperture of f16. High-contrast, high-grain, and razor-sharp photographs were the result, often defined by an ink-black background against which their subjects appeared to float. It was the perfect style for reproduction in the newspapers. In 1935 Weegee, who had grown frustrated seeing his photographs published under a news agency byline, began a career as a freelance news photographer, publishing images in the New York dailies and national magazines. By 1937 his fame as a photographer specializing in violence and disaster between ten at night and five in the morning had led to profiles in *Life* magazine and *Popular Photography*. Only the *New York Times* steadfastly ignored Weegee, not printing any of his photographs until its favorable review of the publication of *The Naked City*.[62]

Weegee's ability to arrive at the scene of the crime in advance of other photographers contributed to his legend. Standing on a corner of Chinatown, he once photographed a building only moments before it inexplicably exploded, capturing before and after shots. His images of a sleeping tramp follow the man from his slumbering on the sidewalk to the interval moments later when he is run over by a car and administered the last rites by a priest. Weegee did not cause these misfortunes, yet his photographs and statements promote the disavowal of this knowledge and multiply the uncanny resonances of his work. "People are so wonderful that a photographer has only to wait for that breathless moment to capture what he wants on film . . . and when that split second of time is gone, it's dead and can never be brought back."[63]

Objective chance, freedom from logical connections, and what film critic Jean Goudal called "conscious hallucination" and "fusion of dream and consciousness" in surrealist film establish compositional principles for many of Weegee's photographs.[64] Their affinity with Surrealism extends to the relationships between text and image in his book *The Naked City*, where photograph and caption converge and diverge with equal frequency. More than mere clarification or commentary, the text in Weegee's book carries its own distinctive authority.

It conveys his journey through the city, providing opportunities for reflections on fame, crime, and social life, not unlike the voice-over narration of Mark Hellinger in the film of the same name. In the nocturnally illuminated stack of newspapers, the third photograph of *The Naked City* calls attention to its own mode of journalistic circulation through the bundles that evoke the countless bodies splattered on countless sidewalks that Weegee reproduced in their pages.

Packed within a typical photograph and text in *The Naked City* is a suggestion of the tenuousness of the social bond itself, the precarious state of

Peaceful scene in the heart of Chinatown. The cops who always patrol the beat in pairs there think I am crazy . . . because I am taking their picture. . . .

Right after I took the photo above . . . the street blew up . . . the water main pipes broke . . . the gas main caught fire . . . followed by an explosion . . . five hundred tenement dwellers in the block were driven from their homes.

Chinatown explosion sequence from Weegee, *The Naked City* (New York: Essential Books, 1945). Copyright © Weegee / International Center of Photography / Getty Images.

Newspaper bundles on sidewalk from Weegee, *The Naked City* (New York: Essential Books, 1945). Copyright © Weegee / International Center of Photography / Getty Images.

an urban reality always on the verge of fraying, if not exploding, in multiple directions. Consider Weegee's account of a typical fire:

> At fires I also make shots of the crowds watching the fires . . . for the detectives and fire marshals who are always on the scene . . . on the look out for pyromaniacs . . . jealous lovers . . . thrill seekers . . . disappointed would-be firemen . . . who having failed in their examinations will start fires . . . Also at fires where there are rescues . . . different

Murder victim on sidewalk from Weegee, *The Naked City* (New York: Essential Books, 1945). Copyright © Weegee / International Center of Photography / Getty Images.

firemen will take credit for such rescues . . . my photos decide who did make the rescue and end all disputes.[65]

Where many discern a catastrophe, Weegee perceives society, a war of competing and sometimes hostile claimants from which even that most benign agent of social self-preservation, the fire department, cannot extricate itself. Implicating himself in the activity of urban surveillance and presenting his photographs as the means of adjudicating disputes, Weegee makes little attempt to conceal what critic John Coplans refers to as the larger "morally dubious" quality of his work.[66] William McCleery, editor of *PM* magazine, in which Weegee often published, observed in his foreword to *The Naked City* that

Loving the City, Weegee has been able to live with her in utmost intimacy . . . Even in slumber he is responsive to her . . . In sickness and in health he will take his camera and ride off in search of new evidence that his city, even in her most drunken and disorderly and pathetic moments, is beautiful. Of course Weegee, being an Artist, has his own conception of what constitutes beauty, and in some cases it is hard for us to share his conception; but insofar as we can share it, we can share his love for the city.[67]

Conjuring a mawkish imitation of Baudelaire's aesthetic of the dandy, McCleery's sentimental prose evokes the literary antecedents of the naked city as cultural trope, a genealogy that encompasses nineteenth-century French urban narrative.[68] Consider as but one example the frontispiece by the illustrator Gavarini to Le Diable à Paris (1845–46), with the black giant crouched over the map of Paris studying the features of the city through his monocle. Literary historian Karlheinz Stierle observes that the basket carried on the giant's map is overflowing with manuscripts and observations by Parisians, reports on the same urban life chronicled in the very book they are now reading.[69] Functioning as a self-reflexive device, the engraving calls attention to the means of representation of the book and its mass circulation. Like the stack of newspapers in Weegee's photographs, it highlights its own narrative voice as essential to revealing the city in its bare truth.[70]

McCleery's comparison of Weegee's city to a female body raises the question of the psychosexual relations such a figure implies. Laura Mulvey's influential essay "Visual Pleasure and Narrative Cinema" suggests two characteristic strategies through which the male unconscious can escape from castration anxiety:

Preoccupation with the reenactment of the original trauma (investigating the woman, demystifying her mystery), counterbalanced by the devaluation, punishment, or saving of the guilty object (an avenue typified by the concerns of film noir); or else a complete disavowal of castration by the substitution of a fetish object or turning the represented figure itself into a fetish so that it becomes reassuring rather than dangerous.[71]

Reading McCleery's trope of the city as female body through Mulvey's Freudian schema, one is struck by the applicability of these varied scopic

Gavarini, frontispiece to *Le Diable à Paris* (Paris, 1845–46).

regimes to many of the photographs in *The Naked City.* In Weegee's photographs the city is continuously feminized as the object of a controlling gaze. The serial repetition of wounds and corpses in his crime and accident photos evokes the anterior trauma of an equally palpable psychic injury that never subsides, even as such violence is aesthetically represented. Devalued, punished by the law, or saved by fire or police rescuers, the subjects of Weegee's urban photographs, even at their most disorderly or pathetic, are still embraced by the photographer; his amorous relation to the "soul of the city I knew and loved" is never questioned.[72] And in their fascination with movie stars, Frank Sinatra, transvestites, and striptease artists, many of Weegee's images reveal the logic of fetishism.

Haunted by absence and presence, oscillating between impassivity and tenderness, lack and fulfillment, real objects and fetish objects, Weegee's photographs conjure an impossible urban body, simultaneously reassuring yet stimulating, capable of providing some measure of psychic equilibrium. Yet the very refusal to disavow the violence he encounters on the job lends the corporeal metaphor in his book title an element of desperation. Searching for photo opportunities night after night in his beloved city, Weegee comes to resemble the melancholic lover of a phantasmatic body described by Christine Buci-Glucksmann:

> The horizon of melancholic loss or withdrawal of the love-object explains why the poetic experience focusses on bodies, and especially on the female body which is confronted with its most destructive othernesses: death and the angelic aura of nostalgic, impossible love . . . And yet, as in all melancholy, desire is gripped by a kind of "heroic fury" or "lovesickness," a sublimity and bodily excess. For the melancholic gaze, as for the baroque gaze, the body always announces itself as lost and overly present.[73]

Reading advertisements for Mark Hellinger's film *The Naked City*, it is not hard to discern the trope of this lost and overly present feminized urban body, confirmation (if this were necessary) together with McCleery's foreword that the gender of Weegee's metropolis is female. "The Soul of a city. Her glory stripped! Her passions bared! Raw life! Real life! Reckless life! Filmed through the eyes of the New York homicide squad. Actually filmed on the sidewalks of New York," one advertisement (illustrated with a female body draped over the film title) intones. Yet Weegee's direct biographical connection to the film noir cycle was minimal. It involved his appearance in bit parts in *The Set-Up* (Robert Wise, 1949) and *M* (Joseph Losey, 1951) and culminated with the sale of his book title to producer Mark Hellinger in 1946. This involved a payment of $6,200, with Weegee being hired to serve as a consultant and to play the role of a press photographer in the film.

Although Weegee's performance as an extra is inconspicuous (perhaps not even present) in the film, at least a few of its shots—those of children opening up fire hydrants and a cleaning woman in a deserted bank—might well have been inspired by his photographs. Hellinger steadfastly denied

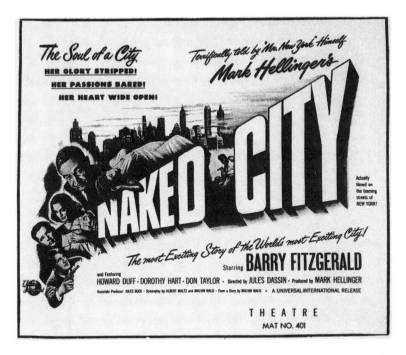

Advertisement from pressbook for *The Naked City* (Jules Dassin, 1948). Courtesy of Mark Hellinger Collection, Cinema and Television Library, University of Southern California.

that Weegee's book could prove valuable to a motion picture.[74] Yet such a claim disavows the key feature shared by the "naked cities" of both men, namely their role as urban narrators whose humanizing discourse imposes order upon the random and often chaotic experience of the metropolis. Both Weegee and Hellinger became identified with the city through their media productions in a manner that guaranteed their sincerity and authority to speak its reality, and lent their pronouncements a reassuring quality.

Hellinger, the successful producer of earlier atmospheric films noir such as *The Killers* (Robert Siodmak, 1946) and *Brute Force* (Jules Dassin, 1947), began his career as a newspaper columnist and covered Broadway for the *New York Daily News* through the 1920s. A close confidant of gossip columnist Walter Winchell, Hellinger, according to his authorized posthumous biographer, Jim Bishop, wrote about New York in a glib, superficial, and charming conversational tone. Often recycled from stories provided by readers and published literary tales, his columns hinged upon cliché and anecdote, yet avoided the gossip disseminated by Winchell. Hellinger shared Weegee's cynicism about human nature, even as his writing expressed "tremendous love of human beings" encountered in the city. Like Weegee, his celebrity made him more famous than the topics he covered, and by the time his syndicated column began appearing in the Hearst newspapers in the 1930s it reached an estimated 25 million readers per week.[75] Long accustomed to nocturnal forays in the metropolis and fascinated by the lives of ordinary people, Hellinger took their heartaches and successes as a theme for a column he called "Unsung Broadwayites."

Hellinger built upon his power as a columnist to establish a career in the film industry and eventually became an associate producer at Warner Brothers, where he worked with director Raoul Walsh on *They Drive by Night* (1939) and *High Sierra* (1940). Malvin Wald, author of the story treatment on which the screenplay was based (and a veteran of the First Air Force Army Motion Pictures unit), claims to have convinced Hellinger to produce a film set entirely in the streets of New York, and to gamble that the vogue for location photography introduced by wartime documentaries, Italian Neorealism, documentarist Louis De Rochemont's *March of Time* newsreels, and *The House on 92nd Street* (Henry Hathaway, 1945) might have commercial potential.[76] While Wald was writing the story treatment for the film, he conducted extensive research in the New York Police Department. He attended detective school and read through unsolved cases of the New York Police Department for inspiration, selecting the unsolved murder of a blonde model called Dot King as the basis for his story.[77]

In the opening sequence of the film, Hellinger's voice-over, often cited as an instance of "voice of god" disembodied first-person narration, alternates between statement of fact and prediction.[78] Later the narrator even addresses the characters directly, an extradiegetic intrusion into the fictional world of the narrative. Hellinger's narration adopts an informal poet-novelist persona influenced by Walt Whitman, according to Wald.[79] This technique is subsequently employed in *The City That Never Sleeps* (John H. Auer, 1953), in which a narrator also speaks as the voice of the city, yet without a distinctive persona. Harold Lightman wrote in *American Cinematographer* that Hellinger "personified The Big City, the brashness of the prohibition era, the 'stop-the-presses' school of journalism. Like his contemporary, the late Damon Runyon, he was a bard of the modern age—a chronicler of the complex, urban, sometimes-hysterical 20th Century in America."[80] As Sarah Kozloff has noted, "since [Hellinger] publicly identified himself so closely with New York (the publicity posters called him 'Mr. New York himself') the voice becomes the voice of The City, secondly since Hellinger was the film's producer and thoroughly in charge at every step, there is no question but that this voice speaks as the film's image maker."[81]

A clue to the significance of the opening aerial cinematography in *The Naked City* can be found in the montage sequence that immediately follows it. Here, imitating Walther Ruttmann's *Berlin: Symphony of a Great City* (1927), emerges a social, economic, and geographic cross-section of a day in the life of New York.[82] This technique borrows heavily from the tradition of the urban novel and its resolution of spatial conflicts by arranging them in a temporal sequence.[83] Yet despite this common narrative structure, significant differences exist between the two films and their presentations of their respective cities.

Ruttmann's Berlin is entered from the surrounding countryside at dawn

Frame enlargement of urban crowd from *Berlin: Symphony of a Great City* (Walther Ruttmann, 1927).

by a speeding locomotive with a camera mounted on it. First seen are the outlying industrial districts, as if to reinforce the subsequent images of assembly lines, machine parts, laboring masses, and Tiller Girl–style revue dancers as the foundation of its urban identity as a site of industrial production. Frequent shots of crowded sidewalks, sidewalk cafés, and residential courtyards convey the impression of a frenetic metropolis of irrepressible kineticism but one still possessing urban centers and the possibility of centralized control, an idea expressed by repeated shots of police conducting automobile traffic.

By contrast, the day in the life of New York in *The Naked City* begins at night, when the city is asleep. The sequence thus contains fewer crowds and more empty streets and buildings, as if to emphasize the separation of the city's inhabitants from one another. New York appears less the hyperbolic unity of movement suggested by Ruttmann's Berlin than a series of discrete topoi that require maintenance by a servile workforce. Hellinger speaks of ordinary New Yorkers playing themselves in the film, and this characterization is vividly conveyed in the scenes of empty factories, banks, and theaters. Apart from a late-night supper club, a morning breakfast at a luncheonette, and a scene on the subway, street life is conspicuously absent, as are neighborhoods and landmarks that might suggest a viable urban center.

A convincing theoretical account of such urban anomie is provided by Jean-Paul Sartre. Visiting New York in 1946 (the same year Weegee sold Hellinger the film rights to his book title), he became fascinated by the predicament of the individual in American mass society and the power of managers and institutions to predict and adjust markets, behavior, and production. Sartre called this mode of cultural production directed simultaneously toward everyone and no one "seriality." He defined it through the constitution of social collectives based upon alterity, a relation of separation, rather than reciprocity. Writing concurrently with the film noir cycle (the anonymous streets in *Phantom Lady* seem to illustrate his concept perfectly), he discerned seriality as omnipresent in the United States but nowhere more evident than in a peculiarly American cultural form: the weekly radio broadcast of the Top Ten best-selling records. In this media practice, if the music consumer "listens to the radio every Saturday and if he can afford to buy every week's No. 1 record, he will end up with the re-

cord collection of the Other, that is to say, the record collection of no one
. . . Ultimately, the record collection which is no one's becomes indistinguishable from everyone's collection—though without ceasing to be no
one's."[84]

In another example, that of the newspaper quiz, "whoever wins—that is
to say, is chosen, selected, publicly named, and rewarded—does so because
he has been more perfectly Other than all the Others."[85] Seriality dominates the metropolis, in whose space, Sartre notes,

> Isolation becomes, for and through everyone . . . the real social prod-
> uct of cities . . . And through the medium of the city, there are given
> the millions of people who are the city, and whose completely invisi-
> ble presence makes of everyone *both* a polyvalent isolation . . . *and* an
> *integrated* member of the city . . . Let me add that the mode of life oc-
> casions *isolated behavior* in everyone—buying the paper as you leave
> the house, reading it on the bus, etc.[86]

Both the aerial cinematography footage and the urban cross-section
employed in *The Naked City* engage the culture of seriality and isolation
that Sartre locates in the capitalist metropolis. The film depicts the city as
a socially produced set of distances between its inhabitants and represents
the metropolis as an accumulation of processed matter, an immense iner-
tial force, produced by the meanings and actions of human beings. Sartre
termed this residue of past human activity the "practico-inert."[87] "Does
money ever sleep, I wonder?" Albert Maltz wrote in a pointed social jab
(omitted from the film) that suggests monetary circulation in the city as
the quintessential serial process, a relation between human beings reified
into seemingly autonomous dynamic.[88]

Repeatedly anthropomorphized in Hellinger's narration, which compares the city to a sleeping body whose pulse never stops beating (again
evoking Weegee), this organicization is nonetheless undermined by the
montage sequence and its presentation of a city as an inexorable sequence
of mechanical processes without any centralized control.[89] Such a conflict
between competing rhetorics of urban description, between the directed
personality of the corporealized metropolis and impersonal mechanical
functions, permeates *The Naked City*. "Do machines in a factory ever need

Frame enlargement of disc jockey from *The Naked City* (Jules Dassin, 1948).

rest?" the narrator inquires. "You put on a record and take it off. You put on another one. Does anybody ever listen to this program but my wife?" the disc jockey complains.

That the response to both questions may well be negative is suggested by the ironic line in the narration spoken in a voice attributable to the linotype operator occupied at his machine: "It's wonderful to work on a newspaper; you meet such interesting people." Unlike Ruttmann's film, *The Naked City* assigns subjectivity and individuality to this character and to the cleaning woman who complains about dirty feet while mopping an immense lobby, as if simultaneously to humanize and to undercut the critical force of their remarks. Isolation within urban technological society defines the city as an ensemble of what Sartre called "indirect gatherings," defined by relations of absence and alterity between citydwellers. He suggested that serial behavior, serial feelings, and serial thoughts exist. Expanding upon his insight, I would argue that there also exist serial modalities of urban space. Take, for example, Sartre's remarkable 1946 account of his pedestrian forays in New York City:

> I feel at ease if I walk quickly; if I stop I get flustered and wonder "Why am I in this street rather than in the hundreds of others like it?" Why am I standing in front of this drug-store, or this Schrafft's or

Woolworth branch, rather than in front of any other of these thousands of identical ones? . . . And suddenly pure space looms into view.
I imagine that if a triangle could become conscious of its position in
space, it would be terrified at the realization of the rigorousness of its
defining coordinates, but that it would also be terrified to discover
that it is merely any triangle, any place . . . In the numerical anonymity of the streets and avenues, I am simply anybody, anywhere . . . But
no valid reason justifies my presence in this place rather than in any
other, since this one is so like another. You never lose your way, and
you are always lost.[90]

Anticipating the critiques of urban and suburban uniformity that would
proliferate during the late 1940s, this account of a spatially homogeneous
New York also prefigures Lefebvre's understanding of abstract space as
well as the concept of simulation later developed by Jean Baudrillard.[91]
One street or drugstore resembles the next, and the anxiety incited by the
experience of pure space threatens loss of subjective identity as a correlate
to a metropolis now experienced as placeless, bereft of historical markers,
and increasingly indistinguishable from other cities. Such a nightmare of
the ubiquitous commodified city, a burden of modern life equally alienating whether present or absent, is evoked by Woolrich in his description of
a small suburban town in *Phantom Lady:* "It was still close enough to have
certain typical features of the metropolitan scene; a well-known five-and-
ten cent store, an A and P, a familiar chain orange juice concession. But
they only seemed to emphasize its remoteness from the originals, instead
of tempering it."[92]

A fear of the statistically average and anonymous urban realm, of its potential to level the metropolis into an isolated and isolating space of everyone and no one, haunts these passages and Sartre's notion of seriality. Film
noir trades heavily upon such an understanding of the city in which cultur-
ally sanctioned anonymity increasingly proves the rule. Countless nocturnal automobile rides through the metropolis in films such as *Cry of the City*
(Robert Siodmak, 1948) and *DOA* (Rudolph Maté, 1949) present the illuminated neon landscape of stores, cinemas, and commercial signage as
geographically nonspecific instances of what David Nye calls the "phenomenology of industrial society."[93]

No longer restricted to familiar neighborhoods, this new and vastly expanded urban space appears self-sufficient. The recognition by many post-war intellectual and cultural practitioners that mass culture and media increasingly were shaping the city and replacing earlier social practices based on direct and collective action expresses another dimension of "the naked city" as a cultural trope. To represent the metropolis adequately is now to treat these relatively new forms of communication beginning in the nineteenth century, maturing after World War I, but truly coming into their own only after 1945, no longer as mere accoutrements but as primary constituents of modern urban civilization. It is also to recognize that in this new social universe of statistical anonymity the buildings in stone invoked by Hellinger and White have lost their former hegemony in the establishment of collective meaning and community. Architecture undergoes a social transformation and suffers the assault of the written word earlier diagnosed by Victor Hugo in his famous proclamation in *Notre Dame de Paris* (1831) "this will kill that."[94]

Yet the built environment of New York experienced an equally palpable physical transformation after 1945 that complements, if not surpasses, Hugo's prediction. Many Manhattan landmarks filmed by director Jules Dassin and his crew on *The Naked City*, such as the Third Avenue elevated subway, disappeared shortly thereafter. Recalling the proclivity of the film noir cycle for urban topoi on the verge of destruction—Bunker Hill in Los Angeles, New York's Pennsylvania Station, the stockyards of Chicago—*The Naked City* included several scenes of the Turtle Bay neighborhood, east of First Avenue, between 42d and 48th Streets, at the precise moment, July 1947, it was being demolished to accommodate the building of the United Nations.[95]

Perhaps like Weegee, Dassin and Hellinger were drawn to this area for reasons they could not articulate. Its outmoded and putrid-smelling slaughterhouses along the East River shorefront that so horrified Theodore Dreiser, popularly nicknamed "Blood Alley," might well have seemed tailor-made for a film noir.[96] Sparsely inhabited, this seventeen-acre site remained a zone of "nonsynchronicity," as Bloch put it, a nonproductive holdover from an earlier moment of history that elicited revulsion and nostalgia in equal measure. By the summer of 1947 it was gone. Writing that July in a report on the construction site of the United Nations, the secretary general announced in vocabulary redolent of Le Corbusier that the complex would provide New Yorkers with the late-modern voids of "radiant space."[97]

Occupying the interstices between the burgeoning postwar spatiality of the large-scale void evident in projects such as Lincoln Center and an older centripetal space organized around the human body, *The Naked City* reveals a sense of loss no less than an awareness of the new possibilities accompanying New York's impending transformation. While a strongly centered metropolis was integral to the urban schemes of Le Corbusier and other modern city planners, the traditional urban fabric, including the street and its low-rise architecture, would inevitably disappear in their large-scale plans.

Weegee's photographs and the film *The Naked City* recognize the ascendance of seriality as a social principle. Each utilizes the mass media of newspaper photography and the cinema to participate in and document a social world now dominated by alterity and the relations of otherness described by Sartre. Conspicuous in their representations of New York City is an evident fascination with the ability of photography and cinema to represent direct (rather than indirect, in Sartre's parlance) social groups. This concern manifested itself in the elaborate publicity campaign that accompanied the release of the film. In the "Showman's Manual" published by its distributor, Universal, local exhibitors were encouraged to organize photographic contests in which participants would submit the best or most characteristic images of their city, especially when it "appears naked in the early morning hours." They were also encouraged to nominate a local person in the community to be their own Mark Hellinger, the voice of their local city.[98] Once again, the humanizing function of urban narration is unmistakable, as is its emphasis upon the reassurance provided by a familiar spokesperson for the city and a recognizable individual persona.

It is within this context that one should understand the rise of the police procedural genre in film noir. Spurred by the Depression, the professionalization of law enforcement from the 1920s through the 1950s entailed an increase in rank-and-file training, bureaucratic restructuring of police chains of command and response mechanisms, and a growing emphasis upon scientific investigation.[99] The introduction of the Uniform Crime Report system in the 1920s, a by-product of management science and public relations techniques, now construed criminality "as a recurrent state of affairs, appearing in predictable locations and, quite often, from a predictable class of perpetrators." Procedure came to be defined as "anticipating future criminal actions by following an actuarial logic based on past cases."[100] The criminal act became a statistical artifact delineated by a serial logic that emphasized its resemblance to other criminal acts and their anonymous perpetrators.

Parallel to this stress upon the average crime and its predictable location, a combination that translated easily into heightened surveillance of specific neighborhoods, a new breed of detective appeared, a college graduate and an intelligent family man rather than a romantic Sherlock Holmes or Sam Spade, as Wald discovered after reading an article in *Time* magazine.[101] Following procedure, this new breed of sleuth employed techniques and scientific analyses no longer specific to his individual genius but identical with those of every law enforcement officer. Nonetheless, the police must, "above all else, be human," as one commissioner noted in 1944, anticipating the ethos of bourgeois humanism radiated by myriad cultural projects after the war, including the lived experience valorized by film noir critic Nino Frank.[102] Thus, a defining tension of the procedural becomes evident in the conflict between the impersonal application of criminological method and the concomitant need "of little people . . . to establish a populist link with the cop."[103] It is hardly surprising that Detective Halloran in *The Naked City* lives not in the Manhattan of statistical anonymity but in the low-rise family-friendly borough of Queens.

Discussions of the police procedural in film noir generally emphasize its appropriation of true stories, collaboration with law enforcement agencies, location cinematography, and voice-of-god narration as elements of a transparent style. These features are understood to implicitly criticize the traditional classical Hollywood cinema through the articulation of a "space of truth" whose own conventions go unquestioned.[104] A film such as *Call Northside 777* (Henry Hathaway, 1948), with its extensive filming on the streets of Chicago and incorporation of actual newsreel footage, is paradigmatic of this approach to urban representation that blurs distinctions between fiction and documentary.

Despite the frequent depictions in these films of scientific techniques of crime detection, the presentation of this technology of police power as evidence of a "postwar cultural consensus" represents only a single strand of their ideological agenda.[105] No less significant, I would argue, is their depiction of the humanity of law enforcement officials and urban residents, epitomized by the jokes and banter of Barry Fitzgerald as Detective Muldoon and the nonprofessional actors in *The Naked City*. Contemporaneously with the introduction of the Uniform Crime Report, the 1920s introduced the culture of newspaper gossip developed by Walter Winchell that provided a common national "backyard fence," in Neal Gabler's apt spatial metaphor. By constructing a shared frame of reference, this popular journalistic mode proved reassuring to a country undergoing transformation from a community to an increasingly urbanized society.[106]

If the Uniform Crime Report rendered the criminal an anonymous statistic without a personality, the gossip column traded in no less extreme speculation about celebrity and character. Equally pervasive in tabloid newspaper coverage and photographic reportage, gossip promotes the seriality of mass culture by dissolving a unique life into a tissue of rumors and conjectures. Incidents of controversy or transgression ultimately matter less for what they might convey about an individual in his or her actuality than for their value in the system of gossip within which they elicit comparison with previous scandals. Juxtaposed with the anonymity of the Uniform Crime Reports and scientific law enforcement procedures on one side and the excess of personality associated with the circulation of gossip in the tabloids (not to mention the cult of the movie star that emerged around 1910) on the other, this accent upon the shared humanity of the police officer and average citizen suggests an effort to circumvent serial culture.[107] Through the articulation of a comforting human personality, it proposes a third option for a cultural identity defined by neither statistical anonymity nor media-dominated celebrity.

Whereas nineteenth-century criminology and photography constructed a juridically specifiable subject useful to the institutions of state power, the human individual proposed by the police discourse of the 1940s and exemplified in *The Naked City* facilitated a mode of subjectivity conducive to the postwar politics of consensus and the emerging society of consumption. Indeed, by the early 1950s the procedural became the object of parody in a film noir such as *The Tatooed Stranger* (Edward J. Montagne, 1950) in which an aerial shot over Central Park and the use of a female scientist as the detective imply a waning of the once-omnipotent combination of large-scale urban surveillance and male criminological prowess.

To humanize faceless citydwellers, to restore an experience of place to an urban realm becoming increasingly homogenized through abstract space, and to recognize the lived dimension of mass cultural seriality, such are the aspirations one might understand as common to the photographs of Weegee and *The Naked City* film. They employ four strategies of aesthetic transfiguration to realize these ends: disaster narrative, aerial views, street scenes, and humanizing narration. Each seeks to overcome distinctions between absence and presence, alterity and reciprocity, isolation and integration, and anonymity and individuality to yield a concrete representation of the metropolis and its inhabitants.

Whether we think of the killings and fires photographed by Weegee or the murder of model Jean Dexter in the film *The Naked City*, these narratives provoke new social groupings such as the temporary gatherings around crime scenes. Throughout the film, lurid tabloid crime coverage, frequently shown being read by characters in group situations such as on the subway, is presented as a social adhesive, a mode of collective reception, that holds together the metropolis. Never is the city more unified than when threatened by a criminal transgressor whose exploits become the subject of journalistic reportage, an idea already developed in *M* (Fritz Lang, 1931). The film suggests that such violence is the rule rather than the exception, a consequence of scarcity in social life.[108]

Frame enlargement of tabloid newspaper coverage of Dexter murder read by subway riders, from *The Naked City* (Jules Dassin, 1948).

The second aesthetic strategy involves the attempt to transcend seriality through elevated views of the city, to obtain a view from the "eye of God" that provides a visual correlative to the narrative reassurances of Weegee and Hellinger. Though rarely pursued by Weegee, such images abound in the film. Aerial and elevated views of Manhattan figure prominently in the opening sequence, in the scene in which Detective Halloran ascends a skyscraper under construction to locate the murderer, and in the final chase on the Williamsburg Bridge. Aspiring to represent the city as a social whole, a complete organism, these images presuppose positions removed from the lived space of everyday experience.

That so many films noir begin with elevated, aerial, or skyline views suggests that an essential feature of the film cycle entails the movement from a clearly delimited synoptic overview of the metropolis toward dark street corners, alleyways, and other relatively inaccessible interior spaces. Peter Hales identifies the earliest instances of elevated urban images in the United States as lithographic "bird's-eye" views of the nineteenth-century city with an aspiration to "enclose and to order" it.[109] These synoptic images and the early-modernist abstractions produced from elevated positions in the city by photographers such as Alvin Langdon Coburn and László Moholy-Nagy reveal a palpable cultural distance.[110] One might also trace these visual overviews to the mass-cultural form of the panorama and its photographic variant, of which Hales writes:

> Panoramas represented one of the most successful mechanisms photographers used to civilize the city and make it comprehensible. By enclosing and encapsulating the city, they gave it holistic identity. And to an urban culture characterized by vague, constantly shifting boundaries and a tenuous unity threatening always to break down into its cultural, economic, or geographic subcategories, closure and identity were precious commodities.[111]

Providing a mode of photographic totality, an experience that might allow the city to be viewed and conceived as a unity, the aerial photograph realizes this panoramic goal but with a twist, for it is also the quintessential serial artifact. Like the phenomenon of the Top Ten records analyzed by Sartre, its views claim universality but often are controlled by aerial photographers and law enforcement agencies.[112] As the view of anyone realized from the position of no one, the city of others rendered by others, the aerial view can never reinforce a directly lived reciprocal social identity, except perhaps among those experiencing it together in the air. Unlike the scene at the beginning of the film, the photographic panoramas of San Francisco created by Muybridge in the 1870s presented a "synthesized whole" whose spatial perspectives were easily accessible to the spectator, who could choose to visit them in person.[113]

No less pervasive in *The Naked City* is the scene in the street, the ground-level representations of the metropolis that link Weegee's photography to the film. Unlike aerial views, they capture a criminal's daily routine, including those traces of spatial practice that serve as clues and facilitate apprehension. Sometimes, as in the two scenes in which the murderer Garza eats an ice cream cone or reads a newspaper before we learn his identity, they recall Weegee's technique of incongruous urban montage. Here, the spectator is not granted more information than the police, and the scene reveals how the second-person mode of narrative address functions in *The Naked City* to delay knowledge and to individuate characters from the urban crowd. Hellinger's initially cryptic comment about a third man in the scene across from the police station (a reference to Garza before his identity is revealed) makes sense to the viewer only at the end of the film.

In the Lower East Side sequence, the space of backyards, dilapidated lots, alleys, and tombstones where the film's concluding manhunt transpires, these images suggest a challenge to the increasingly serial and abstract spatial environment shown in the midtown Manhattan sequences. Unlike the rationalized space of the uptown urban grid or the procedures of the police investigation, the Lower East Side presupposes the bodily familiarity and memory of spatial practice in order to navigate its maze. It is one of the few areas of New York filmed as a continuous nonfragmented space without elaborate montage or synoptic overviews, as if to accentuate its status as a vibrant space of representation. Juxtaposed with the ensuing Williamsburg Bridge sequence, the single instance in which the film appropriates modernist abstraction in its representation of New York, the neighborhood appears a haven of ethnic difference and cultural integrity.[114]

Contrast this depiction of the bridge in the film with Theodore Drei-ser's description of it in his 1923 book *The Color of a Great City:* "Take your place on Williamsburg Bridge some morning, for instance, at say three or four o'clock, and watch the long, the quite unbroken lines of Jews trun-dling pushcarts eastward to the great Wallabout Market over the bridge . . . A vast, silent mass it is, marching to the music of necessity. They are so grimy, so mechanistic, so elemental in their movements and needs."[115]

Dreiser's prose underscores the contrast between these earlier rhythms of human labor and the film's representation of the bridge as an abstract space of modernism and modernity. Every trace of the social relations it once fostered disappears in its formalized depiction in *The Naked City.* Reminiscent of the photographs of the Eiffel Tower by Germaine Krull, the images of the bridge nonetheless eschew cool technological styliza-tion, as well as the ebullience of Joseph Stella's paintings of the Brooklyn Bridge.[116] "Keep in Line: Cutting In and Out Prohibited" reads a sign di-rected to automobile drivers that Garza passes on his ascent to the tower. Though intended as a message to the motorists below, it conveys an alle-gorical message through its linkage of the spatial and social orders and a suggestion that Garza's ascent to the summit entails an equally perilous transgression.

As if announcing the inability of the city to be grasped any longer as a synoptic image, a totality, the view from the "eye of God" briefly occupied by Garza before he is shot down from the summit by the police is rendered literally unsustainable. The final breathtaking view of the Manhattan sky-line from the top of the bridge is succeeded by the no-less-spectacular fall of Garza to his death, powerfully confirming philosopher Bernd Jager's as-sertion that falling entails a loss of lived space.[117] To reflect upon the fact that in *Phantom Lady, The Naked City,* and *The Big Clock* all the criminal protagonists meet their deaths by falling from a tall structure is to lend credence to the identification of this spatial ascent with psychopathology.

As Jager writes, "Vertical space is a *tabula rasa* and a dissolvent of form . . . It is inhabited by all that which is recklessly inward and unworldly. It also is the dimension of madness and suicide."[118] Yet the film returns to this panoramic image a second time, granting the spectator, the everyone and no one addressed by the film, a privilege denied Garza, and underscor-ing the serial character of cinematic spectatorship. In a memo on this final

Frame enlargement of murderer Garza on Williamsburg Bridge, from
The Naked City (Jules Dassin, 1948).

sequence, Hellinger underscores the importance of its filming from the
perspective of the narrator and the bystander, as if to emphasize the syn-
thesis between ostensibly impersonal and personal views as a key element
of the film and to prevent his narrative voice from being usurped by the serial character of elevated images.[119]

Absent from many accounts of the film is a chronicle of the political turmoil that embroiled the makers of *The Naked City*. Hellinger died of a
heart attack on December 21, 1947, shortly after its completion. The distributor, Universal, reedited the film against the wishes of director Jules
Dassin, cutting the many comparisons between wealth and poverty the director claimed to have added to the script. Upon viewing the final release
version for the first time, Dassin felt ready to weep.[120] Both he and screenplay writer Maltz had been members of the American Communist Party.
The latter went to jail as one of the "Hollywood Ten" for his testimony as
an "unfriendly witness" before the House Un-American Activities Committee in October 1947, just months before the world premiere of *The Naked City* in New York on March 3, 1948. Dassin left the United States soon
thereafter and commenced a successful second career in Europe. Despite
Hellinger's alleged hostility to Communism and his reported willingness

to identify members of the party to the FBI, the political convictions of the two men he hired to work on the film scarcely appear to have concerned him.[121]

Film historians have speculated that the disfiguration inflicted upon *The Naked City* may well have reflected a climate of growing fear about Communist subversion in the Hollywood film industry.[122] What seems probable is that the film released by Universal that won an Academy Award in 1948 for best editing and best cinematography bore little resemblance to the ideal of emphasizing the "architectural beauty and squalor that exist side-by-side" that Maltz advocated in his notes for the filming of his screenplay. Had his advice and Dassin's direction been heeded, *The Naked City* might have more closely resembled the work of Weegee, if not the sharper-edged social commentary evident in many films noir.

Yet the Cold War political turmoil at the end of the 1940s echoed other cultural and spatial shifts of the postwar era. It announced an end to the urban media environment familiar to, if not through, Weegee, a fact that he sardonically noted in his 1961 autobiography: "New York was in transition. My beloved slums were disappearing. The place where I had spent my happy childhood was now a housing project for the under-privileged. Everything in New York was becoming regimented. All television programs had to be approved by Paddy Chayevsky. All street fights and rumbles were under the supervision of the Police Athletic League."[123]

Substitute the Lower East Side for the Place du Carrousel marked for demolition by Haussmann in Paris, and the parallel between Weegee and Baudelaire becomes compelling.[124] Like Baudelaire, Weegee retained an affection for crowds, even while he despised the growing significance of the mass in modernity. His carping about the underprivileged, his critique of social regimentation, and his romanticization of spontaneous violence all present him as a social outsider. This egregiously fictitious self-fashioning ignores the extent to which Weegee prospered within the social and media universe and was never simply a passive victim or an outsider ignored by the establishment. Nor does it acknowledge his occasional collaboration with and complicated relation to the police. Weegee's lifelong financial difficulties, and the thirty-four-year gap between his first American solo exhibition in 1941 and his second in 1975, lend credence to the view of him as an outsider, at least to the art world. If, like Baudelaire, he was a transitional figure whose work inaugurated a significant understanding of his culture's modernity, what might this have been?

A suggestive explanation is found in Weegee's attack upon the television medium and the growing centralization of its control. Coinciding with the publication of his book *The Naked City* in 1945 and the release of Hellinger's film three years later was a dramatic increase in the number of television sets in American homes, from 8,000 in 1946, to almost one million in 1949, to over 10 million in 1951. By 1960 the figure reached 45 million (almost 90 percent of American homes).[125] Weegee's antipathy to television suggests nothing so much as an anxiety of influence, for what was the photographer with his automobile police radio (a unique privilege granted him by the authorities) and mobile photo studio but a proto remote television reporter? Toward the end of his career, he even allowed victorious contest participants to accompany him on his nocturnal rounds, thus anticipating the now-familiar programs in which television producers of crime shows accompany the police.

One of Weegee's last portraits was of Andy Warhol, whose pronouncement on the culture of celebrity—"in the future everybody will be world famous for fifteen minutes"—challenges Weegee's Stieglitzian modernist enshrinement of the unique and unrepeatable temporality of the photograph.[126] In a sea of evanescent media images the claim to present the city in its actuality becomes less compelling than the desire to register the very ephemerality of the new media landscape ushered in by television. Disaster imagery figures prominently in both the work of Weegee and Warhol, yet the serial reproduction decisive in Warhol's silk screenings breaks with Weegee's romantic aesthetic of the photograph as a unique fragment of reality and presupposes—perhaps even welcomes—the culture of seriality as its decisive principle. The serial rhythms of the city in Hellinger's film and the tabloid circulation of Weegee's photographs appear muted by comparison with Warhol's stated desire to be a machine.[127]

The irony implied by such an ambition is not far removed from the ending of *The Naked City*, in which the film self-reflexively exposes its own multilevel implication within serial culture. As Hellinger's voice-over revisits the characters of the narrative in the aftermath of Jean Dexter's death, we see Detective Muldoon surveying the Manhattan skyline from a

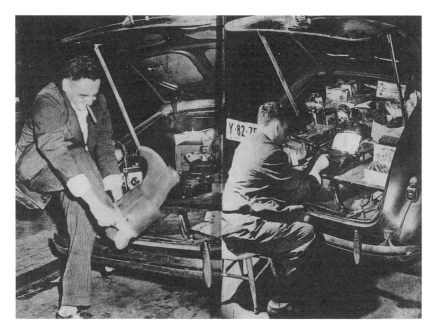

Weegee and his mobile photography studio from Weegee, *The Naked City* (New York: Essential Books, 1945). Copyright © Weegee / International Center of Photography / Getty Images.

distant rooftop, as if to cast doubt upon his control of the metropolis. We also see a crumpled newspaper headline proclaiming the solution of her murder by the police as it is swept up and thrown away by a street cleaner in Times Square—one story out of the eight million possible stories mentioned by the narrator, now forgotten. Both the high point of Weegee's career and the police procedural film were not far behind, soon to be exhausted by the 1950s, recycled in television series such as *Dragnet* and *The Naked City*, and lifted as the title for that most celebrated situationist icon, the 1957 psychogeographical map designed by Guy Debord and Asger Jorn.[128]

In the film's final image, the lights and marquees of Times Square become illuminated, as if to oppose the solidity of the metropolis to the transience of media representations. Yet this trademark film noir cityscape realizes, like Gavarini's drawing, a *mise en abîme*, for what is Times Square but the epicenter of media culture from which even *The Naked City* cannot escape, such overtures toward self-reflexivity and the reassuring voice of

Frame enlargement of newspaper with Jean Dexter newspaper headline being swept in gutter by street cleaner, from *The Naked City* (Jules
Dassin, 1948).

Hellinger notwithstanding? Paradoxically, the publicity and advertising
campaign prepared by the distributor ignored this scene. It went to great
lengths to distance the film from the Runyonesque association of Broadway with fiction and staged spectacle, thereby curiously denying to the
film what might well be its only urban center:

> For background art we use the familiar New York landmarks from the
> picture such as the Williamsburg Bridge, the Eastside, the waterfront,
> the elevated, but at no time Times Square. In fact, we pointedly avoid
> the suggestion that Broadway or Times Square are involved in the
> story. In other words, this is not the often told story of Broadway but
> the real, untold, intimate story of the people of the city.[129]

If there is any truth-telling in the naked cities exposed by Weegee and
Hellinger, it probably consists not in an intimate account of the people of
New York but in a subtle and easily overlooked critique of earlier modernist metaphors—the vibrant pulse and romance of the urban body, the mechanical rhythms of the city, and the objective aerial view—in the service
of understanding the metropolis as a space of greater moral uncertainty in

which broad overviews, clear judgment, and empathic response are complicated by the culture of seriality. The narrative voices of Weegee and Hellinger humanize this cultural transition and offer viewers the illusion of transcending the media spectacle with which all are in fact complicit. Hinging upon the mixed metaphor of the naked city, the modes of address operative in their work remain beholden to a cultural logic that takes the visible body and the charismatic urban personality as its fundamental axioms.

Lefebvre trenchantly analyzes the organicism implied by the naked city as cultural trope:

> When an institution loses its birthplace, its original space, and feels threatened, it tends to describe itself as "organic." It "naturalizes" itself, looking upon itself as and presenting itself as a body. When the city, the state, nature or society itself is no longer clear about what image to present, its representatives resort to the easy solution of evoking the body, head, limbs, blood or nerves. The physical analogy, the idea of an organic space, is thus called upon only by systems of knowledge or power that are in decline. The ideological appeal to the organism is by extension an appeal to unity, and beyond that unity (or short of it) to an *origin* deemed to be known with absolute certainty, identified beyond any possible doubt—an origin that legitimates and justifies. The notion of an organic space implies a myth of origins, and its adduction eliminates any account of genesis, any study of transformations, in favor of an image of continuity and a cautious evolutionism.[130]

Thinking about New York after 1948, we might well conclude that the organic metaphor of the naked city serves the defensive function outlined by Lefebvre and compensates for the declining cultural force of centripetal space. At a moment when the mass media and centrifugal space were challenging the hegemony of the centered city, the continuity and cautious evolutionism implied by the belief in the city as an organic entity might easily have provided a welcome reassurance. For despite the unknowability of the millions of stories in the metropolis, an appeal to its unity and knowable origin was undoubtedly comforting and familiar.

Subsequent centripetal films noir would continue to explore the interrelation between the circulation of the mass media and the city, and further suggest their inextricability. In *Deux Hommes dans Manhattan / Two Men in Manhattan* (Jean-Pierre Melville, 1958), the central characters are employed by *Paris Match* magazine and the Agence France press agency. Melville's film, a historical curiosity filmed in French and English with a bilingual cast (including the film director himself in the lead role) on actual locations in New York, proves a challenging case for inclusion in a national cinema. Is this an American film noir made by a French director, a French film noir set in New York, or a hybrid production that fits uneasily in any single category?[131]

Two Men in Manhattan narrates the quest of a reporter and a photographer for the missing French delegate to the United Nations. Here New York appears less as a nostalgic evocation of its past (unlike *The Naked City*, no horse-drawn carts or ethnically homogeneous neighborhoods are anywhere to be seen) than as a future-oriented world city of global exchange and information production, an emphasis confirmed by the film's obsession with audiovisual reproduction. Commencing with a romantic jazz soundtrack and a nocturnal drive through Times Square with the camera filming from the rear window, upon reaching the midtown neighborhood of office towers the film cuts to a frontal view through the windshield.

A pan across a row of skyscrapers on the East Side concludes with the United Nations building. The voice-over narrator contrasts a 1912 street light "forgotten by urban planners" with "the great glass building on First Avenue" and presents the Italian, Jewish, and Irish children who play beneath it as evidence of the same ethnic and national mix found inside the building. Conjoining the old and the new in an urban film noir, the film celebrates the architecture of Wallace Harrison's United Nations, completed in 1952, with evident enthusiasm. A series of three additional pans emphasizes the vertical mass of the reflective transparent Secretariat, and finally cuts to the inside of the General Assembly.

We soon learn from the narrator that the French delegate has disappeared, a fact that the armies of reporters, photographers, teletype machines, telephones, and assorted sound recording equipment are well placed to register and communicate. In fact, the only form of labor depicted in the film is the reporting accomplished by the professionals shown

Frame enlargement of United Nations Secretariat building, from *Two Men in Manhattan* (Jean-Pierre Melville, 1958).

in the United Nations, as well its two protagonists, the reporter Moreau (Jean-Pierre Melville) and his photographer colleague Delmas (Pierre Grasset), who are charged by the French press agency with the task of learning why the delegate has vanished.

After a cut from the United Nations to Rockefeller Center, a brass horn is heard playing "Silent Night" in Channel Plaza, arguably Manhattan's most famous centered and centering space. Moreau and Delmas pursue a wild trail of leads that takes them to a Broadway theater, a recording studio, a Brooklyn bar, a bordello, and Times Square before they eventually locate the diplomat, dead of an apparent heart attack, in the apartment of his mistress. Arguing about the morality of publishing such incriminating images, Delmas and Moreau stare out upon the New York skyline from the roof of the building, as Delmas attacks the latter for surrendering his opportunity to become a millionaire.

The buildings they are looking at confirm the postwar economic and political supremacy of the United States. Unlike Detective Mulvey in *The Naked City*, who contemplates the skyline from a considerable distance, Moreau and Delmas are effectively in its midst. Yet the towers that surround them also allude to the increasing self-consciousness of the film noir cycle during the 1950s, and of Melville's film in particular. Though clearly intended as a love letter to New York, Melville's representation of the city resonates with the observation of the Agence France director that "history is no longer written but photographed." Contributing to the myth of New York as capital of the twentieth century, Melville romanticizes it to a far greater degree than an earlier French visitor such as Sartre and ultimately fuses the city with the image of its skyscrapers, a *ville radieuse* of the postwar world more gratifying to the filmmaker than it was to Le Corbusier.

The mass media play a prominent role in *The Big Clock*, John Farrow's 1948 adaptation of Kenneth Fearing's novel that presents the attempt of a magazine editor to outwit the efforts of his boss to frame him for a murder that he in fact committed. The opening pan across the dark New York skyline set to a jazz melody evokes the visual form of the nocturne.[132] Such an association is broken by the terminus of the shot, the flat, unadorned facade of the Janoth Building. Tracking into the building through the large plate glass windows of its lobby, the film introduces *Crimeways* magazine editor George Stroud (Ray Milland) as he evades security guards in the marble labyrinth of its lobby.

Stroud hides in the big clock deployed in its nucleus that centrally controls time in each office throughout the structure. A cylinder of flashing lights entered through a winding circular staircase, the interior of the clock evokes a deranged capitalist revision of Vladimir Tatlin's *Monument to the Third International* (1920). Centered control, rather than dynamism, permeates this mechanism, nowhere more evident than on its exterior with a map of the world and the forty-three bureaus of the Janoth organization that maintain the identically synchronized time.[133] Guy Debord's celebrated thesis in *The Society of the Spectacle* that the false consciousness of time pervades late capitalist societies attains vivid presence here.[134] Each floor of the Janoth headquarters houses a different magazine (*Styleways, Airways, Futureways, Urbanways, Pictureways* are but a few depicted in the credits) and seamlessly blends time, space, and the visual images of countless lifestyles. Fearing's novel conveys this omnipotence in Stroud's remarkable description of the clock that anticipates Debord's notion of the spectacle: "The big clock ran everywhere, overlooked no one, omitted no one, forgot nothing, remembered nothing, knew nothing. Was nothing, I would have liked to add, but I knew better. It was just about everything. Everything there is."[135]

This ability of the mass media continually to remake the social world according to the logic of the image constitutes a key facet of the future-directed quality that Sartre attributed to seriality.[136] In his speech to employees of his various magazines at a meeting designed to increase circulation, Earl Janoth (Charles Laughton) expresses a similar point in the film: "We live in a dynamic age, gentlemen. With dynamic competitors, radios, newspapers, newsreels. And we must anticipate trends before they are trends. We are in effect clairvoyants."[137] Little wonder that space is distinctly inferior to time in this domain of social control and renders the synoptic overview, the bird's-eye view or elevated perspective, insignificant.

No longer limited to neighborhoods such as Greenwich Village or the Lower East Side, the criminality explored by many films noir beginning in the late 1940s increasingly entails malfeasance by corporate or institutional employees. The era proclaimed by Peter Drucker's *The New Society* (1949) and analyzed in William Whyte Jr.'s *The Organization Man* (1956) had begun.[138] Both *Two Men in Manhattan* and *The Big Clock* conspicuously feature modern architecture in office towers. As the narrator in the trailer produced for the latter film depicts its star, Ray Milland, his role entails "twisting and turning through all the shadowed byways of the skyscraper city." This shift in the location of shadows from the street to the urban architectural complex neatly encapsulates the arrival of New York City as the center of the new postwar international economic and political order. Writing in *Variety* during the middle of the film's production in March 1947, one reporter noted:

Possibility exists that Paramount set designer Roland Anderson will achieve some sort of global fame as a result of set for "The Big Clock." Architects and furniture houses have been asking for sketches and permission to take a looksee but one New York group has gone even further. Architects are studying design and construction of ingenious clock, focal point of film, which has 25 faces, telling the exact time in each of the world's four time zones. Group is believed to be among the architects commissioned to draw up plans for the new United Nations headquarters along New York's East River in midtown. And because of its global character, design of Anderson's clock may ultimately be used for lobby of UN administration building to keynote One World idea.[139]

There appears to be no supporting evidence besides this report that the clock depicted in the film played any direct or indirect role in the interior design of the United Nations complex; the news item may well have been concocted by the studio press department. Nonetheless, it makes clear that the convergence of the film's architecture with the imminent arrival of the United Nations in New York had not escaped the attention of Hollywood. That the big clock was perceived as an expression of the "One World idea" is as significant as an earlier report (more likely based on the truth) that Anderson's furniture designs in the film elicited significant interest from a public starved for modern design and far surpassed the styles then available in catalogs.

Although the control of time is jeopardized at the novel's conclusion when the clock temporarily stops, the film also hints at moments when urban spatiality portends a loss of individual identity, a new mode of uncanny spatial experience accompanying late modernity. An elevated shot emphasizes the anonymity of tourists walking through the lobby of the Janoth Building. It is a point more powerfully expressed in the novel when Stroud arrives at the terminus of his morning commute, that great hub of centripetal space, the train station.

> Finally, as the train burrowed underground, I prepared myself for the day by turning to the index and reading the gist of the news. If there was something there, I had it by the time the hundreds and thousands of us were intently journeying across the floor of the station's great ant heap, each of us knowing, in spite of the intricate patterns we wove, just where to go, just what to do.[140]

Reading the morning paper, Stroud obtains an informational overview of the city to whose knowledge economy he contributes. If there is anxiety in this passage, it resides in the acknowledgment that a visual image of social life, a coherent synoptic overview of the urban workforce, has come to resemble an antheap, if not the vertical aerial photograph scrutinized by military surveillance analysts. The pretense of depicting the metropolis as a social unity, a conceit vital to the narratives of the city symphony tradition, Weegee, and Hellinger's film, has become impossible.

Expressed in the terms of Gilles Deleuze, it might be argued that the synoptic visual images of skylines, panoramas, and aerial views pervasive in films noir exemplify the spatial concentration and enclosure of the "disciplinary societies" of the eighteenth and nineteenth centuries. Appropriating the work of Foucault, Deleuze describes "the ideal project of these environments of enclosure, particularly visible within the factory: to concentrate; to distribute in space; to order in time; to compose a productive force within the dimension of space-time whose effect will be greater than the sum of its component forces."[141]

With the emergence of what Deleuze terms "societies of control," the decentralized workings of power in an age of corporate capitalism, disciplinary societies come to an end. Here one can relate the demise of the synoptic image to the emergence of new social modalities for which enclosure within a determinate space-time becomes less significant. For example, take the swarm of anonymous urban individuals in "The Beehive," a photograph made from the ceiling of the terminal dome in Grand Central Station by railroad worker Ed Nowak in the 1950s. Opposing the power and grandeur conveyed by older skyline and elevated depictions of the city, let alone the kinetic vibrancy of a film such as *Berlin: Symphony of a Great City*, its abstraction of the urban crowd suggests the railroad terminal as the locus of abstract space.

A surveillance image of a peculiar kind, it proposes a breakdown of the panoptical structure of earlier metropolitan representations with their emphasis upon ordering the city and endowing it with a visual unity. Though containing a center, the photograph offers no insight into the crowd, long a familiar theme in the art of the nineteenth century, and instead suggests what Meyer Shapiro calls an "aggregate of aimlessly moving atoms."[142]

The very surfeit of visual information in "The Beehive" cancels out its potential cognitive value and underscores the distance between this image and the synoptic views of the city that precede it. Compared to a photograph of people leaving a skyscraper and congregating in diverse patterns reproduced in Sir Raymond Unwin's essay on tall buildings, "The Beehive" provides no insight into the space of the city. By the 1950s, this "generalized look" of the metropolis resembles nothing so much as the

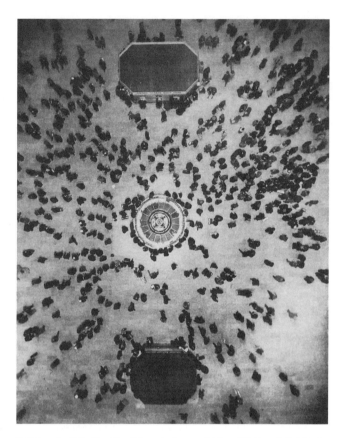

Ed Nowak, "The Beehive," frontispiece to Richard F. Crandell, *This Is Westchester: A Study in Suburban Living* (New York: Sterling Publishers, 1961).

patterns of dots on an empty television screen and is scarcely more revealing.[143]

Despite the ironic transposition of the natural to the social conveyed by the photograph's title, "The Beehive" is indifferent to depicting individual bodies or the city as a coherent entity. Circulation, pulse, temporal sequence, and clear overview matter little in such an image, whose disconnection from the daily rhythms of the city offers no clues about the time of day when it was taken. Like Stroud's description of the station quoted above, it allegorically conveys the flow of capital in the postwar information economy, whose intricate patterns of movement no longer prove amenable to corporeal metaphor. "The Beehive" provides a fitting epi-

Sir Raymond Unwin, "People Leaving a New York Skyscraper
at Evening," from "Higher Building in Relation to Town
Planning (1924)," in *The Legacy of Raymond Unwin: A Human
Pattern for Planning*, ed. Walter L. Creese (Cambridge: MIT
Press, 1967).

taph for the cultural and cinematic figure informing the photographs of
Weegee and the film of Hellinger and Dassin. It suggests that the celebra-
tory mode of much previous urban photography and cinema was losing its
capacity to represent the society of everyone and no one, the other and the
stranger, pursued by film noir in its elusive quest for the naked city.

2
CENTRIPETAL SPACE

Penetrated on every side by the radioactivity of our own space-time thought, our physical surroundings are disintegrating before our eyes. Flattened by the bulldozer of our inexorable logic in action, our cities seem to be on the way to becoming desert parking spaces. They must sooner or later be rebuilt to correspond to the image of the universe we have created. For this purpose, we must someday have kinetic money, but that is another question.

—**George Howe, "Flowing Space: The Concept of Our Time" (1949)**

Swooping down on the city as if to catch it unawares, *Criss Cross* (Robert Siodmak, 1949) begins with a briskly moving aerial sequence. Before any character enters the narrative, the film identifies Los Angeles as its setting by presenting its highly recognizable City Hall as its first image. Moving to the east, it hovers over the downtown business district and toward the low-rise residential structures of Boyle Heights and Bunker Hill. Filmed at night, the city appears a blaze of illuminated buildings, its status as the locus of dramatic possibilities underscored by the powerful strains of the romantic musical score composed by Miklos Rozsa.

Gradually lowering its altitude, the camera eventually settles upon a parking lot, dissolves to a closer view, and introduces the two main characters, Steve Thompson (Burt Lancaster) and Anna Dundee (Yvonne De Carlo). Later in the film we come to realize that this sequence is a flashback. Accessible only to the film spectator, this nondiegetic aerial journey through Los Angeles frames the impulsive actions of the characters in *Criss Cross*, as if to propose the metropolis as an omnipresent catalyst in

Harry Callahan, "New York, 1977." Partial view of the principal facade of the
Seagram Building (1954–1958) showing the pool and the adjacent building,
New York City (Ludwig Mies van der Rohe, Architect). Collection Centre
Canadien d'Architecture / Canadian Centre for Architecture, Montreal.
Copyright © the estate of Harry Callahan, courtesy Pace/MacGill Gallery,
New York.

their eventual self-destruction. Through its initial presentation of Los Angeles as lodged in the past, a gateway through which the narrative must pass,
the film introduces the city through the filters of violence and memory.

Six years later, *The Big Combo* (Joseph H. Lewis, 1955) opens with a similar aerial sequence. Filmed by John Alton at twilight as the sky darkens
over Manhattan, the camera travels across the canyons of its glowing skyscrapers. Set to the strains of the jazz composed by David Raksin, music
that would not be an inappropriate accompaniment for a striptease performance, this introduction of New York City itself suggests an urban
striptease. The city is sighted, surveyed, and gradually opened for exami-
nation by the spectator in a striking prefiguration of the urban mastery

Frame enlargement of Los Angeles from opening credits of *Criss Cross* (Robert Siodmak, 1949).

Frame enlargement of New York from opening credits of *The Big Combo* (Joseph H. Lewis, 1955).

wielded by mob leader Mr. Brown (Richard Conte) over Susan Lowell (Jean Wallace).

Four subsequent shots present closer views from the ground, pulling the viewer into the streets of midtown. A few architectural landmarks (perhaps the Metropolitan Life Building or the Empire State Building) are discernible in these images, yet these matter less than the city in which they are located. In the final shot of the opening, a pan down the side of an arena building ends in the street, where throngs of people are directed by a traffic cop as they arrive at a boxing match. Like the film spectator, they have arrived at the beginning of a violent spectacle with an unpredictable outcome.

Two films, two cities, two decades. Different as these sequences are in content and mood, both deposit the film spectator squarely in the metropolis and frame the ensuing narratives as resolutely urban in character. We might comprehend them as engaged in a centering operation through which the film narrative and the viewer are positioned in the city and, no less crucially, Los Angeles and New York are presented as visible and knowable. Less concerned with portraying them as the cultural and urban opposites they are conventionally thought to be, these films instead assimilate both to a common spatial logic of cities.

Introducing their respective cityscapes with energy and verve, *Criss Cross* and *The Big Combo* assert the tangibility of Los Angeles and New York. Displaying far more of the city than is necessary to commence their narratives and doing so through the complications and expense of aerial cinematography, these films may well raise suspicions by virtue of their grandiloquent openings. Analyzed in relation to postwar urbanism, the bravado of both aerial sequences might well be grasped as an implicit rejoinder to the growing cultural anxiety that the city had been eclipsed and its concentrated centers rendered inconsequential.

Representing the metropolis is never an innocent gesture but one that is always motivated by cultural needs and ambitions. What was at stake in this visual proffering of it and the traffic between the city and violent conflicts pervasive in film noir? The palpable absence of a single prominent center (despite many recognizable landmarks) and the continual motion of the camera in these opening scenes hint at a decisive shift in the identity of the postwar American city. Presented without the clearly delineated plaza, piazza, *place,* or *Platz* that traditionally provided a focal point for collective life in the large city, the metropolis in these two films noir confirms the heightened emphasis upon visualizing the skyline and the cityscape in relation to the trope of the naked city.

To consider the challenges and anxieties that accompany life in this new

Frame enlargement of sign announcing new building, from *Johnny One-Eye* (Robert Florey, 1950).

modality of the uncentered city, now rendered as a single metropolitan expanse on a vast scale, an early scene in *Johnny One-Eye* (Robert Florey, 1950), a film noir based on a Damon Runyon story, is instructive. Here the criminal Martin Martin (Pat O'Brien), sought by the police, takes refuge in Greenwich Village. Happening by chance upon the rundown building on MacDougal Street in which he hides, Martin pauses before a sign on its exterior that reads "Ultra modern apartment to be erected here." The film never clarifies when the announcement was first posted or when the edifice will be built. It is equally silent on the matter of its future stylistic identity, let alone whether the construction will prove a welcome addition to the neighborhood. Yet the placard's initial appearance in a point-of-view sequence and its recurrence in a later scene implies its significance. Contemporaneous with the Federal Housing Act of 1949 and King Vidor's adaptation that same year of Ayn Rand's 1943 novel, *The Fountainhead*, such opposition of modern architecture (often associated with aberrant characters throughout the cinema of the 1940s) to an unrefurbished urban past resonates suggestively with American culture and architecture of the 1940s and 1950s.

Juxtaposing a dilapidated older structure in a low-rise neighborhood with the promise of an architectural clean sweep to be realized in a temporally indeterminate future, the film reveals a key characteristic of the post-1939 American centripetal metropolis: the psychic hazards of dwelling in an urban space whose historical mutation yields real spatial gaps and temporal voids between the modern as "yet-to-come" and the urban past as "yet-to-be-destroyed." Simply, yet unmistakably, this scene conveys the fascination and anxiety generated by a decaying corner of the city located away from the central business district. It introduces the tensions permeating centripetal space.

Charles Baudelaire, Walter Benjamin, Siegfried Kracauer, Marshall Berman, and other critics of modernity have explored the uneasiness provoked by the modern city, locating it in the Parisian *quartiers* destroyed by Haussmann, the empty streets surrounding the Berlin *Mietskasernen* (rental barracks), and the no-man's-land of the freeway ribbons traversing countless cities in postwar America. As a prominent example of twentieth-century American popular culture set in the metropolis, a feature it shares with the contemporaneous forms of jazz and hardboiled fiction, film noir remains unique for its engagement with urban subject matter more often encountered in social and architectural histories than in Hollywood narrative film.

Like jazz, it can also evoke a rich soundscape that engages with the acoustics of the concentrated metropolis. Here we might think of the sounds of the New York subway that pervade the narratives of *Sorry, Wrong Number* (Anatole Litvak, 1948) and *The Window* (Ted Tetzlaff, 1949), as if to juxtapose the private destinies of their characters with the impersonal machinery of the urban transportation infrastructure. Although location cinematography would become common in many films noir from the late 1940s, synchronous or wild recording of the actual city was less frequent. Voice-over narration and nondiegetic music typically substitute for the actual sounds of the metropolis, whose realism even in the most atmospheric of films noir is seldom auditory.

More widespread is the use of jazz in nightclubs and entertainment establishments. Its modalities can vary from the torrid eroticism of the cellar jam session in *Phantom Lady*, to the Latin rhythms in the Round-Up bar in *Criss Cross*, to the melancholy rendition of Nat King Cole's "I'd Rather Have the Blues than What I've Got," first heard on a car radio and later sung by an African-American chanteuse in *Kiss Me Deadly* (Robert Aldrich,

1955), to the 52d Street milieu in which the Chico Hamilton Quartet performs in *The Sweet Smell of Success* (Alexander Mackendrick, 1957). It is the rare film noir without a scene in which jazz or vocal music is performed, lending it a wide range of associations ranging from the angst of bohemian nonconformism, to the liberal political ideal suggested by racially integrated clubs, to expressions of romantic or erotic longing.[1]

Runyon's story "Johnny One-Eye," first published in 1941 and filmed nine years later, exemplifies the customary lag between the urban space initially portrayed in crime fiction and later presented in film noir. Frequently explained in relation to the dynamics of adapting novels for the screen and loosening censorship restrictions, such a temporal discrepancy between the initial publication of a film's literary source and its cinematic adaptation in an actual urban location underscores the hybrid character of many films noir. This gap (ubiquitous in the cinematic transformation of novels by Raymond Chandler and James M. Cain) reiterates the status of film noir as an amalgam of nonsynchronous elements drawn from literature and contemporaneous urban culture and typically complemented by additions introduced by directors, screenplay writers, cinematographers, and the built environment itself.[2]

Johnny One-Eye commences with a credit sequence of still images that introduces the dramatic topoi of the film. A shot of the arch in Washington Square Park designed in 1895 by architect Stanford White, a block of row houses on MacDougal Street, a distant skyscraper, and a street scene introduce the film's New York locations. The first image of the narrative, a shot of the lower Manhattan skyline filmed from the Staten Island Ferry, underscores the urban fabric as an integral character of the narrative. This urban background is further emphasized in a pan shot that begins with criminals Martin Martin and Dane Corey throwing the body of a double-crossing associate called "The Dutchman" into New York Harbor and concludes once more with the skyline.

Such an insistent repetition of these urban landmarks, far more than is necessary to establish the film's setting, presents them as simultaneously background and active agent, object and subject of the camera's gaze, as if the skyscrapers were silent witnesses to the criminal activity before them. Yet the shot of distant buildings from the ferry also elicits comparisons to the earliest views of New York (once a city whose wealth *was* controlled by the Dutch), and invites the viewer to reflect upon its similarity to earlier images of the skyline and its waterfront architecture, many of which also were views from the harbor. As if confirming the opening lines of Martin's voice-over narration, "It all goes back a few years ago," the opening insinuates that the past inhabits the present, not merely according to the logic of temporal succession but also through a process of spatial layering in which the earlier architecture of the city, as well as its lingering phantasms, remains legible as if in a palimpsest.

This vestigial influence is most explicitly conveyed by the tension throughout the film between the vertical and horizontal axes of the city, first suggested in the skyline images and later reintroduced in the series of vertical camera pans of skyscrapers that commences with the apartment building where Martin resides. Now a respectable businessman, he is warned by an associate at the start of the film that the district attorney has obtained the cooperation of Corey and seeks to prosecute him for the unsolved murder of the Dutchman. A surprise visit by the police forces Martin to escape by a vertical slide down the laundry chute in his apartment, his first egress of many from tall buildings.

Seeking to silence Corey, Martin visits him at the Broadway theater where the latter enjoys a new career as a producer. After an exchange of

Frame enlargement of criminal Martin Martin in Times Square, from *Johnny One-Eye* (Robert Florey, 1950).

gunfire with Corey's associate in an alley near the stage door, Martin flees the scene. As he runs into the Times Square neighborhood, the film cuts to a long shot of the Brill Building at the corner of 49th Street and Broadway. It then cuts to a close-up of Martin as he clutches a lamp post for support. A shot from his point of view pans slowly across the feverishly illuminated signs and billboards of the area, settling upon the Brill, home to the music agents and publishers of Tin Pan Alley and the dazzlingly lit Turf Restaurant. For years a notorious gathering spot for figures from the entertainment industry and the underworld, Martin contemplates the eatery from the other side of the street, barred from its dynamism by an imperative to continue moving signaled by the florid strains of jazz.[3]

A low-angle shot of a lamp post confirms its location as 49th Street and Broadway and then pans down to reveal Martin walking along the street, away from the Times Square entertainment district. In the next shot, a vertical pan down the side of a skyscraper depicts Martin in midtown. This is followed by another vertical pan of a tall building that concludes with a vertical neon sign for a liquor store and shows Martin walking past the shop. A third pan down a skyscraper presents him walking through a low-rise neighborhood where he finds a newsstand and sees his photograph emblazoned on the front page of the newspaper, at which point he climbs the stairs of the Third Avenue elevated railway station.

After ascertaining the whereabouts of Corey's actress companion, Martin exits a bus near the Washington Square Arch, shown in the background. His move away from the urban center is now evident. He staggers through the streets of Greenwich Village until he crumples over next to a fire hydrant that seems to loom over him, and later is discovered by a night cop who takes him for a drunk. Martin wanders on until he arrives at the abandoned brownstone on MacDougal Street with a sign announcing the future modern construction. Here he is discovered first by a dog blinded in one eye that he dubs "Johnny One-Eye" and later by its owner, a little girl called Elsie. After he convinces her that he is Santa Claus, she eventually directs her mother's companion, Dane Corey, to the house where Martin and Corey die in a shoot-out. Elsie collects the reward for leading the police to the fugitive, and the dying Martin extracts a promise from a cop to buy her a new dog using the twenty-dollar bill in his pocket.

Mixing brutality and sentimentality in equal measure, *Johnny One-Eye* oscillates between the noir mise-en-scène and cruelty evident in director Robert Florey's previous film, *The Crooked Way* (1949), and the maudlin relationship between Martin and Elsie, appropriated with few changes from Runyon's story. Yet most relevant for my purposes is the spatial trajectory pursued by Martin in his evasion of the police and search for Corey. Central here is the film's recurrent formal device of panning down skyscrapers, repeated three times in the midtown sequence and echoed in other shots of the film that depict tall buildings soaring over Martin, as if to overpower him.

Combined with director Florey's predilection for filming from extremely low angles, these pans consistently reduce Martin in stature with respect to the surrounding urban architecture. No matter where he walks, a tall building rises over him, as if subjugating him by its presence and only grudgingly allowing him to share the space of the city. Yet unlike the depiction of New York's architecture by Florey in his short film *Skyscraper Symphony* (1929), the effect here is less one of intoxicating vibrancy than of violent force.[4] Exhibiting the dynamism associated with skyscrapers in much early-modern culture of the 1920s and 1930s, Florey's early contribution to the genre of the city symphony film playfully renders Manhattan's tall buildings as geometric abstractions and graceful formal compositions, sublime architectural achievements defamiliarized by the use of canted perspectives. By contrast, the skyscrapers in *Johnny One-Eye* suggest a less sanguine assessment of the tall building as an architectural form that causes the central business district to appear menacing and ill-suited to promoting collective life.

Philosopher Bernd Jager persuasively argues for understanding the vertical and the horizontal "as aspects of *lived space* rather than as purely geometrical designations." Read in this manner, Martin's walk through the vertical canyon of New York's towers entails precisely what Jager calls the "absence of the other as faced." Suggesting that the vertical can usher human beings into a world of "private fantasy or even psychosis," Jager notes that it typically involves a space in which people find themselves "alone, unfaced, unaided," a perfect description of Martin's fate in midtown, where he speaks with no one during his walk through the streets.[5]

More than simply a motif of alienation, the vertical architecture of Manhattan's skyscrapers depicted in *Johnny One-Eye* presents an urban scale that thwarts contact and exchange with other human beings.

This phenomenological description can be filled out by a historical account of tensions between the horizontal and vertical dimensions of urban form in New York. Historians William Taylor and Thomas Bender have noted the tendency to assume that "a horizontal monumentalism in buildings implies civic or public purposes, and that vertical structures such as towers represent the power of corporate capitalism."[6]

They trace this opposition back to the nineteenth century and the Beaux-Arts tradition of a unified architectural ensemble organized along axes and linked by street perspectives and uniform cornices, a design strategy epitomized by the 1893 Chicago Columbian Exposition presided over by Daniel Burnham.

Writing of the Flatiron Building, Alfred Stieglitz famously described it in 1903 as the horizontal "bow of a monster ocean steamer." Later constructions such as Pennsylvania Station, designed by McKim, Mead, & White and completed in 1910, utilized their horizontality so as to make the entire block a monument and thereby construct an urban center of transportation and movement paradigmatic of what I call centripetal space. The megablock structure of Grand Central Station (1913), with its ramps channeling crowds into the station lobby, produced a similar effect. Resistance to the vertical architecture of the skyscraper emerging at the end of the previous century remained pervasive at this time. After he returned to the United States in 1904, Henry James complained that tall buildings lacked "the ancient graces" and "overtopped" Trinity Church.[7]

If we accept the thesis of "the essentially horizontal perception of urban form during the nineteenth century" and the growing acceptance of verticality in the early twentieth century, Martin's oppression by towering buildings in *Johnny One-Eye* proposes itself as a nonsynchronous return of the past, a longing for older horizontal forms and a reminder of the discomforts of the elevated city of capitalist commerce, epitomized by the neon freneticism of the Brill Building.[8] For despite the undeniable victory of the skyscraper in New York as an aesthetic and commercial form by the end of World War I, its defects continued to attract criticism. In 1951 Lewis Mumford castigated the Secretariat tower of the United Nations complex for what he termed its perpetuation of the "outmoded form" of the vertical in its architecture.[9] Mumford's remark reminds us that the verticality celebrated in a film such as *Two Men in Manhattan* was scarcely universally admired.

The opposition in *Johnny One-Eye* between the tall buildings of midtown and the low-rise neighborhood of Greenwich Village exemplifies the desire to "find the village within the city" that Taylor finds pervasive in the New York accounts of many writers.[10] Departing from Runyon's story, Florey's film transposes the abandoned brownstone in which Martin hides from "East Fifty-third Street over near Third Avenue" to MacDougal Street in Greenwich Village. Although the reasons for this switch must remain a topic of speculation, one might surmise that the selection of Greenwich Village, a neighborhood where Martin converses with people on the street and rests on a bench in Washington Square Park, provided a greater opposition to the area around Times Square than the closer East 53d Street neighborhood, soon to be transformed by skyscrapers at the end of the 1950s.

After seeking a veterinarian to treat the dog, Martin allows this nebulous figure to remove the bullet from his left side. Operating upon him in a shadowy back room (one of the film's most dramatic moments of noir mise-en-scène), the would-be doctor confides: "I don't understand people like you. In the jungle a man had to kill. He didn't have time to stop and think about it. But guys like you on Broadway and 45th Street. What makes characters like you tick? What goes on in your mind? I always feel sorry for animals that get hurt and for people." Identifying the midtown urban neighborhood with violence and criminal activity, he compares its habitué Martin with the animals he commonly treats.

This scene is absent from Runyon's original story. It serves in the film to convey both the dangers of Times Square and midtown but also the wartime military service of the veterinarian, during which he acquired his dubious medical skills. Nor does the story include Martin's walk through midtown or the modern Greenwich Village apartment (replete with transparent glass walls and a television set that broadcasts Martin's image) in which Elsie lives with her mother and Corey across the street from the row house.

By locating the criminal's hideaway in a Greenwich Village ruin opposed to the modernity of uptown skyscrapers and domestic luxury alike, the film underscores the temporal distance of this site, its nonsynchronicity with respect to the central business district and the surrounding city. Yet it also suggests the status of Martin and Elsie as newcomers to a neighborhood that had begun to experience gentrification by the 1930s. It trades upon a pervasive opposition between the established "local people," often tenement residents, and the more upwardly mobile "villagers."[11] Marked by a tension between a socially and ethnically diverse history and pervasive redevelopment, *Johnny One-Eye* proposes the row house in which Martin hides as an imminent victim of the "ultra modern" destined to replace it.

Entering its dark and uncanny space, surrounded by statues and relics of the past, Martin and Elsie enact a mock domesticity in which she brings him food while he protects the pet banished from her home by Corey. Confined to the floor of the house while he awaits information about Corey, Martin exemplifies the traits of the agoraphobic. Even in the surrounding low-rise neighborhood, his major foray outside the house involves stealing a taxi cab and impersonating its driver so as to visit his lawyer without attracting the attention of the police. No longer menaced by tall buildings, neither does he walk through open space, as he did in midtown.[12]

Dwelling in the abandoned house, Martin befriends both Elsie and her dog, calling the latter the only real friend he has ever had. Such a forced removal from the street is also a distancing from the urban center and its commercial activity, epitomized by Times Square. Despite several violent shootings, a hallucination scene, and the urban iconography, the mawkish sentimentality of Florey's film conflicts with the crime narrative and violence commonly associated with film noir.

Derived from Runyon's story, the film humanizes the city through the appealing character of Martin, the benevolent gangster.[13] Like Runyon's famed use of slang, Florey's adaptation provides an appealing and knowledgeable voice of urban experience and an enticing hint that some refuge from the culture of vertical congestion may be found in the urban village. The contradictory representations of New York in *Johnny One-Eye*, oscillating between vertical nightmare and low-rise sanctuary, convey a nostalgia for older urban forms and deep ambivalence about the centripetal city.

THE EMERGENCE OF CENTRIPETAL SPACE

The late-modern spatiality and cultural anxieties that pervade film noir find their origin in the conflicts and tensions endemic to the centripetal metropolis. Frequent discussions of "centripetal" and "centrifugal" spatial tendencies in writings by architects, urbanists, and geographers confirm the long history of these ideas.[14] My use of the notion of centripetal space emphasizes not simply forms of the built environment of the large metropolis (the street, urban plazas, or downtown business districts) but a range of attitudes, behaviors, and shared interpretations that crystallize around what Edward S. Casey calls "centration" and its sociocultural consequences.[15] These include the lived experience and appropriation of space, as well as representations and conceptualizations of it. More than simply the geographic presence of the central business district at the actual center of a metropolitan area or its functional significance as defined by its tax base, retail sales, or daytime population, centripetal space constitutes a set of cultural attitudes and beliefs.[16]

The specific urban forms, practices, and representations of centripetal space emerge as a product of interrelated developments in architecture, urbanism, and technology that had concentrated population in metropolitan centers since the Industrial Revolution. By the middle of the nineteenth century, steamships and railroads provided the means for transportation of coal and raw materials to factories, initially clustered together because of slow intraurban communication.[17] Industrial cities emerged as labor centers attracting office and factory workers alike. From the Manchester slums described by Friedrich Engels to the foul Coketown of Charles Dickens to the steel mills of Pittsburgh, the nineteenth-century manufacturing city became paradigmatic of overcrowded and insalubrious conditions attending the first industrial revolution of coal, iron, and steam.[18]

Mid-nineteenth-century advances in technology and engineering fueled urbanization and the new building types and spatial conceptions that

transformed the American city. Elisha Graves Otis demonstrated his hy-
draulic elevator at the 1853–54 New York World's Fair; the electric elevator made its debut in 1887. Metal frame construction was incorporated in
William Jenney's Home Insurance Building (1883–1885), often considered
the first skyscraper. Burnham and Root's ten-story Rand McNally Building (1888–1890) utilized the first all-steel frame and hastened the move
toward ever-taller office towers.[19] Unlike the European metropolis, the
American city developed a vertical core of skyscrapers together with an increasingly centrifugal movement of population.

The quintessentially American metropolis that commentators have
called "the walking downtown" emerged in New York's Wall Street by
1810 and was pervasive in many cities by 1850, a product of the evolution
of the mercantile colonial town into the industrial capitalist center.[20] Department stores, train stations, stock exchanges, office buildings, and sites
of entertainment provided its key nodal points. Long axial boulevards and
monumental civic architecture, popularized by the success of the 1893
Chicago Columbia Exposition and the City Beautiful Movement of the
early twentieth century, defined this still predominantly horizontal conception of urbanity and its centering aspirations.[21] The construction of
commercial skyscrapers in the central business district, already beginning
in Chicago by the 1880s, formed its vertical complement. Equally significant for the emergence of centripetal space was what Blumenfeld refers
to as the second technical revolution:

> Finally, shortly before and since the turn of the century, the technical
> revolution reached the second stage. The internal transportation and
> communication of the city were transformed by electric traction and
> the automobile, and by telephone, radio, and television. People could
> do what they had always wanted to do: live in more spacious sur-
> roundings with some green, some fresh air, and sunshine, but work
> and seek work in the great metropolitan labor market. They could
> improve their conditions of living without impairing their chances to
> make a living. The great exodus to the suburbs began and is still gath-
> ering momentum.

To listen to our urban redevelopers, there is something sinful in
this trend toward decentralization that threatens the city's full land

values and tax base; it should be reversed! It is time for these modern
King Canutes to understand that this trend will never be reversed and
that anyone who tries to do so is bound to come to grief. The densely
crowded agglomeration of the nineteenth century with its concomitant, the fantastic skyrocketing of urban land values, was a short-lived
passing phenomenon caused by the time lag between the modernization of interurban and intraurban traffic; once this time lag was overcome, it was bound to disappear forever; and few will regret its passing.[22]

Writing in 1948, Blumenfeld offered one of the earliest accounts of the
bivalent character of urban densification.[23] It entails what he understood as
the two basic trends of twentieth-century urbanism: "concentration from
the country . . . into relatively few metropolitan areas; and decentralization
within these areas." Replacing the former distinction between town and
countryside, the metropolitan area presupposes nearness to both its labor
force and markets. Its urban region develops according to a principle of
"mutual accessibility" governed by the temporal constraints of intraurban
transportation. Within this territory, the central business district houses
retail and business services, cultural and political functions, and other activities that require close interpersonal contact.[24]

An important and easily overlooked component of Blumenfeld's argument is its emphasis upon the simultaneous centralizing *and* decentralizing consequences of new communication and transportation technologies.
Developments such as commuter railroads in the nineteenth century and
automobility and highway construction in the twentieth promoted the
compact metropolis that enabled workers to live outside it, further altering
the relationship between the urban core and the periphery. While facilitating access to the central business district, they also improved access to
outerlying areas.

As Blumenfeld noted, this trend was already apparent in the last two
decades of the nineteenth century and coincided with the development of
large metropolitan areas. This tonic reminder of how the modern metropolis entails both concentration and dispersal complicates efforts to encap-
sulate spatial modernity in a single term such as "urban centralization" or
"suburbanization" or to identify a single technological innovation as the

prime mover of spatial processes that generally admit multiple and contradictory results. It argues as well for the dialectical interrelation of centripetal and centrifugal spatial forms.

ABSTRACT SPACE

In a provocative insight, Lefebvre posits the disintegration of an earlier pattern of Western urbanism as the basis for subsequent developments in the twentieth-century metropolis:

> Yet did there not at one time, between the sixteenth century (the Renaissance—and the Renaissance city) and the nineteenth century, exist a code at once architectural, urbanistic and political, constituting a language common to country people and townspeople, to the authorities and to artists—a code which allowed space not only to be "read" but also to be constructed? If indeed there was such a code, how did it come into being? And when, how and why did it disappear?[25]

Comprehending the transformation of five centuries of urban form and life in relation to the expansion of capitalism, Lefebvre discerns its impact in the rise of abstract space. Most generally, this signifies the advent of the industrialized metropolis, with its increasingly functionalized separation into spaces of production, dwelling, leisure, transportation, and infrastructure. Codified as the basis of modernist city planning in the 1933 Athens Charter of the International Congress of Modern Architecture (CIAM), this spatial differentiation of urban functions became a ubiquitous characteristic of the urbanism realized in the built environment during the latter half of the twentieth century.[26]

The growing loss of urban forms connected to the life of a culture and charged with collective meaning is another consequence of the proliferation of abstract space. Whether one thinks of the traditional market square and its myriad uses as a site of exchange, leisure, and political assembly, or one envisions the gate or portal to the city, a symbolic marker indicating passage into the dominion of a ruler, these spaces possess a semantic richness irreducible to a single purpose. Unlike the abstract spaces of contemporary shopping centers, office parks, and housing developments, which tend to fulfill a sole function, these earlier spatial forms blur distinctions between functions, activities, and publics.

Writing in his 1959 book, *Town and Square: From the Agora to the Village Green* (a study contemporaneous with the spatialities depicted in film noir), architectural historian and theorist Paul Zucker defined urban space in a manner that proves a useful counterpoint for understanding Lefebvre's idea of abstract space:

> Here, "space," designating generally a three-dimensional expansion of any kind, is used more specifically. It means a structural organization as a frame for human activities and is based on very definite factors: on the relation between the forms of the surrounding buildings; on their uniformity or their variety; on their absolute dimensions and their relative proportions in comparison with width and length of the open area; on the angle of the entering streets; and finally, on the location of monuments, fountains, or other three-dimensional accents. In other words, specific visual or kinesthetic relations will decide whether a square is a hole or a whole.[27]

Zucker understood the paradigmatic urban space as the "artistically relevant square" whose void attains shape through adjacent buildings.[28] Designed with attentiveness to visual and kinesthetic relations, the experience of the human beings who traverse it, such a form provides, in Zucker's catachresis, "a psychological parking place" for the urbanite. Recalling the emotionally reassuring qualities of the enclosed plaza promoted by Viennese urbanist Camillo Sitte, Zucker underscored that "the closed square represents the purest and most immediate expression of man's fight against being lost in a gelatinous world, in a disorderly mass of urban dwellings."[29]

Presented in language that suggests an existential imperative, Zucker's espousal of clear spatial delineation is not without a hint of anxiety, as if to proclaim the dangers of a spatial culture in which real parking places now predominate. He insinuates that the disappearance of the spatial frame provided by traditional urban forms portends not merely a shapeless world and a chaotic built environment but also the specter of a similarly formless culture, a reaction to the postwar United States hardly surprising from a scholar educated and trained in Europe.[30]

Read as a commentary on the American built environment, Zucker's remarks are a recognizable instance of the lament over the disappearance of the urban center pervasive in architectural discourses of the 1940s and 1950s. By juxtaposing the chaotic metropolitan settings of the present-day city mentioned in his remarks with the clear articulation of volume and space that Zucker understood as paradigmatic of Renaissance urbanism, it becomes possible to discern how more recent metropolitan spaces, holes rather than wholes in his phrase, support Lefebvre's narrative of abstract space.[31]

Decisive here is an urban space designed with less regard for the corporeal and aesthetic experience of those who navigate it than for the realization of specific economic ends, social policies, or technological functions, a development one might conveniently link to Haussmann's transformation of Paris.[32] Often lacking in formal harmony, the resulting disconnected city frustrates the robust experiences of time and movement that Zucker understood as essential to successful architecture.[33]

Assimilating the constraints imposed by traffic and circulation, public health, housing, production, and civil administration, the modern metropolis appeared to be a different species from Renaissance or baroque cities in which aesthetic considerations were still paramount.[34] For in these earlier municipalities integrated spatial relationships, the expression of rationalizing philosophical schemes, produced centralized buildings such as the domed church and the central city square, with its radiating street pattern. If such architectural and urban forms ultimately communicated the power relation of the sovereign over his subjects, they nonetheless, as Zucker emphasized, acknowledged unified and unifying spatial organization as the foundation of urban design as a civic art.

Acutely registering the loss of these possibilities, many urbanists writing in the United States during the 1940s and 1950s, especially those European by birth, experienced a growing sense of intellectual estrangement from their surroundings. By the time of a late film noir such as *Odds against Tomorrow* (Robert Wise, 1959), its criminal protagonists no longer congregate in the street but limit their meeting places either to private apartments or to Central Park. The older vibrant metropolis of public spaces evident in films made but a few years earlier, such as *Killer's Kiss* and *The Big Combo*, has receded from view.

To make sense of the concept of abstract space and its inflection of centripetal and centrifugal spaces, Lefebvre's notions of spatial practice, representation of space, and space of representation are helpful.[35] Spatial practice (*pratique spatiale*) encompasses the reproduction of the social relations of production, particularly the division of labor, the interaction between people of different age groups and genders, the biological procreation of the family, the material production of the necessities of everyday life (houses, cities, roads), as well as the accumulated knowledge with which societies transform their spatial and social environments.

In the centripetal film noir, a common spatial practice involves walking through a densely populated city where characters experience meetings ranging from the familiar to the unexpected, as when Steve Thompson (Burt Lancaster) and Anna Dundee (Yvonne De Carlo) unexpectedly cross paths in Los Angeles' Union Station in *Criss Cross*. A citydweller's life is frequently divided between several urban locations—public and private—that serve as meeting points and places of conflict, as in a film such as *Scarlet Street*, in which Edward G. Robinson moves between the private club, his apartment, Greenwich Village, and his place of employment.

Representation of space (*représentation de l'espace*) is the second notion in Lefebvre's dialectic of spatial terms, understood to encompass cognitive entities, conceived spaces and concepts, which belong to the history of ideologies and play a role in spatial practices involving the deployment of knowledge and power, such as urban planning. The relationships between interior and exterior or top and bottom constitutive of much architectural signification are also representations of space, and such a tension figures prominently in the film noir *Black Angel* (Roy William Neill, 1946), with its opening boom shot sequence that conveys the social and physical distance from the Los Angeles street to a penthouse apartment.

Similarly, a tracking shot from the window of the Bureau of Narcotics in *Port of New York* (Laslo Benedek, 1949) dissolves to a series of long shots of Manhattan Island followed by shots of skyscrapers filmed alternately from extreme high and low angles, so as to present the city and its movements as surveyable from all positions. In both of these examples, the window figures prominently as the pivot between interior and exterior space and holds out the promise of an unproblematic transition between them, reinforcing its normally uncontested status as a neutral frame.[36]

The third element in Lefebvre's dialectic of spatial terms is the space of representation *(espace de représentation)*, which includes "lived" *(vécu)* environments, once of a mythical, animistic, or spiritual character, and later associated with particular cities (especially Venice), artworks, religious imagery, festival, and the products of the culture industry. Spaces of representation shape subjective experience and imagination and admit a strong temporal dimension. In the centripetal film noir they include darkness, skylines, and street scenes in the metropolis.

Abstract space exemplifies Lefebvre's understanding of abstraction as the hallmark of modernity, a consequence of the industrial and political revolutions of the eighteenth century and the increased prevalence of exchange relations.[37] Opposed to the "concrete" space of everyday users, their lived subjective experience, abstract space corresponds to an economic mode of life in which "reproducibility, repetition, and reproduction of social relationships" attain precedence over nature.[38] It is the space of the factory, of mass production, and the trusted relations of the *Gemeinschaft* yielding to the impersonal relations of *Gesellschaft*.[39] A growing permeation of social life by exchange relations (a consequence of the labor expended in commodity production) yields an increasingly mediated mode of spatiality that alters traditional relations of production and connections to nature.[40]

Though associated by Lefebvre with the modern city and the post–World War II built environment of housing projects, highways, shopping centers, monumental plazas, airports, and tourist sites, the scope of abstract space cannot be reduced to these. The multidimensional scope of Lefebvre's concept speaks against linking it with industrial mass production *tout court*.[41] For example, the gridiron pattern of circulation, a spatial plan organized around two axes of regularly spaced parallel streets intersecting at right angles, already codified in New York City by 1811, possesses the repetition and financial exploitability characteristic of abstract space. Its proclamation in the New York City Commissioners' plan of that year encouraged continued land development.[42] Frequently criticized for its relentless uniformity and indifference to the urban fabric, unlike the morphologies of Renaissance and baroque urbanism, with their attention to the square or piazza, the grid imposed an abstract logic upon the overall metropolis.[43] It minimized the significance of topography, allowed for the extension of the city's area as a united entity (including the annexation of Harlem), and maximized real estate values.[44]

Named after a medieval instrument of torture, the gridiron similarly assails space, a fact that led Edgar Allan Poe in the 1840s to decry its elimination of picturesque sites in New York.[45] Through its infinite extension of street systems "without consideration of buildings and architecture," in the words of one 1930s observer, the New York grid promotes abstract space.[46] Yet this follows from its effects in a specific location rather than from its morphology, since the grid was long a constant in urban history, and Renaissance and baroque urbanists employed it to quite different ends. The significance of the grid in New York must be understood in the context of its symbiotic relations with the social and economic imperatives of American capitalism.[47]

After 1939, criticisms of the inadequacy of the existing metropolis and the laments over what was perceived to have been lost in its development intensified. Unlike earlier exposés of slums or antiquated infrastructures, these late-modern critiques often specifically attack the urban vernacular of the twentieth-century metropolis. Consider, in this context, the melancholy 1944 diagnosis by José Luis Sert of its inhuman qualities and scale:

> *The natural frame of man has been destroyed in the big cities.* Elements hostile to human nature have replaced the natural ones that once constituted man's surroundings. We are obliged to walk on hard pavements, to breathe and see through polluted air, our eyes are constantly disturbed by rapidly changing lights. Our "corridor streets" canalize cold or hot air and noises of all kinds, etc. But besides having substituted the natural surroundings of man for hostile and artificial ones, *cities have fallen short of their main objective, that of fomenting and facilitating human contacts so as to raise the cultural level of their populations. To accomplish this social function cities should be organic social structures.*[48]

Sert also attacks the traditionally closed "corridor street" criticized by Le Corbusier in 1931 for its simultaneous accommodation of traffic and housing.[49] Recalling the Modern Man discourse of the 1940s analyzed by Michael Leja in relation to Abstract Expressionism, Sert's opposition of an earlier and more humane city form to a contemporary urbanism bereft of human scale takes the post-1939 American metropolis as its target.[50] Like Zucker's espousal of the spatial frame provided by traditional urban forms such as the square, it perceives recent urban developments as antithetical to the aspirations of 1940s humanism.

Appropriating Lefebvre's conceptual terminology, one can recognize centripetal space in film noir in a range of contents. These include characteristic architectural forms (skyscrapers, mass transportation facilities, public landmarks, residential neighborhoods), spatial practices (crowd movements, police surveillance, strolls and routines), spaces of representation (darkness, skylines, landmarks, cityscapes), and representations of space (the urban core, the grid, maps, photographs).

Rather than comprehending spatiality in the film noir cycle through categories of realism or mimesis that would establish correlations (or lack thereof) between film and the actual built environment, Lefebvre's model suggests how this dilemma might be circumvented. Film noir does not so much "represent" Lefebvre's concepts (for in what sense could a "representation of space" or "space of representation" be represented?) as realize them in cinematic form. Parallelisms between the built environment, film noir, and other cultural forms present an opportunity to analyze the manner in which space is similarly lived, conceived, and perceived across different cultural and social contexts ranging from the actual city to its representations.

Through its provision of a legible and intelligible backdrop for cinematic narratives of investigation and suspense, centripetal space animated the film noir cycle, which should in turn be understood as a compensatory response to the actual disappearance of older urban forms. The growing sway of abstract space necessitated new and more frequent representations of centrality, for which New York and Los Angeles proved particularly well suited. An indispensable prerequisite for film noir, centripetal space is simultaneously celebrated and mourned in its films as characters traverse the vertical urban center, partake of its dynamism, or succumb to its violence. Hence the elegiac quality common to many of these urban representations, if not the frequently somber tone of many films noir themselves.[51]

THE URBAN CORE AS REPRESENTATION OF SPACE

The urban core is a key representation of space in which the tensions pervading the post-1939 centripetal metropolis become evident. Discerning the spatial pathologies of the 1940s and the arrival of new centrifugal spatial modalities, urban planners and architects developed an anxiety that the city and its center were declining in significance. Although parks and other public gathering places had not altogether disappeared, their ability to foster genuine collective life could no longer be taken for granted in an age of mass media, decentralization, and automobility. Nostalgia for public urban space becomes palpable in the writings of many urbanists in the 1940s, as does a fearfulness about the city center and the loss of position (social, ideological, cultural) accompanying its changed status. This sense of an impending crisis in Western civilization was expressed during the 1940s and 1950s in a rash of articles bearing titles such as "The Invisible City," "The Humane City: Must the Man of Distinction Always Move to the Suburbs?" and "The Deserted City." It culminates in Kevin Lynch's book *The Image of the City*.[52]

Throughout these texts one encounters a concern with *visualizing* one's position in the metropolis. These postwar approaches to the city avoid the statistical abstractions that would shortly reconfigure the discipline of planning as a quantitative discipline and seek instead to imagine the body of the urbanite in space. Consistent with the urbanism of the Italian Renaissance highly valued by many of the German, Austrian, and Swiss historians writing at this time, this spatial frame construed humanism as the basis for urbanism and emphasized the city as an enclave for the pedestrian, a figure whose passage through the urban center is commonly read as an index of its vitality. Faced with a metropolis that seemed to be disappearing, "the walking cure," a spatial practice of urban "cognitive mapping" grounded in the lived experience of the pedestrian, becomes ubiquitous in both theoretical statements and film noir.

In his 1944 essay "The Need for a New Monumentality" Sigfried Giedion lamented the absence of a viable urban centrality and called for the construction of new community centers that would combine the talents of architects and artists. Likening them to the agora, the forum, the medieval square of earlier cities, he opposes these nuclei to the mass media and observes that "neither radio nor television can replace the personal contact which alone can develop community life."[53] In Joseph Hudnut's 1949 essay "The Invisible City" one encounters a similar diagnosis of urban malaise:

> So it was with the city under the fierce impact of the Industrial Revolutions and of that explosive mercantilism which scattered the European peoples over the earth. Our cities grew rapidly to unprecedented dimensions and as they grew shattered that form and character, that humanity of pattern and expression—in a word, that architecture—which had been impressed upon them by collective thought and feeling long continued. Our vast new cities exhibit no framework of social purpose, no trace of that cement of manners, conventions and moralities, of ecclesiastical and aristocratic tradition, built over centuries by patient change and slow compromise, which gave pattern and beauty to the city's life, or of that dignity of environment which sustained the spiritual forces. We are at sea and without home or status.

At the conclusion of his article, Hudnut provides this revealing narrative of his experience of metropolitan wholeness:

> Sometimes when I am in Rockefeller Center, where skyscrapers, theatres, gardens, streets and shops innumerable crowd into an islanded harmony, I imagine that I feel the promise of that reorientation of our art. A city rises about me; I am in an arena prepared for me as if by ancient usage and rehearsal. At such times I like to believe that architecture may indeed re-assume its forgotten importance as outward frame and envelope of a communal life, being shaped once more by the commerce of a society that is civilized, polite and urbane. Civilized, polite and urbane—each word rooted in a word which means *the city*.[54]

Invoking the Greek agora, with its orchestra for choral dancing, Hudnut decries the loss of an urban center for communal life.[55] He surveys

Rockefeller Center (a space best negotiated by the pedestrian) and finds evidence of a consciously shaped urban environment—a viable city center—that he identifies as the enduring legacy of the metropolis as stronghold of civilization.[56] Yet he turns a blind eye to the fact that this "islanded" harmony event is a tourist attraction and media spectacle rather than a domain of everyday spatial practice. Writing at a later date, the architectural historian Manfredo Tafuri reaches a quite different conclusion and interprets Rockefeller Center as the terminal instance of comprehensive urban planning, further evidence for my contention that by 1945 the notion of the city center functioned increasingly as a phantasm of planners, a representation of space whose lack of corresponding spatial practices was conspicuous.[57]

It was precisely the desire to realize city centers that would facilitate human interactions that motivated the CIAM group to meet in 1951 in Hoddeson, England, to discuss "The Core of the City" as the main theme of its eighth congress. The destruction wrought by the war and the experience of European reconstruction led the architects associated with the group to search for "the element that makes a community a community and not merely an aggregate of individuals."[58] They advocated the construction of urban cores that would serve to focus social life in the city. Giedion formulated seven key features of this core:

1. That there should be only one main Core in each city.

2. That the Core is an artifact—a man-made thing.

3. That the Core should be a place secure from traffic—where the pedestrian can move about freely.

4. That cars should arrive and park on the periphery of the Core, but not cross it.

5. That uncontrolled commercial advertising—such as appears in the Cores of many cities today—should be organized and controlled.

6. That varying (mobile) elements can make an important contribution to animation at the Core, and that the architectural setting should be planned to allow for the inclusion of such elements.

7. That in planning the Core the architect should employ contemporary means of expression and—whenever possible—should work in cooperation with painters and sculptors.[59]

One may easily discern in this statement of principles the outlines *in nuce* of now-commonplace urban forms such as the pedestrian zone, shopping mall, office plaza, and neighborhood promenade, soon to become prominent in the reconstruction of war-devastated cities such as Rotterdam and Coventry. As proposed by the CIAM delegates, this notion of the core is among the earliest attempts to theorize a representation of space for the authentic metropolitan experience of the pedestrian in a built environment challenged by increasing automobility. Taking its inspiration from the urban squares of the past (such as the Italian piazza, to which an entire chapter of the book was devoted), the group's prior emphasis on systematization and quantifiable data collection now shifted toward the analysis—and revival—of centrality in an urban environment experiencing rapid technological and social change.[60]

Conceived as a space of representation in Lefebvre's terminology, this notion of the core reiterated the tension between public space as a physical gathering spot and its function as site for receiving media messages.[61] It suggests the continued weakening of a purely spatial conception of urban centrality in which architectural forms alone can promote social solidarity. Contributors to *The Heart of the City* repeatedly defined the core as a space facilitating direct contact and the exchange of ideas in opposition to the passivity and potential for totalitarian control they viewed as inherent in the emerging predominance of the electronic media.[62]

Acknowledging that the "movies, the loudspeakers, television screens have come to the public squares," they defined their notion of the core against these technologies, conceptually empowering urban space through a binary opposition to what they understood as its antithesis. Giedion sought "to turn people back from passive spectators to active participants" through "an emotional experience which can reawake their apparently lost powers of spontaneity."[63] Espousing the humanism of the day, he asserted that "a new stage of civilization is in formation in which the human being as such—the bare and naked man—will find a direct means of expression."[64]

Prefiguring the "construction of situations" later advocated by Debord and the Situationists, such a reanimation of urban centrality sought to transfigure the degraded social life in cities:

The word "Core," in the sense we are using it, does not mean merely the centre of the urban agglomeration, nor the busy heart of the city traffic or economic activity; sometimes it may be united with these areas, but the Core includes other elements, often of an imponderable nature.

The essence of the Core is that it is a rendezvous. Its situation and contents may be planned or spontaneous; drawn from history or from some isolated accident; derived from the convergence of activities or as a refuge against such activities. Whatever the cause the Core should give both an impression of freedom of movement and also a release from loneliness or boredom; an atmosphere of general relaxation, of participation in a spontaneous and impartial performance, a touch of the warmth of human kindness and—at the same time—a recovery of *civic consciousness*.[65]

Here the core is offered as an antidote against the ills of alienation, boredom, and lack of civic consciousness. Under the impact of urban renewal, suburbanization, new communication and transportation technologies, and the "commercial-business dominated Main Street," the experience of traversing the urban center was losing its force. Unlike the Renaissance or baroque city, with its prominent markets, plazas, and squares, the twentieth-century metropolis appeared to these architects in danger of relinquishing its paradigmatic site of spatial practice, no less than a vital space of representation. Illustrated throughout with photographs of Times Square, Piccadilly Circus, and older urban centers, *The Heart of the City* is marked by an unbridgeable tension between new spaces constituted by the mass media and the desire for traditional centers such as the Piazza San Marco.

By the beginning of the 1950s, this dilemma was being addressed by the designs of Peter and Alison Smithson, which sought to appropriate the everyday milieu of advertisements and commercial buildings as viable public spaces.[66] The anxiety about the loss of the urban center, while not completely vanquished, had diminished beneath the wave of historical styles and pop vernaculars forming the nascent culture of postmodernism.[67] To paraphrase Debord, the urban core that once was lived, now was becoming

either a depopulated void or an idealized representation, a point well articulated by Roland Barthes:

> The studies of the urban nucleus of different cities have shown that
> the central point of the city center (every city has a center), which we
> call "solid nucleus," does not constitute the peak point of any particu-
> lar activity but a kind of empty "focal point" for the image that the
> community develops of the center. We have here again somehow an
> empty place which is necessary for the organization of the rest of the
> city.[68]

This empty "focal point" of the metropolitan center forms a key attribute of the centripetal space manifested in films noir. Whether one thinks
of the many films set in Times Square, or the fascination exerted by landmarks such as railroad stations, such elements remain conspicuous. Much
as the city requires the empty center as a focal point, the centripetal film
noir requires it for its narrative coherence. Responding to transformations
in the metropolis and the experiences of nostalgia, loss, and discomfort
they produce, the film noir cycle articulates fantasies about public space
and engages with problems of spatial orientation in a changing urban
fabric. It does so through two principal textual strategies: a set of mapping and surveillance procedures to organize spatial passage and a utopian
modernism whose formal devices transfigure the daily experience of the
city.

New York's revised zoning code, perhaps the ultimate triumph of abstract space in the centripetal metropolis, dramatically extended the ubiquity of the empty center. In the words of one history,

> On December 15, 1960, the city's pioneering zoning ordinance of
> 1916 was completely overhauled and one year later the new code took
> effect. The old ordinance, with its solid roots in the traditional space-
> making of streets and avenues bounded by walls of buildings that
> filled up city blocks to near solidity, was abandoned. The new regu-
> lations encouraged unmodulated, independently spaced skyscraper
> tower slabs rising from generously scaled plazas—an "open" city, a
> city that was space positive rather than mass positive, a city that, were

it to be rebuilt completely along the lines of the new code, would become one with the continuous open space of the essential ruralism of Megalopolis.[69]

Yet the "open" city of office plazas that emerged in the 1960s would scarcely recreate an effective urban centrality for its age, let alone reestablish a connection between the built environment and social experience, despite the occasional success of the office tower plazas at attracting lunchtime crowds.[70] As the concluding effort in a long series of attempts to realize an adequate centripetal space, this new "space positive" metropolis of skyscrapers and office plazas in fact replicated the empty focal point of the center across the entire city.

Far from constituting a radical precedent, the new zoning envelope reiterated and amplified earlier spatial anxieties of late modernity, translating the fears and speculations of artists and architects into common facts of everyday life. This spatiality of vertical masses puncturing a void fundamental to the new zoning regulation was already visible in advance of the new building code in the Seagram Building by Mies van der Rohe (1958). Yet it had also been anticipated by the late 1940s sculptures of Alberto Giacometti. In his *City Square (La Place)* (1948–49) elongated bodies move in separate directions, united by the open space of an empty pedestal and suggestive of nothing so much as the urban multitude converging upon a building surrounded by an empty plaza. The deployment of these figures in a shared space, far from accidental, suggests a "totality of life," a common existential situation.[71] Writing of Giacometti's work, Jean-Paul Sartre described the simultaneous isolation and social bond of its crowds in terms that anticipated his own notion of seriality: "An exhibition by Giacometti is a populace. He has sculpted men who cross a square without seeing each other; they pass, hopelessly alone, and yet, *they are together* . . . Ironic, defiant, ceremonious and tender, Giacometti sees empty space everywhere . . . Between things as between men, the bridges are broken, and emptiness seeps in everywhere, every creature concealing his own. Giacometti became a sculptor because he was obsessed by vacuum."[72]

Empty space and human separation emerge as key concerns in Giacometti's work, with multiple resonances for the post-1939 built environment of abstract space and the film noir cycle. Invoking the architectural

Alberto Giacometti, *City Square (La Place)*, 1948, bronze, 8½ × 25⅜ × 17¼. Digital image copyright © Museum of Modern Art, New York. Licensed by SCALA/Art Resource, Artists Rights Society, New York. Copyright © 2003 Artists Rights Society (ARS), New York / ADAGP, Paris.

figure of the bridge, Sartre describes an alleged *absence* of relation, a vacuum, that masks the fragile social bond asserted by Giacometti's humanism. Isolation, as the philosopher later would write in the *Critique of Dialectical Reason,* becomes the real social product of cities.[73] The detached figures of Giacometti's work still share a common space and human fate. And in an equally urban metaphor (highly apposite for film noir), Sartre observes that Giacometti's art produces "the same shock that we feel returning home late at night and seeing a stranger coming towards us in the dark."[74] Writing in 1946, the same year that Nino Frank formulated his film noir criticism, Giacometti described his own spatial anxieties in language no less suffused with angst: "There was no longer any rapport between things, they were separated by immeasurable abysses of empty space."[75]

Suffering from the agoraphobic fears of the void reported by seventeenth-century philosopher Blaise Pascal, Giacometti was prone to doubt the spatial integrity of his surroundings.[76] As Simone de Beauvoir noted, "for a long time, when he was walking down the street, he had to test the solidity of the house walls with his hand to resist the abyss that opened up next to him." The elongated and frequently tiny figures of his sculptures were intended, she claimed, to save the unity of the artist's human figures "from vertiginous dispersion in space."[77] This vocabulary of nausea and the abyss corresponds as well to the experience of spatial depth, for philosopher Maurice Merleau-Ponty the most existential dimension of space. It "is not impressed upon the object itself . . . it announces a certain indissoluble link between things and myself."[78]

Refracted through the existentialism that would prove an effective (and highly marketable) idiom for promoting his work, Giacometti's spatial anxieties evoke his own experience while also presciently adumbrating the psychic impact of the empty spaces that would become more visible in postwar urban life, the new American metropolis scarred by vacant buildings, endless parking lots, and urban redevelopment projects. Even as his sculpture traded upon the cachet of postwar French intellectual culture, it anticipated the abstract spatiality of the late-modern centripetal metropolis to which it forms an extraordinary parallel.

From the empty centers of American cities bulldozed by urban redevelopers during the 1950s and often depopulated a decade later, to the skyscrapers that emerged in the wake of the revised New York zoning code, fears of "vertiginous dispersion in space" afflicted many contemporaneous observers in an urban realm whose cultural significance had irrevocably shifted.[79] This actual urban space and its real depths briefly impinged upon the Parisian Giacometti in his work upon the commission he received, but never completed, for a monumental sculpture to be placed in the office plaza in front of the Chase Manhattan Bank skyscraper designed by architect Gordon Bunshaft (1961).[80]

In this assignment the spatial anxieties of the artist would have confronted the angst elicited by the open vacuums produced by New York's zoning regulation. His final design for the building plaza was a single larger-than-life female figure.[81] If the desire for an increasingly absent, if not impossible, centrality was among the most ubiquitous of post-1939 urban discourses, no less palpable was a desire to fill this void of social space with a plenitude, conveniently provided here by the form of the female body.

"Giacometti's space is an *erotic* space. His figures exist in it as in his consciousness," one critic wrote of the sexualized vacuum through which the sculptor's figures pass.[82] Yet the psychosexual dynamics of the artist's work transcend his individual subjectivity. As one psychoanalyst suggested, *"open places,* from the dread of which the term *agoraphobia* derives, signify *the castrated mother.* Probably some inner urge prompts us to put a statue, an obelisk and, especially, a fountain in the middle of squares."[83] With its myriad scenes of bodies puncturing the emptiness of the city, the film noir cycle is pervaded by such eroticized spaces, epitomized by the Greenwich Village street devoid of all signs of life where a startled Christopher Cross (Edward G. Robinson) first encounters the alluring Kitty March (Joan Bennett) in *Scarlet Street.*[84]

Whereas the bodies in *La Place* converge toward the female figure at the group's center, Bunshaft's modern bank represents the immaterial flow of capital through its empty plaza, which was eventually filled with a sculpture by Jean Dubuffet. The art committee of client David Rockefeller rejected Giacometti's design for its alleged failure to instill the space with sufficient strength.[85] Had their decision been otherwise, the result would have been notable. Positioned in the heart of the building's void, in the heart of the city, Giacometti's sculpture might well have become the last femme fatale of centripetal space.

3
WALKING CURES

Strange as it may seem, although streets, faces, railway stations, etc., lie before our eyes, they have remained largely invisible so far. Why is this so?

—Siegfried Kracauer, *Theory of Film: The Redemption of Physical Reality* (1960)

Although synoptic overviews of the metropolis are prominent in many films noir, they do not exhaust the film cycle's modalities of representing the city. Indeed, their remove from the street and from the lived experience of the pedestrian proves to be both an asset and a limitation. This chapter analyzes wayfinding, peregrinations, and strolls of characters in centripetal space. Unlike the long-distance depictions of the city in a single elevated or panoramic view, these ground-level cinematic representations often secure temporal as well as spatial coherence.

They emulate the sequentiality of memory and frequently accentuate discrepancies between the urban past and the actual condition of the post-1939 metropolis. Emphasizing parts of the city rather than its whole, the figures of synecdoche and metonymy (rather than metaphor) best describe such cinematic sequences of movement through the street. By condensing the metropolis into a spatial fragment, they realize the reduction that Kenneth Burke understood to define these tropes.[1] Such moments in film noir may also allegorize the larger metropolis and its history from the perspec-

Theodore Seymour Hall, Angels Flight, Los Angeles, date unknown. Courtesy of the Huntington Library, San Marino, California.

tive of the user of the city, whose guise is temporarily adopted by the film spectator.

Whether facilitating narrative resolution or directing a film toward more expansive intellectual reflection, these images from the ground take the micro dimension of the city, the practice of urban passage, as their purview. If the gaze upon the city from an elevated perspective defines the synoptic view, such views from the street exemplify the spatial trope whose diverse manifestations serve as instances of a "walking cure" for the different species of urban malaise that are pervasive in the centripetal film noir.

At once recording the often abstract and alienating space of the metropolis, they may also gesture toward its transcendence.

A decade before the New York City Landmarks Preservation Commission was legally empowered in 1965 to prevent the destruction of buildings of historic significance, a film noir such as *Killer's Kiss* (Stanley Kubrick, 1955) presciently confirmed Benjamin's remark that "anything about which one knows that one soon will not have it around becomes an image."[2] The film noir cycle similarly needs to be grasped as a means of rendering visible the often-overlooked features of the city noted by Kracauer, many of which soon would disappear. For the increasingly dispersed and suburbanized cinema audience of the 1950s, film noir offered a prophylactic encounter with endangered urban spaces whose direct experience might well produce anxiety, if only because of their distance from the ever-more-familiar centrifugal character of the built environment.[3]

By invoking the notion of a walking cure, I refer to a plurality of narrative tropes, cinematic techniques, and representations of the built environment linked by their common engagement with the increasingly functionalized space of the city. It is a figure with antecedents in the flaneur profiled in the literary and cultural criticism of Baudelaire, Breton, Aragon, Benjamin, Kracauer, and Hessel, as well as the walking subject explored by Michel de Certeau and the tradition of cognitive geography.[4] Yet it also engages the urbanism theorized in a film such as *The City*, in which the perils encountered by the pedestrian crossing the street in an automobile-dominated city bolster the argument for greenbelt suburbs.

My deployment of the term *walking cure* acknowledges the emergence in the 1950s of a range of theories and methods, some derived from urbanism such as the work of Kevin Lynch, others with early-modernist cultural antecedents, such as the Surrealist lineage of the Situationists' drift, which sought to register the experience of the pedestrian. That the centripetal film noir flourishes contemporaneously with these attempts to analyze urban experience confirms the ubiquity of the metropolis in the film noir cycle, understood as a key manifestation of post-1939 American culture.

While the activity of walking obviously could not (and cannot) by itself transform the metropolis, its close connection with memory in many films noir, if not the characteristic melancholy understood as one of the film cycle's most pervasive "feeling tones," poses the topics for investigation in this chapter. The idea of a walking cure is intended as a mediating term between the city's occasioning of movement and looking, on the one hand, and the fragmentation of its spaces and the film spectator, on the other.

Whether understood as a celebration of the city, a species of nostalgia for an older environment vanishing under the impact of postwar modernization, a critique of the mechanisms of abstract space, or an attempt to realize the ideal of "redemptive" criticism advocated by Benjamin, the different modes of urban passage evident in the centripetal film noir prove an essential component of the film cycle's representation of the metropolis. Their close connection to the experiences of nostalgia or the fissured subjectivity of the inhabitant of abstract space confirms the significance of the urban walk in a range of films.

REMEMBERING TILLARY STREET

Street of Chance (Jack Hively, 1942), adapted from Cornell Woolrich's novel *The Black Curtain* (1941), engages in an exemplary manner the activities of walking in the street and remembering the city.[5] The film alludes to the scale of urban experience lived by the pedestrian in both its title, resonant of the Surrealist encounter with the unexpected, and in its opening credit sequence, in which drawings of street signs, an apartment building, and a corner luncheonette evoke the New York etchings of Reginald Marsh.[6] The verticality of the metropolis plays a less significant role in this film's cityscape than does the horizontal domain of the pedestrian.

The film's first image is an elevated crane shot moving downward from a street sign announcing the corner of Tillary Street and 22d Street toward a construction site. A fencework sign emblazoned "Empire House Wrecking Company. We Move Anything" is accompanied by the sound of jackhammers. Never does the film indicate the nature of the activity in progress. We do not understand whether the building is being destroyed, rebuilt, or both, for the sign itself conveys a fundamental ambiguity. Yet this is entirely fitting, conveying as it does the notion of an urban modernity in permanent flux, a metropolis continually under construction. Its initial suggestion of demolition and movement is complicated by the ensuing long shot of elevated scaffolds. When one of these collapses and sends debris to the ground, the central character, Frank Thompson (Burgess

Frame enlargement of Tillary Street corner, from *Street of Chance* (Jack Hively, 1942).

Frame enlargement of Thompson being knocked unconscious by falling debris from building, from *Street of Chance* (Jack Hively, 1942).

Meredith), is knocked unconscious after he trips over some equipment littering the sidewalk.

"What part of town is this? What am I doing here? I've never been here before in my life. There's no reason why I should be here. I can't even remember how I got here," Thompson complains to an indifferent police officer. Yet the patrolman's directions to the elevated subway so that Thompson can return to the neighborhood in New York familiar to him cannot erase the fictitious character of Tillary Street. Its nonexistence in his memory (as well as on any actual mental or physical map of Manhattan) parallels Thompson's current uncertainty about his spatial location. Both his hat and cigarette case bear the initials "DN," and Thompson grows nervous when a boy observing his interaction with the cop taunts him for not recognizing his own hat.

Thompson returns home, and the sight of the stairway to his front door, the threshold between public and private space, appears simultaneously reassuring and threatening. He discovers his apartment vacant, a powerful intimation that his intimate domestic space has become foreign, and learns from the landlady that his wife has moved elsewhere in the neighborhood. Upon locating her new residence, identified by her maiden name written over the doorbell, Thompson is told that he has been missing for over a year. As his wife notes to him in her reconciliatory monologue, "We've both heard of cases like this. Amnesia. On the way to your office that last morning something must have happened to you, some accident, some blow, just like what happened tonight. You just didn't know who you were anymore. Forgot where you were going. Forgot to come home to me."

The momentous unspecified event of both the novel and the film, the absent cause of which the above dialogue constitutes the sole mention, concerns the earlier trauma suffered by Thompson that is capable of erasing his memory. Indeed the ideological dilemma of the film involves not merely his current dual identity but the unstated possibility that he actually might *prefer* having shed his past, a narrative option that is finally rejected. What was it that annihilated Thompson's identity for a year and rendered his former life as unfamiliar as Tillary Street? And how is it that the process of urban construction and demolition in the present inadvertently restores his memory?

Arguably the earliest film noir that treats amnesia, *Street of Chance* is equally striking for its treatment of the relationship between subjectivity and spatial remembrance. Unlike later films noir such as *The Crooked Way* (Robert Florey, 1949), in which wartime combat is presented as the cause of amnesia (visible in the x-ray of the shrapnel lodged in the protagonist's head), here the city itself, in the form of debris from a falling building,

provides the catalyst for regaining an earlier life and memories, while losing more recently formed recollections. *Street of Chance* proposes the role
that fortuitous events can play in the dynamics of forgetting and remembrance and the imbrication of the city with the process of memory.

A comparison of Woolrich's novel *The Black Curtain* with the film provides revealing clues about the spatial and temporal gaps in its story. Perhaps most significant is the alteration of the period of Townsend's disappearance from three years in the novel to but a single year in the film. For
in Woolrich's book, his wife notes that he disappeared on January 30,
1938, and returned on May 10, 1941.[7] What such a block of time immediately calls to mind is, of course, the onset of World War II, noted by a
poster at the construction site advertising war bonds. This chronology
makes it even more unlikely that a young man of conscription age could
have adopted a new identity, shed his old one, and remained undetected in
the wartime metropolis. By abandoning his prior identity, Townsend necessarily adopts the persona of a social outcast, an identity minimized in the
film by its shorter presentation of his disappearance.

No less significant in the novel is his wife's telling comment about the
day of his disappearance: "Your suit had just come back from the cleaner's
that morning. You left in kind of a hurry, without taking time to transfer
most of the personal trifles you usually carried around in your pockets
from the old one to the new one. And any one of them—an address on an
old envelope, a receipted bill—would have helped you. But without them
you were cut off completely."[8]

Contained in this passage is a powerful implication that the metropolis
has metamorphosed into a jumble of disconnected details, a spatial disarray analogous to the contents of the amnesiac's suit pockets. Lacking "an
intricate web of existing paths and neighborhood markets or similar open
spaces," found in older cities, the urban realm of the post-1939 American
city fails to bolster the activity of recollection.[9] If, as Edward S. Casey has
claimed, place is "well suited to contain memories—to hold and preserve
them," the unspoken but striking intimation conveyed by the dialogue
above is of a breakdown in the city's traditional function as a substratum
for memory formation. For it is not the urban landmark or conspicuous
architectural detail that could orient Thompson after his amnesia, but
only the printed scraps of paper that he neglected to carry with him when

he suffered his first blow. Through a diminution of its memorable qualities, a process whose cause is unstated but which we might well attribute to the increasing spatial homogenization discussed in the previous chapter, the city no longer facilitates the bodily memory or the alleviation of anxiety that Casey identifies as key features of place.[10]

The psychic costs of negotiating this urban space are suggested repeatedly in the novel, nowhere more vividly than in Woolrich's description of the agoraphobia induced by crossing the space of a large train station:

> Now the station, gained by underground causeway, a lesser risk than the streets above. As he came out into the vast expanse of the main waiting room, the symptoms of agoraphobia struck him full blast. He felt as though the walls were a thousand miles away from him on all sides. He felt as though he were walking alone, with not another moving object to mar his conspicuousness, across this immense expanse of marble and cement. He felt as though a spotlight were focused squarely on him from head to toe, following him across this tremendous amphitheater every step of the way, with nothing to hide behind, nothing to break the *openness*. And all around him, unseen, in a hideous circular line-up, faces scanning, scrutinizing, staring at him.[11]

Once more, the urban void replaces the substantiality of space and the experiential qualities of place with a site of surveillance and anxiety, here contrasted with the constricted space of Tillary Street, whose profusion of bodies and small shops proves less frightening and more reassuring than the station concourse. Though absent from the film, this scene in the train station and its correlation of vast open space with the unwanted gaze of strangers permeate the spaces in *Street of Chance* in other ways. Each site in the film is connected to the identity of Thompson or to that of his alter ego, Danny Nearing. Upon returning to his job in a large office, Thompson is told by his boss that he hardly looks as if he has suffered the nervous breakdown reported by his wife.

The glass windows throughout the office reinforce the effect of being under surveillance, an idea already introduced when the detective tracking Thompson first spots him through the ground-floor window of the office building. On the floor where he works, symmetrically deployed rows

of desks convey the ordered existence of institutionalized capitalist bu-
reaucracy that will reappear in *Double Indemnity* and many other postwar
films.[12] It is a world whose constant specular authority admits no uncertainty about personal identity, once more underscoring the opposition between virulent transparency and the comforting space of darkness, what
Woolrich calls "the anonymity of the night," pervasive in many films
noir.[13]

Yet at the end of his first day back at work, Thompson is once more
chased in the street by the detective. Their confrontation ends in an attempt to smash the window of the taxi cab in which Thompson flees, another reminder of the link between visual penetration and violence ubiquitous in the film noir cycle. Later that evening at home, he looks out of the
window of his apartment and experiences a flashback of the scene earlier in
the day. This space of the street is subsequently occupied by the detective
and two accomplices who force Thompson and his wife to flee their apartment. After they separate, he walks alone down an empty street, filmed
from an elevated angle in darkness after a single street lamp is extin-
guished. In an effort to learn about his new identity, Thompson returns to
the site of his last accident, the place where he regained memories of his
older identity and lost those of his more recent one: "Here we are, Tillary
Street. Somewhere down here is the answer. Someplace there's somebody
that's got to recognize me, remember me, say hello. Nobody I ever saw in
my life. Nobody that ever saw me from the looks on their faces."

Yet the response that he initially encounters suggests a city of indifferent
strangers who can provide little assistance in restoring his memory. Entering a tavern, he requests his usual drink, only to encounter a gruff bartender who fails to recognize him. Upon visiting a pawnshop, Thompson
is recognized, only to be chastised by its owner for repeatedly attempting
to pawn his cigarette case. The last address he provided as his own was actually a vacant lot, a further hint that conveys Thompson's spatial incom-
prehension and rootlessness, if not the rapid change of the urban fabric
itself.

Writing of the mental illnesses of schizophrenia and general paralysis,
the phenomenological psychologist Eugène Minkowski distinguished the
latter in terms of the spatial and temporal disorientation experienced by
those who suffer from it. Unable to identify his or her precise spatial loca-

tion or to relate a series of events to a fixed point in time, the general para-lytic loses the ability to perceive the extent of space. Though incapable of answering the question of where he or she came from, general paralytics nonetheless can understand a change of place. Their psychic world, Min-kowski notes, is unmistakably dynamic: "Everything is movement and nothing but movement, movement that develops with great rapidity, no obstacle is considered, no distance, no duration measurable. That move-ment involves all, overwhelms the individual, blots out all the limits that exist between himself and the universe, transforms them into an ambula-tory world, into a moving space."[14]

Utilizing such an idea, we might begin to analyze Thompson's ambula-tions along Tillary Street. In their compulsive repetition up and down the block, they allude to the moving space described by Minkowski, a contin-ual and restless exertion accompanied by a loss of spatial and temporal bearings. Yet if Thompson's impulse toward motion ultimately derives from the traumas he has undergone and represents an attempt to recapture his personal chronology in the city, it is equally striking to note how the surrounding built environment itself assumes many of same qualities of the "moving space" associated by Minkowski with general paralysis.

The corner of Tillary and 22d Street possesses no obvious connection to Thompson's previous life; in his mind it lacks the measurable duration of space through which any relation to other street intersections can be mapped. Thompson is unable to master the static factors that "place the objects in relation one to the other, in geometric space, where everything is motionless, relative and revertible."[15] Failing to recognize Tillary Street and to coordinate its spatial position, even after convalescing from his blow, Thompson is presented by *Street of Chance* as a stranger to his own past.

His return to the pushcarts, older stores, and walk-up apartments on the block (a neighborhood meant to evoke the Lower East Side of New York) that Woolrich calls "a slum street, swarming with humanity," where he strides up and down its length, now hoping to be spotted by someone who knows him, establishes Thompson as arguably the earliest practitioner of what I call the "walking cure" of the film noir cycle.[16] For like Freud's psy-choanalytic method, this cure also hinges upon memory and repetition as the means by which past and present combine into a comprehensive per-

sonal identity. Yet here the technique employed does not involve a pa-
tient's verbal narration of dreams or earlier events but rather the physical
act of passage through the city. Its goal is the restoration of those memory
impressions that enter experience, comprehended by Benjamin through
the notion of *Erfahrung*, which he presents as "less the product of facts
firmly anchored in memory than of a convergence in memory of accumulated and frequently unconscious data."[17]

Just as Benjamin argues that Bergson's philosophy of experience neglected the large-scale industrialism whose transformation of experience
created the necessity for a "philosophy of life," I would contend that the
film noir cycle similarly presupposes the disruption of older urban forms
and the growing significance of the mass media that no less decisively alter the historical determination of urban memory in post-1939 America.
The replacement of narration by information and sensation that Benjamin
views as a key trait of the growing sway of *Erlebnis*, the mode of experience
of short-term memory, entails an eradication of older urban narratives
generated by the historical fabric of the city as it is transformed by abstract
and centrifugal space.

Street of Chance suggests the strategies by which film noir occupies this
vacuum. Thompson is introduced in the film at the moment when he is literally attacked by the city, felled by the debris from the construction site
that knocks him unconscious. Unlike characters in *The Naked City* and *The
Big Clock*, who ascend and later fall from elevated sites, he is assaulted on
street level, a victim of the chance alluded to by the title. His earlier loss of
memory reinforces the identity of New York as a metropolis in which
severe shocks disrupt the continuity of ordinary routines and supports
Benjamin's assertion via Freud that memory fragments are "often most
powerful and most enduring when the incident which left them behind
was one that never entered consciousness."[18] Thompson's everyday life
and routine, his spatial practice, in Lefebvre's vocabulary, survives his loss
of memory. The spatial identity of New York is contrasted to that of the
suburban manor house in New Jericho, the quintessential bourgeois *in-
térieur*, where the dénouement transpires. This lends *Street of Chance* a particularly bivalent character through its suggestion of two modes of social
and spatial life that fail to coalesce into a whole.

Tillary Street promises to restore a deeper stratum of Thompson's memory, one whose annihilation coincides with the onset of the urban renewal that would transform American cities in the 1950s. While the shocks accompanying psychic readjustment to dramatic change may well appear permanent features of the modern metropolis, as Baudelaire prophetically noted, there are convincing grounds to view the twenty-year period from 1939 to 1959 as anomalous, even in a city such as New York. From the end of the 1930s through the middle of the following decade, the many instances of reconstruction and urban crisis inflicted no shortage of blows upon the city's landscape and its inhabitants alike.

Whether we think of the record number of tenements destroyed on the Lower East Side in 1938, the completion of the East River Houses in 1941, or the beginning of the Stuyvesant Town housing project in 1943, instances of destruction and rebuilding are plentiful.[19] Losses of population in the urban core, a declining tax base, and the aging of much housing stock in the central city signaled a situation that many perceived as a crisis.[20] These dynamics suggest a historical context for *Street of Chance* and propose it as one of the earliest films noir that allude to urban renewal and the violent post-1939 transformations of the metropolis.

Architecture, as John Ruskin famously remarked, acts to preserve social memory. "We may live without her, and worship without her, but we cannot remember without her."[21] The trauma and amnesia experienced by Thompson serve as a powerful allegory for the disappearance of familiar architectural landmarks and neighborhoods in New York City after 1939. It suggests that cycles of memory loss and subsequent recollection may well have been common among citydwellers in the post-1939 metropolis and proposes the unspecified trauma initially suffered by Thompson as an instance of what Richard Terdiman calls the "memory crisis" of modernity. Recognizable as "the failure of organic integration of the past into the lived experience" of individuals living in the present, this breakdown of spatial and temporal convergence in the present pervades film noir.[22]

Such an intuition resonates with the thinking of Siegfried Kracauer, notably his book *Theory of Film: The Redemption of Physical Reality* (1960), which cogently outlines a cinematic aesthetic of the centripetal film noir. Appearing at the close of the film cycle, Kracauer's book adumbrates, in the words of Miriam Hansen, "a theory of a particular type of film experience, and of cinema as the aesthetic matrix of a particular historical experience" contemporaneous with a range of other postwar cultural discourses, including existentialism, jazz, and the New Wave cinemas.[23] The city of growing invisibility that Kracauer diagnoses in the epigraph to this chapter occupies a key locus in *Theory of Film* and its diagnosis of a loss of memory and experience.

Before considering Kracauer's theory and its relevance to film noir, one can profitably relate *Theory of Film* to larger developments in postwar American urbanism. More specifically, one might understand Kracauer's book as a key articulation of late modernity and the crisis of centripetal space analyzed in Chapter 2. Robert Beauregard argues that in the 1960s the integrity of the modernist project in planning that arose after 1945 began to unravel.[24] An earlier belief system that emphasized coherent urban form, the objective logic of scientific inquiry, comprehensive and holistic solutions to metropolitan problems, and the functional integration and organic integrity of the city seemed increasingly precarious.

By the late 1970s, theorists of postmodernism would challenge these assumptions and their underlying "metanarratives" and articulate a tension between the logics of modernity and postmodernity that today pervades both the contemporary built environment and the larger culture.[25] Yet it is useful to grasp *Theory of Film* as demarcating the historical apex of late modernity from the ascendance of postmodernism. Sharing many of the tensions endemic to this era, especially the intellectual uncertainty around the foundations of scientific rationality increasingly noted by many philosophers and social commentators from Karl Popper through Thomas Kuhn, Kracauer's book provides an epitaph of sorts for the crisis of the metropolis and its exploration in the film noir cycle.

The credo that architecture can systematically remake the city on a large scale, an article of faith extending from the early days of CIAM through Rockefeller Center and Wallace Harrison's United Nations and Lincoln Center complexes, began by the early 1960s to appear problematic. Writing a decade later, Colin Rowe and Fred Koetter famously observed that "like the idea of World War I as a war to end war, the city of modern architecture, both as a psychological construct and as a physical model, has been rendered tragically ridiculous."[26] Kracauer's book and the film noir cycle represent cinematic analogues to this more general crisis of faith in scientific rationality and the formative potential of urbanism. De-

nying the possibility of wholeness valorized by earlier modernist architects, the fragmentation analyzed—and valorized—in *Theory of Film* and
represented in film noir corresponds to an actual built environment whose
increasingly fragmented character by the end of the 1950s had become undeniable.

FRAGMENTATION AND CONTINGENCY

Appropriating the discussion of photography in Marcel Proust's *The Guer-
mantes Way*, Kracauer constructs a notion of "psychophysical correspondences" that decisively positions his film theory within the legacy of modernism. Rich with implications for the study of urban spatiality in film
noir, his book delineates an insightful theoretical analysis of the cinematic
representation that grounds the film cycle. Kracauer quotes from the section in Proust's novel in which the narrator enters the living room of his
grandmother and compares his own gaze to that of a photographer.

Proust identifies photography with a detached, fundamentally distanced
mode of perception predicated on a nondiscriminating vision unhampered
by previous memories of its objects. For Kracauer, the foremost virtue of
the photographer is an estrangement from the world that facilitates an
emotionally untainted view of it. As a witness and a stranger (two roles
common in urban life), the photographer does not belong to or appear in
the scenes he depicts. Kracauer suggests that Proust's chief concern lay
with the states of mind conjured up by external phenomena that flood the
mind with involuntary memories.

Rejecting Proust's comparison of the photograph with a mirror, he
thereby undercuts his own emphasis upon the indexical features of photography, further complicating the sense in which he understands the realism of both media. Kracauer criticizes the specular metaphor for ignoring
two dimensions of subjective experience that photographs both presuppose and invite, namely that photographers structure their sense perceptions and that viewers bring a range of emotions to photographic images.
In both instances, subjectivity intervenes, and the meaning of the photograph proves irreducible to an instance of pure mimesis or indexicality. To
account for this predominantly unconscious activity, he proposes the notion of the psychophysical correspondence to comprise "all these more or

less fluid interrelations between the physical world and the psychological dimension in the broadest sense of the word—a dimension which borders on that physical universe and is still intimately connected with it."[27]

The properly cinematic object for Kracauer maintains contact with the surface of physical reality while simultaneously inducing psychophysical correspondences. Our daily "psychic permeation" of objects and places (a process eminently suitable for study by psychoanalysis) frequently blinds us to their physical characteristics.[28] Kracauer's assertion (rife with significance for film noir) that we often fail to see the everyday urban environment follows as a consequence of this "incessant love." Here we might think of the city encountered during the course of daily spatial practice and suddenly transformed into a menacing environment in films such as *Stranger on the Third Floor* and *Scarlet Street.* But one might also think of the shots of urban life in *The Naked City* and their depiction of the city from uncommon perspectives. All confirm Kracauer's argument that film realizes a dialectic that strips away our desires and unconscious attachments to reveal the characteristics of the visible world, of which the metropolis remains a key instance.

Paradoxically, this process renders the film viewer more, rather than less, fragmentized. Instead of providing an experience of spectatorial or urban mastery, the cinema consigns the spectator, in Hansen's words, to "encounters with contingency, lack of control, and otherness . . . an aesthetic experience on par with the historical crisis of experience." Writing in his 1940 Marseilles notebooks, which contained the earliest outlines for *Theory of Film*, Kracauer asserted: "The 'ego' [Ich] of the human being assigned to film is subject to permanent dissolution, is incessantly exploded by material phenomena."[29] Cinema suggests a wound that never heals in which physical reality continually permeates the boundaries of the subject. The fragmented narratives and indelible impression of lived experience identified by Nino Frank in his early analysis of film noir exemplify important traits of the film medium. As Kracauer notes:

> Film renders visible what we did not, or perhaps even could not, see before its advent. It effectively assists us in discovering the material world with its psychophysical correspondences. We literally redeem this world from its dormant state, its state of virtual non-existence, by

endeavoring to experience it through the camera. And we are free to experience it because we are fragmentized. The cinema can be described as a medium particularly equipped to promote the redemption of physical reality. Its imagery permits us, for the first time, to take away with us the objects and occurrences that comprise the flow of material life.[30]

Borrowing from the work of Roland Barthes and the Russian Formalists, Kristin Thompson proposes the notion of cinematic excess to account for those elements in a film unmotivated by its narrative, elements on which Kracauer lays particular stress.[31] They direct the attention of the viewer to the materiality and stylistic level of the film and "skid" it away from literal meaning. In his suggestion that films "alienate our environment in exposing it," Kracauer shares the aspirations of other modernists such as Brecht and Shklovsky to renew our perceptions, as well as the impulse of Benjamin and Kracauer to redeem experience.[32]

In one of the most famous sections in his book, Kracauer compares the spectator to the flaneur:

And how do films gratify the isolated individual's longings? He recalls the nineteenth-century *flaneur* (with whom he has otherwise little in common) in his susceptibility to the transient real-life phenomena that crowd the screen. According to the testimony available, it is their flux which affects him most strongly. Also with the fragmentary happenings incidental to them, these phenomena—taxi cabs, buildings, passers-by, inanimate objects, faces—presumably stimulate his senses and provide him with stuff for dreaming. Bar interiors suggest strange adventures; improvised gatherings hold out the promise of fresh human contacts; sudden shifts of scene are pregnant with unforeseeable possibilities. Through its very concern with camera-reality, film thus permits especially the lonely spectator to fill his shrinking self—shrinking in an environment where the bare schemata of things threaten to supersede the things themselves—with images of life as such, glittering, allusive, infinite life . . . All that has been said so far indicates that the delight he takes in films does not, or need not, stem from their intrigue proper. To quote Chaperot, "sometimes right in the middle of a film whose whole intrigue we know and whose lamentable threads we even anticipate, do we not suddenly have the feeling that the image rises to a superior plane and the 'story' is not more than of secondary importance?" What redeems the film addict from his isolation is not so much the spectacle of an individual destiny which might again isolate him as the sight of people mingling and communing with each other according to ever-changing patterns. He seeks the opportunity of drama rather than drama itself.[33]

Wandering through the film, Kracauer's spectator-flaneur is drawn by images of transient phenomena—crowds, streets, faces, train stations, and ultimately the city itself—and allows these objects to release their psycho-physical correspondences within him- or herself. His account of the bare schemata of things recalls the phenomenology of Edmund Husserl and its similar program to return "to the things themselves."[34] Like Husserl the phenomenologist, Kracauer criticizes the insufficiency of the abstraction and the quantitative thought associated with science as a foundation for human values and experience.[35] In a world of growing formal rationality that he had already labeled *ratio* in his 1920s writings, the spectator-flaneur unquestionably occupies a defensive position.

Perhaps most striking is the congruence between Kracauer's critique of the "abstract manner in which people of all walks of life perceive the world and themselves" in contemporary technological society and Lefebvre's notion of abstract space.[36] Read through this prism, the film viewer in *Theory of Film* seeking to fill a shrinking self appears irreducible to the transhistorical spectator of cinema that the book sometimes appears to posit. The street provides a key anchor for this notion of spectatorship. Inversely, Kracauer's spectator can be recognized as the occupant of an increasingly abstract urban realm, the American city whose disappearing contours and landmarks are rendered visible before their eradication by abstract space through the images of streets, train stations, and bars described in *Theory of Film* and pervasive in the film noir cycle.

Although the literature on film noir emphasizes a sense of narrative foreboding and inescapable fate as defining traits of the film cycle, the significance of chance identified by Kracauer appears no less crucial, if often undervalued.[37] Chance meetings, unexpected coincidences, and empty streets pervade film noir no less than the atmosphere of overdetermination that allegedly dominates its stories.[38] Read as a pretext for the development of more-ephemeral perceptions, film noir narratives assume an entirely different guise, one that reveals their modernist lineage, including an emphasis upon the unconscious and a rediscovery of the urban landscape that links the film cycle to the literary and cinematic legacy of Surrealism.[39]

Here one might reflect on the contingency of events in a centripetal film noir emblematic of Kracauer's analysis, *Killer's Kiss* (Stanley Kubrick, 1955). As we shall see, many of its pivotal narrative events (Albert's murder, the theft of Davey's scarf that leads him to miss their rendezvous, Gloria's employment at the dance hall, her meeting with Davey) occur only because characters appear fortuitously at a certain time and place.

TIMES SQUARE AND THE URBAN FRAGMENT

Perhaps the most remarkable feature of Kubrick's film is its extensive representation of public spaces, at once a depiction of the urban realm as violent and alienating yet potentially open to different appropriations. *Killer's Kiss* presents a veritable catalogue of places for mingling, strolling, waiting, and watching in the New York City of the 1950s. Few films noir profile the activity of *flânerie* more prominently or to greater effect. From the apartment complex shared by the film's two central characters (a boxer and a dance hall hostess) with its common roof and central courtyard permitting residents to see into each other's apartments, to frequent scenes in Times Square, atop Brooklyn industrial buildings, and alongside New York Harbor, it presents actual urban spaces to a degree unparalleled by most of the films noir of the 1940s.

In its depiction of urban spaces (Pennsylvania Station, Times Square, rooftops with panoramic views) that elide the dichotomy between private dwellings and automobile-dominated streets, *Killer's Kiss* holds out the tantalizing prospect of a public spatial realm that is negotiable on foot. Most striking, however, is the film's predilection for those public spaces that Kracauer identifies as uniquely cinematic: crowded streets, railroad stations, and bar interiors. It offers a "walking cure" through which the metropolis is encountered and rendered spatially coherent and productively resonates with the argument developed by Kracauer in *Theory of Film*.

Pennsylvania Station reappears prominently as the site from which the boxer Davey Gordon (Jamie Smith) recites his flashback voice-over narration. Beginning and concluding in the main waiting room (sometimes called "the Great Room") of the McKim, Mead, & White station (1904–1910), the film obsessively treats this space in three flashback scenes.[40] These establish the station's barrel-vaulted ceilings and clerestory windows as both the point of origin of its story and the central spatial anchor in its representation of New York.[41]

Unlike the places of employment of the two protagonists, the waiting room exudes a calmness that is noticeably absent from other spaces such as Times Square and the mannequin factory where Davey exchanges blows with the dance hall owner Vincent Rapallo (Frank Silvera). Filmed in full-frame long takes from ground level, as if to accentuate the activity of waiting, the station we see is full of real travelers. These images of pedestrian movement, the flux and transition of urban life, exploit what Kracauer understood as the essential affinity of the cinematic apparatus for representing public spaces as loci of chance and contingency.[42]

Produced during the booming exodus to the suburbs of the 1950s,

Frame enlargement of boxer Davy Gordon waiting in Pennsylvania Station, from *Killer's Kiss* (Stanley Kubrick, 1955).

Killer's Kiss represents Pennsylvania Station in a manner that evokes the social traffic of the great railroad stations of the nineteenth century. As Wolfgang Schivelbusch notes, "in the railroad station, *the human traffic* literally flows through actively, in the form of travelers streaming in and out of the trains."[43] Although the neoclassical facade of the terminal once functioned like a stimulus shield (the psychic armor of the urbanite first postulated by Simmel) to insulate preindustrial space from the jarring character of locomotive travel, by the postwar period its architectural effect had changed.

A century later, when the metropolis is thoroughly mired in the automobile age, a curious inversion transpires through which the railroad station becomes an anachronistic haven for the pedestrian-flaneur, a proxy for the film spectator and the guarantor of a shock-free urban passage the contemporary city is hard pressed to provide. Hence the fascination that Pennsylvania Station occupies in the film, as well as the tenacity with which it represents the experiences of walking and waiting in the city. Already experienced as antiquated by many New Yorkers, Pennsylvania Station exemplifies Bloch's nonsynchronous contradiction not yet resolved in capitalist terms, in this case by the political economy of urban redevelopment that decisively transformed New York.

As the former *Look* magazine photographer Kubrick filmed *Killer's Kiss* in Pennsylvania Station in 1955, developer William Zeckendorf was secretly entering into an agreement with the Pennsylvania Railroad's president to purchase the air rights above the station.[44] By 1962 the latter had decided to demolish the financially unprofitable structure and to allow the Madison Square Garden Corporation to construct a new sports arena in its place. Protests by renowned architects (Philip Johnson, J. J. P. Oud) and critics (Lewis Mumford, Ada Louise Huxtable) proved ineffective in halting its demolition at the end of 1964. Directors such as Kubrick knew only too well where to point the camera in a city changing even faster than the human heart.[45]

Yet Pennsylvania Station serves as more than mere background in the film, for the "stimulus shield" function that Schivelbusch discerns in railway architecture establishes a prototype for the narrative throughout *Killer's Kiss*. Davey's spatial anchoring in the waiting area through his voice-over narration emphasizes his intention to leave the city and conveys the status of the terminal as a "protected" space, unlike the boxing arena, Times Square, and his apartment building, places where he experiences loss (the match, his scarf, his manager, and his female companion).

The metaphor of the stimulus shield attains literal form when before the boxing match he is rubbed down with alcohol in his dressing room, his body prepared for the blows of his opponent. Similarly, Gloria Price (Irene Kane) makes up her face as a ritual of self-protection before stepping onto the dance floor. Through crosscutting the film establishes a parallel between Davey's boxing career and Gloria's work as a hostess in the Pleasure Land dance hall in Times Square. Both jobs position these characters as objects of an anonymous urban gaze.

By watching the television broadcast of the match rather than actually attending it, Vinnie underscores the growing decorporealization of this gaze in centrifugal space, in which television eliminates the need for the actual spatiotemporal proximity of boxers and the audience. Yet the essential violence performed on both Davey's and Gloria's bodies—the experience of shock each undergoes in the metropolis—is underscored by the montage sequence that cuts between Davey's rout by his opponent and Vinnie's violent seduction of Gloria.

Explaining her employment at the dance hall, Gloria alludes to her objectification but also describes its appeal: "I happened to pass the dance hall. I don't know what possessed me. I went up and I actually took the job. I don't understand any part of it. Every night I worked in that depraved place, a human zoo." One thinks here of Simmel's formulation of the blasé attitude as a characteristic urban personality trait and its devaluation of the world, "which in the end unavoidably drags one's own personality down into a feeling of the same worthlessness."[46] Gloria and Davey seek out jobs that objectify them and signal their internalization of the urban imperative to maximize nervous stimulation. This extirpation of subjective reaction in the metropolis is evident in the scene in which they return home after work and nurse their wounds in isolation, victims of perceptual overload in the metropolis. It is also suggested by the lap dissolve from the swaying punching bags in the gym where Albert works to the gyrating bodies of the two Shriners in Times Square who steal Davey's scarf.

A basic experience of metropolitan life for Simmel involves the development of a reserved urban personality that avoids exchanging gazes with other people, exemplified by the failure of Albert (Jerry Jarret) and Gloria to recognize each other that indirectly leads to the latter's murder by Vinnie's henchmen, who mistake him for Davey. One finds this visual reticence in the pattern of gazes exchanged between Davey and Gloria. At first they spy upon each other from their apartment windows; later they leave their building and continue to ignore each other.

Significantly, the first experience of mutual recognition that punctures their urban reserve occurs not through the sense of sight, but when Davey hears Gloria's scream. It awakens him from his troubling nightmare, a sequence of driving (not walking) through the city at rapid speed that is filmed in negative, as if to identify the automobile-mediated city with a menacing experience of space. Accompanied by the sound of the boxing match and the taunt "Go on home, you're all through," the sequence proves all the more jarring for the fact that Davey dreams it while he is at home.

Killer's Kiss explores multiple parallels between the female body; the mobile gaze as it shifts between characters, film spectator, and citydwellers; and the abstract space of the metropolis. This exploration of the linkages between vision and the metropolis is evident in the sequence that commences immediately after Davey's opening narration in Pennsylvania Station. As he recounts his fight with Rodriguez, the camera dissolves to a close-up photograph of him in boxing gloves. The next shot reveals this photograph as belonging to a flyer advertising the boxing match that evening. In the following image we see the poster clinging to the wet pavement, where it is stepped upon by a pedestrian (recalling a similar shot in *The Naked City*).

Rather than dwelling on the psychological state of the boxer (the vanquished hero presented with the chance to regain his victory), the film presents Davey in his dressing room before the match and then cuts to a series of exterior shots in Times Square. As if emphasizing the violence of the surrounding city, these shots nonetheless fail to advance the narrative and appear as a series of discrete tableaux that encourage psychophysical correspondences. Beginning with a long shot of lights and the anonymous urban crowd of Times Square, we then see a succession of exterior close-ups of store windows, obviously filmed with a handheld camera.

A toy animal, frankfurters roasting on a grill, slices of cake and other

Frame enlargement of photography studio in Times Square, from
Killer's Kiss (Stanley Kubrick, 1955).

desserts on a rotating tray, a photo-studio sign with dozens of cheap studio
portraits on its back wall, and a windup toy in a dish of water—no single
image in this sequence stands out or calls attention to itself. Together they
form a medley of shabbiness familiar to any tourist visiting the urban center: cheap restaurants serving greasy food, souvenir shops filled with tawdry novelties, and everywhere the urban crowd. No character in the film
lives in this district, a fact that confirms our presence in the urban center,
the realm of the empty signified described by Barthes that here appears
identical with the urban environment and its affinity to cinema noted by
Kracauer.

The next image after the windup toy is an exterior long shot of the sign
for the Pleasure Land dance hall. Two subsequent closer shots depict two
women in the advertisement. These images become a metaphor for Gloria. Just as the boxing match flyer becomes Davey's sign, the Pleasure Land
billboard becomes Gloria's. This movement through the detritus of images in Times Square connects the workplaces of both characters, suggesting the impossibility of any connection between them unmediated by the
urban center.

Both images identify the characters with their jobs. Each prepares the
space of Times Square for the events of the narrative, especially the dance

Frame enlargement of Pleasure Land dance hall sign, from *Killer's Kiss*
(Stanley Kubrick, 1955).

hall sign, which serves as an establishing shot of its space throughout the
film. The "event" announced by the marquee—the deployment of the
signs of femininity and commodification of sexuality—recurs daily in Pleasure Land. This proffering of an image of the feminine in the urban center constitutes a recognizable figure of modernity. As Christine Buci-
Glucksmann observes:

> Of this we can be certain: the image engraved upon the *flaneur's* body,
> the Baudelairean passerby barely glimpsed in the intoxication of large
> cities, this multiplicity of emotions are only specific examples of what
> is characteristic of modernity: the cult of images, the secularization/
> sublimation of bodies, their ephemeral nature and reproducibility . . .
> The feminine becomes the inevitable sign of a new historic regime of
> seeing and "not-seeing," of representable and unrepresentable.[47]

Endlessly recirculated on billboards and magazine covers and in advertisements for every conceivable commodity, what is the cult of the image described by Buci-Glucksmann if not a cult of the image of woman?
This "seeing" and "not-seeing" ranges from the billboard model embodying current fashion to invisible sites of prostitution and characterizes the

(empty) urban center as an allegorical topos, a site of ruins and loss, the space of fissured subjectivity. This permeation of the metropolis by images of the feminine may well constitute a key cultural attribute of centripetal space.

From the emblem of woman on its exterior, to the painted tableaux on its dance floor, but most of all in the fusion of space and desire conveyed by its very name—Pleasure Land—the site of Gloria's employment and entrapment lends itself to allegorical interpretation. Here, the romantic strains of ballroom music repeated throughout the film emanate from a phonograph that lulls the dancers into a dream, their reverie interrupted only by the end of a tune and the obligation to negotiate the next dance. The smoothly functioning dance floor, its painted backgrounds and neatly attired hostesses, promises a world of unblemished surfaces whose wholeness is simultaneously proposed as illusory and reified form.

Surrounded by the flux of Times Square, the ruins of Pleasure Land exemplify the Benjaminian understanding of allegory: a visible image or tableau of a petrified and fragmented reality that is imperfect, incomplete, and ambiguous.[48] Its status as an allegory of fragmentation is further suggested by the scene in which Vinnie viciously smashes the mirror in his office after two smirking cartoon characters in a window frame depicted on his wall seem to be looking at him. After he throws an object at the camera, we see a protective sheet of glass swaying in front of it, confirming that Vinnie himself remains under observation in a window—literally shielded from the camera—despite his violent outbreak.

This shattered reality is nowhere more evident than in the film's use of photography. From Davey's photograph on the boxing placard to the contiguous sequence of images of store windows and commodities, *Killer's Kiss* presents photographic images of a reified nature that epitomizes the features of film and photography already noted in 1927 by Kracauer: "If the disarray of the illustrated newspapers is simply confusion, the game that film plays with the pieces of disjointed nature is reminiscent of *dreams* in which the fragments of daily life become jumbled."[49] Here one might think not simply of the fragments of urban reality photographed and reorganized in the film but also of the lives of its two central characters and their reliance upon the image in both their domestic and work environments.[50]

Frame enlargement of Davey in his apartment, surrounded by photographs, from *Killer's Kiss* (Stanley Kubrick, 1955).

One might also recall the urban photography produced in New York around the time that Kubrick was filming *Killer's Kiss*, especially William Klein's 1956 book *Life Is Good and Good for You in New York*. Returning to his city of birth after military service in Europe, Klein captured the atmosphere of anomie and seediness he found around him in grainy images that aspire to the sequencing of cinema. Adopting a diaristic mode that recalls the film's location cinematography, Klein's photography prominently features advertising imagery and the same Times Square neighborhood filmed by Kubrick. American publishers rejected the project, chastising his "noir" images and complaining: "This isn't New York, too black, too one-sided, this is a slum." The initial reception of Klein's book underscores the cultural resistance to such nonconformist urban imagery in 1950s America.[51]

The most stunning meditation on the fragment in *Killer's Kiss* takes place in a mannequin factory and pits Vinnie and Davey in a life-and-death struggle using the plastic female body parts around them as shields and weapons. The scene is not only an allegory for their struggle over the body of Gloria, the figure who brings them together as competitors. Their destruction of the "bodies" around them also suggests the end of the corporeal metaphor of the city and the arrival of a dismembered, if not sym-

Frame enlargement of fight between Davey Gordon and Vinnie Rapallo in mannequin factory, from *Killer's Kiss* (Stanley Kubrick, 1955). Courtesy of Film Stills Collection, Museum of Modern Art, New York.

bolically beheaded, form of centripetal space. Contemporaneous with the collapse of the modernist project of integral urbanism, the scene evokes the relations among the fragmented body, sexuality, and abstract space described by Lefebvre in the following remarkable passage:

> In abstract space, where an anaphorization occurs that transforms the body by transporting it outside itself and into the ideal-visual realm, we also encounter a strange substitution concerning sex . . . The space where this substitution occurs, where nature is replaced by cold abstraction and by the absence of pleasure, is the mental space of castration (at once imaginary and real, symbolic and concrete): the space of a metaphorization whereby the image of woman supplants the woman herself, whereby her body is fragmented, desire shattered, and life explodes into a thousand pieces. Over the abstract space reigns phallic solitude and the self-destruction of desire . . .
>
> . . . Confined by the abstraction of a space broken down into spe-

cialized locations, the body itself is pulverized. The body as represented by the images of advertising (where the legs stand for stockings, the breasts for bras, the face for make-up, etc.) serves to
fragment desire and doom it to anxious frustration, to the non-satis-
faction of local needs. In abstract space, and wherever its influence is
felt, the demise of the body has a dual character, for it is at once symbolic and concrete: concrete, as a result of the aggression to which the
body is subject; symbolic, on account of the fragmentation of the
body's living unity. This is especially true of the female body, as transformed into exchange value, into a sign of the commodity and indeed
into a commodity *per se*.[52]

Whether we think of the geometrically shaped rooftop as an abstract
space that is both "homogeneous and divided," the commodity trade in female bodies at Pleasure Land, or the mannequin factory as a domain of
castration where the two men lunge at each other with sharp instruments,
spaces of fragmentation and fragmented spaces appear throughout the
film. Through their emphasis on repetition and loss, these fragments exemplify the discourses of melancholia and spleen explored by Benjamin
and consign the female body to the domain of the "ideal-visual realm"
purged of actual subjectivity.

That the struggle between Davey and Vinnie employs dismembered female mannequins, lifeless bodies, implies the significance of the sequence
as an allegory for the death of experience in the centripetal city.[53] Also related to the male control of the female body in fetishism (such as the scene
in which Davey fondles the stockings hanging in Gloria's apartment), the
gendered body fragment equally informed the conception of urban space
in the 1950s. The role of the female body and its discrete parts as a model
for the shape of the city, an ideal of aesthetic wholeness, is suggested by
the following 1958 observation by urbanist Grady Clay:

Although a woman's shape may change with fashion, de-emphasized
here, exaggerated there occasionally disappearing in other strategic
areas—the shapeliness of women is a quality which has aroused the
cupidinous interest of mankind since Adam.

Mankind's interest in the shape of his cities is of a different—and

more diffuse—order. Yet few influences more subtly repel our advances or more surely arouse us than the spatial quality of our cities.

Shapely cities have always attracted man's interest, his love, fortune, and sacred honor. This past summer we've watched the world's
tourists flock to such uniquely shaped cities as Venice, Stockholm,
Copenhagen, Rome, and San Francisco. Of course it is not shape
alone which beckons tourists, industries, love, and money. But it is the
molding of exterior space into a recognizable pattern which gives so
many towns and cities their character, and visual qualities to stir men's
souls.[54]

One can easily apply this description to the Times Square scenes in
Killer's Kiss, which transpire in precisely such a molded and recognizable pattern that disrupts the urban grid and realizes the erotic qualities
that "stir men's souls" while remaining silent on the matter of the female
urbanite and *her* desires. The openness of Times Square contrasts markedly with the darkness and constricted movement in the skyscraper canyons of Manhattan and with the warehouse neighborhood where Gloria is
rescued. Unlike the many shots that imitate still photographs, these sequences of bodies strolling in every direction are generally filmed with a
moving camera and eschew the stasis and close range of the former in favor of greater movement in the frame and distance from the object.

A palpable combination of defeat and solace is conveyed by the scene in
which Gloria walks against the flow of traffic through Times Square after
her violent encounter with Vinnie, while cars pass by on a perpendicular
avenue. A highly public, if not dangerous, area of the city for a single
woman to be walking at night, this scene is among the few in the film in
which Gloria is not oppressively surveyed at a close range. Suggesting the
nearly overpowering isolation and alienation produced by the city, her
promenade through a possibly threatening neighborhood also reveals her
own spatial practice, a walking cure whose filming in an elevated traveling
shot calls attention to her act of spatial and temporal appropriation. Gloria
bears the impact of the metropolis in her sullen facial expression, yet her
walk nonetheless suggests an alternative to the wholly impassive acceptance of urban shock.

Killer's Kiss exemplifies the proclivity of the centripetal film noir to wrest fragments of the past—a building, a style, a corner of the city—from obscurity and to facilitate awareness of the city's existence in time. If, as Kracauer claims, the spectator's own fragmentation forms the condition of possibility for a redemptive criticism of urban reality, this fissured subjectivity should be grasped as integral to late modernity and its enlarging sphere of abstract space. As the physical face of the city is transformed, the psychophysical correspondences provoked by film noir facilitate an encounter with an urban environment undergoing physical alteration and challenged by the modalities of centrifugal space.

FOOTSTEPS IN THE CITY

Contemporaneously with the release of *Killer's Kiss* there emerged a body of European and American writing on the experience of passage through the city. Attentive to the physical details of the urban environment, this discourse was notably attuned to the urban past and thus formed a striking contrast to the future-oriented pronouncements of many postwar modernists. French Situationists such as Guy Debord began in the mid-1950s to chronicle their walks through Parisian neighborhoods on the verge of redevelopment. Calling these "strolls," inspired by the earlier *flânerie* of Baudelaire and the Surrealists, the drift *(dérive)*, they walked (occasionally as long as twenty-four hours) to chart the ambience of streets and neighborhoods.[55] These ideas and activities led to the mapping activity they called "psychogeography" that would later garner the Situationists an influential position among critics of postwar urbanism.[56]

French analogues to the redevelopment of the post-1945 American built environment, including the construction of enormous public housing projects and the destruction of neighborhoods such as Les Halles in Paris, provided fertile soil for the reception of the Situationists' ideas.[57] Yet it is equally striking to consider the historical overlap of early Situationist discourse with the French critical reception of film noir. Here one might think not merely of Debord's affection for *The Naked City*, but also of the aesthetic of the *insolite* valorized by film noir critics Raymond Borde and Etienne Chaumeton and the relation of this shock experience to the exploration of the energy flows radiated by the city undertaken by the Situationists and the Surrealists before them.[58]

Several years later, the most influential attempt to theorize the experience of the urban space in an American context appeared, Kevin Lynch's
book *The Image of the City* (1960). Based upon research he had begun to
conduct at the beginning of the 1950s, contemporaneous with the urban
drifts of the Situationists, Lynch's study was the first to investigate how
city inhabitants construct mental images or "maps" of the surrounding
metropolitan environment.[59] Writing primarily for urban designers and
planners, he analyzed existing urban forms as the basis for designing new
cities. The desideratum of good city design lay in what Lynch termed "legibility," the ability of city users to recognize and to organize parts of the
urban environment as features of a coherent whole.

Poorly designed cities lack discernible features capable of evoking
strong mental images in their inhabitants, thereby promoting spatial disorientation and an impoverished relation to the surrounding environment.
Through a combination of interview techniques, field analyses, and requests that survey participants draw maps of the urban environments of
Boston, Los Angeles, and Jersey City, Lynch identified the characteristic
"public images" of these cities shared by large segments of their popula-
tions. His research marked an early and significant instance in which planners conducted experiments in the actual city rather than in the controlled
setting of the laboratory, a fact that links it to the earlier empirical studies of urban psychopathology by Carl Otto Westphal and Eugène Minkowski.[60]

Lynch classified the physical forms of the city into five types of elements: paths, edges, districts, nodes, and landmarks. The task of the city
planner consists in the harmonious deployment of these elements at the
level of the city scale. These serve in turn as the raw material of the environmental image, the temporally evolving mental map whose pragmatic
function and emotional charge correspond to what Lefebvre calls spaces of
representation and representations of space. Film noir presents many instances of the elements described by Lynch, and one might understand instances of walking in the film cycle as analogous to the mapping of urban
space he describes. Spatial itineraries of characters can be construed as attempts to overcome urban formlessness and to connect parts of the city
into a coherent environmental image.

This strategy appears in *Footsteps in the Night* (Jean Yarbrough, 1957), a film noir about a Los Angeles murder investigation. Although the police readily apprehend a resident of the Sunset Villa Motel in connection with the crime, one of their detectives remains unsatisfied that this suspect is actually the killer. Returning to the scene of the crime, a drab West Hollywood bungalow court motel, he discovers a nearly identical motel across the street called the Sunset Vista and conjectures that the murderer may have inadvertently mistaken them, thus killing the wrong man. After planning a trap and mapping out the space between them, the police find the real offender.

Most suggestive in *Footsteps in the Night* is the connection posited between an urban environment lacking recognizable landmarks and the individual's loss of spatial position: a disorientation in centripetal space that leads to murder. Although the film does not depict the global Los Angeles environment (street plans, landmarks, centers) that Lynch describes, it suggests an architectural homogeneity on the much smaller scale of the neighborhood block. The bungalow motel—a curious hybrid between private residence, apartment, and commercial structure—already signifies the social atomization and separation of its residents.

It provides no clues about the spatial practices of its inhabitants, their daily routines, or the nature of their lives, while its inhospitable social material repels any speculation about its potential to facilitate a memorable space of representation. The numerical ordering of the motel rooms exemplifies the dominance of the abstract representation of space, as well as the power of contingency discussed by Kracauer, underscored by the murdered man's unlucky occupation of Bungalow 8 in the Sunset Villa, the same number occupied by the intended victim in the adjacent Sunset Vista.

Although the murderer is not shown getting lost in the bungalow courts, the film depicts both the detective's initial retracing of the space between them and the subsequent police mapping of the area in preparation for trapping the killer.[61] The formless quality of this urban space—the absence of distinguishing features between the two courts—is marked. The detective's own cognitive mapping of it (a procedure he accomplishes on foot while his partner dozes in their squad car) provides a solution to the crime, a narrative resolution for the film that furnishes a critique of illegible space and a walking cure through which it is rendered coherent.[62]

REPRESENTING BUNKER HILL

Unlike the descriptions by Lynch and other commentators of many Los Angeles neighborhoods as distended nuclei with no apparent relation to one another, one former locality pervasive in film noir, Bunker Hill, exhibited a marked spatial coherence. Formerly located between the central business district and the civic center in the northwest sector of the city's downtown, it was bounded by First Street on the north, Hill Street on the east, Fifth Street on the south, and the Harbor Freeway to the west. Born in 1874 with the creation of Bunker Hill Avenue, the neighborhood's major north–south axis advocated by Los Angeles land speculator and future mayor Prudent Beaudry, Bunker Hill became the city's most exclusive residential neighborhood during the 1880s and 1890s.

By the end of World War I, Bunker Hill was increasingly populated by transients, pensioners, and derelicts and developed a crime rate double the city average. Raymond Chandler's widely touted description in *The High Window* (1942) became permanently associated with the neighborhood, almost to the point of usurping its actual physical identity:

> Bunker Hill is old town, lost town, shabby town, crook town. Once, very long ago, it was the choice residential district of the city, and there are still standing a few of the jigsaw Gothic mansions with wide porches and walls covered with round-end shingles and full corner bay windows and spindle turrets. They are all rooming houses now, their parquetry floors are scratched and worn through the once glossy finish and the wide sweeping staircases are dark with time and cheap varnish laid on over generations of dirt. In the tall rooms haggard landladies bicker with shifty tenants. On the wide cool front porches, reaching their cracked shoes into the sun, and staring at nothing, sit the old men with faces like lost battles.[63]

Bunker Hill became the site of one of the earliest post–World War II urban redevelopment projects mandated by the 1945 California Community Redevelopment Act and the establishment of the Los Angeles Community Redevelopment Agency (CRA) in 1948. In 1951 the agency designated it an official urban renewal area, a move made possible by the

Federal Housing Act of 1949.[64] Initially designated as a site for 10,000 units of severely needed low-income housing, Bunker Hill was subsequently reclaimed by real estate and business interests, whose formation of a "Committee against Socialist Housing" carried the day and led to the adoption of a commercial development plan in 1959.

By 1966 the CRA had acquired title to nearly all of Bunker Hill. It was bulldozed out of existence by the end of the decade and replaced by parking lots and later additions such as California Plaza, the Museum of Contemporary Art, the Bonaventura Hotel, and, most recently, Frank Gehry's Disney Concert Hall. As the great absent presence of the city's urban past, the Ur-instance of metropolitan density seldom associated with Los Angeles, Bunker Hill remains among the most politically charged places/chapters in the city's history. Depending on the views of the observer, it can provoke rueful nostalgia or confirm the wisdom of postwar urban redevelopment policies.

Already by the end of the 1950s, Lynch noted the peculiar relation of inhabitants to the neighborhood, a place that they could not precisely locate

Theodore Seymour Hall, view from Los Angeles City Hall of Bunker Hill (1940).
Courtesy of the Huntington Library, San Marino, California.

Theodore Seymour Hall, view from Los Angeles City Hall of Bunker Hill redevelopment (1960). Courtesy of the Huntington Library, San Marino, California.

but nonetheless perceived as changeless in a Los Angeles whose features were constantly altering:

> Another frequent theme was that of relative age. Perhaps because so much of the environment is new or changing, there was evidence of widespread, almost pathological, attachment to anything that had survived the upheaval. Thus the tiny Plaza-Olivera node, or even the decayed hotels of Bunker Hill, claimed the attention of many subjects. There was an impression from these few interviews that there is an even greater sentimental attachment to what is old than exists in conservative Boston.[65]

Kenneth Burke observed that "the basic strategy of metonymy is this: to convey some incorporeal or intangible state in terms of the corporeal or tangible . . . to speak of 'the heart' rather than 'the emotions.'"[66] Metonymy and synecdoche are the master tropes of Bunker Hill, for the neighborhood's very name eliminates other properties characteristic of its 133 acres and fuses its identity with its topography. Conveying the idea of an elevated fortified projection, Bunker Hill became unavoidably identified with, if not overdetermined by, its elevation early in its history.

On December 7, 1912, an article appeared in *Southwestern Contractor* magazine urging that the hill be removed to facilitate the growth of the downtown business district.[67] In 1931 the engineering firm Babcock and Sons was hired to explore the feasibility of its regrading and noted in its report: "This densely populated section contains many obsolete buildings, mostly frame residences and old apartment houses. Due to its topography and location there has been practically no real estate development in this territory in recent years . . . The Hill and its improvements are in the main unsightly. The elevations are such that this section constitutes a barrier to the free flow of traffic into the Central Business District and the Civic Center."[68]

The 1931 Babcock plan was never implemented, a likely casualty of the Great Depression, yet arguments about the redevelopment of the Hill would continue into the postwar decades. Twenty years later, in 1951, the firm recommended that the buildings on the Hill be razed and that thirty-seven thirteen-story middle-income apartment buildings be constructed in their place. Urban developers and newspaper editorialists suggested that the Hill had long been psychologically and physically isolated from the rest of the city. Their plans and development schemes consistently approached the area as a void in need of elimination or redevelopment.

Yet the Hill's steep topography struck other observers as one of its prime assets. The construction of the Angels Flight funicular at Third and Hill Streets by Colonel J. W. Eddy in 1901 provided residents with an easy means of reaching the downtown business district without an automobile. Bertram Goodhue, architect of the Los Angeles Central Library, completed two years after his death in 1924, urged the municipal government to locate his commission on Bunker Hill. "That hill should be made your acropolis," he told his client in words that would reverberate throughout the 1950s.[69]

Newspaper commentators observed with some puzzlement that while the Hollywood Hills were being gentrified, Bunker Hill's inviting proximity to the central business district was all but ignored by residents in search of "cliff dwelling."[70] As an editorial in the *Los Angeles Mirror* noted in 1951, "Bunker Hill with its commanding position and excellent views could be turned into a show place. It could and should become one of the city's most attractive areas."[71] Yet in the postwar climate of urban renewal and increasing centrifugal movement, this prospect failed to attain many supporters.

During the 1950s newspaper journalists and city planners displaced the characterizations of Bunker Hill as traffic barrier or acropolis with discussions of its centrality and urban blight. As the *Mirror* argued in 1956, "For thousands employed in downtown offices, stores, and industry, residence on the hill would be a great convenience. They could forget long trips to work and traffic jams. In fact, the CRA development of the Hill would have a tendency to lessen traffic congestion in the central area."[72]

Citing Bunker Hill's proximity to the civic center and central business district as evidence of its overlooked centrality, commentators endorsed redevelopment as a means of enhancing its value. Yet a proposal to turn a refurbished neighborhood into a proper city center ran counter to the tendency toward centrifugal growth in the region. In 1960 *Highland Park News-Herald and Journal* publisher Oran Asa decried such a project. Anticipating the work of urbanists such as Reyner Banham, Asa recommended that Angelenos develop an appreciation for the multinucleated character of their city:

> We think it is time to . . . interject a note of dissent into the appearance of general approval spuriously manufactured by the downtown interests and given currency by the downtown press . . . Los Angeles is a headless city they say . . . They allege that by putting together their magnificent dream "central city" they will have supplied the head, the intelligence center, which will draw the indifferent population together in common purpose . . . Their trouble is that their view of present Los Angeles is clouded by nostalgic memories of the past. With a 1920 map in front of them, they are prescribing a radical operation for the Los Angeles of 1960 . . . If these facilities are designed for the convenience of the people, would it not be more sensible to put them out where the people live? . . . We submit that the Los Angeles of today is not a city at all but a conformation of pleasant towns

and villages, each with its own traditions and group interests. The people, by searching out for a little greenery and clean air for themselves and their children, have brought this about and that's the way they like it.[73]

Urban blight on the Hill was frequently described in terms of the organic metaphors of degeneration and social pathology: "Bunker Hill, a once high-class residential district which sat snootily on a knob of land overlooking the city center, is now a decaying sore on the body of downtown Los Angeles. Having long outlived its beauty, it has been invaded by poverty and filth," wrote one reporter in 1954.[74]

Often elaborately feminized and described as in need of a "facelifting" or as marred by ringed slums that looked "like a dirty necklace," Bunker Hill's appearance in the 1950s was inevitably juxtaposed between a prelapsarian past and an idealized future, as in this 1955 newspaper article:

In years long gone Bunker Hill was dotted with mansions of the wealthy. But today most of these examples of ginger bread are rooming houses or hotels. They have the forlorn, unpainted, rundown look of a dowager who has lost her fortune, her figure and her self respect . . . A woman office worker, imagining herself one day occupying a chic, bachelor-girl apartment in the area from which she could walk to work, said of Bunker Hill: "It's always been the wart on the city's nose."[75]

What precisely was the metropolitan disease that elicited such reactions to Bunker Hill? According to the 1959 CRA report, 63 percent of all structures and 62 percent of all dwellings on the Hill were substandard, well in excess of the 50 percent figure required by federal law for an area to qualify for redevelopment funding. Eighty-four percent of all buildings had been constructed before 1916. The average crime rate per 1,000 population in Los Angeles was 43, while for Bunker Hill it was 88. And the average city arrest rate per 1,000 population was 71, while on Bunker Hill it was 618.[76]

Authorities pronounced the neighborhood of predominantly wooden frame dwellings to be one of the worst firetraps in the city, while a health

Theodore Seymour Hall, elderly residents of Bunker Hill (no date). Courtesy of the
Huntington Library, San Marino, California.

department survey declared 17 percent of its structures slums, 23 percent
substandard, 39 percent acceptable, and 21 percent poor. City service costs
for police, fire, and health exceeded tax revenue by $648,000 annually.
Downtown businesses, especially large department stores, complained of a
loss of customers as Bunker Hill's population declined and consumers
flocked to malls and shopping centers in the San Fernando Valley and on
the west side of Los Angeles, echoing the expansion that had already begun in the 1920s.

   The absence of any scholarship analyzing the very meaning, if not the
accuracy, of these official statistics suggests the need to proceed cautiously
with them. Photographs of the neighborhood and testimonials from its
primarily elderly residents suggest a less harsh portrait. As one woman
wrote in a letter to a newspaper in 1951: "There are many of us living on
Bunker Hill who have nice homes. We appreciate these homes. For the record, too, there are many of us on Bunker Hill who are teetotalers. In
short, I think more could be done to clean up the slum areas of our cities
by restraint on the issuance of liquor licenses than by tearing down and re-

building any particular section of the city to conform to changing conceptions of civic beauty."[77]

While residents often noted the sense of community in the neighborhood, whose small scale and easy access to shopping made it convenient for elderly residents, property owners protested that the threat of condemnation hanging over the area had long discouraged improvements and new building. The mixed ethnic and racial composition of its population—Mexican, Filipino, and European immigrants, and pensioners—has been repeatedly emphasized in discussions of the Hill, often as proof of its social harmony. If the high crime statistics produced by the city are to be believed, life in the area was frequently violent and disruptive.

Given its manifest architectural appeal and nineteenth-century charm, would it not have made more sense to rehabilitate rather than redevelop Bunker Hill with less disruption to residents and owners? In 1956 the City Planning Commission and the CRA rejected eleven alternative plans submitted precisely toward that end. William T. Sessnon Jr., the CRA chairman, claimed that "rehabilitation is not the answer."[78] William McMann, AFL-CIO housing director, no doubt anticipating major union building contracts, suggested that tenants "would be better off moving away from this dilapidated area."[79]

On March 30, 1959, the City Council approved the Redevelopment Plan for the Bunker Hill Urban Renewal project, a mixed-use scheme encompassing residential, motel, commercial, and office buildings. Utilizing Title I federal funds, the CRA eventually relocated more than 5,600 residents and 440 businesses and demolished nearly 400 structures. After years of prolonged legal challenges, it began to acquire the first parcels of land for redevelopment in 1964. In January 1956 Los Angeles newspapers featured articles announcing the return of Sessnon from "a 10-day fishing expedition to New York and Washington" where he obtained pledges of $150,000,000 in private capital, toward Bunker Hill redevelopment.[80]

Bunker Hill figures prominently in many films noir throughout the 1940s and 1950s. Its streets and alleyways were the object of attention by location scouts when the neighborhood exemplified the period's ambivalence toward the aging urban center. As Mike Davis notes, "The Hill was broodingly urban and mysterious—everything that Los Angeles, suburban and banal from birth, was precisely not. With such star qualities, it is

not surprising that it so quickly lodged itself in our nocturnal imagination."[81]

In *Night Has a Thousand Eyes* (John Farrow, 1948), Bunker Hill makes an
early appearance in film noir. Based on a Cornell Woolrich novel, it tells
the story of John Triton (Edward G. Robinson), a man with the gift of cor-
rectly predicting the future, including the moment of his own death. He
lives on Bunker Hill, the perfect correlate to a world containing "secret
things still hidden from us, dark and mysterious." Significantly, Bunker
Hill is absent from the original novel.[82] The film introduces it through an
elaborate pan up the length of Angels Flight that eventually rests upon his
residence, a decrepit residential hotel. As the camera follows him inside,
his voice-over narration comments: "It was an odd part of the city but I
liked it. It was a strictly no questions asked area. People minding their own
business and letting you mind yours. Even after fifteen years my social
conversation didn't exceed twenty-five words a day."

Equally noteworthy is the Hill's representation in *Act of Violence* (Fred
Zinnemann, 1949), whose filming involved what its director called "many
sleepless nights . . . shooting exteriors in the slums of downtown Los Angeles" and an elaborate description of the area's decrepitude in the screenplay.[83] Divided between an imaginary bedroom community of Los Angeles
called Santa Lisa (filmed in Santa Monica) and Bunker Hill, this rigid spatial dichotomy deploys a range of oppositions between daylight and evening, center and periphery, modernity and tradition. It is as if the neighborhood assumes the role of the repressed historical unconscious of Los
Angeles in juxtaposition to its recently constructed suburban present.[84]

Act of Violence recounts the postwar reencounter of two Army soldiers
who survived internment in a German prisoner-of-war camp. Frank Enley
(Van Heflin) was the commanding officer of his group. Joe Parkinson
(Robert Ryan) was his bombardier and close friend. All the incarcerated
men were close to starving. When Enley learned that Parkinson and others were plotting an escape through the tunnel located beneath their barracks, he implored them to reconsider. In the interest of avoiding blood-
shed and obtaining food for himself, he informed the S.S. commandant of
the camp of the planned escape. All the would-be escapees were brutally
murdered except Parkinson, who survived with a crippled leg and vowed
to murder Enley.

In its highly economical opening the film's narrative oppositions unfold according to an almost crystalline structuralist logic. These include the oppositions of the war cripple and the healthy veteran, the vertical and darkly forbidding cityscape of New York and the sunny warmth of southern California sprawl, and the apartment-dweller war cripple and the suburban home-builder veteran. Juxtaposed to the men who march from left to right in the Memorial Day parade, Parkinson appears as the disgruntled loner who crosses their line, an ironic commentary on postwar patriotism.[85] Hailed as a war hero in his community, Enley has become a successful housing contractor whose recent completion of a development of tract homes, mass-produced domesticity, is celebrated at the film's beginning.

Introduced in the presence of his wife and young son, Enley is filmed in tight medium shots, his point-of-view shot from the podium directed back at his adoring wife and child. Parkinson's unexpected arrival in Santa Lisa triggers the return of the repressed, the memories of the war that evade displacement. Just as the war reasserts itself, so does the metropolis. Enley attends a builders' convention in downtown Los Angeles, where he is followed by Parkinson. To escape from his pursuer, he leaves the convention hotel and runs through Bunker Hill.

A montage sequence of shots presents spatially disconnected views of Angels Flight and Clay Street, a jumble of images that fails to present the cohesion and integrity of Bunker Hill as a neighborhood. Descending an interminable flight of stairs and running through empty streets, as if entering an underground purgatory, Enley finally goes into a bar, where he encounters the stock characters of the gruff bartender and the kindhearted prostitute, Pat (Mary Astor). She leads him to a gangster leader who arranges for Parkinson to be murdered. Trading upon popular associations of Bunker Hill as a haven for alcoholics and criminals, the film's representation of the area recalls the description by Raymond Chandler.

After the mobsters have agreed upon Parkinson's murder, Enley enters the Third Street Tunnel, at which point the film juxtaposes voice-over audio flashbacks of the mobster and the German S.S. commandant. Enley runs screaming through the tunnel, whose roadway disappears into the vanishing point of the horizon. His anguished attempt to undo the past and prevent the violent murder of Parkinson in the present registers three distinct spatiotemporal settings: the German camp, the film's diegetic

Frame enlargement of Frank Enley (Van Heflin) running through
Third Street Tunnel, from *Act of Violence* (Fred Zinnemann, 1949).

world of postwar Los Angeles, and the neighborhood of Bunker Hill,
which would soon undergo urban redevelopment.

Together with such temporal slippage, widely encountered in film noir,
one recognizes in this scene a no less profound spatial slippage between
the tunnel of the prisoner-of-war camp and that under Bunker Hill.
Enley's scream alludes to multiple spatial traumas of modernity, the "unhomely" condition of the postwar metropolis in which space acquires a
complex layering of temporalities and resonances of the past erupt with
explosive force. Once again, it is the activity of walking through the city,
here presented in Enley's feverish run through the tunnel, that proposes
postwar urban redevelopment as a latent content of the film. When he attempts to prevent Parkinson's murder, Enley becomes the assassin's victim,
and the moral order of the community is restored at the conclusion of the
film.

Bunker Hill's steep inclines, decrepit boardinghouses, navigable streets
and stairways, and ornate Victorian homes emerge as the single spatial
zone in *Kiss Me Deadly* (Robert Aldrich, 1955) with any pretense to being a
coherent pedestrian space in Los Angeles. It is a marked contrast to the
Westside high-rise building in which Hammer lives and whose view from
the window affords only racing automobile traffic, a universe of abstract

space later made palpable in the overhead shot of the traffic intersection near his apartment. Here the synoptic view connotes less a sense of visual mastery than a recognition of spatial homogeneity. Yet people walk on the streets and stairways of Bunker Hill. Palpably dilapidated, it nonetheless remains a neighborhood, and one whose residents prefer stability to mobility, as is made clear when an Italian man confesses to Hammer that he has lived there for sixty-three years. Complaining of his walk up the flight of stairs adjacent to Angels Flight, Hammer is confronted by a surly hotel desk clerk with the retort "Who invited you?"—a response that might well have been directed at representatives of the Community Redevelopment Agency founded a decade earlier. Carefully scouted by the film's screenplay writer, A. I. Bezzerides, the structures filmed on Bunker Hill were selected with an awareness that their days, like those of the hapless protagonists who resided there, were numbered.[86]

Looming prominently in one of the first scenes on Bunker Hill, the Angels Flight funicular was the neighborhood's most prominent landmark. Entering Bunker Hill in his automobile, Hammer drives beneath the railway's tracks, a suggestive spatial metaphor for the encroachment of the Harbor Freeway on the neighborhood's western edge. After parking at the base of the Hill, he climbs up the stairway adjacent to the railway, a con-

Frame enlargement of Mike Hammer looking out of the window of his Westside Los Angeles apartment, from *Kiss Me Deadly* (Robert Aldrich, 1955).

cession to pedestrians mandated by the City Council to prevent Angels
Flight builder Colonel J. W. Eddy from enjoying a transportation monopoly.[87] Constructed in 1901, while Bunker Hill was a prosperous residential
district with mansions inhabited by doctors, lawyers, and town fathers
such as Judge R. M. Widney, a founder of the University of Southern California, the railway obviated the need to begin the day with a steep climb.
Angels Flight rose 335 feet to a summit on Olive Street where Eddy built a
park with easy chairs, an observation tower 100 feet high, and camera
obscura to provide a view of the surrounding city and mountains. Gardens
and pedestrian promenades composed the early citadel of Los Angeles.
More illustrious still is the case of the most famous landmark on Bunker
Hill, Angels Flight. Its purchase by the CRA was authorized by the Los
Angeles City Council in 1962. In 1969 it was dismantled as one of the final
components of the Bunker Hill urban renewal project, a casualty of what
Mike Davis calls the need to sever accessibility to the newly renovated
downtown from the adjoining neighborhoods to the east in the interests
of "resegregated spatial security."[88] In 1996 "the shortest railroad in the
world" resumed operations half a block south of its original 1901 setting.
Today it carries passengers from Hill Street to California Plaza.[89] Whereas
once urban planners considered relocating Angels Flight to Disneyland,
today downtown Los Angeles, like so many other American cities, has
come to resemble a theme park, a site together with the shopping mall
where the walking cure becomes yoked to the activity of consumerism, its
ability to generate insight less clear.[90] Countless cities have destroyed historical districts and neighborhoods. Some have relocated significant buildings. Yet Los Angeles, home to the world entertainment industry, remains
among the few instances of a metropolis that has sought to trademark surviving fragments of its urban past. As the CRA 1996 Progress report
noted, "During the past two years, the Agency was able to resolve out-
standing issues related to the ownership of the Angels Flight name and
trade name. The Angels Flight Foundation will be coordinating use of the
trademark for merchandising and marketing efforts."[91]

    Killer's Kiss and *Kiss Me Deadly* share a further historical irony: their rep-
resentations of significant urban landmarks have entered the news as future redevelopment sites. Recent plans to relocate Pennsylvania Station to

another McKim, Mead, & White building, the James A. Farley post office occupying two city blocks between 31st and 33d Streets and Eighth and Ninth Avenues, evince a similar nostalgia for the early twentieth-century built environment. Amtrak spokesman R. Clifford Black reported to the *New York Times* that urban stations such as those in Chicago, Philadelphia, and Washington enjoyed tremendous success "because they exhibit a sense of optimism and grandeur, an esthetic beauty which we feel is a very important psychological factor in marketing rail services to passengers."[92]

Pending receipt of the requisite funding, Amtrak hopes to relocate into the post office (complete with sweeping parabolic arch, skylight, and "deference and reference" to the old station).[93] Born (1901/1910), demolished (1964/1969), and likely to reappear (1996/200?) within a decade of each other, Angels Flight and Pennsylvania Station offer an instructive lesson in the vicissitudes of the twentieth-century American built environment. Although their cameo appearances in films noir such as *Killer's Kiss* and *Kiss Me Deadly* could not prevent their destruction, the role of cinema in stimulating the contemporary postmodern inclination to recreate earlier urban landmarks appears striking.[94] Through its depiction of endangered metropolitan topoi that later return as elements of architectural and cinematic spectacle, film noir reveals the logic of an urban uncanny. As Freud noted, the "uncanny is in reality nothing new or alien, but something which is familiar and old-established in the mind and which has become alienated from it only through the process of repression."[95] Buildings, landmarks, spaces that were once familiar and later destroyed or simply forgotten, continually reappear from the dead, resurrected first on the cinema or television screen and then often in the actual city itself.

As Kent Barwick observed about the destruction of Pennsylvania Station:

> There's a funny cycle that occurs in the history of a building. It is very much appreciated when it is put up, then it sort of disappears into the city when other buildings become more noticeable and celebrated. And just a little while before it is rediscovered, it is thought to be absolutely worthless. That's a dangerous moment for a building. If Penn Station was given five more years—maybe three more years, a little more time—Penn Station would have been here and alive today.[96]

The walking cures of many centripetal films noir appeared precisely during this dangerous moment when they were able to sensitize film viewers to those features of the urban environment that Kracauer realized spectators were already ignoring. Occupying a tenuous threshold between an older urban modernity no longer capable of mounting a credible cultural defense and a nascent postmodern sensibility, the film noir cycle embodies what Svetlana Boym calls the "reflective nostalgia" of modernism.[97] The affinity between the cinema screen and the theme parks that soon would infiltrate American cities under the guise of postmodern urbanism was greater than anyone in the 1950s could have imagined. Where movie directors first scoured for locations, urban developers often later followed. For countless buildings and neighborhoods of the postwar period, cinematic representation in film noir augured the kiss of death.

4
CENTRIFUGAL SPACE

The renaissance painter constructed the scene to be painted from *an unchangeable, fixed point* following the rules of the vanishing point perspective. But speeding on the roads and circling in the skies has given the modern man the opportunity to see more than his renaissance predecessor. The man at the wheel sees persons and objects in quick succession, in permanent motion.

—László Moholy-Nagy, *Vision in Motion* (1947)

CITY OUT OF TIME

Los Angeles pervades the crime fiction of Raymond Chandler, together with Cornell Woolrich the most influential literary contributor to the film noir cycle. Whereas Woolrich portrayed the agoraphobia and spatial constriction of New York, Chandler excelled in representing the fading grandeur and distended spaces of Los Angeles, the city that constitutes the inexhaustible specular object of his fiction.[1] Seen from afar ("The lights of the city were an endless glittering sheet. Neon signs glowed and flashed") or observed up close ("Newton Street, between Third and Fourth, was a block of cheap clothing stores, pawnshops, arcades of slot machines, mean hotels in front of which furtive men slid words delicately along their cigarettes, without moving their lips"), Los Angeles reveals an infinite array of spatial details, the condition of possibility for Chandler's narratives.[2]

Recalling the naturalism of Zola with its similar proclivity for visual description, Chandler's stories reflect what Fredric Jameson terms the logic of modernism, entailing an "autonomization of ever smaller segments."[3]

The city serves as a character or agent throughout his fiction, its isolated particulars derailing the reader from the plot. Juxtaposing long shots and close-ups, Chandler's prose functions akin to cinematic montage by alternating different scales and perspectives. Had they never been adapted for the screen, his narratives still would remain illustrious screenplays of twentieth-century Los Angeles.

Murder, My Sweet (Edward Dmytryk, 1944), based upon the 1940 novel *Farewell, My Lovely,* reveals a uniquely Chandlerian approach to the space of Los Angeles. Its opening sequence depicts Philip Marlowe (Dick Powell) with a bandage across his eyes as he retrospectively recounts the narrative of several murders to the detectives who question him. His temporary loss of vision from exposure to gunfire is underscored by the bright light of a desk lamp. As Marlowe begins his narration, the camera pans to a window through which the illuminated signs of Hollywood Boulevard flash on and off. It slowly focuses upon these as it continues to track into

John Divola, MGM film studio, New York lot with encroaching suburbia, Culver City, California, 1979. Courtesy of the artist.

the window. A montage of four short shots connected by lap dissolves introduces the view of the city from ground level. We see a man walking down a street illuminated with overhead marquees, a car passing a darkened office building, street traffic, and a view of telephone wires and the corner of an office building.

The sequence realizes a perfect symmetry by concluding with the camera, now on the exterior of the building, slowly tracking toward Marlowe through the window of his office as he sits at his desk. From inside to the street outside, from the street back to the office interior, and from the end of the film's story to its beginning, a view from a window organizes the relation between interior and exterior space. These shots articulate the degree to which the action in the film (but also in Chandler's fiction) is inflected by Los Angeles, where the boundaries between interior space and the metropolis remain permeable. This idea is conveyed by Marlowe's monologue as he sits at his desk: "Something about the dead silence of an office building at night. Not quite real. The traffic down below was something that didn't have anything to do with me." At once separated from the city yet unable to resist contemplating it, Marlowe's position as observer is reiterated throughout the film, as by the shots of city lights continually visible through his office window.

Simultaneously dematerialized and encircled by the night, valorized yet presented as tawdry and insubstantial, this illuminated city also suggests the perceptual modality of the automobile. It is as if each view of Los Angeles were seen from the window of a moving car, a discrete snapshot carried away from a scene with no further thought as to its utility. Chandler's stories may well count among the first to grant automobile-framed views prominence in their narratives, instances of the perceptual dynamism that Moholy-Nagy describes in the epigraph above.[4] Marlowe perceives much of Los Angeles through the automobile windshield as he travels on surface streets and the outlying roads predating the highway system that emerged at the end of the 1930s.[5] The surrounding communities he encounters, such as the African-American neighborhood of South Central and its main thoroughfare, Central Avenue, are minimized in the film *Murder, My Sweet*.[6]

Though identified with the gritty cityscape of Los Angeles, Chandler's fictions also chronicle the centrifugal identity of southern California. Ir-

reducible to specific urban forms or demographic trends such as suburbanization, centrifugal space initiates novel perceptual and behavioral
practices—new experiences of time, speed, and distance—no less than
new features of the everyday landscape. While the broad transformations
in cities that arose in the 1920s have been widely noted, corresponding
changes in spatial perception have received far less attention, as has the
role of cinema in the promulgation of this new geography.[7] More than
simply a product of suburbanization and decentralization, centrifugal spatiality reconfigures bodily experience and valorizes speed.

Yet if the oppositions between attention and distraction, substantiality
and dematerialization, close-up and long shots structure the Los Angeles
depicted in *Murder, My Sweet*, an equally significant range of oppositions in Chandler's fiction involves temporality. Consider his attentiveness
to the rhythms of urban labor conveyed in this passage from *The High
Window*:

> It was getting dark outside now. The rushing sound of the traffic had
> died a little and the air from the open window, not yet cool from the
> night, had that tired end-of-the-day smell of dust, automobile ex-
> haust, sunlight rising from hot walls and sidewalks, the remote smell
> of food in a thousand restaurants, and perhaps, drifting down from
> the residential hills above Hollywood—if you had a nose like a hunt-
> ing dog—a touch of that peculiar tomcat smell that eucalyptus trees
> give off in warm weather.[8]

Conjuring the close of the workday and the ensuing race toward home
and distraction, this excerpt powerfully evokes the unseen population of
the metropolis, the people for whom food is being cooked and whose bodies fill the automobiles and buses driven along its roads. Their labor, the
unseen catalyst of the city's activity, is evident only through its residual
traces. To the emptiness of Los Angeles, associated in Chandler with the
frequent descriptions of its deserted neighborhoods and urban landmarks
("They went casually through a red light, passed a big movie palace with
most of its lights out and its glass cashier's cage empty"), the passage above
counterposes the metropolis as a complex temporal organization of social
interdependencies.[9] The problem of representing this urban reality per-

vades the film noir cycle, and Chandler's rhetorical predilection for evoking the totality of Los Angeles through the metonymic signs of its inhabitants finds ample cinematic expression in the streets and the urban crowds that pervade the films noir of the 1940s and 1950s.

One might also note the opposition throughout Chandler's writing between older elements of Los Angeles and the continual influx of more recent constructions, one of the city's features most remarked upon by commentators.[10] The Pacific Electric streetcar tracks already described as abandoned in *The Lady in the Lake* (1943) provide a suggestive instance of the former, while the mass production of ersatz Spanish-style homes noted by Walter Neff as he pays his first visit to the Dietrichson household in *Double Indemnity* is but one of many examples of Chandler's contempt for Californian modernity. His fascination with nonsynchronous remnants from earlier historical moments, specific architectural landmarks, as well as the Bunker Hill neighborhood described in *The High Window*, summon up nostalgia for the past. But which one? The moment around 1912, when Chandler first moved to the neighborhood near Pershing Square? Or the era of the 1930s, whose disappearance his novels seem to chronicle?[11]

What seems undeniable is that by the early 1940s the Los Angeles streetscapes pervasive in Chandler's earlier stories and novels from the 1930s radically diminish in his fiction. The metropolis now oscillates in function between a structuring absence and an object of contempt. A late novel such as *Playback* (1957) dispenses with the city entirely and creates a small town modeled after La Jolla (where he moved in 1946) as its setting. By the end of the 1940s, Chandler's writings frequently excoriate Los Angeles as a vapid wasteland and California as "the department-store state." As private investigator Philip Marlowe observes in *The Little Sister*: "Real cities have something else, some individual bony structure under the muck. Los Angeles has Hollywood—and hates it. It ought to consider itself damn lucky. Without Hollywood it would be a mail-order city. Everything in the catalogue you could get better somewhere else."[12]

By 1949 Chandler was railing against what he termed the impossibility of maintaining "public taste . . . and a sense of style . . . in the Coca-Cola age . . . the age of the Book-of-the-Month and the Hearst Press."[13] This statement lends itself to interpretation as a conservative rejection of popular culture in favor of some older, class-inflected snobbery of manners and behavior. Yet read in tandem with Marlowe's remark about authentic cities retaining a deep structure beneath their exterior transformations, Chandler's reproach also captures the urban changes undergone by Los Angeles, as if the dematerialization realized by its nocturnal illumination had penetrated to its core and drained off some vital marrow. Writing in a letter of 1957, two years before his death, he registered a sense of defeat: "I have lost Los Angeles as a locale. It is no longer the part of me it once was, although I was the first to write about it in a realistic way."[14] The "individual bony structure" of Los Angeles that had disappeared in his fiction was becoming no less elusive in the actual city itself.

Far from unique to Los Angeles, the transformation of urban structure and the ensuing tension between centripetal and centrifugal spatial modes are pervasive in both the post-1939 built environment and the film noir cycle. While often opposed in historical studies as well as in popular consciousness, both Los Angeles and New York were marked by the clash between an earlier centripetal trend that had emerged in the early nineteenth century and the accelerating challenge of centrifugal modalities. If we juxtapose the 1936 completion by Robert Moses of the Grand Central Parkway in New York with the 1939 opening of the Arroyo Parkway in Los Angeles, the first stretch of freeway in the city, some sense of this common historical legacy and the growing centrifugal character of both cities becomes evident.

As a private investigator, Marlowe is in a privileged position to grasp the social and spatial structure of Los Angeles; hence the prominence of specular diversions and opportunities for gazing at the city throughout his urban journeys.[15] In an environment increasingly devoid of a single spatial center, the private eye functions as a vital surrogate for readers and film viewers, a kind of mobile perceptual center that links concrete experience with a social and political structure of growing complexity. Similarly, the film noir cycle can be comprehended as a means of generating spatial knowledge, a cultural strategy to bridge the gap between everyday life and institutions.

Tensions between centripetal and centrifugal spatial tendencies provide an important key to understanding the film noir cycle of the 1940s and 1950s. While both centripetal and centrifugal films noir spaces manifest traits of abstract space, each reveals distinct modalities of urban anxiety.

For if the former elicits the agoraphobic sensation of being overwhelmed by space, fears of constriction, or the fear of losing one's way in the metropolis, its fundamental legibility can generally be assumed, despite the disorienting features of particular cities or neighborhoods noted by Kevin Lynch. By contrast, the anxieties provoked by centrifugal space hinge upon temporality and the uncertainty produced by a spatial environment increasingly devoid of landmarks and centers and often likely to seem permanently in motion.

SPEED TRAPS

Walter Neff (Fred MacMurray) enters the first shot of *Double Indemnity* (a 1944 film cowritten by Chandler and Wilder) in a nocturnal drive through downtown Los Angeles to the Pacific All-Risk Insurance Company on Olive Street, where he confesses his crime to his employer Barton Keyes (Edward G. Robinson). Traveling at breakneck speed, his car first becomes visible in a long shot as it approaches a crew of the Los Angeles Railway Corporation Maintenance Department. A welder is engaged in repairing the streetcar tracks, and Neff is signaled by another worker and a set of flares to veer away from the construction site, toward which he initially seems to be heading.[16]

Walter Neff in his car approaches streetcar repair crew, from *Double Indemnity* (Billy Wilder, 1944).

Already decrepit and ailing in 1944 (if not the year 1938, in which the film is set), the once-extensive public-transportation system of Los Angeles no doubt struck many contemporaneous viewers as in need of permanent repair, if not retirement.[17] Gravitating in large numbers toward the automobile since the 1920s, Los Angeles residents perhaps recognized a kindred spirit in Neff and his near attack upon the trolley infrastructure, if not his running of a red light in the following scene.[18] *Double Indemnity* juxtaposes this older public-transportation technology with the automobile and proposes the speed of automotive travel as the fundamental experience of passage through the city.

Though appearing early in the film noir cycle, *Double Indemnity* portends the growing sway of centrifugal space through the relative absence of the city, as well as the significance of the automobile as the modality through which the now-diffused metropolis is primarily encountered. Apart from the principal sites of the action (the Pacific All-Risk Building, Neff's apartment, the Dietrichson house, Jerry's Market), Los Angeles itself is strangely absent from the film. We see it in the four shots of the opening sequence, in the Glendale train station, the Corner of Vermont and Franklin where Lola Dietrichson (Jean Heather) meets Nino Zachette (Byron Barr), the Olvera Street Mexican restaurant, and the wooded path behind the Hollywood Bowl where Neff takes Lola. Rarely do characters walk through its streets, and the film features few conspicuous urban landmarks.

Taken as a whole, these relatively fleeting scenes reinforce the geography of the film as one of separate spatial monads with little overlap. We see Neff initially walking from his apartment and arriving at the Dietrichson house but none of the city between those points. When we do see Los Angeles, it is often through the windows of Neff's automobile, where the murder of Dietrichson takes place. While evoking spatial dispersion, freedom, and mobility, this emphasis upon the car also underscores the characters' dependence on technology, as when Neff and Phyllis Dietrichson (Barbara Stanwyck) encounter a recalcitrant ignition cylinder immediately after they dump the body of Mr. Dietrichson (Tom Powers) on the railroad tracks.

The film's rhetoric of technological determinism and inextricable causality, exemplified by Neff's willingness to live out the consequences of the murder "straight down the line" and the comparison by Barton Keyes (Edward G. Robinson) of killers to people forced to ride a streetcar to the end of the line, finds an apposite parallel in a nearly contemporaneous discussion of technology by Herbert Marcuse:

> A man who travels by automobile chooses his route from the highway maps. Towns, lakes, and mountains appear as obstacles to be bypassed. The countryside is shaped and organized by the highway: what one finds en route is a byproduct or annex of the highway. Numerous signs and posters tell the traveler what to do and think; they even request his attention to the beauties of nature or the hallmarks of history . . . Business, technics, human needs and nature are welded together into one rational and expedient mechanism. He will fare best who follows its directions, subordinating his spontaneity to the anonymous wisdom which ordered everything for him.[19]

Double Indemnity explores the logic of this "rational and expedient mechanism," exemplified by the Pacific All-Risk Insurance Company, introduced as Neff enters the building at the beginning of the film and the camera hastens ahead of him, so as to direct the spectator to the rows of identical desks on its main floor. If the corporate enterprise represents one spatial modality of "the apparatus that has mechanized and standardized the world," in Marcuse's words, then the highway and the automobile, two elements of centrifugal space, surely constitute another.[20]

Michel Foucault alluded to the constellation of forces that defines the identity of this late-modern space. Responding to Paul Rabinow's suggestion that "architects are not necessarily the masters of space that they once were, or believe themselves to be," Foucault answered: "That's right. They are not the technicians or engineers of the three great variables—territory, communication, and speed. These escape the domain of the architects."[21] Foucault emphasized the complex imbrication of three factors—territory, communication, and speed—in spatial forms that exceed received understandings of the architectural and usefully define centrifugal space.[22] A determinant feature of the built environment of modernity, it finds expression in the geographic arrangement of the United States commencing in the 1920s and challenges conventional understandings of the metropolis.

A vivid example of these transformations appears in *Odds against Tomorrow* (Robert Wise, 1959), a late film noir set in a New York whose luminous daylight and wide open spaces contrast markedly with earlier depictions of the city in the film cycle. Absent are the horse-drawn carts and Lower East Side of *The Naked City* and the anxiety-saturated and constricted spaces of *Phantom Lady*. Replacing this earlier substratum of the centripetal city, a new Manhattan appears, negotiated by the automobile and filmed entirely in daylight. From the shots of Riverside Drive with the West Side Highway in the background to the footage of the Triboro Bridge and the surrounding highway network, the film basks in a profusion of distended spaces and transportation infrastructure that dwarfs its protagonists. Its wide open spaces find their acoustic complement in the vibraphone-inflected strains of the Modern Jazz Quartet playing compositions by John Lewis on its soundtrack, music that oscillates between the romantically sentimental and the melancholy.[23]

Whether in the Central Park Sheep Meadow or walking down an empty street pummeled by the wind, characters in *Odds against Tomorrow* consistently appear diminished by the urban backdrop in a New York that conspicuously lacks a center. Times Square, Pennsylvania Station, and other nodal points are absent, and the film's chief characters leave Manhattan

Meeting of Dave Burke (Ed Begley) and Bacco (Will Kuluva) in Central Park, from *Odds against Tomorrow* (Robert Wise, 1959).

and drive to upstate New York to rob a bank. The small city in which they arrive suggests the horizontal suburban community as an alternative to the metropolis and likens them to commuters who must travel to their workplace. In the film's final scene, two members of the criminal gang meet their end in an explosion of gas storage tanks in a sprawling yard quite unlike the dense fabric of the metropolis.

The decreased significance of metropolitan density and agglomeration in centrifugal space accompanies the shift from urban verticality to the horizontal sprawl of suburbs and larger territorial units.[24] But one might also discern centrifugal space in the redeployment of surveillance mechanisms away from the bodies of citydwellers toward the automobile, the proliferation of electronic media, and the collection of traffic statistics as a strategy of control. Replacing the older discourses of Bertillonage and physiognomy, these new technologies accompany the transformation of the nature of surveillance itself in late modernity.[25]

Centrifugal spaces include suburban settlements, industrial landscapes, shopping malls, but also urban regions that have lost their former centripetal features (perhaps through renewal projects, suburban exodus, or economic blight) or have become incorporated into conurbations such as Jean Gottmann's Eastern Seaboard "Megalopolis" or the type of extended development or "edge city" now omnipresent throughout the United States.[26] They are historically transitional between the older centripetal metropolis of the street and promenade and the still-developing domains of cyberspace and virtual reality.

From the opening long shots of cityscapes serving to establish the position of both spectator and characters, to the frequent views through or into open windows, to the continual attempts of figures to orient themselves within the city, centripetal films noir presuppose the urban center and its complex weave of meanings and spatial practices. Criminals move from obscure locations to more centralized positions, often shuttling between a hiding spot and a center. Ambiguous, easily mistakable spaces may provoke crime and later be investigated by a figure of authority who ascertains their truth. Characters from different social strata converge in a common location. In each instance, spatial positions and relations to the urban center assume narrative meaning, as well as a broader cultural significance.

To comprehend centrifugal space is to grasp the multiple implications of a spatiality that redefines the notions of the center and centrality that have long dominated Western thought.[27] Irreducible to a style, a form of the built environment, or a theoretical system, centrifugal spaces can determine or be determined by each of these through a dialectical logic. Yet centrifugal spaces should not be construed as incompatible with centripetal space, for many elements of the built environment reveal both.

A shopping center with a pedestrian mall located on the outskirts of a city is one example of a centering activity brought to the edge of a metropolis, while an urban fabric composed of the sprawling "superblock" citadels or the "tower in the park" urbanism associated with Le Corbusier is another.[28] At stake in this distinction are not fixed identities or pure types but shifting terms and oppositions between center and periphery with corresponding forms of culture and subjectivity.

Although both types of space can coexist in the film cycle, 1949 appears to be a pivotal year in which centrifugal spatiality decisively manifests itself in films noir such as *Thieves' Highway* (Jules Dassin), *Criss Cross* (Robert Siodmak), and *White Heat* (Raoul Walsh). One might also note a confluence of factors that year, ranging from a dramatic increase in television ownership, to the passage of the Federal Housing Act, to the establishment of the New Jersey Turnpike Authority, to the successful testing of the first atom bomb by the Soviet Union, to the first transcontinental flight by the U.S. Air Force in under four hours, each of which in its own way introduced a new understanding of space.

We may define centrifugal space historically as the set of consequences resulting from the tendency, already evident by the middle of the nineteenth century in the United States, toward movement from the urban center to its boundaries. This was initially made possible by the development of commuter railroads and streetcar networks as precursors of the automobile.[29] Yet to avoid a technologically determinist argument, the actual desire of many people to live outside the urban core should also be noted as a factor in this history.

If centripetal space is characterized by a fascination with urban density and the visible—the skyline, monuments, recognizable public spaces, and inner-city neighborhoods—its centrifugal variant can be located in a shift toward immateriality, invisibility, and speed. Separation replaces concentration, distance supplants proximity, and the highway and the automobile supersede the street and the pedestrian. Where centripetality facilitates escape or evasion by facilitating invisibility in an urban crowd, centrifugality offers the tactical advantages of speed and superior knowledge of territory. Frequently lacking visible landmarks, centrifugal spaces substitute communication networks and the mass media to orient those who traverse them.

The most striking feature of centrifugal space remains its frequently *nonarchitectural* character, its introduction of technologies that facilitate speed and communication into the experience of a built environment once exclusively defined by architecture, urbanism, and landscape. Monuments, pedestrian zones, and those urban areas identified by CIAM, Lynch, and the Situationists as centers of life and activity may exist within centrifugal space as remnants of an older spatiality but do not capture its specific identity. In addressing the declining role of the street as a meaningful artifact, Thomas Czarnowski summarizes the factors that displace its former hegemony:

What one should recall is the obvious trend toward an independence of personal movement. This trend has been supported by a growing network of personalizable communication, the telephone, the growth of the mass media, indeed of the mass industrial product and of its attendant means of distribution—which has allowed a widely dispersed population to exist with a lessened reference to the older urban centers and greater reference to a polynuclear structure of local nodes of meeting and exchange. As a result of these changes, the communicational functions of the street have been transformed, both in the old urban centers and in the new suburban areas that, almost by definition, have low density and scattered communicational intensity. These three events, the replacement of the street as a system of access and movement by other channels of communication, the alteration of the street by the superimposition of modes of communication requiring varying scales of operation, and the development of configurations of streets that rely on mechanized movement and form greatly distended regional patterns, constitute a metamorphosis and a narrowing of the role of the street as a locus for communication.[30]

Dispersal of the population, elimination of the city center, and planning for new transportation technologies were also central components of the city plans developed by twentieth-century modernist architects such as Frank Lloyd Wright and Le Corbusier. By the middle of the 1930s each had already articulated the importance of speed, efficient traffic flow, and communication in the modern city. Their prescient theorizations suggest that centrifugal space is irreducible to changes in population density and land use but also entailed a new conception of the city.

In his 1932 book *The Disappearing City*, later revised and published as *The Living City*, Frank Lloyd Wright adopted the terms *centrifugal* and *centripetal* to describe the predicament of centralization in the modern city, to which he proposed his conception of the Broadacre City as an alternative. Throughout the evolution in his thinking about Broadacre, Wright never deviated from a steadfast opposition between it and the centralized metropolis, whose pathology is vividly represented by a photograph of a polluted city, practically invisible behind thick clouds of smog and smoke. He spared no mercy for the metropolis, which he frequently likened to a malignant growth.[31]

Spatial decentralization and an agricultural economy did not imply provincialism, however, for intrinsic to Broadacre was a conception of a new spatial order linked to the surrounding world by emerging communication and transportation technologies. Electricity, airplanes, automobiles, printing, radio, and television would expand the reach of the city, substituting travel and communication for spatial propinquity. Within this centerless settlement, "The bad form of centralism that built the great railway stations as gateways to the old city *(Bahnhof)* will be gone . . . because 'the great station,' owing to lack of the great concentration, is no longer desirable."[32] Wright's designs for Broadacre were never carried out except in piecemeal form. But his ideas proved wildly successful and prefigured the dispersed character of major metropolitan areas throughout the world that today reflect its legacy most strongly.[33]

Le Corbusier's deliberate elimination of the city center and the street from his plan for the City of Three Million is another instructive case. It does contain a center, a railway station that he likens to a hub in a wheel, but one of greater functional than symbolic significance, a fact suggested by its underground location and the use of its roof two stories above the ground as a landing strip for airplanes. Le Corbusier was even more adamant than Wright in his attempt to eliminate streets from the City of Three Million. He advocated reducing the number of streets within it by two-thirds, so as to eliminate cross-streets, which he deemed "an enemy to traffic."[34] The basic thoroughfare of the city was to be a standard length of 400 yards, replacing residential "corridor streets," with their dark courtyards and awkward siting of buildings.

Throughout the city, pedestrian traffic and motor vehicle traffic were rigorously separated by a three-part system of levels. Tramways and fixed-rail transportation were rejected, and arterial roads provided for the rapid, unidirectional flow of traffic. Efficient circulation of people and goods through the city would be paralleled by growing contact between the metropolis and the countryside through the construction of modern highways.[35]

After World War II, sociologists and urban scientists discerned broad changes in the social character of many large American cities. The concentrated urban metropolis of the past, though not likely to disappear, had already begun to mutate into a sprawling metropolitan region increasingly filled by single-family homes. Tracy Augur argued in 1948 for the historical obsolescence of cities:

> The present pattern of cities in the United States—their locations and relative size and relationship to one another, as well as their basic arrangements of streets and buildings—was pretty well set by the end of the nineteenth century. It was not planned to meet the needs of the mid-twentieth century and does not meet them. It was established before many of today's most effective instruments of transportation, communication, production, and organization were in use. It is in fact, a pattern carried over from a bygone day, grown bigger and more clumsy through a curious momentum that has led us to repeat past practices long after they have ceased to be efficient or profitable to the community.
>
> Fifty or sixty years ago there were reasons for having large aggregations of people living and working in tightly constricted areas and for having management concentrated in a few big cities, but those rea-

sons have been largely dissipated by the invention of telephones and
radio and automotive transportation and other commonplace devices
of modern life. The urban pattern that grew in response to nineteenth century reasons had its drawbacks even then, but in its time it
had compensating advantages. Now it has the drawbacks in intensified form and few of the compensations.[36]

Social commentators and students of the city during the postwar period
quickly seized on changes in population and technology as the basis for
proclaiming the concentrated urban settlement an endangered species.
Brandishing concepts such as "postcivilization," "megalopolis," "road-
town," "the anti-city," and "urban sprawl," they announced the impending
crisis of metropolitan civilization and predicted diverse social and economic consequences following from its dissolution.[37]

If one seeks to explain the proliferation of centrifugal space, one encounters accounts of the rise of transportation technologies such as the
commuter railroad and the automobile, suburbanization, population
shifts, changes in urban planning, the growth of mass media, highway construction, and growing antiurban sentiments. Yet which of these factors
are causes, and which effects? Most of these social and technological developments were in place by the end of World War I, and some as early as
the second half of the nineteenth century. Although the increased cultural
emphasis upon speed is commonly associated with greater spatial decentralization, automobile usage, and highway travel, does this alleged causality not cut both ways? Is it not also equally plausible to conceive these
other developments as expressions of a growing cultural desire for the experiences of velocity and mobility?

HIGHWAYS WITHOUT FRICTION: NORMAN BEL GEDDES
AND THE FUTURAMA

Largely ignored by architects, the highway may well be the preeminent
centrifugal space of the twentieth century.[38] Arguably as significant to
post-1930 cinema as the street and the railroad were to those earlier films
engaged in charting a centralized and navigable centripetal space, cinematic representations of the motorway remain far less studied than filmic

treatments of the metropolis.[39] Precariously situated on the intellectual
meridian between the disciplines of architecture, geography, urban planning, landscape design, and traffic management, the freeway occupies an
ambiguous status in the branches of knowledge devoted to the study of
modern space.[40]

Frequently imagined as a spatial superconductor for transporting vehicular traffic in an unimpeded, frictionless flow, the motorway has become
the most extravagantly romanticized structure of the late twentieth-century built environment. As the last refuge of the myth of a pure functional-
ism long since disavowed by architects, the freeway conveniently evades
the faintest hint of contingency; its allegedly utilitarian vocation is imagined as the product of disinterested traffic engineers and transportation
planners.

Richard Guy Wilson has characterized the 1920s and 1930s as the decades during which America was rebuilt.[41] Great construction feats; dams,
superhighways, underwater tunnels, bridges, and giant radio towers infiltrated the landscape, while a social cult of the engineer blossomed around
those who designed them. It was during this period that a new breed of
transportation specialist emerged, the highway engineer, road/landscape
architect, and traffic planner, now charged with expediting the increasing
automobile circulation still thwarted by primitive road conditions and a
dearth of travel routes.[42]

Separation of fast vehicular from local and pedestrian traffic, already a
basic tenet of the urban schemes of Wright and Le Corbusier, permeated
thinking about highways. Writing in a classic 1931 essay, Benton Mackaye
and Lewis Mumford called for complete segregation of residential areas
from automobile routes, what they called "Townless Highways":

> Once we have grasped the essential notion of the automobile as a pri-
> vate locomotive, the example of the railroad will give us a clue to its
> proper treatment. It must have a related but independent road system
> of its own, and this system must be laid down so as to bring into use
> all the potential advantages of the automobile for both transportation
> and recreation. This means a kind of road that differs from the origi-
> nal turnpike, from the railroad and, above all, from the greater part of

the existing automobile highways. One can perhaps characterize it best by calling it the Townless Highway, to denote its principal feature—the divorce of residence and transport.[43]

In the shifting and contentious history of relations between the highway and the city—initial avoidance, later deployment on the urban outskirts and separation by overpass and tunnel, and finally the elimination of urban neighborhoods by freeways—the segregation advocated by Mackaye and Mumford would find growing acceptance in the 1930s. Though today commonplace, the notion of spatial isolation of automobile traffic on freeways from business and residential districts was once radical and untried. The "Townless Highway" becomes a prime example of the growing sway of abstract space, the zoning of speed and its introduction into the landscape.

The 1920s marked the effective entry of the federal government into the road-building business. The landmark Federal-Aid Road Act of 1916 provided $75 million in state aid for highways, but it was plagued by wartime shortages, construction delays, and administrative confusion that retarded its influence until the following decade. The Bureau of Public Roads (BPR) continued the program of technical and scientific assistance to state highway agencies that it had begun around the turn of the century.[44] This provided local governments with advanced information and techniques of road planning such as the origin and destination surveys for motorists that the BPR increasingly advocated to regional authorities as a highway-planning technique after 1921. From its inception, the BPR regarded its primary mission as one of dispensing objective technical information and ensuring uniformity in the collection of traffic-sampling data.[45] Whether designing revised highway surveys in 1936 or working with engineers from the IBM Corporation on an automatic traffic counter (whose locations by the roadside it assigned), the BPR sought to provide accurate and impartial data.

By the beginning of the 1940s, the technocratic thinking of the BPR directed a new attention to the role of highways in cities. In its 1939 report, *Toll Roads and Free Roads*, the bureau claimed: "Only a major operation will suffice—nothing less than the creation of a depressed or an elevated artery (the former usually preferred) that will convey the massed movement pressing into, and through, the heart of the city, under or over local cross streets without interruption by their contending traffic."[46]

Recognizing the need to move traffic efficiently in and out of large cities—an imperative corresponding to their growing centrifugality—the BPR report outlined a highway-building strategy that was to gain growing acceptance after the war. By 1951 the BPR noted that all major cities were working on such arterial highway improvements. Yet significantly enough, as the above quotation suggests, the underlying logic of this construction scheme questioned neither the planning of cities themselves nor the place of highways in an evolving transportation system. The supremacy of the automobile and the social implications of the highway system for cities remained its blind spots. As highway historian Bruce Seely notes:

> At various points in the committee deliberations, the planners raised the possibility that highways could revitalize urban business districts, control decentralization, and guide urban land use and growth. The report did mention these points, recognizing that highways in cities had a permanent impact on urban development. But traffic service always ranked first among the purposes of highways . . . Any broader social or economic purposes achieved by the new roads were coincidental to the need for express highways.[47]

In this context one may profitably consider the attempt to promote the economic, political, and defensive significance of highways undertaken by the industrial designer Norman Bel Geddes. Part activist, part publicist, Bel Geddes occupied a unique position in 1940s American highway development, gliding effortlessly between the roles of professional visionary, corporate imagemaker, motorway lobbyist, and popularizer of European modernist trends in architecture, design, and city planning.[48] Best known for his book *Horizons* (1932), one of the first treatises on streamlined design, Bel Geddes was also a knowledgeable cinephile and one of the few industrial designers trained to create sets for the theatrical stage. He approached his mission as a highway prophet in the spirit of a film director.[49]

In 1940 Bel Geddes published his book *Magic Motorways* in conjunction with the Futurama show of the General Motors Highways and Horizons

Exhibit mounted during the summer of 1939 at the New York World's Fair, an exhibition notably concerned with urban form through its premiere of the film *The City* and the popular Democracity pavilion. It was the most popular exhibit at the fair: between 5,000 and 15,000 people often waited for hours each day to gain admission to the General Motors pavilion, which one visitor described as combining "the thrills of Coney Island with the glories of Le Corbusier."[50]

Visitors to this "Futurama" designed by Bel Geddes were transported in rubber-tired trains wired for sound along a motorized conveyor belt below which an illuminated model of cities, farms, and highways of the future was presented to their gaze.[51] At the conclusion of their trip they emerged at a full-scale reproduction of a street corner from the "City of 1960."[52] Its multilevel division of vehicular and pedestrian traffic and streamlined, silver-painted walls (suggestive of automobile styling) were clearly indebted to the designs of Le Corbusier, Harvey Wiley Corbett, and Erich Mendelsohn and underscore the fair's importance in the American reception and diffusion of architectural modernism.[53]

Yet the very appropriation of the diorama and panorama, nineteenth-century protocinematic technologies, as chosen media for the Futurama, suggests a key link between cinema and the concept of urban space articulated by Bel Geddes.[54] One historian of the 1939 fair notes that over 500 films were shown during its festivities, the most famous of which was *The City*.[55] Industrial, promotional, travel, and educational films were also exhibited, lending truth to the exclamation of one pundit that "the best way to build a World's Fair is not to build it at all, but to make a motion picture of it."[56]

Coinciding with the growing trend of many corporate displays to avoid the representation of industrial labor, dioramic, panoramic, and cinematic representations were particularly well suited to depiction of the more ethereal processes of consumption and mastery of centrifugal space.[57] Here cinema was indirectly evident in the many exhibits that employed "architecture as environmental control" and relinquished "the mere enclosing of space."[58] Such an emphasis upon the constitution of a spatial environment through media messages would become increasingly prevalent under the sway of centrifugal space.

The convergence of cinematic and dioramic images with the experience

Norman Bel Geddes, Futurama exhibit for General Motors pavilion at 1939 New York World's Fair. Courtesy of the Norman Bel Geddes Collection, Performing Arts Collection, Harry Ransom Humanities Research Center, University of Texas at Austin, by permission of Mrs. Edith Lutens Bel Geddes Estate.

of passage through real physical space—exemplified in the Futurama's transition from model to lifesize street scene—underscores the exhibit's profoundly filmic character. Roland Marchand offers a persuasive reading of the mechanisms through which the Futurama appealed to and constructed its spectators:

> As visitors acclimated themselves to this new world of 1960, Bel Geddes introduced a narrative plot to guide their comprehension. The audacious technique of moving the audience through the exhibit

provided, in itself, a major advance in solving one of the central problems in exposition displays—how to control the flow and attention of
visitors so that they could be told the corporation's story in a focused
and sequential way and at a pace determined by the company. To this
particular structured control, Bel Geddes added a story-line, physical
"blinders," and rotation of the chairs to shift the spectator's line of vision—all to insure the desired pattern of audience attention. By controls on the visitors' line of sight, by the eye-catching motion of a particular vehicle in the initial rural panorama, and by promptings by the
unseen voice, spectators were induced to follow the progress of a certain truck as it pulled out of a farmyard, traveled a country road, and
then entered the superhighway system.[59]

Drawn through the exhibition while their vision was controlled by
blinders and the involuntary shifting of their chairs, the Futurama spectators viewed the highway from overhead, until they found themselves without warning in the middle of the street of 1960.[60] As Bel Geddes writes:
"Suddenly the spectator, in his chair, is swung about! He can scarcely believe his eyes. He is confronted with the full-sized intersection he was just
looking down on. He gets out of his chair and becomes part of the city."[61]

Bel Geddes' 1940 book, *Magic Motorways*, is both visual essay and intellectual argument, a highway sermon for a Depression-era America on the
verge of entry into World War II.[62] Juxtaposing images of old and new
travel routes, traffic jams and animal herds, futuristic cities and congested
urban centers, its striking photographs present binary oppositions between archaic and modern transportation technologies, human and animal
movement, urban and rural travel, and aerial and roadway vistas.

Photographs of highway models in *Magic Motorways* depict an immacu-
late system of predominantly eight-lane motorways. Unlike the Germans,
who sought to mold their Autobahn to the contours of the local landscape,
Bel Geddes was primarily interested in speed. He cared less about the geographic location of his ideal highways and their aesthetic or ecological virtues and stressed instead their uniformity.

Motorways . . . will overpass and underpass each other, using wide-
flowing developments of present day cloverleaf; their traffic streams
in the opposite direction will be completely separated, and individual

lanes in the same direction will be segregated by separators. Although in the map they look like solid lines shooting across the country, actually they are complicated mechanisms which differentiate sharply between through and maneuvering traffic, and which provide automatically safe means for entering and leaving the motorways. Their lanes are designed for three separate and constant speeds of 50, 75, and 100 miles an hour. Their grades are constant, never excessive. Their curving radii are constant, always generous. All over the United States, the motorways are uniform and function in exactly the same way.[63]

General Motors was made understandably nervous by the prediction of freeway speeds as high as 100 miles per hour, despite frequent attempts by Bel Geddes to convince them of the safety of his motorized world. Yet there can be little doubt that a key selling point of his scheme was speed. As Bel Geddes confessed to an interviewer, "If I had described the new highway as accommodating three lanes of traffic at 20, 30, and 40 miles per hour, it would have caused no indignation. It also would have caused no headlines."[64]

This conception of the national highway network as a rapidly functioning mechanical device exemplifies what may well be the most original component of the motorway scheme of Bel Geddes: its union of a machine aesthetic inspired by European modernism with a political and economic discourse of highways as instruments of American economic growth and national integration. Valorizing speed as both an aesthetic experience and a functional demand of modern life, the highway of Bel Geddes participates in the social ideology that David Nye describes as "the American technological sublime."[65]

While fairgoers were waiting in line to experience the Futurama, architectural historian Sigfried Giedion was delivering the Charles Eliot Norton Lectures at Harvard, the basis for his 1941 book, *Space, Time and Architecture: The Growth of a New Tradition*. Praising both the highway and the landscaped parkway, Giedion devoted three illustrations in his book to the Randalls Island Cloverleaf, the "Pretzel" intersection of the Grand Central Parkway, Union Turnpike, Interboro Parkway, and Queens Boulevard, and the Henry Hudson Parkway running along the West Side of

Manhattan. Echoing Giedion's interest in the Randalls Island Cloverleaf as "expressive of the space-time conception both in structure and handling of movement," the former Bauhaus artist Herbert Bayer selected it as a key motif for his design of the book jacket for the first edition.[66]

Giedion shared his friend Le Corbusier's advocacy of the separation of different forms of circulation and equally admired the Pretzel as "one of the most elaborate and highly organized of all recent solutions of the problem of division and crossing of arterial traffic."[67] Giedion understood the parkway, the predecessor of the larger and less manicured highway, as a quintessential manifestation of the space-time conception of the modern age: "The meaning and beauty of the parkway cannot be grasped from a single point of observation . . . It can be revealed only by movement, by going along in a steady flow as the rules of traffic prescribe. The space-time feeling of our period can seldom be felt so keenly as when driving, the wheel under one's hands, up and down hills, beneath overpasses, up ramps and over giant bridges."[68]

Space, Time and Architecture explicates what Giedion called the "space-time" of the contemporary age, a post-Renaissance worldview that he identified with the arrival of non-Euclidean geometries in the nineteenth century and the relativity theory of Albert Einstein in the twentieth. It understands the early-modernist historical avant-gardes, including Cubism, purism, Futurism, De Stijl, and Constructivism, as prefiguring the spatiality of modern architecture. Writing about Cubism, Giedion describes it in terms that echo his account of the multiperspectival character of the parkway: "The essence of space as it is conceived today is its many-sidedness, the infinite potentiality for relations within it. Exhaustive description of an area from one point of reference is, accordingly, impossible; its character changes with the point of view from which it is viewed. In order to grasp the true nature of space the observer must project himself through it."[69]

In praising the Randalls Island Cloverleaf as "modern sculpture of numberless single or triple cloverleaves," Giedion removed the highway from consideration within a larger social or political framework. Unlike Bel Geddes, who discerned economic or ideological benefits in freeways even while praising the speed of travel they permitted, Giedion admires their abstract embodiment of the space-time of the modern age and its new perceptual modalities.[70] Speed and politics matter less in his valorization of highways than the abstract flow of movement and energy, for which reason he emerges together with Bel Geddes as a prescient theorist of highway modernism, a crucial mediator between pre- and postwar conceptions of space and automobility.

By contrast, through his valorization of speed and machine production, which he grafted onto the already decades-old controversy around the establishment of an interstate highway system, Bel Geddes offered a stunning preview of postwar American politics, specifically the vast increase in the power of the federal government precipitated by New Deal regional projects such as the Tennessee Valley Authority and later the interstate highway system of the 1950s.[71] Once administered by municipalities or states, the "object" of planning was now radically redefined.

As the economic necessity of highways and other transportation facilities became apparent, American planners enlarged the scope of their activities from the local to the "regional," or, following Foucault, what one might call the territorial. This new administrative entity overcame isolationist and antagonistic relations among states and empowered centralized federal planners and highway engineers to shape the space of cities and larger settlement areas in an unprecedented manner.[72]

The highway depicted in the Futurama and in *Magic Motorways* offered no clues about the labor and financing of its construction, let alone social relations in the world of 1960. The obvious contradiction between the Futurama's understated celebration of laissez-faire economic policy (required by the intense hostility of General Motors toward the New Deal) and the centralized government authority necessary to build the interstate highway system it depicted, did not escape the attention of astute observers at the time.[73] Yet Bel Geddes tended to remain silent about the political will required to realize his plans.

Within the domain of the Futurama, labor conflicts, unemployment, poverty, urban blight ceased to exist. Pulled along its trajectory like workers on an assembly line (production never *really* disappeared from these exhibits), spectators were addressed as consumers and drivers. The unsavory drama of American transportation policy (antidiversionary measures to ensure continued highway funding, corrupt land-condemnation deals, hidden subsidies for automobility, and the systematic disregard of mass-transit planning) playing out beyond its walls was nowhere to be seen.[74] Despite an unprojected $5 million cost overrun, the Futurama was judged a smashing success by General Motors executives and other captains of industry. Perhaps the greatest (if not the most ironic) compliment came from Paul Hoffmann, president of Studebaker, who praised Bel Geddes for "blasting open the minds of men as to our highway needs."[75]

TRAFFIC PLANNING, MOBILIZATION, AND THE "TOTAL PROBLEM OF MOVEMENT"

From the Federal Highway Act of 1916, to the Pershing Map of 1922 that outlined significant military travel routes, to the enabling interstate bill of 1956, few significant pieces of American highway legislation were proposed without their supporters proclaiming their alleged military objectives or significance.[76] Studying the development of the interstate system, one is struck by the apparent impossibility of conceiving a national highway system apart from its strategic or defense implications, if only as a pretext or justification.[77] While many planners or politicians apprehended the highway as a tool for military conveyance, Bel Geddes simultaneously understood it as a communications system and emphasized the advantages of speed and mobility to national defense.[78]

The dispersal of the American population accompanying the war effort must surely count as one of the great demographic and spatial shifts in its history. Fifteen million servicemen were moved to military bases, a million blacks migrated from the South to the North in search of better-paying industrial jobs, and millions of Americans left farms and cities to become workers in plants established at 275 national defense areas.[79] While total urban growth rose 7.9 percent in the 1930s, population increases in outerlying municipalities were far greater. Portland grew by 1.2 percent, its suburbs by 31.3 percent. Los Angeles and Detroit gained in inhabitants by 21.5 percent and 3.5 percent, while their surrounding towns enlarged by 29.6 percent and 25.4 percent. The population growth in new war production centers such as the Willow Run bomber plant of the Ford Motor Company (twenty-eight miles from downtown Detroit), which employed 100,000 workers at the peak of its production, contributed to this pattern of growth on the urban fringe.[80]

Measurements of highway traffic were conducted by the Bureau of Public Roads as early as the 1920s, although wartime congestion and transportation disruptions appear to have been the catalyst for introducing traffic-planning research into cities. Few urban surveys seem to have been conducted before the early 1940s, but their continuing value and interest to traffic planners at the end of the 1950s is suggested by the undiminished publication of such analyses. Freeway construction bills such as the Federal-Aid Highway Act of 1944 increasingly involved the federal government in the construction of urban highways and forced its engineers to include cities in their planning process.[81]

The essential purpose of all traffic-planning research is to ascertain common travel patterns, routes, and destinations in a region as the basis for developing new thoroughfares. Its most fundamental tool was the "origin and destination" survey. Utilizing a series of calculations for distance traveled, the economic value of time saved, the anticipated construction costs, and the data obtained from these surveys, traffic planners would determine the priority of highway projects, such as a freeway bypass through a busy section of a city. With their complex traffic patterns, congestion, and aesthetic features irreducible to efficient routing, cities posed a challenge to traffic researchers, and urban drivers often proved less than compliant.

To conduct traffic-planning surveys in cities, planners developed three sampling techniques: cordon-station studies, license-number compilations, and questionnaires. The military connotation of these cordons, a phalanx of survey stations encircling a strategic point to ensnare the hapless driver, is difficult to ignore. Although there is no evidence that military personnel were ever involved in traffic surveys, the engineers at the Bureau of Public Roads lost no opportunity to mobilize willing sectors of the civilian population in their work, including the Boy Scouts.[82] Direct surveillance of automobile traffic and the division of the city into different traffic "zones" were distinctive contributions of license-plate surveys.

Traffic-planning surveys were undoubtedly valuable resources for highway and road planners. During the postwar period the Bureau of Public Roads conducted them in more than 100 American cities and amassed sufficient statistical data to allow for comparative study of travel patterns in different urban settings. Statistics on trip purposes, modes of conveyance, and travel frequency in different cities were used to determine general patterns of movement according to population size, as well as national averages for activities such as traveling to a doctor or conducting business.[83]

Fixated on destinations and origins spread throughout a city, urban traffic surveys reflect the increasingly centrifugal character of postwar American space by virtue of their conspicuous omission of landmarks and the city center and their reconceptualization of urban passage as a temporal process. They also propose a new mode of surveillance organized around the automobile and its travel routes. If the pedestrian map is a quintessential representation of centripetal space, then the highway survey may be considered its equivalent for centrifugal space.

HOW FAST CAN YOU GET OUT OF TOWN? *PLUNDER ROAD* AND THE END OF HIGHWAY HAGIOGRAPHY

In 1957 and 1958 *Fortune* magazine published a series of articles on the state of American cities later collected in a volume provocatively titled *The Exploding Metropolis.* Containing essays on the revitalization of downtown neighborhoods, the challenges faced by local government, and the enduring problem of urban blight, the magazine series and subsequent book not surprisingly also included an essay on the city and the automobile. Its author, Francis Bello, noted the impact of changing modes of transportation in the American metropolis—the disappearance of the streetcar, ineffective bus routes, deteriorating commuter rail and subway service, and the new expressways, each pouring more traffic into the city center. He then observes:

> Perhaps the central question is whether the city will continue to serve as a unifying core for its surrounding metropolitan region, or whether it will be utterly fragmented. The key to this problem is transportation. Planners fear that if urban transportation costs—not only in money but in time and wear and tear on the rider—rise much further, they will cancel out all the advantages of the city. The basic dilemma: building more and more transportation facilities to keep the central core accessible may carve so much space out of the city that little worth while will remain.[84]

The *Fortune* article provided mileage figures of *exactly* how far from the urban center one could travel in thirty minutes during rush hour in the twenty-five largest American cities. Urban egress, the daily escape from the city by millions of suburbanites, was reborn as an object of scientific inquiry. The survey, complete with population figures, bar graphs, and the costs of all-day parking, treated time, space, and distance with the matter-of-fact clarity of American social science of the 1950s. Careful selection of research objects and isolation of variables, and the precise measurement of data and formulation of conclusions, characterized its approach. One imagines teams of *Fortune* researchers boarding trains to Greenwich and Princeton, turning ignition keys in cars, stopwatch in hand, harried commuters of the exploding metropolis, set upon answering the question posed by the survey's title: How Fast Can You Get Out of Town?

Together with graphs for each of the twenty-five cities surveyed, Bello provided the following summation of the research project:

> What is most surprising about automobile use in America's biggest cities is not that the ratio of automobile to public-transit riders varies so widely, but that automobile traffic seems to flow at just about the same speed everywhere, regardless of the size of the city, its age, its geographical assets or handicaps, the number of its expressways, or the cleverness of its traffic engineers. This is perhaps the most striking conclusion that can be drawn from a series of nationwide driving experiments, to determine how fast it is possible to get out of town at the peak of the evening rush hour in the twenty-five largest U.S. cities. The results are summarized in the chart on pages 60–63. It shows how far a motorist can drive in thirty minutes if he starts from the busiest corner in town and travels over the most heavily used outbound artery. With remarkable consistency, the outbound traffic averages just about 20 mph. In only three cities, Boston, St. Louis, and New Orleans, was the average speed as low as 16 mph. And how fast does the transit rider get home? Against the motorist's average speed of 20 mph, riders using the busiest transit routes in the same cities can expect to average only about 13 mph. The three big exceptions are New York, San Francisco, and Newark, where rail commuters travel at about 34 mph. The slowest transit speed, 8 mph, was recorded in Pittsburgh and San Antonio.[85]

While population, density, and land-use surveys had long been familiar to planners and demographers, the consideration of how far and how fast one could travel within a city marked a new stage in thinking about urban form. The attention to the city and passage through it as an object amenable to quantitative study and analysis (already evident in the BPR traffic surveys), a phenomenon to be studied through the introduction of time into a discourse once defined primarily by space, was indeed symptomatic of an emerging conceptualization of speed, communication, and territory in the postwar era.

Although Bel Geddes' City of 1960 and plans for an interstate highway allowing twenty-four-hour coast-to-coast travel never materialized, they did capture the attention of the planning professionals and politicians and popularize interest in the construction of transcontinental roadways.[86] By the end of World War II opposition to the construction of long-distance motorways virtually disappeared as the United States began the largest road construction program in its history. Commencing shortly before the end of the war, the Federal-Aid Highway Act, signed into law by President Roosevelt in December 1944, established four classes of roads (trunk, farm-market, urban, and interstate) with guaranteed funding for all but the last.

In 1945 the federal government contributed $76 million toward the construction of 308,741 miles of highways. Twelve years later, in 1957, the expenditure had increased over twelve times, to $968 million, and the actual amount of constructed roadway grew more than two and a half times, to 780,989 miles.[87] The Federal-Aid Highway Act of 1956, the enabling legislation that funded the interstate highway system, was approved by President Eisenhower in June 1956. After its establishment of the Highway Trust Fund, supported by taxes on gasoline, tires, and automobiles, road constructors could depend on an expanding budget without fearing its diversion or the specter of the introduction of toll roads.

It may well have seemed to many observers at the time that Thomas MacDonald, chief of the Bureau of Public Roads, was correct when he asserted to Congress in 1944 that "everybody in the United States is waiting for the close of the war to get in a car to go some place."[88] By the end of the 1950s, highway enthusiasm among professional planners reached an almost religious fervor, as evinced by the words of one landscape architect who wrote: "The modern automobile and its highways are as integral to our lives as the market place, forum, or acropolis to the ancients; as integral as our homes and our clothing . . . the complete highway . . . expresses an aspiration of mid-twentieth-century America, just as the functional structures of the ancient Greeks expressed their aspiration of beauty in everyday life."[89]

Freeway engineers and proselytizers continued to offer visions of the construction of the future, just as they had before the war.[90] A vivid example of this is found in the 1959 book *Highways to Tomorrow*, whose opening chapter, titled "Commuting, 1975," reads:

> THIS IS THE FUTURE, and it is yours.
>
> You've finished your breakfast coffee and you move toward the garage and the car. It's 90 miles to work and, glancing at your watch, you see you have an hour to get there. Plenty of time.
>
> You've worked late last night and you're still tired. No matter. You'll rest on the way.
>
> A few miles from your home, following the red, white and blue signs, you swing gently onto a handsomely landscaped access road, clinging to its long, easy curve as it slowly dips down to the highway.
>
> Seconds later, your right hand leaves the steering wheel and touches several buttons on the dash. A small green light flashes on. For the next 50 minutes, your call will be a mechanical robot, an electronic wizard with glowing vacuum tubes dimly lighting its infallible brain. This genie of yours will accept every radioed command and drive your car, with complete safety. You will do nothing . . .
>
> Fifty minutes later, a buzzer sounds, awaking you to the nearness of your destination—the city. You raise your electronically controlled seat and punch the phosphorescently lit button that permits the outside light to flood your car and bathe the lingering sleep, somewhat harshly, from your eyes. You squint involuntarily and off to the right, rapidly approaching, its shining steel and glass spires slowly piercing the mist, you see the city.[91]

Yet the role of Washington as patron of the interstate system raised the vexing problem of coupling expressways with the metropolis and coordinating the distinct mandates of local and federal planning agencies.[92] For many planners and urbanists, the radical changes in urban morphology accompanying urban highways were deeply troubling. In his 1958 essay

"The Highway and the City" Lewis Mumford minced few words with his acerbic suggestion that "perhaps our age will be known to the future historian as the age of the bulldozer and the exterminator; and in many parts of the country the building of a highway has about the same result upon vegetation and human structures as the passage of a tornado or the blast of an atom bomb."[93]

New territories (the interstate highway system, suburban residential districts), expanded communication networks (the coordination of radio and television), and the fantasy of escape to more "natural" and increasingly elusive settings define the centrifugal films noir contemporaneous with these developments, which do not relinquish the city so much as they incorporate it into larger spatial units. Passage through the metropolis, the veritable cornerstone of the literature of detection from the nineteenth-century through the 1930s novels of Chandler, becomes less crucial to these films, in which the urban landscape is either absent or strangely muted. No longer readily mappable through the presence of cohesive urban neighborhoods or familiar landmarks, the city signifies differently in these films noir of centrifugal space; its earlier confident stability and electric vitality are less readily evident.

An inkling of these transformations is suggested by *They Drive by Night* (Raoul Walsh, 1940) and *Thieves' Highway* (Jules Dassin, 1949), two films noir in which highways figure prominently, based upon novels by A. I. Bezzerides, the truck driver turned screenplay writer and novelist responsible for the screenplays for *Kiss Me Deadly* and *On Dangerous Ground*.[94] Relentlessly downbeat in tone, the novels of Bezzerides sketch a world of struggling farmers, truckers, and working-class protagonists against the background of the economic ills of the 1930s and 1940s. Dysfunctional families, violent confrontations between produce wholesalers and truckers, and passionate romances unfold against the background of the natural fecundity of California.

Their vivid descriptions of orange groves or light hitting city streets, fascinating accounts of the state economy before the rise of agribusiness, and desperate attempts by ordinary people to escape from economic impoverishment and the dangerous life of wildcat trucking contribute a flavor of homegrown naturalism to the novels of Bezzerides, whose relevance to the film noir cycle resides precisely in this specificity of place. In the case of *Thieves' Highway* extensive location cinematography in the wine and apple country around Sebastopol and Calistoga, as well as in the produce market and waterfront districts of San Francisco, makes the Californian location of the film evident.[95]

Apart from these sequences in the produce market, where Nick Garcos (Richard Conte) confronts the crooked produce dealer responsible for his father's loss of limbs and is aided by the kindhearted prostitute Rica (Valentina Cortesa), *Thieves' Highway* scarcely represents the urban environment. Much of the action of the film transpires on the highway in the army-surplus trucks that Nick and a friend purchase to haul apples from south to north. Here the open road is presented in an unromantic light as a series of physical hazards leading to mental and motor fatigue and possible death. The Californian setting of this relatively primitive state highway, not yet part of an interstate network, is never in doubt, and its adversarial nature derives as much from the avarice of the characters who travel through it as from the dangers of mechanical breakdown.[96]

Among the most arresting films noir of centrifugal space, and perhaps also the least known, is *Plunder Road* (Hubert Cornfield, 1957). Released a year and a half after passage of the legislation creating the interstate highway system, *Plunder Road* seems best read as an allegory of that epochal event.[97] From its opening credit sequence of highway divider lines seen from a rapidly moving vehicle, *Plunder Road* introduces speed as its dominant trope. The road markings appear to move faster as the credits progress, their visual regularity punctuated by the random appearance of arrows.[98] For the spectator the effect of this velocity is pleasure, a willing identification with the camera and its movement. As Paul Virilio notes: "Like the war weapon launched at full speed at the visual target it's supposed to wipe out, the aim of cinema will be to provoke an effect of vertigo in the voyeur-traveler, the end being sought now is to give him the impression of being projected into the image."[99]

Plunder Road is indeed vertiginous, propelling and interpellating its viewers not only into the cinematic image but into the American highway system itself. Decades of spatial fantasies about motorways and speed culminate in this film and its melancholy verdict about the promise of the open road. Few works of cinema more forcefully propose the analogy between driving, cinema, and criminality. And few films noir set in Los Angeles so resolutely abandon the traditional landmarks and topoi that make up its defining cinematic iconography.

Frame enlargement of highway arrow, from *Plunder Road* (Hubert Cornfield, 1957).

Through its interminable scenes of driving and constant attention to time, *Plunder Road* dispenses with many traits associated with film noir, including low-key lighting, expressionistic cinematography, elaborate character psychology, and misogyny. The flatness of its acting style and lighting serves as an objective correlative to the flat expanse of the highway, and the film functions simultaneously as symptom and critique of the spatiality that it represents.

Largely missing as well from *Plunder Road* are night and the city.[100] Lacking density or visual landmarks, urban topoi in the film become pure spaces of passage devoid of centers or familiar points of orientation. It is difficult to think of another film in the noir cycle that represents Los Angeles with such coolness and detachment from common landmarks and stereotypes. Significantly, the most important source of spatial orientation provided remains the constant radio bulletins monitored by the gang members.[101] The space of *Plunder Road* is precisely that quantifiable and measurable variety described by Henri Lefebvre as abstract space:

> The person who sees and knows only how to see, the person who draws and knows only how to put marks on a sheet of paper, the person who drives around and knows only how to drive a car—all contribute in their way to the mutilation of a space which is everywhere

sliced up. And they all complement one another: the driver is concerned only with steering himself to his destination, and in looking about sees only what he needs to see for that purpose; he thus perceives only his route, which has been materialized, mechanized, technicized, and he sees it from one angle only—that of its functionality: speed, readability, facility . . . Space is defined in this context in terms of the perception of an *abstract subject*, such as the driver of a motor vehicle, equipped with a collective common sense, namely the capacity to read the symbols of the highway code, and with a sole organ— the eye—placed in the service of his movement within the visual field. Thus space appears solely in its reduced forms. *Volume* leaves the field to *surface*, and any overall view surrenders to visual signals spaced out along fixed trajectories laid down in the "plan." An extraordinary— indeed unthinkable, impossible—confusion gradually arises between space and surface, with the latter determining a spatial abstraction which it endows with a half-imaginary, half-real physical existence. This abstract space eventually becomes the simulacrum of a full space (of that space which was formerly full in nature and history).[102]

Plunder Road begins with a series of shots that cut between the cab of the gang's truck, driven by Eddie (Gene Raymond), and the cargo area, in which two of the robbers anxiously watch a bottle of nitroglycerine bounce up and down as they drive on a bumpy road. The initial few minutes of dialogue are interior monologues of each gang member. In the first spoken words of the film Eddie alludes to time pressure: "Seven minutes late. Didn't figure on rain." Temporal exactitude is to the caper film what scientific management is to assembly line, optimal productivity organized around the time segmentation of human movement. Spatial positions and the time allotted for moving from one to another are meticulously circumscribed in this film narrative, in which the criminals *time themselves.* Compared with the problem of dividing up the loot and evading the police, the execution of the robbery itself appears relatively unproblematic, so much so that it occupies only the first ten minutes of *Plunder Road.*

The film's narrative, a rather ordinary heist involving the seizure of a trainload of gold bullion, obtains its twist from the struggle of its perpetrators to render ten tons of gold invisible in the new centrifugal space of highways and surveillance networks. After successfully hijacking this valuable payload, the criminals must labor to render it undetectable. Deflected from its metropolitan destination, San Francisco (the city in film noir persistently associated with the previous century), the treasury train signifies an older spatiality now in retreat before the emergence of abstract space.

The railroad, the great nineteenth-century transportation mode identified by Le Corbusier and Wright with the urban concentration and present in popular literary, historical, and cinematic genres, appears under siege. Its fixed routes, timetable, and terminal point in the metropolis are powerless before the highway and its new cargo vehicle, the truck. Where the train possessed visibility and a fixed itinerary, the truck substitutes a relative invisibility and the possibility of travel in many directions in a landscape conspicuously devoid of geographic features and landmarks, unlike the California road system in *Thieves' Highway*.

Most of the gang members are apprehended as the materiality of their cargo alerts the highway patrol to the true nature of their load. For in an age of increasing immateriality, a world in which knowledge, wealth, and culture circulate at ever-greater speeds, stealing ten tons of gold is an obsolete criminal project. But no more so than is shipping it by rail across country. *Plunder Road* suggests a metamorphosis in the definition of value from a material commodity to a signifier in an abstract and intangible sign system.

Within this new social space of invisibility and immateriality, capitalism and crime become at one and the same time more immaterial and more subject to the "friction" of the material world. In a transportation system organized around the optimal organization of movement, measurement applies to all who circulate through it, criminal and trucker alike. We see this most clearly in the capture of the second group of the heist team at a highway weighing station as the identity of their load is revealed by its being 4,500 lbs. overweight. A dragnet spread over twenty-three states and the simultaneity of radio communication are less effective in locating the criminals than the sheer weight of the gold itself. The materiality of their heist, rather than any personal or moral failing, leads to the robbers' detection. We find another example of this in the gang's near brush with the law when they are served with a summons for the smog produced by their foundry. Once again, the materiality of their production catches up with them.

A moral reading of the film would interpret this ending as evidence of a fatalism characteristic of film noir as a genre, or perhaps as an obligatory representation of punishment for a criminal act. But it may be more rewardingly understood as the return of the repressed of abstract space-time. For what belongs more to everyday life in centrifugal space than the daily commute, that ritualized movement between the urban center and its environs that organizes the schedules of so many who dwell within it? By concluding with road congestion on the Harbor Freeway, *Plunder Road* represents a fundamental experience of lived centrifugal space.

The traffic jam exemplifies the breakdown of social rationality in the planning of space, for it is *an everyday aberration*, a predictable daily event in passage through centrifugal space. Presented with this evidence of a social will to dispersal that returns as unwanted concentration, the cunning of history transforms the freeway into a parking lot. For who has not had the experience of being snarled in congestion, gazing at the crowd of cars on the freeway, and wondering what bond exists between one's automobile-encased subjectivity and that of the other motorists? solidarity? animosity? contiguity? Each driver a separate monad, the traffic jam realizes the perfect figure of the chaotic spatial order of capitalism.

A telling illustration of the failure of highways to circulate traffic effectively through the city, the traffic jam scene in *Plunder Road* recalls the following puzzled assessment by one historian of the 1956 highway bill:

Frame enlargement of traffic jam, from *Plunder Road* (Hubert Cornfield, 1957).

Was the highway program a triumph for the federal and state high-way engineers, the automobile manufacturers, the oil companies, and the speculators who hoped to make "killings" by subdividing fringe areas? Was it a defeat for city planning, advocates of metropolitan government, and humanists who believed in compact centers as ex-pressions of the civilization that man had taken thousands of years to develop? The planners for the most part thought of it as a revelation of their own inadequacies as exponents of the idea of foresighted con-sideration of alternatives and rational choice of means to ends.[103]

Under the haze of Californian smog, the breakdown of rational highway planning meets the impossibility of realizing a gold heist in an age when wealth has become increasingly immaterial. Police and surveillance net-works may be avoided, but space casts its own nets, for which traffic sci-ence provides little salvation. *Plunder Road* explodes the technocratic faith in perfectly engineered highways and in apolitical feats of design and con-struction. Through its depiction of the irrationality of centrifugal space it evinces the crisis of reason that Kracauer would shortly outline in his *The-ory of Film*. If there exists a moral agent in *Plunder Road*, it is not the police or legal authority but rather the parcelized space of Los Angeles, which ex-tracts its revenge through the traffic jam, the new nightmare of centrifugal space. After following Eddie to the highway ledge from which he jumps to his death, a crane shot tracks along the faces of the crowd gathering on the highway. The sound of police whistles and commotion accompanies its final image: undeveloped land on the urban periphery.

Yet the group does manage to arrive in Los Angeles, where it is ulti-mately apprehended by the police as a result of traffic congestion on the Harbor Freeway. Once fantasized as a spatial system yielding unrestricted movement and predictable speed, driving in centrifugal space is now char-acterized by the dystopian metaphor of the traffic jam. Failing to account for the predictable morning rush, the criminals fall prey to the revenge of time on the abstract space of the highway. The thoroughfare that would later be understood as the "Main Street" of Los Angeles had already ceased to function in the manner for which it had been designed.[104]

Fully resonant with the emphasis upon chance present in much film noir, the ending of *Plunder Road* suggests the nascent unraveling of the great narratives of centrifugal space during the 1950s. Serenely indifferent

Final shot of Los Angeles periphery, from *Plunder Road* (Hubert
Cornfield, 1957).

to the ends of its travelers, thwarting criminal transgressors and morning
commuters alike, the highway gridlock in the film alludes to a crisis of belief in the possibility of spatial mastery. For the malevolent urban environment of cinema, "the asphalt jungle" of dead ends and uncanny encounters
that extends from the gangster, thriller, and caper genres into film noir,
this state of affairs was to prove rich with possibilities.

Appropriating the traditional film noir ideologeme of "the combo,"
the social or underworld organization against which individuals struggle,
Plunder Road pits its criminal protagonists not against a corrupt judicial
system or syndicate, but against the irrational and unpredictable social order of centrifugal space itself.[105] Friction finally overtakes the highway, for
the traffic jam depicted in the film (no less than those occurring in the real
Los Angeles of 1957) connotes the now-dysfunctional character of the
metropolitan region.[106] The fantasy of escaping from the metropolis to begin life elsewhere (as in *The Asphalt Jungle*) appears frustrated by a physical
environment that defeats the attempt to leave its confines.

To watch *Plunder Road*'s criminal mastermind meet his death by jump-
ing into a stream of morning traffic on the Harbor Freeway is to witness a
powerful image of the end of highway hagiography. Envisioned as a means
of attaining ever-greater mobility, the dream of the American highway as a
frictionless utopia of speed and movement finally comes to a screeching
halt. Decades of lobbying to construct highways through the city had pro-

duced more travel routes, but also increased congestion, a state of affairs grimly confirmed by the *Fortune* magazine survey. The master narrative of centrifugal space on which highway modernism had thrived was beginning to show its age.

An older centripetal space based upon the scale of the human body no longer adequately describes this new lifeworld of the automobile and the freeway, with its poetics of distance, speed, pleasure, and technologically mediated solitude.[107] Commonly submerged in histories of urban political economy and "real" transportation needs, the fantasies and desires stimulated by centrifugal space delineate the qualitative lived experience of social transformations too frequently rendered invisible by quantitative analyses.

The American embrace of freeways reveals the profound ideological resonance of the motorway, its function a vehicle for the social imagination rather than merely an engineering solution for moving traffic.[108] One might understand quantitative traffic analyses and the 1950s dread of the traffic jam in *Plunder Road* as paradigmatic highway metaphors in which the flow of automobiles through the built environment represents fantasies of technological efficiency and dystopian breakdown. In each instance the abstract space of the highway emerges as a new medium for the articulation of political aspirations and cultural tensions.

No less than buildings and constructions, centrifugal space pervades the representational practices of our age. From the spectators who crowded before the Los Angeles freeway (or their television sets) to follow the flight of O. J. Simpson, to Helmut Kohl's election promise to maintain the fast driving speeds on Germany's Autobahn, highways continue to promote an increasingly circumspect identification of speed with individual freedom. If today one confronts the social legacy of motorway construction as a series of broken promises and roads not taken, a film such as *Plunder Road* suggests the value of an investigation into the complicity of cultural representations with the spatial restructuring of the twentieth century. As centrifugal space proliferates, so does the desire to represent it in images that might provide some comfort or critique in the face of often hostile social material.

Here one thinks of the driving sequence in *On Dangerous Ground* (Nicholas Ray, 1952), in which a violent police officer flees the city that has cor-

rupted him and in which black streets and shadows give way to the blind-
ing white snow of the countryside. It conveys the impossibility of shedding
the past and seeking transcendence in a spatial domain whose twin poles
are defined by the barren winter landscape and the decrepit city. Cinema
gravitates toward the highway, and in *Plunder Road* the result is a rare work
of social criticism that punctures the generally affirmative character of
1950s American culture. More often, however, abstract space casts the
road movie's shadow and incites this popular genre to romanticize the
uniquely twentieth-century spatial pleasures to which we have grown accustomed. The song of the motor is indeed contagious: I drive, therefore
I am.

5

SIMULTANEITY, THE MEDIA ENVIRONMENT, AND THE END OF FILM NOIR

Since 1896, three agencies have profoundly and directly affected the lives of all Americans. For none of us has been left untouched by the influence of the motion picture, the automobile and the radio. Probably never before in human history have three instruments of such incalculable social power been developed in so short a time. All three were perfected in the United States, within the memory of a generation still active today. Yet together, they have completely transformed our society, civilization and culture.

—Lloyd Morris, *Not So Long Ago* (1949)

Five years after the end of World War II, the production of films noir reached its peak. According to one standard filmography, from a record high of 57 films in 1950, production figures dropped to 20 films in 1955, and plummeted to a mere 7 per year in 1958 and 1959.[1] Regardless of the fine points of definition, few would argue that the film noir cycle disap-

Theodore Seymour Hall, urban redevelopment on Bunker Hill (no date). Courtesy of the Huntington Library, San Marino, California.

pears by the early 1960s and that subsequent invocations of its legacy entail greater nostalgia and self-consciousness than prevailed during the previous two decades of its existence.

Film historians have proposed various theories to account for this transformation. Most obviously, the appearance of crime series such as *Dragnet* and *The Naked City* transplanted many noir conventions to television, thereby siphoning ticket sales away from the box office.[2] One might also propose the decline of the B movie within changing industrial practices, audience boredom with familiar story conventions ("genre fatigue"), and the desiccation of the film industry by blacklisting as possible explanations for the eventual disappearance of the cycle.[3] While films noir (including many today regarded as canonical) would continue to be produced throughout the 1950s, Raymond Borde and Etienne Chaumeton assert that by 1949 the cycle had reached a turning point:

> From 1949 on, the career of the noir genre, properly so called, comes to an end. There were hints of this effacement in the preceding period, and it seems mainly to have to do, on the one hand, with a certain crisis of the subject, which the theme of "the strange" [*insolite*] had duly brought about and, on the other hand, with a strong taste for realism shared by both directors and audiences, in which the influence in the USA of European and especially Italian productions has to be perceived, at least in part. From now on, the idea is to "make it real" down to the very last detail, and even minor B-movies will be shot on location. This move, in fact, was much more compatible with the traditional series of criminal psychology and gangster films. It was even more so with the police documentary, which, beginning that year, is to experience a major boom. As things stand, the noir style doesn't disappear, it *tends to be absorbed* into adjacent series; and, at the very moment neorealism modifies certain of its traits, it ups the dosage of atrocity, psychopathology, or sensuality that it already contained.[4]

If one accepts the notion of a privileged relation between centripetal space and the narrative patterns in film noir, then how does the growing sway of centrifugal spatiality in postwar America manifest itself in film noir? Can its ascendance be related to mutations in narrative form and ideological content, including the alleged increase of realism noted above? Or should it be understood instead as a consequence of transformations in industrial structure? And what of the psychopathology, and the theme of *insolite*, conveyed by the film cycle after 1949? Although I claim that both centripetal and centrifugal spatial modes inflect film noir, in this chapter I argue for the expanded significance of the latter in films made after 1949. The formal and narrative features of these post-1949 films noir differ from earlier films both visually and through the increasing prominence of the mass media. They introduce a new range of spatial fears and anxieties.

For 1949, the year that Borde and Chaumeton select to demarcate the shift in the film cycle, is also the moment when television attains new prominence in American culture, complementing the significance of the radio, automobile, and cinema noted in the epigraph to this chapter.[5] While in 1946 only 8,000 American homes had television sets, in 1949 almost one million did, and by 1951 the figure reached over 10 million.[6] Around that same year urban planners began to debate the civil-defense merits of "defensive dispersal" settlements as an alternative to the concentrated centripetal city. Finally, 1949 was the year in which Claude Shannon published his mathematical theory of communication and scientists at the University of Illinois built one of the earliest computers, thereby inaugurating the information age.

Though still sharing many recognizable centripetal film noir conventions, centrifugal films noir diverge from them in several key respects, most evident in their increasingly nonurban settings. New spaces (the interstate highway system, suburban residential districts), expanded communications networks (the interlinking of radio and television), and the fantasy of escape from the networks of centrifugal space to more "natural" settings determine the changing spatial practices of these films. No longer grounded in the pulsating nocturnal metropolis of neon signs and dark alleys, the films of centrifugal space represent social life in an increasingly decentralized America knitted together by highways, radio, and television.

Patterns of spatial movement by characters in film noir attain growing complexity as the film cycle develops. Thus, in the films of the 1950s one observes a noticeable tendency toward the increased movement of characters between different locations. Early significant films noir such as *Stranger on the Third Floor* (1940), *The Maltese Falcon* (1941), *Phantom Lady* (1944), *Double Indemnity* (1944), *Murder, My Sweet* (1944), *Scarlet Street* (1945), *The Dark Corner* (1946), and *The Naked City* (1948) are set in a single clearly identifiable city where all events of the narrative transpire. Whether conveying the ethos of Hammett's San Francisco, Chandler's Los Angeles, or New York neighborhoods such as Greenwich Village or the Lower East Side, these films fundamentally transmit a sense of place. Saturated with what Lefebvre calls the "space of representation" of the city, centripetal films noir may transfigure the metropolis through characteristic aesthetic strategies (such as nocturnal filming) while nonetheless remaining rooted in it.

Films in which the dramatis personae move between cities such as *This Gun for Hire* (Frank Tuttle, 1942), *Detour* (1945), and *The Postman Always Rings Twice* (Tay Garnett, 1946) are still relatively uncommon before 1947.[7] Around this time three spatial tendencies become apparent: characters increasingly move from city to city in such films as *T-Men* and *The Lady from Shanghai* (both 1948); from the city to the country or vice versa in *Desperate, Out of the Past* (both 1947), and *On Dangerous Ground* (1952); or through the countryside itself in *They Live by Night* (1949) and *Gun Crazy* (1950). By the middle of the 1950s, characteristic urban markers disappear from a film such as *The Killer Is Loose* (Budd Boetticher, 1956), which is set in Los Angeles but offers little evidence of that fact. The growing contiguity of suburban and urban space appears prominently in other films noir set in that same city such as *The Pitfall* (Andre de Toth, 1948) and *Act of Violence* (1949).

Although centripetal urban space never disappears entirely from film noir, toward the end of the 1940s it loses its former monopoly as the dominant spatial mode of the film cycle. While Borde and Chaumeton emphasize the expanded use of location photography during this period in films such as *Side Street* (Anthony Mann, 1950) and *Force of Evil* as evidence of a renewed role for the city, such arguments must be counterbalanced by a recognition of the growing significance of centrifugal spaces. As in the case of *The Naked City*, changes in film technology or economics are often insufficient to explain spatial transformations in the film noir cycle and their cultural significance.

As the tendency toward spatial deconcentration becomes increasingly evident after 1939 in both the actual built environment and the discourses of architecture and planning, what changes in cinematic representation is less the presence of centralized legal authority—no longer monopolized by the police, but just as easily represented by a treasury or FBI agent—nor even the criminal (just as likely a white-collar lawbreaker as a burglar or murderer), but rather *the mechanisms of surveillance*, now no longer dependent upon synoptic modes of observation such as aerial or panoramic views.

The magnitude of centrifugal space requires new modes of detection and observation, techniques of power uncoupled from the body of the traditional citydweller in centripetal space. Foucault's invocation of the Panopticon still presupposes an immobile centralized site of observation and a geography of overseeable spaces and subjects over which power may be exercised. Anthony Vidler has shown how the representational modalities of photography and cartography enabled nineteenth-century French city planners to realize a holistic vision of an entire city.[8] I would argue for a similar historical break in the emergent conception of centrifugal space as a mappable and surveyable domain that was facilitated by radio, television, and the interstate highway system, new surveillance mechanisms.

The centripetal metropolis with its rhythms of the workday; the daily commute; the circulation of workers and merchandise through its streets; the evening promenade through the pleasure spaces of nightclubs, cinemas, and bars tend to disappear in centrifugal space, a topos without temporal coordinates in which the time of day, the season, and the experience of duration itself seem to recede, as in a film such as *Nightfall* (Jacques Tourneur, 1957), in which the artificial rhythms of the all-night city seem in the opening sequence to eclipse natural ones.

Centrifugal space must be understood in relation to its characteristic media technologies, radio and television. Early accounts of radio valorize the simultaneous transmission and reception of information and extol the benefits that would accrue to rural areas through their cultural urbanization.[9] Describing his vision in 1916 for the new medium, one of its earliest pioneers, David Sarnoff, wrote:

> I have in mind a plan of development which would make radio a household utility in the same sense as a piano or a phonograph. The idea is to bring music into the home by wireless . . . A radio telephone transmitter having a range of say 25 to 50 miles can be installed . . . Receiving lectures at home can be made perfectly audible; also events of National importance can be simultaneously announced and received. This proposition would be especially interesting to farmers . . . They could enjoy concerts, lectures, music, recitals, etc., which may be going on in the nearest city.[10]

Although radio news transmissions began in the 1930s, Paul Virilio, Alice Yaeger Kaplan, and Stephen Kern have traced the instantaneous transmission and receipt of radio to news reportage during World War I.[11] Media simultaneity, like highway planning and traffic studies, is spurred by the military uses of space. Consider, for example, the reactions of broadcasters and communications scholars to the Soviet launch of the Sputnik satellite in 1957. Writing in a 1958 issue of the *Journal of Broadcasting*, Frank Stanton, president of Columbia Broadcasting, surveyed the new media environment in which "radio and television brought an exciting new dimension to journalism. Ours is the strength of immediacy in reporting, often in transmitting the very event as it is happening. Combining sight, sound and action, television has brought the world into almost every American home, giving remote places reality and revealing the important figures of the world as both more and less than legendary names."[12]

Nor did the political stakes of simultaneity escape Stanton's attention:

We need to remind ourselves that since the eve of World War II, broadcasting has become the major source of news for the people in this country. As early as 1942, the American Institute of Public Opinion revealed, 62 percent of the American people preferred to get foreign and national news over the radio; 82 percent of all respondents said that they heard the news first over the radio . . . Added to all this is the fact that, alone among media, broadcasting can reach all the people at the same time. It can reach them immediately. And it can reach them at any hour of the day or night. In a democracy, which grinds to a halt without an informed people, this is a profoundly serious responsibility that has been placed on us. In an age over which hangs the threat of ICBM warfare, with all of the speedy, unpredictable devastation that it implies, it is a responsibility of critical importance.[13]

The defining features of simultaneity are not merely the reception of a message concurrently with the event that it describes but also a mobile and *spatially distanced* recipient. Unlike the fixed cinema spectator or newspaper reader, the portable radio listener is mobile. He or she can simultaneously react to information (such as a traffic report) without stopping. In fact, by receiving such information (whose source might itself be mobile, such as a traffic helicopter) the automobile driver travels more efficiently. Automobile driving-condition updates, instantaneous television news coverage, and portable transistor radios are examples of simultaneous communication practices that arose after World War II.[14]

Marshall McLuhan was quick to grasp the spatial implications of radio simultaneity: "One of the many effects of television on radio has been to shift radio from an entertainment medium into a kind of nervous information system. News bulletins, time signals, traffic data, and, above all, weather reports now serve to enhance the native power of radio to involve people in one another. Weather is that medium that involves all people equally. It is the top item on radio, showering us with fountains of auditory space or *lebensraum*."[15]

A civilian target audience could receive information around the clock while mobile or in transit between two points.[16] In the increasingly diffuse centrifugal space of postwar America, the temporal contiguity produced by radio simultaneity compensated for the waning of urban concentration and constitutes the "indirect" social group noted by Sartre. As the geographer Melvin Webber presciently argued in 1964, the conception of the city as a unitary place, a static arrangement of people and objects in space, was giving way to a notion of a "non-place realm" in which community flowed from common interests pursued over distance rather than from propinquity.[17]

In its most extreme incarnation, simultaneity allows one to become subject and object of media discourse, to watch (or hear) oneself being watched (or heard) by others, a possibility brilliantly grasped by McLuhan in this excerpt from his book *The Mechanical Bride:*

SEE SELVES ON "VIDEO"   THEN TWO DIE IN CHAIR
Chicago, April 21, 1950—(AP)—Two condemned murderers saw themselves on television last night and a few hours later died in the electric chair . . . The doomed men . . . were filmed in death row yesterday afternoon. The film was then put on a 7 P.M. newsreel show and viewed by the men on a set loaned them by the warden.

This situation is a major feat of modern news technique. Hot spot news with a vengeance. What a thrill these men must have got from being on the inside of a big inside story. Participating in their own audience participation, they were able to share the thrill of the audience that was being thrilled by their imminent death.[18]

Anticipating the popularization of live television news transmissions throughout the 1950s, McLuhan recognizes the cultural significance of what media scholars today understand as "liveness." As Mary Ann Doane observes, "While the realism of film is defined largely in terms of space, that of television is conceptualized in terms of time (owing to its characteristics of 'liveness,' presence, and immediacy)."[19]

Though not an incident of real-time broadcasting such as a sports event or a domestic catastrophe, the television appearance of the condemned men attains a high degree of presence by virtue of their impending death. The possibility that they could become a media event (of which they in turn become spectators) leads McLuhan to discern a full-fledged cultural epiphany. "Being on the inside of a big inside story, participating in their own audience participation," the convicts become both subjects and objects of media discourse; they watch and hear the television report of themselves as it is being watched and heard by others.

Yet it would be a mistake to reduce this story to an instance of McLuhan's fascination with the nascent television medium, though it clearly is that. Far from being specific to a single medium, he apprehends this experience of reflexivity and heightened temporal immediacy in relation to the legacy of modernism. Explicating comic heroes Superman and Tarzan, a Coca-Cola advertisement, Humphrey Bogart, and the *Reader's Digest* among many other instances of popular culture, *The Mechanical Bride* is equally rooted in a high-modernist cultural tradition. Stéphane Mallarmé, James Joyce, Henri Bergson, Pablo Picasso, André Malraux, Sigfried Giedion, and Le Corbusier appear cheek by jowl with Walter Winchell and Little Orphan Annie in McLuhan's text. Its use of newspaper headlines and advertisements owed much to the work of Wyndham Lewis, McLuhan confided to Ezra Pound shortly before its publication.[20]

Emphasizing the significance of Mallarmé's symbolist aesthetic for the development of modern artistic form, McLuhan finds its supreme manifestation in the front page of the modern newspaper. "How does the jazzy ragtime discontinuity of press items link up with other modern art forms? To achieve coverage from Peru to China and also simultaneity of focus, can you imagine anything more effective than this front page cubism? You never thought of a page of news as a symbolist landscape?" Here the key terms are clearly *discontinuity* and *simultaneity*. Like the poetry of Mallarmé with its abrupt parataxes, the newspaper juxtaposes uncoordinated columns, words, and headlines that can be consumed at a glance in a single instant, rather than in a linear sequence. This emphasis upon contemporaneity also inspired the "simultaneous poetry" produced in 1913 by Blaise Cendrars, also a cinephile and a filmmaker deeply influenced by Hollywood.[21]

In his 1945 essay "Spatial Form in Modern Literature" (a text that McLuhan almost certainly knew), Joseph Frank wrote of modern poetry: "The meaning relationship is completed only by the simultaneous perception in space of word-groups that have no comprehensible relation to each other when read consecutively in time."[22] Like Frank, McLuhan valorizes simultaneity over sequentiality, and identifies the fusion of disparate concepts in a single image, what Pound called "an intellectual and emotional complex in an instant of time," as the defining trait of the modern imagination.[23] Understanding such cultural practice as a species of montage, McLuhan confirms his awareness of cinema (strangely subdued in *The Mechanical Bride*) in an enthusiastic report to Pound of Eisenstein's notion of the ideogram outlined in the Soviet filmmaker's recently translated *Film Form*.[24]

The Mechanical Bride remains a fascinating exploration of vernacular modernism in which theory and practice, high culture and mass culture, remain inextricably intertwined. McLuhan's discussion of simultaneity resists precise localization in a single medium or practice. It owes much to literary modernism but is no less indebted to the mass media and social institutions of modernity. Yet simultaneity also needs to be grasped as spatial no less than temporal, capable both of uniting distant places and creating revealing geographic epiphanies. The montage practices of Joyce, Picasso, and the *New York Times* imply that "henceforth this planet is a single city." They "evoke the image of a world society" and produce the new spatiality that McLuhan would delineate in his 1959 notion of the global village.[25]

Considered as a discursive practice, simultaneity can be understood as the convergence of three separate events: the activity of an agent or an event (a fugitive on the run, a traffic accident); the narrativization and broadcasting of this activity as an event by a media source; and the reception of this narrative by a listener or spectator. In the case above, the agents and spectators of the event (the criminals awaiting their impending execution) are identical, as is the space of their action and reception (prison). More typically, simultaneity implies two agents spatially separated during the moment of reception.

Instances of simultaneity today abound in film, television, cyberculture, and everyday life and have become a fixture of postmodern culture, from the live broadcast to the closed-circuit television camera to the urban webcam. Following McLuhan's persuasive argument that an earlier communication medium becomes the "content" of its successor, I would propose radio as the ancestral content of contemporary media simultaneity, be it the continuous broadcasting of CNN or the live webfeed, both of which obviously emulate television as well.[26] The content of radio might best be viewed less as a single medium than as a continuum that ranges from what McLuhan understands as an atavistic, tribalizing force to more individualizing modes of interpellation:

Radio provides a speed-up of information that also causes acceleration in other media. It certainly contracts the world to village size, and creates insatiable village taste for gossip, rumor, and personal malice. But while radio contracts the world to village dimensions, it hasn't the effect of homogenizing the village quarters . . . Radio is not only a mighty awakener of archaic memories, forces, and animosities, but a decentralizing, pluralistic force, as is really the case with all electric power and media.[27]

To understand the significance of simultaneity in films of centrifugal space, one would do well to reflect on McLuhan's understanding of radio as a medium that speeds up the circulation of information, overcomes spatial separation, and promotes decentralization—three of the tendencies I discern in centrifugal space. At stake in the introduction of simultaneity into cinema, a repetition of radio's transformation from an entertainment technology into a "nervous information system," is a textual adaptation of cinema to the dispersal of space, power, and media after World War II, a dynamic whose presence is especially evident in Joseph Losey's 1951 remake of Fritz Lang's film *M.*

SIMULTANEITY AND THE MEDIA ENVIRONMENT

In an interview Joseph Losey related his initial aversion toward the idea of remaking *M:*

> [Lang's *M*] is and remains a classic, which one doesn't want to compete with, so for a variety of reasons I somewhat reluctantly undertook my version. One was that there was a considerable Hollywood pinch because of political pressures, and I didn't want to go a long time without work. Another was that I was very much interested in David Wayne, whom I thought brilliant and extraordinarily right for the part. And I undertook it with a restriction on the structure and basic story line, because the censorship office wouldn't pass it as a new script, only as a remake of a classic. Therefore my treatment of the central figure came into direct conflict with the whole structure . . . All that emerges from the film, really, is a couple of—I think—remarkable sequences, some previously unseen aspects of Los Angeles, and a fantastic performance from Wayne.[28]

A fundamental difference between the two versions of *M* involves the significant role assumed by the television medium in Losey's 1951 remake. Whereas the citizens of Berlin learn about the child murders from the newspaper and the reward posters plastered throughout the city, the residents of Bunker Hill in Los Angeles obtain their information primarily from television broadcasts they watch together in public. In the very first image, a long-take tracking shot, a stack of newspapers remains immobile on the street as the Angels Flight funicular ascends, as if to suggest the increasing distance between the cultures of print and television.

The special police report to warn parents to protect their children is viewed as a live broadcast in a television store window by a group of citydwellers, framed as a tight group in a tracking shot. Watching the static photographs of city neighborhoods and listening to the chief recite

Frame enlargement of citizens watching television police report on
child murderer, from *M* (Joseph Losey, 1951).

his "Five Don'ts" replaces reading the posters distributed throughout the
city, the activity that bonded isolated individuals into a community in the
Weimar Berlin of Lang's *M*.[29] In Losey's film the murderer Harrow never
writes to the newspaper, an insinuation that in the social world constituted
by television in 1950s America communication was increasingly visual.
Produced only three years after *The Naked City*, a film whose crucial reliance upon the culture of newspaper journalism we already have considered, the remake of *M* confirms the arrival of television as a cultural force.

Live television coverage of news events became a fact of daily life for
Los Angeles residents in the late 1940s and early 1950s. The twenty-
seven-hour live broadcast by KTLA in April 1949 of the attempt to rescue
Kathy Fiscus, a young girl trapped in a San Marino well, is a frequently
cited instance of the origins of the now-familiar television media event.[30]
By February 1951 local television stations had positioned cameras atop
Mount Wilson to catch flashes of atomic tests being conducted near Las
Vegas. The live transmission the following year of the Eisenhower-Nixon
presidential race in 1952 conveys the growing political significance attached to the constitution of a community of television viewers. Losey's *M*
grants the mass media a more prominent role than they possess in Lang's
film and presents the newspaper publisher as the third agent of power (to-

gether with the police and the underworld) engaged in ruling the city.[31] Yet despite his prominent role, it suggests the growing force of television to shape urban experience and community in Los Angeles.[32]

Unlike many other films noir in which Bunker Hill appears dominated by illicit criminal activity, Losey's *M* depicts it as a decrepit but still respectable neighborhood inhabited by middle-class families, members of the underworld, and the psychologically disturbed child murderer. Fluid camera movements and tracking shots emphasize the cohesion of the neighborhood and its accessibility to pedestrians. In 1951, sixteen months after principal photography of *M* on Bunker Hill concluded, the Community Redevelopment Agency of Los Angeles voted to condemn most of the buildings in the neighborhood.[33]

The Los Angeles depicted in Losey's film bears witness to the decentralizing dynamic of centrifugal space.[34] It dramatizes an unresolved conflict between the representation of Los Angeles as receptive to the future and "forward-looking" and an ambivalence among many residents toward the

Publicity still of child murderer playing flute on Bunker Hill, from *M* (Joseph Losey, 1951). Courtesy of Film Stills Collection, Museum of Modern Art, New York.

history of their built environment.[35] Though ultimately unsuccessful, the efforts to prevent the redevelopment of Bunker Hill and the public outcry against its destruction suggest that the embrace of urban renewal and modernist planning principles was hardly universal.[36]

Losey's *M* can be approached as a site for the cinematic analysis of this postwar geographic metamorphosis, an opportunity for recording architectural and urban fragments of earlier historical moments before their imminent disappearance. Unlike Lang's studio-filmed *M*, in which the urban specificity of Berlin nearly vanishes, Losey's remake emphasizes those older nonsynchronous landmarks. In an age of rampant suburbanization and spatial deconcentration, urban centrality and a traversable scale could no longer be taken for granted. *M* explores Bunker Hill as an instance of centripetal space displaced in 1951 Los Angeles, the spatial and temporal anomaly of a downtown core in the process of disappearing.[37] The city attracted its share of prominent visitors after World War II, one of whom, Jean-Paul Sartre, described it as follows:

> Los Angeles, in particular, is rather like a big earthworm that might be chopped into twenty pieces without being killed. If you go through this enormous urban cluster, probably the largest in the world, you come upon twenty juxtaposed cities, strictly identical, each with its poor section, its business streets, night-clubs and smart suburb, and you get the impression that a medium-sized urban center has schizogenetically reproduced itself twenty times . . .
>
> This is due to the fact that these cities that move at a rapid rate are not constructed in order to grow old, but move forward like modern armies, encircling the islands of resistance they are unable to destroy; the past does not manifest itself in them as it does in Europe, through public monuments, but through survivals. The wooden bridge in Chicago which spans a canal two steps away from the world's highest skyscrapers is a survival. The elevated railways, rolling noisily through the central streets of New York and Chicago, supported by great iron pillars and cross-girders, nearly touching the facades of houses on either side, are survivals. They are there simply because no one has taken the time to tear them down, and as a kind of indication of work to be done.

I remember this Los Angeles landscape in the middle of the city, two modern apartment houses, two white cubes framing an empty lot with the ground torn up—a parking space . . . When one turned around the block of houses, the hill disappeared; its other side had been built up, covered with asphalt, streaked with tar roads, and pierced with a magnificent tunnel.[38]

Sartre's description of a decentralized Los Angeles divided into smaller cities echoes the urban planning literature of the period and accurately captures the character of Bunker Hill in Losey's *M* and in other films noir. According to the creed of the postwar planners, each smaller "nucleated" city in Los Angeles would contain commercial and industrial centers and what Sartre calls "survivals," echoing the combination of nostalgia and nonsynchronous "explosive" force. Surrounded by the encroaching Harbor Freeway and the Third Street Tunnel to the west, Bunker Hill in 1951 was indeed an "island of resistance" and a challenge to the postwar expulsion of residential dwelling units from the city's central business district.

Unlike the concentrated centripetal space of Berlin in Fritz Lang's *M*, the space of Los Angeles in Losey's film has mutated into an abstract centrifugal space organized around the automobile and its uniquely mobilized gaze, no longer tied to the body of the pedestrian and the space of the street.[39] From the construction of parking structures and streets designed for the automobile to the building of the vast network of freeways, urban form in Los Angeles follows what one 1949 metropolitan theorist calls "the cardinal principle of movement": "all conflict or interference must be removed."[40] The army of beggars mobilized by the underworld in Berlin is replaced in Losey's remake by a fleet of radio-networked taxi drivers in Los Angeles.

Driving through Bunker Hill, the cab driver surveys the street through the windshield of his car, a clue that the automobilized gaze has supplanted the overhead angle as a constituent element in the perception of abstract space.[41] Spatial surveillance in Losey's film substitutes the roving, horizontal view from the automobile and the road for the fixed and vertically elevated perspective in the centripetal metropolis and the maps of Berlin on which the police draw concentric circles in Lang's *M*. Even when Harrow sits in a café, the camera mechanically approaches him through a fence, as

Pursuit of child murderer in Bradbury Building, from *M* (Joseph Losey, 1951). Courtesy of Film Stills Collection, Museum of Modern Art, New York.

if to prevent the viewer from confusing its technological vision with human sight.

The film's appropriation of the Bradbury Building as the site of the manhunt for the child murderer—a Los Angeles landmark associated before its appearance in *Blade Runner* (Ridley Scott, 1982) with films noir such as *DOA* (1950) (also filmed by Losey's cinematographer Ernest Laszlo) and the 1953 *I, the Jury* (filmed by John Alton)—evokes the plight of public space and the pedestrian in the postwar American city. Built in

1893 by mining millionaire Lewis Bradbury, who commissioned an unknown draftsman, George Wyman, to design the structure, the building's
open central courtyard remains a prime example of French wrought-iron
decorative architecture with the trademark glass skylight illumination associated with the typological form of the arcade.[42]

Wyman's design has been apocryphally understood to bear the influence
of Edward Bellamy's 1887 utopian novel, *Looking Backward*, and the book's
description of commercial architecture bathed in light. Once associated by
writers and critics such as Emile Zola and Walter Benjamin with the phantasmagoria of capitalist visuality, the iron and glass architecture that appears in *M* in the form of the Bradbury Building is a degraded remnant of
this earlier thinking, the "new" of the modern that has long since become
antiquated.[43] But its manifestation in a 1951 film set in Los Angeles suggests an earlier mode of urban public space in danger of becoming forgotten. In the words of Esther McCoy and Raymond Girvigian, "The aesthetic quality of the Bradbury Building is largely derived from the superb
environment of an inner court flooded with light. It is an early and excellent example of a break with façade architecture and the acknowledged un-
pleasantness of a busy city street. By treating the inner court as façades, the
architect has supplied an off-street leisurely and enriched space which de-
nies the bustle of Third Street and Broadway."[44]

The Bradbury Building functions in *M* as a nonsynchronous remnant,
an unexpected fragment of the past that calls the present into question.
Transposed from Europe to Los Angeles, its nineteenth-century grandeur
and pedestrian-friendly space are as anomalous in 1951 Los Angeles as
were the arcades encountered by Benjamin and the Surrealists in Paris
during the 1920s. It appears in the film without masses of consumers or
pedestrians, an uncomfortable hybrid between an interior and exterior
realm, much like New York's Pennsylvania Station, that is, spatially and
temporally displaced, a telling comment on the social predicament of the
American city in late modernity that would soon be assailed by the bull-
dozers of urban redevelopment and had already encountered the automobile.

Unlike Lang's depiction of the display windows in his *M*, Losey's remake adopts a less enthusiastic stance toward this mode of capitalist visual
display. Filmed by daylight on actual Los Angeles streets, the one display-

window scene before a toy store displaying a model railroad (a metaphor for the circle of pathological desire in which the murderer Harrow remains trapped) exudes a less violent and seductive character than in Lang's film. Lacking the knives and reflections that seem to allegorize the murderer's psyche in Lang's *M*, the deeper space and pan from the store to the surrounding street emphasize the store's setting and the point of view of the characters.

This skepticism toward the urban-commodity spectacle is most apparent in the scene in which members of the underworld search the Bradbury Building for the murderer and destroy its many glass windows. At once a critique of the culture of the phantasmagoria, the surface and the gaze, Losey's representation of this structure also presents it as a viable public space threatened by the mindless destruction of the capitalist plunderers.

While at the end of the courtroom scene in both films the police seize the child murderer and protect him from the angry crowd, Losey's *M* presents Langley, the underworld lawyer and defender of the rule of law who attains a more prominent role in the remake, as a victim of this process.[45] Produced in the spring and summer of 1950, during the height of the House Un-American Activities Committee (HUAC) witchhunts, Losey's *M* takes the political persecutions of the Hollywood blacklists as its allegorical subtext, a subject of obvious personal interest to a man who joined the American Communist Party and was subject to intense FBI surveillance in the early 1940s. The suspension of the rule of law during the American Cold War conflict with Communism is alluded to in the film's frequent references to corrupt policemen, victims, and retribution.[46] Released in the same year as the heavily televised HUAC hearings in Washington, *M* suggests the political valence of media simultaneity.

That Lang's *M* film was remade at all by Losey is a consequence of both the German and the American versions' sharing the same producer, German exile Seymour Nebenzal.[47] Besides *M*, Nebenzal is known for his German films, *Menschen am Sonntag* (1923), *Westfront 1918* (G. W. Pabst, 1929), and *The Testament of Dr. Mabuse* (Fritz Lang, 1933). He also worked in the United States, where he produced two films directed by Douglas Sirk, *Hitler's Madman* (1942) and *Summer Storm* (1944), as well as an early film noir, *The Chase* (Arthur Ripley, 1946). *M* was the last film Nebenzal ever produced, and his decision to remake it with Joseph Losey led Fritz

Lang to claim its ownership. Writing in a Los Angeles newspaper at the end of the film's production, Nebenzal offered this account of his fight with Fritz Lang and his motivations for remaking *M*:

> Mr. Lang makes the statement that the old picture was built around the sex criminal being caught and tried by a group of organized beggars in a kangaroo court. He also says that because there is no organized group of beggars in the United States, therefore the premise of the original film is not valid here. I am surprised to hear that the matter of organized beggars should be the premise of the old picture. I always thought, and still think, that the problems connected with a sex criminal of this type, his menace to the community and the treatment of such criminals, was the basic premise of the story—a problem which is much more acute today in the United States than the few isolated cases were in Germany in the early 1930s.
>
> Mr. Lang further states that "M" is a classic and it is stupid to try to improve on it. My reasons for making an English version of the picture are the following:
>
> 1. The German language picture is by now antiquated in its psychological approach to the problem.
>
> 2. As I have already pointed out, the problem is becoming more and more acute.
>
> 3. The German picture was never generally released in the United States, but was shown only in some art houses and by the Museum of Modern Art. Only a very small percentage of theater goers have seen it—and they had to depend on subtitles.[48]

Produced between the HUAC hearings conducted in Washington, D.C., from October 20 to 30, 1947, and resumed in March 1951, the remake of *M* appears as a canny strategy on the part of Nebenzal and Losey to circumvent censorship restrictions and to confront political repression, the real problem, "becoming more and more acute" in 1950 in Hollywood. Indeed, by August 1950, three months after principal photography on *M* was completed, *Variety* reported that Nebenzal had optioned the film rights to a far less controversial story called "The Marines First Spy" about an American soldier killed by the Japanese in the 1930s.[49] A month later, the last of the Hollywood Ten went to jail after their legal appeals proved unsuccessful. As Larry Ceplair and Steven Englund note, by 1951 no one without a political clearance approved by HUAC could work in the Hollywood film industry.[50] By the time Karen Morley, who plays the murdered Elsie's mother, was called by Losey to act in *M*, she had been blacklisted for involvement in a United Auto Workers documentary against racism. Waldo Salt, the dialogue writer for Losey's film and an unfriendly witness before the committee in 1947, was once more subpoenaed in March 1951.

Writing of the film's premiere, a newspaper reviewer noted: "Many in the cast, whose names have been associated with communistic fronts and activities, brought about a picket line in front of the two theaters, the pickets' signs protesting the use of 'known reds' in the film and therefore urging non-patronage."[51] With their common stories of victims, murderers, surveillance, the mass media, lawyers, guilty parties, the desire for retribution, and the reestablishment of legal authority, both *M* films construct cultural narratives about social scapegoats in German and American societies, each of which was undergoing political and social crises.[52] They also demonstrate the inextricable role of the mass media in the public negotiation of these societal traumas.

Whether we think of the elaborate security system in the Berlin warehouse or the Bradbury Building, the prominence of television and automobile-dominated space in Losey's remake, or the eradication of an older centripetal space organized around the corporeal experience of pedestrians, Losey's *M* betrays a fascination with other communications media. The culture of late modernity presented in the film is productively understood as a response to the new experiences of space, time, speed, and social control brought about by the convergence of cinema with television, the automobile, and surveillance technologies. By suggesting the political stakes of these new perceptual modalities and the imbrication of the mass media with larger social conflicts, it confirms the growing inextricability of space and representation throughout the twentieth century.

Instances of media simultaneity appear frequently in other centrifugal films noir of the 1950s, precursors of the mobile communication today facilitated by the cellular telephone, the pager, and the Internet. A common example is the presence of a radio in a public facility such as a restaurant or gas station in *The Devil Thumbs a Ride* (Felix Feist, 1947) over which the description of a criminal fugitive is broadcast while he or she is on the premises. The space and time of narrative action and surveillance temporarily converge, while the authorities continue their search in a different setting. We see a comparable instance in *He Walked by Night*, in which the killer, a former police department employee, monitors the activities of officers on patrol over a police radio receiver. A variation on this theme occurs in *The Hitch-Hiker* (Ida Lupino, 1953) when the police and the radio transmit *disinformation* over the radio so as to convince a murderer holding two passengers hostage that the authorities believe he is moving in another direction. The incursion of simultaneity into centrifugal space is thematized repeatedly in *Plunder Road* through the radio broadcasts that accompany the criminals during their escape. These news bulletins on the robbery (always announced by the identical newscaster in Salt Lake City, whose fixed position and identity underscore the mobility and anonymity of the gang) function as an important narrative device. They facilitate cross-cutting between the three trucks carrying gold and allow each of the three groups to monitor the progress of the police investigation, as well as to learn of one another's capture. Listening to both police radio and commercial broadcasts, the heist perpetrators intend to outwit the authorities by anticipating roadblocks, the ultimate benefit of radio simultaneity for a criminal on the lam.

Utilizing the terminology of Barthes, we might think of radio as a narrative "informant" that spatially and temporally locates the protagonists of *Plunder Road.*[53] Only by means of these radio broadcasts can the spectator position the protagonists, for not until quite late in the film do we learn that Eddie and Frankie are headed for Los Angeles. Yet the geographic information gained from these reports is always in the past tense, and the ironic function of radio in the film is to provide a steady stream of information useless for ascertaining the location or destination of the criminals at a specific moment. Radio is even mentioned explicitly in the remarks of the gas station attendant to Eddie: "They'll catch them. They can't help but catch them. Fellas like that hardly have a chance with radio and all that science against them. Back a few years ago it was different. A man had a real chance. But nowadays, everything has got a system that's pretty hard to beat."

Throughout *Plunder Road* radio simultaneity holds out the threat of imminent detection and capture by the perfect "system" alluded to by the gas station attendant. Thus, when Eddie and Frankie enter a roadside restaurant they find a group of teenage boys discussing the heist with the waitress and speculating on the route taken by the criminals. And after two groups of heist members have been captured, the authorities conclude that the third truck may be destined for California because the other two were intercepted on roads leading there.

Yet the high opinion of the gas station attendant of "radio and all that science" is presented as groundless by the film, for simultaneity neither assists the police in the apprehension of the gang members nor enables them to avoid capture. Nonetheless, his telling remark alludes to a nascent fear of the possibility of a perfect system of surveillance. Although the heist fails, *Plunder Road* suggests that a total "system" of electronic surveillance may well prove ineffectual in the age of centrifugal space and an interstate highway saturated with traffic and stretched over great distances. As in so many other films noir, chance and random bad luck, rather than organized and rationally planned deterrent measures, prove the eventual undoing of the criminals.[54]

Upon entering the Harbor Freeway, Frankie initially misinterprets the traffic congestion as evidence of a roadblock. Eddie quickly disabuses him of his paranoia and identifies the traffic as "the morning rush—the people who have to work for a living." A traffic bulletin on the radio—the only simultaneous moment between receipt of a news report and direct spatio-temporal experience of the event it narrates in the film—reports the bottleneck in which they are caught.[55] Like the condemned men in prison described by McLuhan, the heist members simultaneously participate in and witness their own "event," as the golden bumper they have fashioned for their automobile is discovered by the police when their vehicle is hit from the rear on the freeway. Despite their confidence that they have thought of every possible contingency, the ubiquity of the traffic jam as a fact of life in centrifugal space totally eludes Frankie, Eddie, and Fran.[56]

TIME

What is the time of centrifugal space? Its spatial practices and representations of space (urban planning, traffic surveys, commuting routines, and freeway congestion) all present time as a finite and valuable resource, a measurable commodity to be maximized (or reduced) wherever possible. But what of those individuals who opt out of the temporal orders of simultaneity and centrifugal space? One finds a clue to such questions in Lefebvre's notion of appropriation, the purposive use of space that he opposes to domination:

> Yet abstract space is the outcome not of an ideology or of false consciousness, but of a practice. Its falsification is self-generated. Conflicts nevertheless manifest themselves on the level, precisely, of knowledge, especially that between *space* and *time*. The oppressive and repressive powers of abstract space are clearly revealed in connection with time: this space relegates time to an abstraction of its own— except for labor time, which produces things and surplus value. Time might thus be expected to be quickly reduced to constraints placed on the employment of space: to distances, pathways, itineraries, or modes of transportation. In fact, however, time resists any such reduction, re-emerging instead as the supreme form of wealth, as locus and medium of use, and hence of enjoyment. Abstract space fails in the end to lure time into the realm of externality, of signs and images, of dispersion. Time comes back into its own as privacy, inner life, subjectivity . . . Within time, the investment of affect, of energy, of "creativity" opposes a mere passive apprehension of signs and signifiers . . . The "real" appropriation of space, which is incompatible with abstract signs of appropriation serving merely to mask domination, does have certain requirements.[57]

The struggle by the inhabitant of abstract and centrifugal space to appropriate a time and space—a rhythm—capable of withstanding the leveling forces of the metropolis, is not difficult to discern in film noir. In *The Asphalt Jungle* nature and sexuality provide the basis for an appropriation of space incompatible with schedules, measurements, itineraries, or the demands of production, a space of fantasy that allows for the contestation of abstract space.

Set in neither Los Angeles nor New York, *The Asphalt Jungle* begins in the center of an anonymous midwestern city whose dilapidated streetscape resembles the barren topoi of the Italian neorealist films with which it is

contemporaneous.[58] Its abstract space is not that of the "morbid geom-
etrism" of the urban grid noted by Minkowski nor that of the highway but
rather the ruins of the centripetal industrial metropolis, in which surveillance depends heavily upon the police radio transmissions audible in the
opening sequence.

Characteristically for a centrifugal film noir, the film shifts between the
urban center and locations outside it. Its two final scenes depict Doc
Riegenschneider (Sam Jaffe) as he is captured by the police, and Dix
Handley (Sterling Hayden) as he dies on the ground of the family farm in
Kentucky. As perhaps the classic heist film, *The Asphalt Jungle* moves between the underworld bars and gambling joints of its criminal protagonists
to an elaborately organized (timed) robbery and concludes with the death
or capture of all its perpetrators.

The significance of Handley and Riegenschneider to the film's narrative
is suggested by their introduction at the beginning of the film as Handley
escapes from a robbery into a luncheonette and Riegenschneider, fresh out
of prison, enters a gambling joint in search of a bankroller for his next job.
Riegenschneider exemplifies the ethnically marked criminal mastermind
characteristic of the caper film genre. As played by Sam Jaffe, his German accent bestows a worldliness and sophistication on his character that
differentiate him from both the underworld and the upper-class milieu
in which he circulates. His planning skills and reputation are legendary
among the criminal community and allow him easily to raise the needed
$50,000 to prepare for his jewel robbery.

Riegenschneider's uncontrollable sexuality manifests itself several times
throughout the film and seems to contradict his efficient persona, as well
as his mastery of urban space itself. We first see this as he visits Cobby's
bookmaking operation and steals a furtive glance at some pinup images on
a calendar. Later he recounts a date with a young girl from whom he learns
more about Emmerich. And finally as he flees from the police he sits in a
café watching a young girl dance to a jukebox.

The film clearly emphasizes the temporal implications of this last scene,
the occasion of Riegenschneider's capture. Sitting in the roadhouse watching the young woman gyrate, Riegenschneider is urged to leave by the cab
driver he has hired to drive him to Cleveland: "Mr., Mr. It's getting late.
We's better be moving along," says the driver. "Plenty of time, my friend,

plenty of time," the older man replies as he watches transfixed and totally immobile as the young girl dances. The camera moves progressively lower, tightly framing the dancing girl's body as his point of view. While the song on the jukebox continues to play, he is spotted by the police, who watch him through the window as he gazes in rapture. After he has been identi-fied, Riegenschneider learns that the police have been watching him for the past few minutes—the precise duration of the song.

Without wishing to deny the voyeuristic component of his behavior, I also would call attention to its temporal dimensions. An interlude of un-characteristically irrational behavior for the normally careful criminal, the café scene depicts Riegenschneider's sexuality as the basis for a different relation to time, one based on pleasure and the rhythms of the body. It is a time whose concentration and depth of experience evoke the Benjaminian notion of *Erfahrung* while contrasting markedly with the space-time com-pression presented by David Harvey as omnipresent in the contemporary world.[59] The voyeurism of Riegenschneider promises an intensification of experience and an absorption in temporality rendered fragile by the cul-ture of media simultaneity. The café is the ill-fated locus of his spatial ap-propriation, a dynamic involving eroticism no less than rhythms. In the words of Lefebvre: "What we *live* are rhythms—rhythms experienced sub-jectively . . . A rhythm invests places, but is not itself a place; it is not a thing, nor an aggregation of things, nor yet a simple flow. It embodies its own law, its own regularity, which it derives from space—from its own space—and from a relationship between space and time."[60]

Lacking the crowds depicted in Ruttmann's film of Weimar Berlin, punctuated only by the changing pulses of its illumination, the American city comes to resemble a sovereign machine in which the mechanical pat-terns eclipse the rhythms of place and body described by Lefebvre and em-bodied in the behavior of Riegenschneider. It confirms the omnipresence of seriality and abstract space located by the noir writer W. R. Burnett in an anonymous midwestern city that provides the setting for his novel *The Asphalt Jungle* (1948), from which the film was adapted:

River Boulevard, wide as a plaza and with its parkways and arched, or-ange street lights stretching off into the misty horizon in diminishing perspective, was as deserted as if a plague had swept the streets clean.

The traffic lights changed with automatic precision, but there were no cars to heed or disobey them. Far down the boulevard, in the supper-club section of the city, elaborately glittering neon signs flashed off and on to emptiness. The night city, like a wound-up toy, went about its business with mechanical efficiency, regardless of man.[61]

Unlike Riegenschneider, Dix Handley appears scarcely interested in sex; he allows Doll Conovan (Jean Hagen) to stay in his room on condition that she doesn't get "any ideas." During the night she hears him talking in his sleep. He explains an unfortunate change of luck, the grounds for his move from the country to the city, as well as his lingering distrust of the latter:

And then everything happened at once. My old man died and we lost our corn crop. That black colt I was telling you about, he broke his leg and had to be shot. That was a rotten year. I'll never forget the day we left. Me and my brother swore we'd buy Hickory Wood Farm back someday. Twelve grand would have swung it, and I almost made it once. I had more than 5,000 in my pocket. Panpoon was running in the suburban. I figured he couldn't lose. I put it all on his nose. He lost by a nose. The way I figure, my luck's just got to turn. One of these days I'll make a real killing. Then I'm gonna head for home. First thing I'm gonna do when I get there is take a bath in the creek and wash this city dirt off me.

This scene, occurring early in *The Asphalt Jungle*, establishes Handley's connection to the Kentucky farm where he will die surrounded by horses in the film's final shot. A compulsive gambler forever in debt to bookies— the typical film noir "loser" trapped in a downward spiral—Handley seems obsessed with horses, a character trait traceable to his childhood. His bond to the family land reappears in the frenzied drive he makes with Doll to Kentucky—his return to Hickory Wood Farm, whose appropriation coincides with the moment of his death. In the case of both Handley and Riegenschneider, the space of appropriation overlaps the space of individual fantasy and desire. Its strategy of resistance, the attempt to escape from "the asphalt jungle" of the city, fails.

Neither Riegenschneider nor Handley triumphs over the metropolis, despite their ability to escape its physical limits. The former is apprehended as a consequence of his erotic compulsions, while the latter falls prey to an equally compulsive attachment to the place of his childhood. Succumbing to the lure of these differential temporalities of sexuality and spatial memory, they relinquish the logical calculation of time and space evident in their planning and realization of the jewel robbery. They are trapped not by the mechanisms of surveillance but by their own subjectivity.

THE MEDIA ENVIRONMENT

From the very first shot of *The Big Carnival*, a close-up of the dry New Mexican earth, spatial themes and images recur consistently throughout the film. Were this story set in some other country one could easily imagine its central character, Charles Tatum (Kirk Douglas), as the haughty representative of a colonial foreign power who has come to dominate the local natives. Yet despite his remarkable condescension to those around him, Tatum arrives in New Mexico with the goal not of extracting riches but of obtaining a more intangible commodity—news. Indeed, one of the film's most remarkable narrative feats is to thwart the presentation of Tatum as an outsider to the Escudero community, for by the end nearly all its residents have aided or abetted his work for their own opportunistic motives. Although the colonialist power relation initially seems an appropriate metaphor for Tatum's relation to the locals, the film ultimately suggests that the source of his power exceeds the person of the reporter and must be sought in the dispersed media environment that organizes space and agency alike.

A spatial reading of *The Big Carnival* may profitably begin by surveying oppositions between different types of space in the film. Organized around Tatum, the most powerful antagonism is surely that between centripetal and centrifugal space. Once employed by eleven newspapers in different cities across the country, Tatum enters Albuquerque riding in his car as it is towed into the town center for repairs. His first movement is entry into the city. Although we soon learn of Tatum's fervent desire to return to the metropolis, we rapidly come to understand that he is living out a sentence of exile from it. Having been fired because of his alcoholism and opportunistic journalism, Tatum cannot return to the city.

His search for a story that will allow him once again to work as a metropolitan reporter forms his main narrative quest in the film. It fuels the extraordinary enmity toward his local surroundings, expressed in this monologue in the *Albuquerque Sun Bulletin* office:

> When the history of this sun-baked Siberia is written, these shameful words will live in infamy: No chopped chicken liver. No garlic pickles. No Lindy's. No Madison Square Garden. No Yogi Berra . . . You know what's wrong with New Mexico, Mr. Wendell, too much outdoors! Give me those eight spindly trees in front of Rockefeller Center any day. That's enough outdoors for me. No subways smelling sweet and sour. What do you use for noise around here? No beautiful roar from 8 million ants, fighting, cursing, loving. No shows. No *South Pacific*. No chic little dames across a crowded bar. Worst of all, Herbie, no eightieth floor to jump from when you feel like it . . . When I came here I thought this was going to be a thirty-day stretch, maybe sixty. Now it's a year. It looks like a life sentence. Where is it? Where's the loaf of bread with a file in it? Where's that big story to get me out of here?

Throughout the film New York acts as a lure, a lost spatial object just beyond Tatum's attainment. His agreement to report on the Minosa event for the New York newspaper for which he once worked is conditional on its rehiring him after the rescue. Although Tatum dies before he can return, he does obtain a connection to the metropolis in the form of his telephone conversations with Nagel (the *New York Daily* editor shown briefly in the window of his Manhattan office) and the teletype machine installed in his temporary bedroom at the Minosa trading post. Later, the arrival of metropolitan reporters and tourists from other locations increases the pressure to bring Escudero within the orbit of centrifugal space. Significantly, it is only by leaving Albuquerque and venturing farther from the city that Tatum first obtains the gist of his story, although throughout the film he remains outside of the metropolis and mired in centrifugal space.

The opposition between what Lefebvre understands as abstract and absolute space is no less significant in *The Big Carnival*. Absolute space

> has the effect of setting up reserved spaces, such as places of initiation, within social space. All holy or cursed places, places characterized by the presence or absence of gods, associated with the death of gods, or with hidden powers and their exorcism—all such places qualify as special preserves. Hence in absolute space the absolute has no place, for otherwise it would be a "non-place"; and the religio-political space has a rather strange composition, being made up of areas set apart, reserved—and so mysterious.[62]

Leo Minosa becomes trapped in the cave of the Mountain of the Seven Vultures while searching for Indian pots, a space whose natural darkness contrasts markedly with the metropolitan streets of a film noir such as *Double Indemnity*, to which *The Big Carnival* refers. Its status as a sacred space for the Indians does not deter Minosa from entering it to seek curios to sell to tourists. As he says to Tatum: "I guess I crawled into it too far this time. I guess maybe they didn't want me to have it . . . The Indian dead . . . They're all around here. This is a tomb, mister, with mummies 400 years old . . . I guess maybe they've been watching me all the time I've been taking things out and they got mad."

More than a graveyard vandal, Minosa is also a businessman whose livelihood is based on selling access to the Indians' sacred site. A shot of the sign outside his trading post confirms the essential hubris of this enterprise: "Visit Old Indian Cliffs Dwelling. 450 Years Old. OK to Take Pictures. Films on Sale at Trading Post. Leo Minosa Proprietor."

Named and packaged by a non-Indian outsider, the cliff dwellings are incorporated into a larger, nonabsolute space by Minosa's activities. Although once trapped in the cave he becomes superstitious about the Indian dead, Minosa never expresses remorse about his more subtle expropriation of their tradition. By the film's conclusion the mountain undergoes a full semiotic transformation and regains its original function as tomb. Leo dies within it, the carnival disappears, and in a gesture that mimics the huge drill boring down as part of the rescue operation, Tatum's body is pierced by a pair of scissors wielded by Minosa's wife. The fusing of spatial realms (religious, commercial, private, public, natural, urban) that progresses throughout the film abruptly reverses itself. By its conclusion absolute and abstract space become terms of a spatial chiasmus and once again reassert their former identities, claiming their erstwhile mediator Tatum as victim.

Shortly after he emerges from his first visit with Minosa in the cave, Tatum remarks: "I don't make things happen; all I do is write about them." By the end of *The Big Carnival*, the gap between these two allegedly separate activities—writing or organizing discourse and influencing behavior—narrows to an imperceptible degree.[63] Publication of Tatum's initial newspaper story turns Escudero into a tourist attraction and constitutes a new social space—the city of onlookers camped at the base of the mountain.

Positioned on the mountaintop, the camera slowly pans across the scene below as in a television newscast, and reveals a large crowd of cars, commercial vehicles, and spectators, the type of scene whose growth in suburban communities during the 1950s was conspicuous. It is a moment of heightened reflexivity in the film that proposes the kinship between cinema and the mass medium of television. Whereas an earlier film noir such

Frame enlargement of city of onlookers with Chuck Tatum (Kirk Douglas) about to announce the death of Leo Minosa, from *The Big Carnival* (Billy Wilder, 1951).

as *The Naked City* proclaimed its affinity with the filmic tradition of the city symphony or the newspaper, Wilder's film acknowledges the growing power of television, while still consigning the cinema a privileged role for cultural criticism and analysis. Acknowledging the crowd of onlookers, a voice-over narrator from one of the local electronic media exclaims: "Ladies and gentlemen, something phenomenal is going on here. Right in front of this 400-year-old cliff dwelling a new community is springing up. A veritable town of tents and trucks and trailers. Standing here I can pick out license plates from California, Arizona, Texas, Oklahoma."

This oxymoronic conjunction of the cliff dwelling and the city of onlookers, each representing a different social and spatial organization, dramatically concretizes Lefebvre's thesis of the intercalation of historically distinct spaces. By suggesting how an older spatiality is overlaid by contemporary users, it also demonstrates the potential of the media environment to constitute space. As Jean Baudrillard observes: "With the disappearance of the public place, advertising invades everything (the street, the monument, the market, the stage, language) . . . It determines architecture and the creation of super-objects . . . Today our only architecture is just that: huge screens upon which moving atoms, particles and molecules are refracted. The public stage, the public place have been replaced by a gigantic circulation, ventilation, and ephemeral connecting space."[64]

Written in the 1980s, Baudrillard's diagnosis of mutations in public space is presaged by the tent and trailer city of *The Big Carnival*. If the radio narrator's description of it as a community is correct, the agglomeration of onlookers is nothing more than a community of consumers intent on devouring the spectacle of Leo Minosa's rescue. Commencing as a news story, it soon metamorphoses into a media event.[65] The rescue operation functions precisely as the connecting space described by Baudrillard, a carnival of consumption whose public, social character is eclipsed by its value as an advertising stunt. As a lightly veiled allegory about the crassness of American society in the 1950s, *The Big Carnival* suggests nothing so much as the gap between the space of mass society and the space of true community, the latter invoked only by its glaring absence.[66] As German philosopher Max Picard writes about radio:

The radio does more than substitute for man's own perception. It gathers what is and what happens so unfailingly that it seems as if the things and events not only were perceived and registered, but were produced by it. The radio not only reports history; it seems to make history. The world seems to originate in the radio. True enough, the individual still sees the things and events as they happen, but what happens becomes real to him only as the radio reports the event, or as the illustrated paper depicts it.[67]

A skillful manipulator of people and events, Tatum feels no qualms about "writing" roles for other people. *The Big Carnival* presents its characters as people who accept as real only that which Tatum and the news media report. After Leo's wife, Lorraine, explains her plan to leave Escudero, he replies: "Your husband's stuck under a mountain; you're worried sick. That's the way the story goes." Although she claims to have no religious beliefs, Tatum later insists that Lorraine visit a church for a photo opportunity. He also demands the exclusive right to interview Minosa in the cave, thereby edging out competition from other reporters. Even after it has become clear that Leo is dying of pneumonia, Tatum offers the following rationale for abandoning the drilling operation and directly entering the cave: "When you've got a big human interest story, you've got to give it a big human interest ending. When you get people steamed up like this, don't ever make suckers out of them. I don't want to hand them a dead man." Ever attentive to placing the optimal narrative "spin" upon an event, Tatum aspires to a total mastery of his media discourse. He is motivated less by compassion than by the requirement of providing a proper ending to his news story. The eventual realization of the irreversible character of his decision to drill into the ground rather than shore up the walls of the cave destroys his claim to be a neutral observer of the Minosa rescue he "writes" about.

By the conclusion of *The Big Carnival* our belief in Tatum's ability to wield the power of discourse is revealed as an illusion. Throughout the film there are subtle hints that point to his unstable position. Tatum speaks of an earlier man trapped in a cave as an inspiration for his handling of the story, appealing to prior "media events" as the inspiration for this one. Although "being first" (the first reporter to file a story, the first visitor to the site) is valorized by those who participate in the media spectacle, the narrative categories that process these events inevitably do so by emphasizing their status as repetitions of earlier events.

One might also discern here the relevance to a reading of *The Big Carnival* of Deleuze's characterization of the postwar cinema as determined by clichés after the collapse of the action image:

> The criminal conspiracy, as organization of Power, was to take on a new aspect in the modern world, that the cinema would endeavor to follow and to show. It is no longer the case, as in the *film noir* of American realism, of an organization which related to a distinctive milieu, to assignable actions by which the criminals would be distinguishable . . . There is no longer even a magic centre, from which hypnotic actions could start spreading everywhere as in Lang's first two Mabuse films . . . Occult power is confused with its effects, its supports, its media, its radios, its televisions, its microphones: it now only operates through the "mechanical reproduction of images and of sounds."[68]

Deleuze's insight is further strengthened if one compares Wilder's film with *Double Indemnity*, a parallel made by *The Big Carnival* itself through the narrative structure of Tatum's death and the fact that a spectator of the media spectacle, Mr. Federber (Frank Cady), announces his employer to a reporter as the Pacific All-Risk Insurance Company, the same concern for which Walter Neff worked in the earlier film. Yet whereas Neff encountered the fatal consequences of pursuing illicit erotic desire and committing murder, Federber is presented as a sedate family man drawn to the Minosa rescue carnival by his stated desire to provide an educational experience for his children.

The insurance trade, designed to minimize risk, no longer furnishes the temptation to "crook the house" that it did to Neff. The fate of Leo Minosa renders its concern with statistics irrelevant, just as the narrative structure of *The Big Carnival* substitutes media surveillance for the discovery of clues, once the mainstay of the literature of detection.[69] Now the great risk is neither the loss of a phantasmatic object of desire nor discovery by the police but rather missing the media spectacle. As in *Double Indemnity*, Tatum is murdered by a vengeful woman and returns to his place of employment to die in the presence of a benevolent paternal figure, here the newspaper publisher Jacob Q. Boot (Porter Hall).

Released contemporaneously with the widespread entry of television into the American home, *The Big Carnival* explores many themes later associated with films by Robert Altman, Martin Scorsese, and much postwar American cinema.[70] To watch Minosa's father walk through the garbage-strewn site of the carnival in one of the film's last shots is to encounter a radically different space from the Los Angeles that Billy Wilder depicted in *Double Indemnity* seven years earlier. The centripetal city with its characteristic landmarks has disappeared, replaced by the centrifugal spaces of simultaneity and the media environment. Passage through the city no longer requires its physical traversal, but now comes closer to the experience of space that Fredric Jameson identifies as exemplary of the postmodern in his description of small towns (like Escudero) in the 1950s: "This small-town content was not, in the postwar period, really 'provincial' any longer (as in Lewis or John O'Hara, let alone Dreiser); you might want to leave, you might still long for the big city, but something had happened—perhaps something as simple as television and other media—to remove the pain and sting of absence from the center, from the metropolis."[71]

Films of centrifugal space such as *Plunder Road* and *The Big Carnival* reveal this transformation of spatial experience. They declare the presence of a new spatiality organized around highways, simultaneity, and the media environment in which the older forms of centripetal space no longer play a determinant role. Geographic centrality has ceded its once-fundamental cultural and social significance, a state of affairs that seems especially familiar today when the flow of information in our daily lives derives from multiple sources, and the metropolis is but one of many centers.

DOMESTICITY AND THE 1950S MEDIA ENVIRONMENT

Lefebvre observes that an apparently solid house is "permeated from every direction by streams of energy which run in and out of it by every imaginable route: water, gas, electricity, telephone lines, radio and television signals." Despite its apparent solidity and impermeability, this space of domesticity is infiltrated by multiple forces, and he notes: "As exact a picture as possible of this space would differ considerably from the one embodied in the representational space which its inhabitants have in their minds and which for all its inaccuracy plays an integral role in social practice."[72]

For a Hollywood film genre of the 1950s such as the melodrama, the home constitutes, as Laura Mulvey suggests, a protected psychic space of desire and anxiety, an enclosed sphere of female emotions opposed to the outside masculine space of adventure, movement, and cathartic action.[73] By the mid-1950s the entry of television into the American domestic environment had decisively altered what Mulvey refers to as the "dialectics of inside and outside," by bringing sometimes chaotic and violent images of the external world into the average living room.[74] In the words of Victor Burgin, "The regressive unconscious defense mechanisms invoked by television, as it funnels suffering and excitation into our box in the world theater, as it pours all the world's broken cities into our *interior*, are different from those invoked by photography and cinema photography. They produce a different space."[75]

The Killer Is Loose (Budd Boetticher, 1956) explores this new cultural reality of television and its attendant spatial logic. In the credit sequence, which depicts a drawing of a criminal figure set against parallel lines, the camera slowly tracks away, reducing the size of the figure while increasing the size of the surrounding expanse. No longer at the center of centripetal space, the human body is here surrounded by an empty centrifugal space that envelops and overtakes it without providing reassuring orientation points or landmarks.

This sense of spatial disorientation is further conveyed in the opening sequence. Though set in Los Angeles, the only indicator of this geographic location is a street sign marked Roxbury Drive. In a series of long shots whose central relationship is difficult to ascertain, the city appears as a disconnected series of traffic-conveying streets and strip-mall buildings. Once again, the impression conveyed by this neighborhood is that of little cohesive spatial identity and an overwhelming spatial expanse that frustrates the pedestrian who waits for a traffic light to cross the street. The bank he enters for the purpose of robbing is architecturally distinguished by a long glass storefront that connects it to the surrounding city, evident in the sounds of traffic that permeate its interior space.

This sense of untrammeled spatial expansion is explicitly alluded to by the bank teller Leon Poole (Wendell Corey) when he remarks to a customer: "Another new home owner. Holly Road. The city is spreading out, isn't it?" It is echoed in the depiction of Los Angeles as a series of disconnected neighborhoods of single-family homes, as it is by the enormity of the kitchen in the home belonging to Detective Sam Wagner (Joseph Cotten), which seems to overwhelm him and his wife, Lila (Rhonda Fleming). After being convicted for aiding the bank robbery, Poole is sentenced to a prison term that he serves out working on a state farm. Vowing to avenge the accidental shooting of his wife by Wagner during his capture by the police, Poole escapes from the farm and returns to Los Angeles with the intent to murder Lila.

Despite a series of roadblocks and traffic jams, the police are unable to prevent Poole's entry into the city, shown on the map in the police department as a series of discrete zones. Throughout the film, television viewed by the characters in their homes provides commentary on the state of the manhunt for Poole and a cue for cutting from one home to the next. As Grace Flanders (Dee J. Thompson) prepares dinner for her husband, Otto (John Larch), she watches the manhunt on television. Several minutes later, Poole appears in her kitchen to await the return of Otto, the next murder victim. Unlike the bourgeois home in much filmic melodrama of the 1950s, here domestic space combines interior and exterior reality in a paroxysm of the televised event and the simultaneous real experience of it.

"Can you believe they really think I'm there?" Poole says to the woman.

Frame enlargement of Otto Flanders (John Larch) watching manhunt on television while murderer Leon Poole (Wendell Corey) stands behind him in kitchen, from *The Killer Is Loose* (Budd Boetticher, 1956).

Upon arriving home and finding the manhunt on television, the man, still unaware of the killer in his kitchen, innocently asks his wife: "Where is this going on?" Here the space of the news event and domesticity blurs: the "this" thought to be somewhere else turns out to be no farther away than the family living room. In contrast with the stereotypical depiction of the suburban home as a sanctuary and isolationist refuge, *The Killer Is Loose* presents it infiltrated by violence and trauma, a breakdown of television's proleptic force to ward off anxiety by allowing spectators to maintain their distance from its sources. Even a young child remains glued to the coverage of Poole's capture, announced as imminent by the news team, and is chastised by his mother for sitting too close to the television set.

In the final sequence of the film, Poole and Lila walk along the block where the Wagner home is located as the police train their rifles upon him in an ambush. After he dies on the front lawn of the detective's home, Sam and his Lila enter through the front door, their anxiety at last vanquished. The camera slowly begins a crane shot and tracks away from the body of the dead criminal to reveal the single-family home and the growing crowd of onlookers and police who arrive on the scene. Composing a visual rhyme with the opening credit sequence, this movement away from the characters again locates them in a large spatial expanse.

Frame enlargement of Sam Wagner (Joseph Cotten) and Lila Wagner (Rhonda Fleming) with corpse of Leon Poole (Wendell Corey) on their front lawn, from *The Killer Is Loose* (Budd Boetticher, 1956).

Conveying the safety of the single-family idyll, a state in which the neighborhood has been restored "to the kids and the dogs," as a police officer phrases it, the film also alludes to the fragility of this protected space and the new pressures that media simultaneity exerts upon it.[76] Although television may produce security as well as anxiety, it decisively banishes the illusion of separation from the surrounding world. A centrifugal film noir such as *The Killer Is Loose* evokes the contemporaneous 1950s critique of suburban homogeneity and isolation and proposes a link between the film cycle and the social and cultural criticism of the period.[77]

Murder by Contract (Irving Lerner, 1958) further confirms the transformation of the suburban home into a dangerous space, but one that simultaneously allows for an effective mode of female agency.[78] It suggests the waning of the femme fatale in the film noir cycle at the end of the 1950s and the potentially greater agency of women in centrifugal space. A contract killer named Claude (Vince Edwards) accepts a final assignment that takes him to Los Angeles, where he is to murder a key witness named Billie Williams (Caprice Toriel), who is prepared to testify in a trial against an underworld leader.

Claude arrives in Los Angeles on a train from Ohio, and his introduction to the region is brokered by two gangsters named George (Herschel Bernardi) and Mark (Philip Pine) who drive him along its freeways. Disembarking at the Glendale train station featured in *Double Indemnity*, the film presents this quintessential noir topos in broad daylight and substitutes these two parodic imitations of gangsters for Fred MacMurray and Barbara Stanwyck. The effect is to uproot this site from noir mythology and to reinsert it in the dispersed reality of 1950s Los Angeles. Claude expresses a desire to see the local sights and proceeds to spend the next few days as a tourist, swimming and fishing, rather than planning his crime, much to the consternation of his bodyguards. "I don't like women. They don't stand still. When they move, it's hard to figure out why or where for. They're not dependable. It's tough to kill somebody who's not dependable," he complains, ironically underscoring his punctiliousness.

Claude seeks to identify Billie's domestic routine so that he can devise a means of piercing the heavy security barrier around the isolated Coldwater Canyon split-level home where she is held in protective custody by the police, a variation on the familiar captive-woman narrative in a film such as *Beware, My Lovely* (Harry Horner, 1952). He accomplishes this by spying

upon Billie from a distance and conducting interviews with people who
have known her. The film chronicles her successful efforts to thwart his attacks by defying his expectations of her behavior. When Claude attaches a
high-voltage wire to Billie's television, she avoids electrocution by switching on the set with remote control, as if to assert her power within a domestic environment permeated by the energy of television, shown to be
dangerous yet controllable.

Reversing the customary pattern of domestic melodrama, Billie exerts
control over all aspects of her life while in police custody, and it's she,
rather than Claude, who controls the narrative in the final section of *Mur-*

Police witness Billie Williams (Caprice Toriel) watches as detective Henry
Randolph vacuums, from *Murder by Contract* (Irving Lerner, 1958). Eddie
Brandt's Saturday Matinee.

der by Contract. Like many films noir of centrifugal space, the flat lighting, absence of camera movement, and avoidance of noir mise-en-scène deviate from common representations of the environment of the sexualized woman. In a curious inversion of gender roles, the police officer assigned to protect Billie is seen from her point of view vacuuming and performing housework. Later Billie objects to the presence of the "sex-crazy" policemen staring at her and demands that they be replaced by a policewoman. She spends her day playing the piano, a reminder of her former career as a musician and a suggestion of an independent mind that is reasserted by her preference for protective custody in suburbia rather than in a jail cell. A shot of Billie practicing at the keyboard dissolves into an extreme long shot of the Los Angeles basin, a reminder of the contiguity of the urban and the suburban and the difficulty of distinguishing them in southern California.

After his first two attempts at murder fail and Claude learns that the newspapers have printed a false report of Billie's death, he is taken to the dilapidated Charlie Chaplin movie studio on La Brea Avenue by George and Mark, who offer him the choice between a final try against Billie or his own death. "What is this place?" he asks. Upon learning that it is a movie studio, he drolly replies: "Not much business." Utilizing actual locations and interiors, *Murder by Contract* similarly proposes the ossification of studio filming conventions. After a visit to the city Hall of Records, Claude obtains a map of the area around Billie's house, and he eventually enters it through an underground storm-drain system, a metaphor that compares the pathway of the male criminal with the removal of domestic waste, but also confirms the belief in a mappable underground space of the Los Angeles storm-drain system dubbed "700 miles of hidden highways" in *He Walked by Night*.

Billie quickly realizes that he is impersonating a police officer and dissuades him from killing her with an entreaty to flee: "Give me a break, and I'll give you one; I won't scream." Claude's loss of nerve when he proves unable to strangle her confirms the breakdown of his male authority. He is soon shot dead by the police in the storm drain, his upturned hand protruding from the pipe in a quasi-Expressionist gesture. Billie picks up his necktie from the floor, as if to gain access to this masculine symbol, and treats it with a bemused indifference.

Like *The Killer Is Loose*, *Murder by Contract* challenges the ideal of the inviolability of the suburban home, a space presented in the film as no longer impregnable but now overrun by energies and forces that challenge those who inhabit it. Yet the film also contests the stereotypes of the helpless female victim or the male sexual predator through its depiction of a protagonist who survives both police and criminal aggression by means of her intelligence. The death of the femme fatale in *Murder by Contract* suggests the birth of a different female subject—and a different male subject—in the centrifugal spaces of late modernity.

CITY OF FEAR AND DEFENSIVE DISPERSAL

The fascination of film noir with transient urban phenomena is accompanied by an equally palpable concern with what Edith Wyschogrod calls the "deathworld," whose traces remained only too vivid after 1945.[79] As postwar French critics appropriated Hollywood cinema, often as a means of reckoning with their experience of the Occupation and its aftermath, urban planners in the United States confronted a different set of anxieties about the future of the American city. In August 1946 (the same month in which the film noir criticism of Nino Frank and Siegfried Kracauer appeared), the *American City* published an article titled "The Atomic Bomb and the Future City."[80] Urging decentralization as a precautionary measure, the essay established the equation, asserted repeatedly throughout the postwar period, between urban concentration and military vulnerability.

Increased political tension with the Soviet Union after the announcement of its atomic bomb test in September 1949 and the onset of the Korean War in 1950 spurred the introduction of civil-defense measures early in the decade.[81] In the words of one commentator, "Since June of 1953, Val Peterson, the administrator of the Federal Civil Defense Administration, has been telling the American people who live in prime target areas that they have three choices, 'dig, die, or get out.'"[82] But they also had a fourth choice: spread out.

Postwar urban planners noted that of the two atomic-weapon targets, the number of deaths at Nagasaki were half those at Hiroshima, a consequence of the dispersal of the urban population in the former city. "In an

atomic war, congested cities would become death traps," wrote Edward
Teller and two economists in 1948.[83] Political scientist Ernest Oppenheimer claimed:

> If Russia puts most of her industries underground, decentralizes her
> population, and manufactures atomic bombs, while the United States
> continues to concentrate her population and industries in cities, the
> day of world empire may have arrived, and it will not be an American
> empire . . . To make the United States safe against any attack by
> atomic, bacteriological, or other weapons . . . concentrations of any
> kind, be they concentrations of industry, of population, or of trans-
> portation facilities, must be avoided or at least minimized.[84]

Fear of density pervades much planning discourse of the early 1950s and
in its most extreme form equated urban concentration *tout court* with susceptibility to military attack. As Tracy Augur claimed in 1948: "An urban
structure that is vulnerable to attack is likely to invite it. And if it is vulnerable, it can do little to support the retaliatory action needed for final victory . . . Our contemporary urban structure presents an inviting target for
the machines of modern war because it is dominated by a few dozen key
centers."[85]

Two years later, in November 1950, Paul Windels, president of the New
York Regional Plan, extended this argument. "Decentralization has been
termed insurance against war. But insurance only makes good for losses after damage has occurred. Decentralization is much more than insurance.
It is a powerful deterrent to the outbreak of war."[86] Among the most
prominent advocates of defensive dispersal was Ludwig Hilberseimer, who
as early as 1945 claimed that "security, once provided behind walls, can
only be found in the dispersion of cities and industries," a theme he repeated in his books *The New Regional Pattern* (1949) and *The Nature of
Cities* (1955).[87] Other architects shared this sanguine view of the potential
for the built environment to intervene in political life on behalf of peace
and endorsed the construction of dispersed rural settlements. Even Albert
Mayer, an architect of the enormous (and scarcely dispersed) Manhattan
House apartment project (1950), jumped on the bandwagon: "We must
have civil defense, but it will be a viable, useful mechanism only if we can

look forward to happier solutions. We must achieve the safety of space . . . The continuing sprawl of our cities won't do it."[88]

Translated into a plan for the built environment, this "safety of space" appeared in the form of narrow "ribbon" or "linear" cities that would form parallel, continuous settlements running from east to west crossed by a network of cities built from north to south. The grid that resulted from this plan, punctuated by an interval of twenty-five miles of agricultural land between each urban settlement, was intended to dissipate the destructive force of aerial bombing.[89] Other schemes called for building urban centers with a population of one million inhabitants divided into twenty units of 50,000 people separated by intervals of four to five miles of open country, as well as the construction of decentralized underground factories and the stockpiling of strategic industrial materials.[90]

Defensive dispersal also entailed the rapid removal of the civilian population from urban areas. Speed, no less than decentralization, appeared a universal panacea for nuclear-generated anxiety. Writing in *Life* magazine, Norbert Wiener proposed an urban evacuation system composed of highway belts and railroad lines encircling a dispersed metropolis.[91] Anticipating Paul Virilio's discussion of the overexposed metropolis, Air Force Brigadier General Dale O. Smith suggested in 1955: "The wall of the modern city is its ability for rapid evacuation . . . New high-speed arteries, bridges, and tunnels probably will have to be built."[92] Civil-defense officials busied themselves developing plans for the most efficient utilization of existing road networks, and their efforts buoyed the passage of the Federal-Aid Highway Act of 1956, which established the National System of Interstate and Defense Highways.

As we have seen, throughout the 1940s film noir approached the metropolis, the classic setting of its narratives, with a serene indifference to the spatial anxieties voiced by the advocates of defensive dispersal. Menacing alleys, the shabby asphalt jungle of bars and fleabag hotels, and the pulsating neon cityscape situated the film cycle in a centripetal urban landscape seemingly far removed from the new spatiality of fallout shelters and a scattered and relocated urban population.

Yet by the early 1950s spatial representations in film noir began to evolve in tandem with the "nuclear anxiety" film and a growing cultural fear of mass annihilation.[93] From the radioactive toxin that poisons the protagonist in *DOA* (1950) to the narratives of nuclear espionage by Communist agents in *The Thief* (Russell Rouse, 1952), *Pick Up on South Street* (1953), and *Kiss Me Deadly* (1955), these films explore the tortured subjectivity of avaricious protagonists who possess the dangerous secrets of mass destruction.

One such film rich with significance in this context is the appositely titled *City of Fear* (Irving Lerner, 1959). It narrates the story of an escaped convict from San Quentin named Vince Ryker (Vince Edwards), who has taken flight with what he believes to be a canister containing one million

Vince Ryker (Vince Edwards) with canister of radioactive cobalt-60 tries to fence it to Crown (Joe Mell), from *City of Fear* (Irving Lerner, 1959). Eddie Brandt's Saturday Matinee.

dollars' worth of pure heroin but which in reality holds a deadly form of radioactive cobalt-60. The police must locate Ryker within seventy-two hours, or before the canister is opened, if the city is to avoid radiation contamination. Realizing the uncontrollable panic that news of the contents of the canister would produce, Chief Jensen (Lyle Talbot), Lieutenant Mark Richards (John Archer), and Dr. Wallace (Steven Ritch) of the Radiological Section of the Los Angeles Air Pollution Control District must conduct their investigation "with desperate speed and in top secrecy," qualities that characterize the labor of detection in the 1950s nuclear-terrorism genre.[94]

Ryker steals the car and clothing of a traveling salesman and enters Los Angeles, evading detection by the authorities. Unrecognizable because of his disguised appearance and stolen automobile, he is nonetheless easily detectable through the radiation emitted by the canister that remains by his side and steadily disintegrates his body. Driving through the streets of Los Angeles with Geiger counters mounted on police cars, an image that secures the significance of *City of Fear* in any history of the modalities of postwar cinematic and spatial surveillance, the radiological squad divides the city into quadrants and begins to track his movements.

Commonly assailed for its alleged lack of density, Los Angeles typifies the concentrated urban target decried by the proponents of the urbanism of defensive dispersal. Lerner's film presciently shifts the source of anxiety from the Cold War threat of nuclear conflict to the activities of an unknowing domestic terrorist. Though cryptically invoking "controlled volunteer" experiments conducted at the prison hospital, the film never explains why San Quentin possesses a canister of deadly radioactive material in the first place, and it is tempting to read the prison as a codeword for the type of secret military facility that would appear in films of the 1960s, such as *The Manchurian Candidate* (John Frankenheimer, 1962).

Dialogue exchanged between the two principal police investigators suggests the spatialization of fear associated with the nuclear threat.

JENSEN: Just one man holding the lives of three million people in his hands. People should know.

RICHARDS: That Ryker is loose with a cylinder of death that could wipe out a city. That we don't know where he is. It would start a first-class panic.

Lieutenant Mark Richards (John Archer) and Dr. Wallace (Steven Ritch) of the Los Angeles County Radiological Section of the Los Angeles Air Pollution Control District pursue the trail of missing radioactive material in Vince Ryker's room, from *City of Fear* (Irving Lerner, 1959). Eddie Brandt's Saturday Matinee.

JENSEN: We could evacuate.

RICHARDS: Where could we put three million people with no guarantee that Ryker would be in the middle of them no matter where we send them?

Once reassuring and familiar, urban density now appears the root cause of the defensive vulnerability of the 1950s city. As the exchange continues, the problem of Ryker's invisibility becomes evident. "What good are roadblocks if we don't know what to look for? We know he's somewhere, but where?" Urging that the public be informed, the detective exclaims, "Look at the English during the blitz," to which Richards replies: "They knew where the bombs were coming from."

Concluding this scene, the film cuts to an extreme long shot of the Los Angeles basin, described in the screenplay as a "wide panoramic view of the countless blinking lights. (This could help to show the magnitude of the task before this handful of men.)"[95] Recurring throughout *City of Fear*, this image anchors the film's narrative in Los Angeles and provides virtually the only evidence of the urban location in which it is set, for the streets, stores, and neighborhoods in the film are otherwise entirely anonymous. As Ryker enters a store, the camera pans to consider the reflections of the surrounding city in a display window, as if to suggest the heightened reality of the commodity world denied to this urban environment.

Ryker becomes increasingly ill and delirious as a result of his exposure to the radioactive canister, and his automobile travels through Los Angeles present his deteriorating body against the backdrop of the city's already vaporized urban space. The film's moment of great panic occurs when he loses the steel canister in a gas station, a glass and white-walled modernist box from which he subsequently retrieves it lying innocently in the display window. In such scenes, with which *City of Fear* is replete, the film intimates the lapsed innocence of an earlier modernism. It proposes both the International Style gas station and nuclear terrorism as products of technological civilization and its telos of self-destruction.

Understood within the legacy of film noir, *City of Fear* exemplifies the film cycle's immersion and ultimate dissolution in centrifugal space, a posturban environment where familiar landmarks, boundaries, and recognizable neighborhoods of the city fuse into a dispersed region. Once detectable through the control mechanisms of surveillance, roadblocks, and police lineups, the transgressive criminal body, no longer a potent agency, is now traceable only through the nervous sputtering of Geiger counters. Vince Edwards (not yet recognizable from his role in the *Dr. Kildare* television series) performs the male subject of film noir in crisis, his very body on the verge of collapse as he wheezes and retches a radioactive path through Los Angeles.

Ryker, finally located by the police, refuses to hand over the canister, which he tenaciously insists is worth a million dollars. He dies in the film as rapacious as he began, a victim of the contents of his own private *pharmakon* (the cure and the poison in one) and the capitalist ethos of film noir in which criminal plunder radiates an always-unattainable *promesse de bonheur*.[96] After the police drape Ryker's body with a blanket and a radiation sign, the film dissolves to a long shot of the downtown skyline, a sunset surrounded by multiple TV antennas, and a final long shot of the Los Angeles basin.

It is tempting to identify *City of Fear* as one of the very last films produced in the original noir cycle.[97] Filmed in seven and a half days and produced for under $100,000, it appeared during the twilight era of the B movie.[98] Growing competition from television—suggested by the film's penultimate image of rooftop antennas—and changes in the vertical integration of the motion picture industry had come to eliminate the double bill.

By the early 1960s, the generation of literate filmmakers formed by European culture that created the many films noir and memorable low-budget films of the 1940s and 1950s was aging and had ceased to be a vital force, while the younger generation of Martin Scorsese, Francis Coppola, and Robert Altman would not attain prominence through their films until later in the decade.

The end of film noir also coincides, and not fortuitously, with the end of the metropolis of classical modernity, the centered city of immediately recognizable and recognized spaces. Why does centrifugal space invigorate film noir yet ultimately fail to stem the film cycle's demise? One might speculate that as spatial dispersal became a ubiquitous cultural reality, centripetal space began to appear excessively archaic while centrifugal spatial forms could be more effectively romanticized or negotiated through other genres such as the road movie.

Although atomic weapons never fell on New York or Washington, the alleged dangers of urban density were a favorite weapon of the advocates of urban renewal. As Augur writes:

The dispersal of cities has been considered thus far as a means of defense against overt military attack. It has equal value as a defense against the type of enemy penetration that has become so effective in

modern times and which depends on the fomenting of internal disorder and unrest . . . What fertility there is in this country for the
growth of subversive ideas and actions is furnished by the decay of the
city structure in which increasing millions of people spend their lives
. . . Scattered slum clearance and redevelopment projects do not get at
the heart of the problem. It will take a much more comprehensive attack to eliminate the areas that are unfit to live in . . . Because a national program of defensive dispersal does provide a comprehensive
and constructive approach to this problem it offers as good a defense
against internal enemies as against those whose attack is launched
from outside.[99]

Many urban planners were only too happy to enlist in this war against
enemies, both external and internal, and the comprehensive attack recommended by Augur in 1948 met with considerable—if questionable—enthusiasm by the mid-1960s. In the name of urban renewal American city
centers were gutted, communities and neighborhoods were eradicated,
and the metropolitan fabric was transformed into an unrecognizable maze
of construction sites and redevelopment, little of which would become
public housing.[100]

The destructive force and fear associated with the weapons of the military enemy in the Cold War were now redeployed against domestic targets. A booklet published in 1947 to chronicle the relocation of tenants
evicted during the construction of the Stuyvesant Town housing project
captioned its photograph of a rubble-strewn lot with the reassurance "Not
an atom bomb, just the result of tearing down certain buildings which had
become unsafe, before the general demolition in the fall."[101] Writing that
same year of Hiroshima, Georges Bataille presciently discerned this new
civilizational logic of the Cold War world:

In truth, if ones singles out Hiroshima for lamentation, it is because
one does not dare to look misfortune in the face . . . As a consequence
one takes refuge in the world of activity, dominated by the principles
of a virile reason. But instead of responding to the concern about an
impossible horror, one serves the end of a narrow system . . . Anxiety

and concern, which are the foundations of civilization, always necessi-
tate certain patterns of activity . . . Each civilized unit . . . proclaims
the primacy of its undertakings—by which it means to secure the future—over all considerations of feelings . . . It is strange that concern
for the future at the level of the State immediately diminishes the individual's security and chances of survival . . . The need to make life
secure wins out over the need to live.[102]

The virile mastery described by Bataille characterizes the prowess identified by many critics as the most salient feature of the male investigative
figure central to the film noir cycle.[103] Viewed in this light, the activities of
these investigators and agents of the law can easily be related to a generalized need for security and respite from cultural anxiety. Yet it is no less
striking to reflect upon the literal dissolution of Ryker's body at the conclusion of *City of Fear*, its decomposition an equally powerful allegory of
the dissolution of urban form and of the unraveling of a postwar concept
of masculinity.

Yet the films noir of centrifugal space never entirely abandon the metropolis; they continue to provide insights into the impact of dispersal
upon citydwellers, ever faithful to the project of registering lived spatial
experience. Consider in this context the following review of *City of Fear*,
published in a November 1959 issue of *Variety*: "If watching passing automobiles constitutes entertainment, free drama festivals are available to all
of us every day on any traffic island on any freeway. This can be seen on innumerable TV shows at almost any hour. Yet this is just about the only bait
City of Fear offers to lure the public into the theater."[104]

At a moment when film noir's representation of the centripetal city had
already run its course, the *Variety* reviewer seemed to yearn for the shadowy spaces of an older cinematic "city of fear" no longer evident, if even
possible. In a world threatened by nuclear weapons, darkness no longer
posed the most frightening prospect. Nostalgia for the centered metropolis would largely disappear from the neo-noir cinema of the 1960s in films
such as *Point Blank* (John Boorman, 1967) but would return with a vengeance in the incipient postmodernism of the 1970s of *Chinatown* (Roman
Polanski, 1974). Along with an older image of the Hollywood cinema, the

revival of neo-noir commencing in the 1970s and continuing with vigor into the present betrays a no less palpable longing for an older image of the metropolis whose existence it simultaneously mourns and resurrects.

In his autobiography Lerner observed that "documentaries, at least in the form I produced them, had no chances [sic] anymore. Many things changed with the coming of television. Especially, it was clear to me, that in the changed political climate of the postwar period the documentary had lost its power, which it possessed before. It could not be used to try new ideas and techniques."[105] Yet for the better part of the 1950s, the centrifugal film noir could still be used to explore new modalities of cinema, and Lerner's film is best viewed as an ambitious, if ultimately unsuccessful, attempt to document public space in 1959 Los Angeles. For a filmmaker whose first assignment was to record the 1931 May Day Rally in New York's Union Square, this change of spatial venue may well have presented a daunting challenge. If *City of Fear* provides no solution to the conundrum of cultural politics in an age of urban dispersal and density, especially in a city such as Los Angeles, which is both dispersed *and* dense, it does function as a striking allegory of the disappearance of the city, the urban subject, and the semidocumentary impulse in the age of nuclear war, urban sprawl, and electronic communication.

"People had always expected," Spencer Weart notes, "that atomic bombs would signal the apocalypse, and that traditionally included the social order."[106] *City of Fear* depicts Los Angeles surviving the threat of annihilation, and in so doing emphasizes the uncertain status of the city's social order. Repeatedly returning to the establishing shot of the twinkling lights of the Los Angeles basin, the film juxtaposes this wishful image of collectivity with impending catastrophe, even as it appears to acknowledge the insufficiency of such urban representations, or the possibility of creating new synoptic imagery to encompass the changed realities of the metropolis.

In his knowing analysis of the Los Angeles basin, a topos he dubbed "the great plains of Id," Reyner Banham wrote: "In addition the great size and lack of distinction of the area covered by this prospect make it the area where Los Angeles is least distinctively itself. One of the reasons why the great Plains of Id are so daunting is that this is where Los Angeles is most like other cities: Anywheresville/Nowheresville."[107] Filmed from above the metropolis, Lerner's radiant image of a dispersed Los Angeles—a view that might well be that of Anywheresville or Nowheresville—forms an apposite epitaph for the film noir cycle and its imbrication with the spaces of late modernity. Lacking nostalgia, *City of Fear* signals the end of one form of urban culture and embraces the dispersed city with an eerie hopefulness, signaled by the quiet strains of Jerry Goldsmith's musical score. Its optimism contrasts with the melancholy tenor of many films noir but might profitably be emulated when contemplating the challenges posed by inhabiting the spaces—real and virtual—of the twenty-first century.

NOTES

INTRODUCTION

1. A search of the University Microfilms International (UMI) dissertation abstracts proves telling in this regard. From the nineteenth century through 1982, a mere six doctoral dissertations included the term *film noir* in their abstracts. For the period from 1983 through 1998, the number increased to forty-six. For a discussion of film noir and postmodernism, see James Naremore, *More than Night: Film Noir in Its Contexts* (Berkeley: University of California Press, 1998), 10.

2. Ernst Bloch reworks the idea of uneven development formulated by Karl Marx as the basis for his notion of the *nichtgleichzeitig* in his book *Heritage of Our Times* (1935), trans. Neville Plaice and Stephen Plaice (Berkeley: University of California Press, 1991). There he writes: "The *objectively* non-contemporaneous [*nichtgleichzeitig*] element is that which is distant from and alien to the present; it thus embraces *declining remnants* and above all an *incomplete past* which is not yet 'sublated' in capitalist terms"; 108, translation modified. Throughout this study I translate *nichtgleichzeitig* as "nonsynchronous," although it is frequently rendered as "non-contemporaneous" (in the English translation of Bloch's book) or as "non-simultaneous." For discussions of this notion see Anson Rabinbach, "Unclaimed Heritage: Ernst Bloch's *Heritage of Our Times* and the Theory of Fascism," *New German Critique* 11 (spring 1977): 5–21; and Tony Phelan, "Ernst Bloch's 'Golden Twenties': *Erbschaft dieser Zeit* and the Problem of Cultural History," in *Culture and Society in the Weimar Republic*, ed. Keith Bullivant (Manchester and Totowa: Manchester University Press and Rowman and Littlefield, 1977), 94–121.

3. Bloch, *Heritage of Our Times*, 62.

4. On the relation of film noir to the cinema of Weimar Germany see Edward Dimendberg, "Down These Seen Streets a Man Must Go: Siegfried Kracauer,

'Hollywood's Terror Films,' and the Spatiality of Film Noir," *New German Critique* 89 (spring/summer 2003): 113–144.

5. Bloch, *Heritage of Our Times*, 193.

6. For this last description see "Inside Hollywood," *Daily Variety*, March 30, 1945, 2, in which the author notes that "the psychological chiller-diller is surpassing the cops and robbers detective story picture as a box office puller."

7. See Naremore, *More than Night*, esp. 9–39, for an account of this received history.

8. Nino Frank, "The Crime Adventure Story: A New Kind of Detective Film," trans. R. Barton Palmer, in *Perspectives on Film Noir*, ed. Palmer (New York: G. K. Hall, 1996), 23. This text was originally published as "Un nouveau genre 'policier' l'aventure criminelle," *L'Ecran Français* 61 (August 28, 1946): 8–9, 14. Contemporaneously with Frank's essay, Siegfried Kracauer published a text that identified many of the same features in what he termed "Hollywood's terror films." See Siegfried Kracauer, "Hollywood's Terror Films: Do They Reflect a State of Mind?" *Commentary* 2 (August 1946): 132–136. For a discussion of it see Dimendberg, "Down These Seen Streets."

9. Frank, "The Crime Adventure Story," 23.

10. The classic texts presenting pre–World War I French vitalist understandings of temporality are Henri Bergson, *Time and Free Will* (1889), trans. F. L. Pogson (London: George Allen and Unwin, 1919); idem, *Creative Evolution* (1907), trans. Arthur Mitchell (New York: Henry Holt, 1911). A recent critical study of Bergson is Gilles Deleuze, *Bergsonism*, trans. Hugh Tomlinson and Barbara Habberjam (New York: Zone Books, 1988). Discussions of the cultural resonances and receptions of Bergson's work are found in Leszek Kolakowski, *Henri Bergson* (New York: Oxford University Press, 1985); and Mark Antliffe, *Inventing Bergson* (Princeton: Princeton University Press, 1992). Later receptions of Bergson's ideas include Eugène Minkowski, *Lived Time* (1933), trans. and ed. Nancy Metzel (Evanston: Northwestern University Press, 1970). Jean-Paul Sartre's philosophy may well have influenced the notion of temporality at work in Frank's essay. See Jean-Paul Sartre, *Being and Nothingness: An Essay on Phenomenological Ontology* (1943), trans. Hazel Barnes (New York: Philosophical Library, 1956). Charles O'Brien has persuasively demonstrated the circulation of the term *film noir* as a pejorative epithet in French film culture of the 1930s. See his "Film Noir in France: Before the Liberation," *Iris*, no. 21 (spring 1996): 7–21. The shift away from denunciations of certain late 1930s French films for being "too noir" toward the later valorization of these same qualities by Frank in his postwar analyses of American cinema underscores the significance of film noir as a barometer of postwar cultural transformations.

11. Frank was himself a knowledgeable commentator on the European avant-garde whose interest in modernism preceded his writing on film noir by two decades. See his "Italien per Auto," *Der Querschnitt* 4 (1924): 310–316.

12. See Henri Lefebvre, *The Production of Space*, trans. Donald Nicholson-Smith (Cambridge, Mass.: Basil Blackwell, 1991).

13. For two recent examples see Alain Silver and James Ursini, eds., *Film Noir*

Reader 2 (New York: Limelight, 1999); and Foster Hirsch, *Detours and Lost High-ways: A Map of Neo-Noir* (New York: Limelight, 1999).

14. The most judicious and scholarly overview of film noir published to date is Naremore, *More than Night*. The first and most influential book in French remains Raymond Borde and Etienne Chaumeton, *Panorama du film noir américain* (Paris: Editions de Minuit, 1955), translated by Paul Hammond as *A Panorama of American Film Noir, 1941–1953* (San Francisco: City Lights, 2002). An influential collection of essays is contained in E. Anne Kaplan, ed., *Women in Film Noir*, 2d ed. (Bloomington: Indiana University Press, 1999). Recent interpretations are found in Joan Copjec, ed., *Shades of Noir: A Reader* (London: Verso, 1993). A standard overview of the film cycle is Foster Hirsch, *Film Noir: The Dark Side of the Screen* (New York: Da Capo, 1981). Two helpful reference volumes are Alain Silver and Elizabeth Ward, eds., *Film Noir: An Encyclopedic Reference to the American Style* (Woodstock, Vt.: Overlook Press, 1979); and Spencer Selby, *Dark City: The Film Noir* (Jefferson, N.C.: McFarland, 1984). The former contains detailed film descriptions and credits, the latter a thorough filmography. A recent work that focuses on film noir narrative and includes an extensive bibliography of writing published in the 1980s is J. P. Telotte, *Voices in the Dark: The Narrative Patterns of Film Noir* (Urbana: University of Illinois Press, 1989). Other recent studies include Frank Krutnik, *In a Lonely Street: Film Noir, Genre, Masculinity* (London: Routledge, 1991); and R. Barton Palmer, *Hollywood's Dark Cinema: The American Film Noir* (New York: Twayne, 1994). The relation of film noir to other modes of cultural representation is treated in Paula Rabinowitz, *Black & White and Noir: America's Pulp Modernism* (New York: Columbia University Press, 2002). Two doctoral dissertations, Robert Gerald Porfirio, "The Dark Age of American Film: A Study of the American *Film Noir* (1940–1960)," 2 vols. (Ph.D. diss., Yale University, 1979); and Paul Steven Arthur, "Shadows on the Mirror: Film Noir and Cold War America (1945–1957)" (Ph.D. diss., New York University, 1985), are also useful.

15. Kevin Lynch, *The Image of the City* (Cambridge, Mass.: MIT Press, 1961).

16. For a discussion of this theme see Paul Arthur, "No Place like Home: City versus Suburb in Film Noir," *Aura* 6 (1998): 32–37.

17. By ideology, I understand what Michael Leja calls "an implicit structure of belief, assumption, and disposition—an array of basic propositions and attitudes about reality, self, and society embedded in representation and discourse and seemingly obviously true and natural. If not always beyond challenge or question, these propositions are incessantly restated, resecured, and naturalized; they are woven into the fabric of experience by virtue of their structuring all representation, including perception, analysis, argument, interpretation, and explanation"; Michael Leja, *Reframing Abstract Expressionism: Subjectivity and Painting in the 1940s* (New Haven: Yale University Press, 1993), 6.

18. Here the work of Pierre Macherey has been important to my thinking. See his *A Theory of Literary Production*, trans. Geoffrey Wall (London: Routledge and Kegan Paul, 1978).

19. Besides Lefebvre's *The Production of Space*, other works in this tradition

include David Harvey, *Consciousness and the Urban Experience* (Baltimore: Johns Hopkins University Press, 1985); idem, *The Condition of Postmodernity* (Cambridge, Mass.: Basil Blackwell, 1989); Edward Soja, *Postmodern Geographies: The Reassertion of Space in Critical Social Theory* (London: Verso, 1989); Michael Dear, *The Postmodern Urban Condition* (Oxford: Basil Blackwell, 2000); and Michael J. Dear and Steven Flusty, eds., *The Spaces of Postmodernity: Readings in Human Geography* (Oxford: Basil Blackwell, 2002).

20. For a helpful introduction to these discussions see Lary May, ed., *Recasting America: Culture and Politics in the Age of Cold War* (Chicago: University of Chicago Press, 1989).

21. See Henry Churchill, "What Shall We Do with Our Cities?" *Journal of the American Institute of Architects*, August 1945, 62–65, for an account of the "physical decay" and "economic constipation" plaguing the postwar American metropolis.

22. M. Christine Boyer, "Mobility and Modernism in the American City," *Center* 5 (1989): 102.

23. For a discussion of this dynamic in the German context see Brian Ladd, *The Ghosts of Berlin: Confronting German History in the Urban Landscape* (Chicago: University of Chicago Press, 1997).

24. The analysis of the city in Michel Cieutat, "La ville dans le film policier américain," *Positif*, nos. 171–172 (1975): 26–38, fits this description. More historical investigations are found in David Reid and Jayne L. Walker, "Strange Pursuit: Cornell Woolrich and the Abandoned City of the Forties," in Copjec, *Shades of Noir;* and Paul Arthur, "Murder's Tongue: Identity, Death and the City in Film Noir," in *Violence and the American Cinema*, ed. J. David Slocum (New York: Routledge, 2001), 153–175. Apart from the inclusion of a book by Lewis Mumford in its bibliography, Nicholas Christopher's deceptively titled *Somewhere in the Night: Film Noir and the American City* (New York: Free Press, 1997) rarely addresses the realms of urban or spatial history.

25. For a discussion of this point see Fredric Jameson, "Ideology, Narrative Analysis, and Popular Culture," *Theory and Society* 4 (1977): 546–547. My use of the concepts of content and form adopts Jameson's notion of the "ideology of form," a transposition of the Marxist notion of uneven development to the cultural text. See his *The Political Unconscious: The Narrative as Socially Symbolic Act* (Ithaca: Cornell University Press, 1981), esp. 99–148.

26. Although films noir, or films recognizably similar to them, were produced in other countries, including France, Italy, and Mexico during the 1940s and 1950s, I limit my discussion in this book to those made in the United States.

27. Warren Susman with the assistance of Edward Griffin, "Did Success Spoil the United States? Dual Representations in Postwar America," in May, *Recasting America*, 19–37.

28. See Georges Bataille, *The Accursed Share: An Essay on General Economy*, trans. Robert Hurley (New York: Zone Books, 1988).

29. Richard Terdiman, *Present Past: Modernity and the Memory Crisis* (Ithaca: Cornell University Press, 1993), 5, 127.

30. Maurice Halbwachs, "The Social Frameworks of Memory," in *On Collective*

Memory, ed. and trans. Lewis A. Coser (Chicago: University of Chicago Press, 1992), 40.

31. Maurice Halbwachs, *The Collective Memory*, trans. Francis J. Ditter and Vida Yazdi Ditter (New York: Harper and Row, 1980), translation modified in Terdiman, *Present Past*, 32.

32. Terdiman, *Present Past*, 136–137.

33. Siegfried Kracauer, *History: The Last Things before the Last* (New York: Oxford University Press, 1969), 5.

34. On the problem of the textuality of film see John Mowitt, *Text: The Genealogy of an Interdisciplinary Object* (Durham, N.C.: Duke University Press, 1992), esp. 141–176.

35. Naremore, *More than Night*, 10.

36. On this point see Catherine Gallagher and Stephen Greenblatt, *Practicing New Historicism* (Chicago: University of Chicago Press, 2000).

37. Two notable exceptions are Dana Polan, *Power and Paranoia: History, Narrative, and the American Cinema, 1940–1950* (New York: Columbia University Press, 1986); and Anton Kaes, *M* (London: British Film Institute, 2000).

38. For an articulation of this position see Paul Kerr, "Out of What Past? Notes on the B Film Noir," *Screen Education* 32–33 (autumn–winter 1979–80): 47. A useful critique of the alleged nonconformist character of film noir is found in David Bordwell, Kristin Thompson, and Janet Staiger, *The Classical Hollywood Cinema: Film Style and Mode of Production to 1960* (New York: Columbia University Press, 1985), 74–77.

39. Naremore notes that by 1954 half of the films produced in Hollywood were filmed in color; *More than Night*, 186.

40. For an account of some of these technical changes see Ezra Goodman, "Post-War Motion Pictures," *American Cinematographer* 26 (May 1945): 160, 176.

41. For an analysis of film noir as harmless entertainment that provided postwar spectators with innocuous thrills see Geoffrey O'Brien, "The Return of Film Noir," *New York Review of Books*, August 15, 1991, 45–48. That film viewers and reviewers often reacted vociferously to specific films can be ascertained through a reading of film criticism contemporaneous with the film noir cycle.

42. David Bordwell, *Making Meaning: Inference and Rhetoric in the Interpretation of Cinema* (Cambridge, Mass.: Harvard University Press, 1989).

43. As Tom Gunning has demonstrated, discourses of urban detection also pervade early cinema. See his "Tracing the Individual Body: Photography, Detectives, and Early Cinema," in *Cinema and the Invention of Modern Life*, ed. Leo Charney and Vanessa Schwartz (Berkeley: University of California Press, 1995), 15–45.

44. See Karlheinz Daniels, "Expressionismus und Technik," in *Technik in der Literatur*, ed. Harro Segerberg (Frankfurt am Main: Suhrkamp, 1987), 351–386.

45. For analyses of earlier criticisms of the American city see Morton White and Lucia White, *The Intellectual versus the City* (New York: New American Library, 1962); and Eugene Arden, "The Evil City in American Fiction," *New York History* 35 (July 1954): 259–279.

46. The late film director Abraham Polonsky admitted to me that he provided the cinematographer on *Force of Evil* with a book of reproductions of paintings by Edward Hopper as an example of the visual mood he was seeking in the film; personal conversation, Beverly Hills, Calif., September 17, 1995.

47. Edward Hopper, interview by John Morse, *Art in America* 48 (1960): 60, quoted in Gail Levin, *Edward Hopper: An Intimate Biography* (New York: Alfred A. Knopf, 1995), 388. A palpably different and far more dynamic entry into the city by train appears in the opening sequence of Walther Ruttmann's 1927 film, *Berlin: Symphony of a Great City.*

48. John Alton, *Painting with Light* (New York: Macmillan, 1949), 57.

49. Hans Blumenfeld, "The Urban Pattern" (1964), in *The Modern Metropolis: Its Origins, Growth, Characteristics, and Planning*, ed. Paul D. Spreiregen (Cambridge, Mass.: MIT Press, 1967), 50.

50. Lewis Mumford, "Prefabricated Blight" (1948), in *From the Ground Up* (San Diego: Harcourt Brace Jovanovich, n.d), 109.

51. Miriam Bratu Hansen, "Introduction," in Siegfried Kracauer, *Theory of Film: The Redemption of Physical Reality* (1960; reprint, Princeton: Princeton University Press, 1997), xxxiii.

52. Kracauer, *Theory of Film*, 170.

53. Hansen, "Introduction," xxxii.

54. Lefebvre, *The Production of Space*, 332.

55. See Mike Davis, *City of Quartz: Excavating the Future in Los Angeles* (London: Verso, 1990), esp. 17–46.

56. See Fredric Jameson, *Postmodernism, or the Cultural Logic of Late Capitalism* (Durham, N.C.: Duke University Press, 1991), 287.

1. NAKED CITIES

1. For the filmmaker's account of this scene and the film in which it figures see Samuel Fuller with Christa Lang Fuller and Jerome Henry Rudes, *A Third Face: My Tale of Writing, Fighting, and Filmmaking* (New York: Alfred A. Knopf, 2002), 292–308.

2. Georg Simmel, "The Metropolis and Mental Life," trans. Hans Gerth, and idem, "Sociology of the Senses," trans. Mark Ritter and David Frisby, in *Simmel on Culture*, ed. David Frisby and Mike Featherstone (London: Sage, 1997), 174–185, 109–120. For a contemporaneous American discussion of the experience of being "ignored" by the urban crowd see O. Henry, "The Making of a New Yorker," in *The Complete Works of O. Henry*, 2 vols. (Garden City, N.Y.: Doubleday, 1953), 2: 1411–15.

3. See Georg Simmel, "The Stranger," in *On Individuality and Social Forms: Selected Writings*, ed. Donald Levine (Chicago: University of Chicago Press, 1971). For further discussions of the stranger see Margaret Mary Wood, *The Stranger: A Study in Social Relationships* (New York: Columbia University Press, 1934); Maurice Natanson, *Anonymity: A Study in the Philosophy of Alfred Schutz* (Bloomington: Indiana University Press, 1986), esp. 23–24; and Richard Sennett, "The Foreigner," in

Body Building: Essays on the Changing Relation of Body and Architecture, ed. George Dodds and Robert Tavernor (Cambridge, Mass.: MIT Press, 2002).

4. Walter Benjamin, "The Paris of the Second Empire in Baudelaire," in *Charles Baudelaire: A Lyric Poet in the Era of High Capitalism*, trans. Harry Zohn (London: Verso, 1973), 40.

5. For an insightful discussion of the *physiologie* see Richard Sieburth, "Same Difference: The French *Physiologies*, 1840–1842," in *Notebooks in Cultural Analysis* *1*, ed. Norman F. Cantor and Nathalia King (Durham, N.C.: Duke University Press, 1984), 163–200. The relation between the flaneur and the detective is explored by Walter Benjamin throughout *The Arcades Project*, trans. Howard Eiland and Kevin McLaughlin (Cambridge, Mass.: Belknap Press of Harvard University Press, 1999), esp. 442. See also David Frisby, "The City Detected: Representations and Realities of Detection," in *Cityscapes of Modernity* (Cambridge: Polity, 2001), 52–99.

6. See Anthony Vidler, "The Scenes of the Street," esp. 68–76, in *On Streets*, ed. Stanford Anderson (Cambridge, Mass.: MIT Press, 1986), 29–112, for a discussion of corporeal metaphors in nineteenth-century French urbanism. See also Richard Sennett, *Flesh and Stone: The Body and the City in Western Civilization* (New York: W. W. Norton, 1994), esp. 255–316.

7. David Marshall, *Grand Central* (London and New York: Whittlesey House/McGraw Hill, 1946), 126–127.

8. According to one account, since the 1880s the police have enforced a visual ban on recognized criminals entering the Fulton Street jewelry and financial district in Manhattan with instructions to "arrest on sight any known criminal who ventured south of Fulton Street." See "Criminals Keep Out," in Federal Writers' Project of the Works Progress Administration, *Almanac for New Yorkers 1939* (New York: Modern Age Books, 1938), 126.

9. Describing the "speaking portrait" produced by application of Bertillon's technique of description, Edmond Bayle wrote: "even to-day members of the Police Force who are taught this method can, without any photograph, pick out the individual so described from passers-by in the street." Bayle was a disciple of Bertillon and published his essay "The Scientific Detective" in the memoir by Paris police chief Alfred Morain, *The Underworld of Paris: Secrets of Sûreté* (New York: E. P. Dutton, 1931), 14.

10. See Foster Hirsch, *Film Noir: The Dark Side of the Screen* (New York: Da Capo, 1981), 79.

11. Walter Benjamin, "Paris of Second Empire in Baudelaire," 43.

12. See Carlo Ginzburg, "Morelli, Freud and Sherlocke Holmes: Clues and Scientific Method," trans. Anna Davin, *History Workshop* 9 (spring 1980): 5–36, for a discussion of the clue as trace in nineteenth-century criminological discourses.

13. See Jeremy Bentham, *The Panopticon and Other Prison Writings: Wo Es War*, ed. Miran Bozovic (London: Verso, 1995); Cesare Lombroso, *Criminal Man* (1876) (New York: G. P. Putnam and Sons, 1911); Alphonse Bertillon, *Signaletic Instructions: Including the Theory and Practice of Anthropometrical Identification* (Chicago: Werner, 1896); Michel Foucault, *Discipline and Punish: The Birth of the Prison*, trans.

Alan Sheridan (New York: Pantheon, 1977), esp. 195–228; John F. Kasson, *Rudeness and Civility: Manners in Nineteenth-Century Urban America* (New York: Hill and Wang, 1990), esp. 80–111; and Marie Christine Leps, *Apprehending the Criminal: The Production of Deviance in Nineteenth-Century Discourse* (Durham, N.C.: Duke University Press, 1992). On the history of surveillance see the essays collected in Thomas Levin, Ursula Frohne, and Peter Weibel, eds., *CTRL [SPACE]: Rhetorics of Surveillance from Bentham to Big Brother* (Karlsruhe and Cambridge, Mass.: Center for Art and Media/MIT Press, 2002).

14. An important exception is M. Christine Boyer, *Dreaming the Rational City: The Myth of American City Planning* (Cambridge, Mass.: MIT Press, 1983). See especially her discussion of the surveillance of nineteenth-century American cities on 31–32.

15. Christoph Asendorf, *Ströme und Strahlen: Das langsame Verschwinden der Materie um 1900* (Gießen: Anabas, 1989), 32.

16. The German word *Rasterung* employed by Asendorf is based on *Raster*, which can also mean grid. It commonly refers to the pattern of lines and dots, the screen, in offset photographic reproduction processes or a television image.

17. See the spatial dissection of a crime scene described by Edmond Bayle in "The Scientific Detective," in Alfred Morain, *The Underworld of Paris: Secrets of Sûreté* (New York: E. P. Dutton, 1931), 13–25. One thinks here as well of Edgar Allan Poe's "The Purloined Letter" (1845) and its precise segmentation of space, as well as Jacques Lacan's analysis of it in "Seminar on 'The Purloined Letter,'" trans. Jeffrey Mehlman, in *The Poetics of Murder*, ed. Glenn W. Most and William W. Stowe (San Diego: Harcourt Brace Jovanovich, 1983), 21–54.

18. See Marta Braun, *Picturing Time: The Work of Etienne-Jules Marey (1830–1904)* (Chicago: University of Chicago Press, 1992). On the temporal segmentation of cinema see Mary Ann Doane, *The Emergence of Cinematic Time: Modernity, Contingency, the Archive* (Cambridge, Mass.: Harvard University Press, 2002).

19. On this history see Simon A. Cole, *Suspect Identities: A History of Fingerprinting and Criminal Identification* (Cambridge, Mass.: Harvard University Press, 2001).

20. Allan Sekula, "The Body and the Archive," *October* 39 (winter 1986): 7. This essay remains among the most perceptive studies of nineteenth-century discourses of criminology and surveillance.

21. Entry on *The Street with No Name*, in *American Film Institute Catalog of Motion Pictures Produced in the United States Feature Films, 1941–1950*, vol. 2 (Berkeley: University of California Press, 1999), 2363. For a discussion of the changes in film technology during the 1940s, especially new cameras and lighting equipment that facilitated location cinematography, see Barry Salt, *Film Style and Technology: History and Analysis*, 2d ed. (London: Starword, 1992), 227–240. For an assessment by a witness to these transformations see Ezra Goodman, "Postwar Motion Pictures," *American Cinematographer* 26 (May 1945): 160, 176.

22. Such an "urban time budget" would later be investigated by postwar planners. See Richard L. Meier, *A Communications Theory of Urban Growth* (Cambridge, Mass.: Joint Center for Urban Studies of the Massachusetts Institute of Technology and Harvard University/MIT Press, 1962), esp. 45–59.

23. Robert Fogelson notes that with the exception of the Third Avenue line demolished at the end of the 1940s, all of New York's elevated railways had been torn down a decade earlier. See Robert Fogelson, *Downtown: Its Rise and Fall, 1880–1950* (New Haven: Yale University Press, 2001), 277–278.

24. Jean-Paul Sartre, "Individualism and Conformism in the United States," in *Literary and Philosophical Essays*, trans. Annette Michelson (New York: Collier, 1955), 109.

25. For an insightful analysis of the role of sound in this sequence see Lutz Koepnick, *The Dark Mirror: German Cinema between Hitler and Hollywood* (Berkeley: University of California Press, 2002), 168–172.

26. William Irish [Cornell Woolrich], *Phantom Lady* (New York: P. F. Collier and Son, 1942), 19.

27. Ibid., 23.

28. Relevant cinematic analogues are *Laura* (Otto Preminger, 1944) and *The Woman in the Window* (Fritz Lang, 1944).

29. Irish [Woolrich], *Phantom Lady*, 103. One might note in this connection Simmel's characterization in "The Metropolis and Mental Life" of the urbanite as likely to perceive everything in a gray tone because of the prevalence of the money economy.

30. Ibid., 68, 70, 117.

31. For representative examples see "10 Minutes of War in the Raw," *Variety*, June 14, 1944, 1; "400 Cameras Shoot Invasion," ibid., July 5, 1944, 1; and "Camera Rated as One of Four Big War Weapons," ibid., December 8, 1944, 10.

32. "On Target," *Variety*, January 14, 1944, 45.

33. Paul Virilio, *War and Cinema: The Logistics of Perception*, trans. Patrick Camiller (London: Verso, 1989), 20. This metaphor is suggested by another ad in the Kodak series in which a motion picture cameraman is characterized as "equally adept with a gun."

34. "You Press the Button, It Does the Rest," *Variety*, April 10, 1944, 17. This advertising slogan actually dates from 1888. For its history see Douglas Collins, *The Story of Kodak* (New York: Harry N. Abrams, 1990), 46.

35. Kodak advertisement, "Movies . . . vital records of war," *Daily Variety*, July 28, 1944, 11.

36. Arthur L. Mayer, "Fact into Film," *Public Opinion Quarterly* 8 (summer 1944): 206. A copy of this article is found in the Irving Lerner Papers, UCLA Arts Library Special Collections.

37. "Ten Days after the Allies launched their June, 1944 invasion of France, troops in Normandy were whistling appreciatively at Rita Hayworth in *Cover Girl*. Soldiers who led our advance into Germany saw a movie three days later on German soil. Shortly after General MacArthur's fighters went ashore on Leyte, in the Philippines, they were watching a double-feature program fresh from Hollywood"; *Movie Lot to Beach Head: The Motion Picture Goes to War and Prepares for the Future by the Editors of Look* (Garden City, N.Y.: Doubleday, Doran, 1945), 104.

38. Kodak advertisement, "Movies tonight . . . and when the lights go down, morale goes up," *Daily Variety*, November 17, 1944, 9.

39. "Servicemen prefer musicals, comedies, mysteries, romantic dramas, docu-

mentaries, newsreels showing authentic war action. Best of all are movies whose components—street scenes, normal people on the streets, women who look like mothers, wives, sweethearts—bring them near home"; *Movie Lot to Beach Head,* 105.

40. On the spatial preconditions of nostalgia and its relation to urbanization see Jean Starobinski, "The Idea of Nostalgia," *Diogenes* 54 (summer 1966): 81–103.

41. *Movie Lot to Beach Head,* 36, 41, 54–55.

42. "Shocking sight of German atrocities as depicted in current issues of newsreels has led Warner Pacific Coast Theaters to prepare a special recording warning patrons of what is coming up. Record states that scenes are ghastly and horrifying and suggests that if there are any patrons who wish to retire to the lounge or lobby they will be notified when the newsreel is over. So far theaters report few walkouts"; "Hollywood Inside," *Variety,* May 8, 1945, 4.

43. *From Movie Lot to Beach Head,* 53.

44. Mayer, "Fact into Film," 225, 223, 217, 222, 278.

45. Alfred Schutz, "The Homecomer," in *Collected Papers II: Studies in Social Theory,* ed. Arvid Brodersen (The Hague: Martinus Nijhoff, 1964), 106–119, esp. 116.

46. Jim Bishop, *The Mark Hellinger Story: A Biography of Broadway and Hollywood* (New York: Appleton-Century-Crofts, 1952), 303.

47. See Kevin Moore, "Eyes in the Sky: Alex S. MacLean and the Tradition of Aerial Imagery," *Cite* 48 (summer 2000): 38. The most trenchant discussion of aerial photography remains Allan Sekula, "The Instrumental Image: Steichen at War," *Artforum* 14 (December 1975): 26–35.

48. See Beaumont Newhall, *Airborne Camera: The World from the Air and Outer Space* (New York: Hastings House and George Eastman House, 1969), 43–46. See also Grover Heiman, *Aerial Photography: The Story of Aerial Mapping and Reconnaissance* (New York: Macmillan, 1972); and Peter Bacon Hales, *Silver Cities: The Photography of American Urbanization, 1839–1915* (Philadelphia: Temple University Press, 1984). On the significance of bird's-eye views of the city see Kasson, *Rudeness and Civility,* esp. 70–80.

49. E. B. White, *This Is New York* (New York: Harper and Brothers, 1949), 50–51.

50. Ibid., 53.

51. See Andreas Feininger, *New York in the Forties* (New York: Dover, 1978); idem, *The Face of New York* (New York: Crown, 1954); idem, *Chicago: Photographs by Arthur Haug. Text by Robert Cromie* (Chicago: Ziff Davis, 1948).

52. See Bonnie Yochelson, *Berenice Abbott: Changing New York: The Complete WPA Project* (New York: New Press/Museum of the City of New York, 1997).

53. Consider the following account from *Variety,* August 30, 1945, 10, titled "Air Photos Did Sherlock Job on Enemy, Army Says": "Washington, August 29.— Use of aerial photographs to determine the shape, height, and even the construction materials of enemy ground installations was described to the Visual War Workers yesterday by Major Lewis J. Stevens of the Plans and Policies Staff of the Air Corps Staff intelligence.

"By keeping an accurate record of the height of the plane, distance from the objective and other data on a succession of shots from different points this information was learned from photographs, said the major.

"Seven thousand interpretive reports were compiled from aerial reconnaissance photographs dealing with such assorted material as shipping activity, population density, transportation and communications layouts as well as troop movements and installations.

"Many things show up in air films which would not otherwise be observed, said Stevens, explaining that the lines of an airport drainage system are clearly visible in an aerial photograph even though the field is so well camouflaged that no other evidence is to be found. Repair or construction work or any earth movements are more plainly visible on photographs than by any other means, Stevens said."

54. *Focusing on Facts: Fairchild Covers the World*, 19 (n.d.), brochure in Fairchild Aerial Photography Collection, Whittier College, Whittier, California. For a recent history of Fairchild see Thomas J. Campanella, *Cities from the Sky: An Aerial Portrait of America* (New York: Princeton Architectural Press, 2001). More general postwar discussions of the relevance of aerial photography to urban planning can be found in Melville Campbell Branch, *Aerial Photography in Urban Planning and Research* (Cambridge, Mass.: Harvard University Press, 1948); and René A. Huybens, *La photographie aérienne et l'urbanisme* (Linkebeek: A. Pinkers, 1955). It is not insignificant that by the end of the 1940s the literature on aerial photography no longer emphasizes forestry applications but comes to encompass census data collection. See Norman Carls, *How to Read Aerial Photographs for Census Work* (Washington, D.C.: U.S. Government Printing Office, 1947).

55. See Mike Davis, *City of Quartz: Excavating the Future in Los Angeles* (New York: Verso, 1990); and Steve Herbert, *Policing Space: Territoriality and the Los Angeles Police Department* (Minneapolis: University of Minnesota Press, 1997).

56. For examples of these less politically charged appreciations of aerial views of New York see H. I. Brock and J. W. Golinkin, *New York Is like This* (New York: Dodd, Mead, 1929), 1–13; and the opening sequence of the film *The Saint in New York* (Ben Holmes, 1938).

57. See Michel Foucault, "Space, Knowledge, and Power," trans. Christian Hubert, in *The Foucault Reader*, ed. Paul Rabinow (New York: Pantheon, 1984), 239–257; and Paul Virilio, *The Aesthetics of Disappearance*, trans. Philip Beitchman (New York: Semiotext(e), 1991).

58. See Friedrich Kittler, *Gramophone, Film, Typewriter*, trans. Geoffrey Winthrop-Young and Michael Wutz (Stanford: Stanford University Press, 1999), for an essentialist argument concerning the ontology of cinema and militarization.

59. I am indebted to the thoughtful treatment of Weegee's New York photographs by Ellen Handy, "Picturing New York, the Naked City: Weegee and Urban Photography," in *Weegee's World*, ed. Miles Barth (Boston: Little, Brown, and International Center for Photography, 1997), 148–159. Other recent treatments of this work include Miles Orvell, "Weegee's Voyeurism and the Mastery of Urban Disorder," in *After the Machine: Visual Arts and the Erasing of Cultural Boundaries*

(Jackson: University of Mississippi Press, 1995), 71–96; Carol Squiers, "'And So the Moving Trigger Finger Writes': Dead Gangsters and New York Tabloids in the 1930s," in *Police Pictures: The Photograph as Art* (San Francisco: San Francisco Museum of Modern Art/Chronicle Books, 1997), 41–49; and William Hannigan, *New York Noir: Crime Photos from the Daily News Archive* (New York: Rizzoli, 1999).

60. A comprehensive cultural biography of Weegee has yet to be written. My biographical chronology comes from Miles Barth, "Weegee's World," in *Weegee's World*, 11–35.

61. Although Weegee made eight short films, there is no evidence for the impact of his films or photography upon the early development of the film noir cycle. Nor, *contra* the argument of Alain Bergala in "Weegee and Film Noir," in Barth, *Weegee's World*, 69–77, do I find any basis for claiming that his work shares the allegedly "Central-European derived aesthetic" of 1940s film noir. For a list of Weegee's films and involvement with cinema (including his role as a consultant on Stanley Kubrick's *Dr. Strangelove*) see the filmography in Barth, *Weegee's World*, 255.

62. Russell Maloney, "Portraits of a City," *New York Times Book Review*, July 22, 1945, 5.

63. Weegee, *Naked City* (New York: Essential Books, 1945), 241.

64. Jean Goudal, "Surrealism and Cinema" (1925), in *The Shadow and Its Shadow: Surrealist Writings on Cinema*, ed. Paul Hammond (London: British Film Institute, 1978), 49–56.

65. Weegee, *Naked City*, 52.

66. John Coplans, "Weegee the Famous," in *Weegee's New York: 335 Photographs, 1935–1960* (Munich: Schirmer Art Books, 1982), 7–14.

67. William McCleery, foreword to Weegee, *Naked City*, 6.

68. This discourse also circulated in Weimar Germany. See Gerhard Venzmer, *New York ohne Schminke* [New York without Makeup] (Hamburg: Weltbund-Verlag, n.d.).

69. Karlheinz Stierle, *Der Mythos von Paris* (Munich: Deutscher Taschenbuch Verlag, 1998), 267.

70. The nineteenth-century literary antecedents of the trope of the naked city constitute a topic worthy of a separate study. Valuable contributions to it include Volker Klotz, *Die Erzählte Stadt. Ein Sujet als Herausforderung des Romans von Lesage bis Döblin* (Munich: Carl Hanser Verlag, 1969); Raymond Williams, *The Country and the City* (New York: Oxford University Press, 1973); Andrew Lees, *Cities Perceived: Urban Society in European and American Thought, 1882–1940* (Manchester: Manchester University Press, 1985); Richard Maxwell, *The Mysteries of Paris and London* (Charlottesville: University Press of Virginia, 1992); and Richard Lehan, *The City in Literature: An Intellectual and Cultural History* (Berkeley: University of California Press, 1998).

71. Laura Mulvey, "Visual Pleasure and Narrative Cinema," in *Narrative, Apparatus, Ideology: A Film Theory Reader*, ed. Philip Rosen (New York: Columbia University Press, 1986), 205.

72. *Weegee by Weegee: An Autobiography* (New York: Ziff Davis, 1961), 76.

73. Christine Buci-Glucksmann, *Baroque Reason: The Aesthetics of Modernity*, trans. Patrick Camiller (London: Sage, 1994), 156.

74. Bishop, *Mark Hellinger Story*, 330.

75. Ibid., 206, 86, 98.

76. A comparison of the budgets on two Hellinger productions, *The Killers* (1946) and *The Naked City* (1948), suggests that cost cutting probably was not the most significant motivation behind the trend toward location cinematography commencing in the 1940s. The former, mostly filmed in the studio, spent $113,675 on set construction, operations, striking, and dressing. The latter utilized extensive location cinematography and spent $95,500 on these same expenses plus a $10,000 contribution to the Police Athletic Fund and $7,500 in gratuities and entertainment for the New York Police Department. These expenditures resulted in a nearly identical total of $113,000. Hellinger borrowed $878,800 to produce the film, a high sum whose expense is made obvious when compared with the $615,065 that James Naremore (*More than Night: Film Noir in Its Contexts* [Berkeley: University of California Press, 1998], 141) presents as the cost for producing *Secret beyond the Door* (Fritz Lang, 1948). Film budget data found in box 15, Mark Hellinger Collection, University of Southern California Library. Individual productions may undoubtedly have been able to economize by utilizing actual locations; RKO claimed to have saved $1 million by doing so in the filming of *The Window* (Ted Tetzlaff, 1949). See "RKO Saves $ Million on 'Window,'" *Variety*, December 8, 1947. Yet the obvious aesthetic significance of location cinematography combined with the conflicting evidence about savings realized (or not) by individual productions undermines sweeping generalizations about economic incentives determining this trend. For the standard presentation of such an economic argument see William Lafferty, "A Reappraisal of the Semi-Documentary in Hollywood, 1945–1948," *Velvet Light Trap* 20 (summer 1983): 22–26.

77. Wald spent three years making military films on navigation, bombing, and survival skills. In preparation for a film titled *Bombardier Navigator*, he was sent to Texas to attend a preflight navigation course, another instance in which wartime training films entailed the documentation of technical procedures later associated with the procedural film. After the war he came into contact with Ben Maddow, who regularly screened documentaries such as *The City* and *Berlin: Symphony of a Great City* for aspiring filmmakers. His late encounter with Ruttmann's film confirms that the influence of Weimar cinema upon film noir could also be delayed and did not presuppose direct involvement with the German film industry. Wald claims both films as an influence upon his story treatment for *Homicide*. It was later retitled *The Naked City* after he brought Weegee's book to the attention of Hellinger. Interview with Malvin Wald, Studio City, Calif., February 22, 2001.

78. Though fully scripted by Malvin Wald in his first treatment for the film, the voice-over narration spoken by Hellinger may well have been suggested by his brief career in radio as well as the narrator employed in *The Roaring Twenties* (Raoul Walsh, 1939).

79. Malvin Wald, "Afterword" to *The Naked City: A Screenplay* (Carbondale: Southern Illinois University Press, 1979), 142. Wald has confirmed that the final

narration of the film later was written by Hellinger and that he decided to be the narrator.

80. Herb A. Lightman, "'The Naked City': Tribute in Celluloid," *American Cinematographer* 29 (May 1948): 152, 153, 178, 179.

81. Sarah Kozloff, *Invisible Storytellers: Voice-Over Narration in American Fiction Film* (Berkeley: University of California Press, 1988), 84–85.

82. In a memo conveying his concept for the film its screenplay writer Albert Maltz describes cinematography in a manner that suggests a prior acquaintance with the work of Dziga Vertov: "That the CAMERA EYE, whenever possible, reflect the rich and infinite detail of the daily life of New York . . . the infinite variety of faces and national types; the architectural beauty and squalor that exist side-by-side. Wherever possible, the main characters should be seen as part of, and in connection with, this city background and life"; "Homicide Production Notes for Mark Hellinger," April 7, 1947, Mark Hellinger Collection, batch 152:14, University of Southern California Library.

83. See Franco Moretti, "Homo Palpitans: Balzac's Novels and Urban Personality," in *Signs Taken for Wonders: Essays in the Sociology of Literary Forms*, trans. Susan Fischer, David Forgacs, and David Miller (London: Verso, 1983), 112.

84. Jean-Paul Sartre, *Critique of Dialectical Reason I: Theory of Practical Ensembles*, trans. Alan Sheridan-Smith, ed. Jonathan Reé (London: NLB, 1976), 650, 652.

85. Ibid., 650–651. For a discussion of the contests organized by Mark Hellinger see Bishop, *Mark Hellinger Story*, 92–109. One might also note, as evidence of the fascination with statistics common during the 1940s, the description by Woolrich in *Phantom Lady* of Terry as "a Gallup poll," 17. In 1946 sociologist Alfred Schutz wrote critically of the tendency of "polls, interviews, and questionnaires to try to gauge the opinion of the man on the street . . . which is public opinion as it is understood nowadays"; "The Well-Informed Citizen: An Essay on the Social Distribution of Knowledge," in *Collected Papers II: Studies in Social Theory*, 120–134, esp. 134.

86. Sartre, *Critique of Dialectical Reason I*, 257.

87. Ibid., 67, 318–341. Helpful presentations of Sartre's ideas are found in Mark Poster, *Existential Marxism in Postwar France: From Sartre to Althusser* (Princeton: Princeton University Press, 1975), esp. 264–305; idem, *Sartre's Marxism* (Cambridge: Cambridge University Press, 1982).

88. This line of dialogue first appears in the draft of the script dated April 7, 1947. Maltz's name does not appear on the script drafts until April 2, 1947. This fact combined with the anticapitalist thrust of the remark implies his authorship.

89. For a discussion of the nineteenth-century literary antecedents of the motif of the city as a living organism see Italo Calvino, "The City as Protagonist in Balzac," in *The Uses of Literature*, trans. Patrick Creagh (San Diego: Harcourt Brace Jovanovich, 1986), 182–189.

90. Jean-Paul Sartre, "New York: The Colonial City," in Sartre, *Literary and Philosophical Essays*, 128–129. See also Jean-Philippe Mathby, *Extrême-Occident: French Intellectuals and America* (Chicago: University of Chicago Press, 1993), 104–

136, for a trenchant discussion of Sartre's journalistic writings on America as "a brilliant exercise in applied existentialism."

91. See Jean Baudrillard, *Selected Writings*, ed. Mark Poster (Stanford: Stanford University Press, 1988).

92. Irish [Woolrich], *Phantom Lady*, 212.

93. David Nye, *American Technological Sublime* (Cambridge, Mass.: MIT Press, 1994), 197. For a detailed analysis of Nye's argument see my review of his book, "The Geist in the Machine," *Terra Nova* 1 (winter 1995): 120–129.

94. See Anthony Vidler, "Notes on the Sublime: From Neoclassicism to Postmodernism," *Canon* 3 (1988): 165–191, for an insightful presentation of Hugo.

95. Lightman, "'The Naked City,'" 179.

96. For a discussion of the construction of the United Nations see Robert A. M. Stern, Thomas Mellins, and David Fishman, *New York 1960: Architecture and Urbanism between the Second World War and the Bicentennial* (New York: Monacelli, 1995), 601–640; George A. Dudley, *A Workshop for Peace: Designing the United Nations Headquarters* (New York: Architectural History Foundation; Cambridge, Mass.: MIT Press, 1993). For Dreiser's allusion to the neighborhood see *The Color of a Great City* (New York: Boni and Liveright, 1923), esp. 133–137.

97. Secretary General of the United Nations, *Report to the General Assembly of the United Nations on the Permanent Headquarters of the United Nations* (Lake Success, N.Y.: United Nations, 1947), 11.

98. "Universal Showman's Manual," 1, box 15:19, Mark Hellinger Collection, University of Southern California Library.

99. Here I am indebted to the argument provided by Christopher P. Wilson in *Cop Knowledge: Police Power and Cultural Narrative in Twentieth-Century America* (Chicago: University of Chicago Press, 2000), 63.

100. Ibid., 68, 69, 63.

101. Interview with Malvin Wald, February 22, 2001. On page 1 of "A Publicity and Advertising Campaign for *The Naked City*" (February 2, 1948), Universal writes: "It would seem to us that every local police department would cooperate fully because of the fine job this picture does in authentically portraying the efficient inner workings of a homicide bureau. This at long last is one picture in which there are no 'dumb cops.' That alone will make any police chief thankful"; box 15:11, Mark Hellinger Collection, University of Southern California Library.

102. Wilson, *Cop Knowledge*, 68. For a discussion of the cultural significance of humanism in postwar America see Michael Leja, *Rethinking Abstract Expressionism: Subjectivity and Painting in the 1940s* (New Haven: Yale University Press, 1993), esp. 203–253. For the situation in France see Michael Kelly, "Humanism and National Unity: The Ideological Reconstruction of France," in *The Culture of Reconstruction: European Literature, Thought and Film, 1945–1950*, ed. Nicholas Hewitt (Houndmills: Macmillan, 1989), 103–119.

103. Wilson, *Cop Knowledge*, 85.

104. J. P. Telotte, *Voices in the Dark: The Narrative Patterns of Film Noir* (Urbana: University of Illinois Press, 1989), 139.

105. Wilson, *Cop Knowledge*, 72.

106. Neal Gabler, *Walter Winchell: Gossip, Power, and the Culture of Celebrity* (New York: Alfred A. Knopf, 1994), 81.

107. See also Warren I. Susman, "'Personality' and the Making of Twentieth-Century Culture," in *Culture as History: The Transformation of American Society in the Twentieth Century* (New York: Pantheon, 1984), 271–286, especially his telling comment that Walt Whitman, cited by Wald for his characterization of New York City as possessing a distinctive persona, was one of the first American writers to use the notion of personality in its modern sense. Whitman's writings on the city, many of them panoramic in tone and description, are usefully collected in Henry M. Christman, ed., *Walt Whitman's New York: From Manhattan to Montauk* (New York: Macmillan, 1963).

108. An unfilmed soliloquy by Lieutenant Mulvey in the screenplay articulates this idea and confirms the Darwinian view of capitalism that undergirds the humanism of the film. "People get so pounded and pounded in this life. It's a jungle, a city like this. Eight million people struggling for life, for food, for air, for a bit of happiness. Seems like there ain't enough of everything to go around . . . and so sometimes it breaks out in . . . violence"; *The Naked City: A Screenplay*, 70.

109. Peter Bacon Hales, *Silver Cities: The Photography of American Urbanization, 1839–1915* (Philadelphia: Temple University Press, 1984), 29.

110. For a literary analogue see the short story by O. Henry, "Psyche and the Skyscraper," in which he complains: "From this high view the city itself becomes degraded to an unintelligible mass of distorted buildings and impossible perspectives; the revered ocean is a duck pond; the earth itself is a lost golf ball. All the minutiae of life are gone"; *Complete Works of O. Henry*, 2: 1564.

111. Hales, *Silver Cities*, 73. For a detailed history of the panorama see Stephan Oetterman, *The Panorama: The History of a Mass Medium*, trans. Deborah Lucas Schneider (New York: Zone, 1997).

112. "*The other*, as a formula of the series and as a factor in every particular case of alterity, therefore becomes, beyond its structure of identity and its structure of alterity, a being common to all . . . Alterity as the unity of identities must always be elsewhere"; Sartre, *Critique of Dialectical Reason I*, 266–267.

113. Hales, *Silver Cities*, 79.

114. On this history see Hasia R. Diner, *Lower East Side Memories: A Jewish Place in America* (Princeton: Princeton University Press, 2000).

115. Dreiser, *The Color of a Great City*, 5.

116. See Kim Sichel, *Germaine Krull: Photographer of Modernity* (Cambridge, Mass.: MIT Press, 1999). For Joseph Stella's painting of the Brooklyn Bridge, also titled *Voice of the City* (1920–1922), see Wanda Corn, *The Great American Thing: Modern Art and National Identity, 1915–1935* (Berkeley: University of California Press, 1999), esp. 135–190.

117. Bernd Jager, "Horizontality and Verticality: A Phenomenological Exploration into Lived Space," in *Duquesne Studies in Phenomenological Psychology*, vol. 1, ed. Amedeo Giorgi, William F. Fischer, and Rolf Von Eckartsberg (Pittsburgh: Duquesne University Press, 1971), 219.

118. Ibid., 222, 226.

119. "Our story, is to see Garza through the eyes of the bystander, and the narrator—and it is when we get away from that realization, that we fumble and stumble so badly"; Mark Hellinger, "Notes on Chase Sequence—'The Naked City,'" 4, box 15:19, Mark Hellinger Collection, University of Southern California Library.

120. Cynthia Grenier, "An Interview with Jules Dassin," *Sight and Sound* 27 (winter 1957–58): 142. Malvin Wald supports Dassin's account of the fate of the film after its completion.

121. For a discussion of Hellinger's alleged collaboration with the FBI in naming communists in the motion picture industry see Bishop, *The Mark Hellinger Story*, 284.

122. See Carl Richardson, *Autopsy: An Element of Realism in Film Noir* (Metuchen, N.J.: Scarecrow, 1992), 106–107.

123. *Weegee by Weegee*, 135.

124. See Richard Terdiman, *Present Past: Modernity and the Memory Crisis* (Ithaca: Cornell University Press, 1993), for an insightful discussion of Baudelaire's relation to Parisian topography.

125. Statistics cited in Steven Lubar, *Info Culture: The Smithsonian Book of Information Age Inventions* (Boston: Houghton Mifflin, 1993), 248.

126. Quoted in Andy Warhol, Kasper König, and Pontus Hulten, eds., *Andy Warhol* (Stockholm: Moderna Museet, 1968), 460.

127. For comparisons between the art of Weegee and Warhol see Kirsten Hope Bigelow, "Warhol's Weegee," *New Art Examiner* 22 (October 1994): 21–25; and Ludger Derenthal, "Andy Warhol, Photographic Tradition and Zeitgeist," in *Andy Warhol Photography*, ed. Hamburg Kunsthalle and Andy Warhol Museum, Pittsburgh (Thalwil/Zurich and New York: Editions Stemmle, 1999), 33–39. A thoughtful interpretation of Warhol's work as a "peinture noire" is found in Thomas Crow, "Saturday Disasters: Trace and Reference in Early Warhol," in *Modern Art and the Common Culture* (New Haven: Yale University Press, 1996), 49–65.

128. That Weegee's photographs were not exhibited in Paris until 1962 suggests the film, rather than Weegee's book, was more likely to have gained the attention of Debord and Jorn. For a discussion of their "The Naked City" see Thomas McDonough, "Situationist Space," *October* 67 (winter 1994): 58–77.

129. "A Publicity and Advertising Campaign for *The Naked City*" (February 2, 1948), 2, box 15:11, Mark Hellinger Collection, University of Southern California Library.

130. Henri Lefebvre, *The Production of Space*, trans. Donald Nicholson-Smith (Cambridge, Mass.: Basil Blackwell, 1991), 274–275.

131. For discussions of the film see Rui Nogueira, ed., *Melville on Melville* (New York: Viking, 1972); Jacques Zimmer and Chantal de Béchade, *Jean-Pierre Melville* (Paris: Edilig, 1983); and Ginette Vincendeau, *Jean-Pierre Melville: An American in Paris* (London: British Film Institute, 2003). Many of its interior scenes were filmed in the French Jenner and Billancourt film studios.

132. See William Sharpe, "New York, Night, and Cultural Mythmaking: The Nocturne in Photography, 1900–1925," *Smithsonian Studies in American Art* 2 (fall

1988): 3–22, for a discussion of the photographic form whose images from as early as 1909 prefigure the nocturnal cityscapes of film noir.

133. In Fearing's novel, the painting by artist Louise Patterson that Stroud purchases in a Third Avenue junk shop depicts a pair of hands exchanging a coin and is titled by the artist *Study in Fundamentals* and later dubbed *The Temptation of St. Judas* by Stroud.

134. See Guy Debord, *The Society of the Spectacle*, trans. Donald Nicholson-Smith (New York: Zone, 1994).

135. Kenneth Fearing, *The Big Clock* (1946; reprint, New York: Mysterious Book Club, 1987), 171.

136. Sartre, *Critique of Dialectical Reason I*, 642–654.

137. A similar idea is expressed by George Stroud in the novel: "What we decided in this room, more than a million of our fellow citizens would read three months from now, and what they read they would accept as final"; Fearing, *The Big Clock*, 27.

138. See Peter Drucker, *The New Society* (New York: Harper, 1949); William H. Whyte, *The Organization Man* (Garden City, N.Y.: Doubleday, 1956).

139. "Hollywood Inside," *Daily Variety*, March 31, 1947, 2.

140. Fearing, *The Big Clock*, 17.

141. See Gilles Deleuze, "Postscript on the Societies of Control," *October* 59 (winter 1992): 3.

142. See Meyer Shapiro, *Impressionism: Reflections and Perceptions* (New York: George Braziller, 1997), 148, for a perceptive discussion of the crowd in French Impressionist painting. See also Rudolf Arnheim, "Accident and Necessity of Art," *Journal of Aesthetics and Art Criticism* 16 (1957): 18–31.

143. See Sir Raymond Unwin, "Higher Building in Relation to Town Planning" (1924), in *The Legacy of Raymond Unwin: A Human Pattern for Planning*, ed. Walter L. Creese (Cambridge, Mass.: MIT Press, 1967), 138.

2. CENTRIPETAL SPACE

1. On jazz in film see Krin Gabbard, *Jammin' at the Margins: Jazz and the American Cinema* (Chicago: University of Chicago Press, 1996). For more general surveys of the jazz contemporaneous with the film noir cycle see Scott DeVeaux, *The Birth of Bebop: A Social and Musical History* (Berkeley: University of California Press, 1997); and David Ake, *Jazz Cultures* (Berkeley: University of California Press, 2002), esp. 62–82.

2. See William Luhr, *Raymond Chandler and Film* (New York: Frederick Ungar, 1982); and Gene D. Phillips, *Creatures of Darkness: Raymond Chandler, Detective Fiction, and Film Noir* (Lexington: University Press of Kentucky, 2000), for discussions of the cinematic adaptations of Chandler's work.

3. For a discussion of the Brill Building see William R. Taylor, *In Pursuit of Gotham: Culture and Commerce in New York* (New York: Oxford University Press, 1992), 167. The history of Times Square is helpfully outlined in Lynne B. Sagalyn, *Times Square Roulette: Remaking the City Icon* (Cambridge, Mass.: MIT Press, 2001), esp. 31–67.

4. For discussions of *Skyscraper Symphony* in relation to the modernist experimentation of the 1920s see Brian Taves, *Robert Florey: The French Expressionist* (Metuchen, N.J.: Scarecrow, 1987), esp. 40, 97, 98; and Brian Taves, "Robert Florey and the Hollywood Avant-Garde," in *Lovers of Cinema: The First American Film Avant-Garde, 1919–1945*, ed. Jan-Christopher Horak (Madison: University of Wisconsin Press, 1995), 94–117.

5. Bernd Jager, "Horizontality and Verticality: A Phenomenological Exploration into Lived Space," in *Duquesne Studies in Phenomenological Psychology*, vol. 1, ed. Amedeo Giorgi, William F. Fischer, and Rolf Von Eckartsberg (Pittsburgh: Duquesne University Press, 1971), 217. For the philosophical origin of the idea of the other as faced, see Emmanuel Levinas, *Totality and Infinity: An Essay on Exteriority*, trans. Alphonso Lingis (Pittsburgh: Duquesne University Press, 1969).

6. William R. Taylor with Thomas Bender, "Culture and Architecture: Some Aesthetic Tensions in the Shaping of New York," in Taylor, *In Pursuit of Gotham*, 52.

7. Ibid., 62, 57.

8. Ibid., 57.

9. Lewis Mumford, "A Disoriented Symbol" (1951), in *From the Ground Up* (San Diego: Harcourt Brace Jovanovich, n.d.), 51.

10. Taylor, *In Pursuit of Gotham*, xvi.

11. For a discussion of gentrification in Greenwich Village see the volume published by writers in the Works Progress Administration, *New York City Guide* (New York: Random House, 1939), esp. 124–131. The opposition between "local people" and "villagers" is developed by Caroline F. Ware in *Greenwich Village, 1920–1930* (1935; reprint, Berkeley: University of California Press, 1994), 105–126.

12. For a suggestive analysis of the fear of open spaces as a retreat from the public sphere of commerce see Gillian Brown, "The Empire of Agoraphobia," *Representations* 20 (fall 1987): esp. 136–137.

13. See Taylor, *In Pursuit of Gotham*, 163–182.

14. I have not attempted to identify the earliest discussions of centrifugal and centripetal spatial tendencies, concepts that began to circulate by the early 1930s, if not earlier. One of the first architectural discussions of them appears in Frank Lloyd Wright, *The Disappearing City* (New York: William Farquhar Payson, 1932). An early appropriation of the concepts by an urban geographer is Charles C. Colby, "Centrifugal and Centripetal Forces in Urban Geography," *Annals of the Association of American Geographers* 23 (March 1933): 1–20, reprinted in Harold M. Mayer and Clyde F. Kohn, eds., *Readings in Urban Geography* (Chicago: University of Chicago Press, 1959), 287–298. Colby cites articles and dissertations from as early as 1924 in discussions of the two spatial modes and notes that his own article was first presented as a paper at a scholarly meeting of geographers in 1930. Two more recent yet suggestive discussions are Northrop Frye, "City of the End of Things," in *The Modern Century* (Toronto: Oxford University Press, 1967), 13–49; and Jean Gottmann, "The Evolution of Urban Centrality: Orientations for Research," *Oxford University School of Geography Research Papers* 8 (1974).

15. See Edward S. Casey, "The Experience of Place, Space, and Site in Urban

Life," unpublished paper. See also idem, *The Fate of Place: A Philosophical History* (Berkeley: University of California Press, 1997).

16. For discussions of the differences between geographic and functional definitions of the central business district see Robert Fogelson, *Downtown: Its Rise and Fall, 1880–1950* (New Haven: Yale University Press, 2001), 184–186.

17. Hans Blumenfeld, "Theory of City Form: Past and Present" (1949), in *The Modern Metropolis: Its Origins, Growth, Characteristics, and Planning* (Cambridge, Mass.: MIT Press, 1967), 29.

18. For a discussion of the literary representations of the nineteenth-century industrial metropolis see Raymond Williams, *The Country and the City* (New York: Oxford University Press, 1973).

19. For discussions of these technical developments see Sigfried Giedion, *Space, Time and Architecture: The Growth of a New Tradition* (Cambridge, Mass.: Harvard University Press, 1941); and Cecil D. Elliot, *Technics and Architecture: The Development of Materials and Systems for Buildings* (Cambridge, Mass.: MIT Press, 1992).

20. See Anastasia Loukaitou-Sideris and Tridib Banerjee, *Urban Design Downtown: Poetics and Politics of Form* (Berkeley: University of California Press, 1998), esp. 4–18.

21. Classic formulations of these ideas remain Charles Mulford Robinson, *Modern Civic Art or The City Made Beautiful* (New York: G. P. Putnam's Sons, 1903); and Daniel H. Burnham, *Plan of Chicago* (Chicago: Commercial Club, 1909). For a contemporary assessment see William H. Wilson, *The City Beautiful Movement* (Baltimore: Johns Hopkins University Press, 1989).

22. Hans Blumenfeld, "Alternative Solutions for Metropolitan Development," in *The Modern Metropolis*, 43.

23. A slightly earlier recognition of this dynamic was reached by the Viennese planner Ernst Fooks in his 1946 book *X-Ray the City! The Density Diagram: Basis for Urban Planning* (Melbourne: Ruskin, 1946), 46: "There is a perpetual interchanging process between these two trends, a never-ending contest between centralization and decentralization, between central growth and outward spread, the one trend partially neutralizing the other. This holds true of the mononucleated cities of the older world, of Paris, Vienna or Moscow, as well as of metropolitan regions, such as Melbourne, originating simultaneously from various points."

24. Blumenfeld, "Alternative Solutions," 44, 43, 70.

25. Henri Lefebvre, *The Production of Space*, trans. Donald Nicholson-Smith (Cambridge, Mass.: Basil Blackwell, 1991), 7. Lefebvre's argument about urban history is prefigured by Lewis Mumford in *The Culture of Cities* (New York: Harcourt, Brace, 1938) and *The City in History* (New York: Harcourt, Brace, 1961), though uncited in *The Production of Space*. I am grateful to Robert Fishman for drawing this parallel to my attention.

26. See Le Corbusier, *The Athens Charter*, trans. Anthony Eardley (New York: Grossman, 1973). For an early example of the American reception of these ideas see "Remaking a City: Excerpts from the Second Report (Zoning and Master Plan) of N.Y. Chapter, A.I.A. Committee on Civic Design and Development," *Journal of the American Institute of Architects* 2 (September 1944): 107–113.

27. Paul Zucker, *Town and Square: From the Agora to the Village Green* (New York: Columbia University Press, 1959), 3.

28. "It is only the clear legibility of its geometrical characteristics and aesthetic qualities which allows us consciously to perceive external space as urban space"; Rob Krier, *Urban Space*, trans. Christine Czechowski and George Black (New York: Rizzoli, 1979), 15.

29. Zucker, *Town and Square*, 2, 9. In *The Birth of Modern City Planning*, trans. George R. Collins and Christiane Crasemann Collins (New York: Rizzoli, 1986), 154, Camillo Sitte observes that "in the Middle Ages and Renaissance there still existed a vital and functional use of the town square for community life and also, in connection with this, a rapport between square and surrounding public buildings."

30. Zucker's remarks also recall the spatial anxieties that Wilhelm Worringer labels "Raumscheu" and "Platzangst" in his book *Abstraktion und Einfühlung: Ein Beitrag zur Stilpsychologie* (1908), 3d ed. (Munich: R. Piper Verlag, 1911), esp. 17–18, translated by Michael Bullock under the title *Abstraction and Empathy: A Contribution to the Psychology of Style* (New York: International Universities Press, 1953). The discussion of "dread of space" appears on p. 15. See also Anthony Vidler, *Warped Space: Art, Architecture, and Anxiety in Modern Culture* (Cambridge, Mass.: MIT Press, 2000), 44–46; and Paul Zucker, "The Paradox of Architectural Theories at the Beginning of the Modern Movement," *Journal of the Society of Architectural Historians* 10, no. 3 (1951): 8–14, esp. 12.

31. See Zucker, *Town and Square*, 99–142; and the account of the development of Rome in the fourteenth and fifteenth centuries in Leonardo Benevolo, *The History of the City*, trans. Geoffrey Culverwell (Cambridge, Mass.: MIT Press, 1980), 564–597.

32. Useful presentations of Haussmann are found in David H. Pinckney, *Napoleon III and the Rebuilding of Paris* (Princeton: Princeton University Press, 1958); and Anthony Vidler, "The Scenes of the Street: Transformations in Ideal and Reality, 1750–1871," in *On Streets*, ed. Stanford Anderson (Cambridge, Mass.: MIT Press, 1986), esp. 86–96.

33. See Paul Zucker, "Der Begriff der Zeit in der Architektur," in *Repertorium für Kunstwissenschaft*, vol. 44, ed. Karl Koetschau (Berlin: Walter de Gruyter, 1924), 237–245.

34. For a helpful introduction to this history see Jürgen Pahl, "The Public Square from the Middle Ages to the Era of Baroque," trans. R. W. Roome, *Cultures* 5, no. 4 (1978): 40–41.

35. For more-detailed treatments of these ideas see Edward Dimendberg, "Henri Lefebvre on Abstract Space," in *The Production of Public Space*, ed. Andrew Light and Jonathan M. Smith (Lanham: Rowman and Littlefield, 1998), 17–48; and Rob Shields, *Lefebvre, Love and Struggle: Spatial Dialectics* (London: Routledge, 1999).

36. The ideological sophistication of the picture window has been noted by architects Elizabeth Diller and Ricardo Scofidio: "As advanced technology strives to dematerialize its hardware, leaving only its effects, is not the picture window, in fact, a more advanced technology than the television set, in that its socially and economically driven mechanisms are virtually invisible, leaving only a simple

frame?"; *Flesh: Architectural Probes* (New York: Princeton Architectural Press, 1994), 248. For an overview of the window as a cultural motif see Suzanne Delehanty, ed., *The Window in Twentieth-Century Art* (Purchase: Neuberger Museum, State University of New York, 1986); and Anne Friedberg, *The Virtual Window: A Cultural History from Alberti to Microsoft* (Cambridge, Mass.: MIT Press, forthcoming).

37. "Modernity is doomed to explore and live through abstraction. Abstraction is a bitter chalice, but modernity must drain it to the dregs and, reeling in simulated inebriation, proclaim it the ambrosia of the gods. Abstraction perceived as something concrete, antinature and a growing nostalgia for nature which has somehow been mislaid—such is the conflict lived out by 'modern' man"; Henri Lefebvre, *Introduction to Modernity: Twelve Preludes, September 1959–May 1961*, trans. John Moore (London: Verso, 1995), 193. This passage demonstrates that Lefebvre's engagement with the problem of abstraction and modernity predates *The Production of Space*.

38. Ibid., 120.

39. See Ferdinand Tönnies, *Community and Association*, trans. Charles P. Loomis (London: Routledge and Kegan Paul, 1955).

40. For a discussion of incipient abstraction and commodification in the eighteenth century see Christoph Asendorf, *Batteries of Life: On the History of Things and Their Perception in Modernity*, trans. Don Reneau (Berkeley: University of California Press, 1993), 2–3.

41. Lefebvre traces his interest in urban space to his experience watching the construction in 1953–54 of the abstract space of the "nouvelle ville" in the oil town of Lacq-Mourenx. See Kristin Ross, "Lefebvre on the Situationists: An Interview," *October* 79 (winter 1997): 69–84.

42. On the grid in New York City see Peter Marcuse, "The Grid as City Plan: New York City and Laissez-Faire Planning in the Nineteenth Century," *Planning Perspectives* 2 (1987): 287–310; and Edward K. Spann, "The Greatest Grid: The New York Plan of 1811," in *Two Centuries of American Planning*, ed. Daniel Schaffer (London: Mansell, 1988), 11–40.

43. Thomas Adams, *The Building of the City*, vol. 2 (1931; reprint, New York: Arno, 1974), 38.

44. "The Grid makes the history of architecture and all previous lessons of urbanism irrelevant. It forces Manhattan's builders to develop a new system of formal values, to invent strategies for the distinction of one block from another"; Rem Koolhaas, *Delirious New York: A Retroactive Manifesto for Manhattan* (Rpt. New York: Monacelli, 1994), 20.

45. Edgar Allan Poe, *Doings of Gotham*, ed. J. E. Spannuth and T. O. Mabbott (Pottsville, Pa.: J. E. Spannuth, 1929), 25–26, quoted in Spann, "The Greatest Grid," 23.

46. Adams, *The Building of the City*, 50.

47. Lefebvre perceptively analyzes distinctive social iterations of the urban grid in *The Production of Space*, 150–158.

48. José Luis Sert, "The Human Scale in City Planning," in *New Architecture and City Planning*, ed. Paul Zucker (New York: Philosophical Library, 1944), 395.

49. For a discussion of the corridor street see J. L. Sert and CIAM, *Can Our Cities Survive?* (Cambridge, Mass.: Harvard University Press, 1947), 48.

50. See Michael Leja, *Reframing Abstract Expressionism: Painting and Subjectivity in the 1940s* (New Haven: Yale University Press, 1993).

51. Here one might note a pervasive limitation of much writing about film noir, namely the tendency to focus upon urban landmarks represented in films, to the exclusion of spatialities, which may be equally significant as structuring absences. Images of decrepit metropolitan cores and the central business districts must be understood in relation to highway construction and the lowering of urban densities, just as portrayals of suburban comfort need to be read in relation to centripetal space. Only through an investigation of multiple spatial options available to America of the 1940s and 1950s, not all of which necessarily appear in a given scene or film, does it become possible to understand the ideological signification of space in the film noir cycle. For the notion of structuring absence see Louis Althusser, *For Marx*, trans. Ben Brewster (London: Allen Lane, 1969); and Pierre Macherey, *A Theory of Literary Production*, trans. Geoffrey Wall (London: Routledge and Kegan Paul, 1978).

52. See Joseph Hudnut, "The Invisible City," *Journal of the American Institute of Urban Planners* 15 (summer 1949): 4–10; Ian L. McHarg, "The Humane City: Must the Man of Distinction Always Move to the Suburbs?" *Landscape Architecture* 48 (January 1958): 103–107; Paul N. Ylvisaker, "The Deserted City," *Journal of the American Institute of Planners* 25 (February 1959): 1–6; Kevin Lynch, *The Image of the City* (Cambridge, Mass.: Harvard University Press, 1960).

53. Sigfried Giedion, "The Need for a New Monumentality," in Zucker, *New Architecture and City Planning*, 556.

54. Hudnut, "The Invisible City," 9, 10. This essay was revised and reprinted in a less strident version in Hudnut's book, *Architecture and the Spirit of Man* (Cambridge, Mass.: Harvard University Press, 1949), 157–168. See also Jill Pearlstein, "Joseph Hudnut's Other Modernism at the 'Harvard Bauhaus,'" *Journal of the Society of Architectural Historians* 56 (December 1997): 452–477.

55. For helpful discussions of concepts of public space in classical antiquity, see Guy P. R. Métraux, "Public Space and Place in Antiquity: The Greek *Agora* and the Roman *Forum*," *Cultures* 5, no. 4 (1978): 11–26; and Joseph Rykwert, *The Idea of a Town: The Anthropology of Urban Form in Rome, Italy, and the Ancient World* (Princeton: Princeton University Press, 1976).

56. The status of Rockefeller Center as urban center of Manhattan is scarcely a topic of unanimity among architectural historians. For a positive assessment of its value as urban "forum" see William H. Jordy, "Rockefeller Center and Corporate Urbanism," in *American Buildings and Their Architects* (Garden City, N.Y.: Doubleday, 1972), 1–85, esp. 13–27, 84–85.

57. See Manfredo Tafuri, "The Disenchanted Mountain: The Skyscraper and the City," in Giorgio Ciucci, Francesco Dal Co, Mario Manieri-Elia, and Manfredo Tafuri, *The American City: From the Civil War to the New Deal*, trans. Barbara Luigi La Penta (London: Granada, 1980), 480–481.

58. Statement of English CIAM group quoted in Sigfried Giedion, "The Heart of the City: A Summing-up," in *CIAM 8: The Heart of the City*, ed. J.

Tyrwhitt, J. L. Sert, and E. N. Rogers (New York: Pellegrini and Cudahy, 1952), 160.

59. "Short Outlines of the Core," in Tyrwhitt, Sert, and Rogers, *CIAM 8*, 164.

60. Eric Mumford, *The CIAM Discourse on Urbanism, 1928–1960* (Cambridge, Mass.: MIT Press, 2000), 202.

61. "In the talk given at the Congress, Sert argued that in developing countries, the cores could be places where new technologies such as television screens would soon be available, and this could 'put these people in immediate contact with the world.' People without access to radios could 'listen to the loud speaker on the public square,' and 'could see the images on the television screen,' which would enhance the importance of these places. In the published version, however, Sert followed Giedion's arguments about community centers in 'The Need for a New Monumentality,' justifying these Cores based on their facilitation of direct personal contact and discussion between people"; ibid., 206.

62. J. L. Sert, "Centres of Community Life," in Tyrwhitt, Sert, and Rogers, *CIAM 8*, 6.

63. Giedion, "The Heart of the City: A Summing-up," 161.

64. Idem, "Historical Background to the Core," in Tyrwhitt, Sert, and Rogers, *CIAM 8*, 17. The humanism of the CIAM project is well analyzed in Barry Curtis, "The Heart of the City," in *Non-Plan: Essays on Freedom, Participation and Change in Modern Architecture and Urbanism* (Oxford: Architectural Press, 2000), 52–64.

65. "Short Outlines of the Core," 165. One need not expend great effort to discern an entire range of Situationist motifs in this passage, ranging from the emphasis on the rendezvous, spontaneous and accidental activity, and the freedom of movement epitomized in the Surrealists' walks and the Situationists' "dérive." The principal Situationist texts developing their notion of the drift through city are Ivan Chtcheglov, "Formulary for a New Urbanism" (1953), and Guy Debord, "Introduction to a Critique of Urban Geography" (1955), both translated and reprinted in *Situationist International Anthology*, ed. and trans. Ken Knabb (Berkeley: Bureau of Public Secrets, 1981), 1–8. Other relevant texts include Guy-Ernest Debord, "Two Accounts of the Dérive" and "Unitary Urbanism at the End of the 1950s," both translated by Thomas Y. Levin and published in *On the Passage of a Few People through a Rather Brief Moment in Time: The Situationist International, 1957–1972*, ed. Elisabeth Sussman (Boston and Cambridge, Mass.: Institute of Contemporary Art and MIT Press, 1989), 135–139, 143–147.

66. Paradigmatic here would be the design of Peter and Alison Smithson for the competition entry for Housing, Golden Lane, City of London, 1951–52, with its frank acknowledgment of the street as a commercial space. See *Urban Structuring: Studies of Alison and Peter Smithson* (London: Studio Vista, 1967), 22. For an overview of the career of the architects see Alison Smithson and Peter Smithson, *Charged Void: Architecture* (New York: Monacelli, 2001). An American analogue would be the entry by Robert Venturi and Denise Scott Brown to the National College Hall of Fame competition, New Brunswick, N.J., in 1967 and its incorporation of image projection and graphics to realize a media iconography. See A. Sanmartín, ed., *Venturi, Rauch & Scott Brown* (Stuttgart: Karl Krämer Verlag, 1986), 52.

67. One might also cite in this context the 1955 opening of Disneyland and its centerpiece, Main Street, U.S.A. See Karal Ann Marling, "Imagineering the Disney Theme Parks," in *Designing Disney's Theme Parks: The Architecture of Reassurance*, ed. Marling (Montreal and Paris: Canadian Centre for Architecture / Flammarion, 1997), esp. 79–85, for a discussion of its idealized urban center.

68. Roland Barthes, "Semiology and the Urban," trans. Lily Stylianoudi and Kitty Rouanet, in *The City and the Sign*, ed. Mark Gottdiener and Alexandros Ph. Lagopoulos (New York: Columbia University Press, 1986), 94.

69. Robert A. M. Stern, Thomas Mellins, and David Fishman, *New York 1960: Architecture and Urbanism between the Second World War and the Bicentennial* (New York: Monacelli, 1995), 9. Awareness of this spatial problem antedates the new 1960 zoning legislation. Consider the following assessment of the 1931 Regional Plan: "What New York lacks is not so much beauty in individual buildings as lack of that harmonious treatment and spaciousness in surroundings of buildings which is a characteristic of great capital cities. New York when compared to Washington, Paris and London suffers more from want of space in its central areas than from deficiency in monumental buildings. Its most striking architectural feature is its mass of high buildings as seen from the surrounding areas of open water, which give it the benefit of open space from which its buildings can be seen"; Adams, *The Building of the City*, 75.

70. See William Whyte, *The Social Life of Small Urban Spaces* (Washington, D.C.: Conservation Foundation, 1980).

71. Reinhard Hohl, *Alberto Giacometti* (New York: Harry N. Abrams, n.d.), 140. For a more recent assessment of the artist's work and career see Christian Klemm, *Alberto Giacometti* (New York: Museum of Modern Art, 2001).

72. Jean-Paul Sartre, "The Paintings of Giacometti" (1954), in *Situations*, trans. Benita Eisler (Greenwich, Conn.: Fawcett, n.d.), 126.

73. Jean-Paul Sartre, *Critique of Dialectical Reason I: Theory of Practical Ensembles*, trans. Alan Sheridan-Smith, ed. Jonathan Rée (London: NLB, 1976), 257.

74. Sartre, "The Paintings of Giacometti," 135. In a conversation with de Beauvoir, Sartre casts a valuable light upon his essay on Giacometti by relating that during the years 1950–1952 he began thinking about the *Critique of Dialectical Reason* and reading the crime novels published in Marcel Duhamel's Série Noire. See Simone de Beauvoir, *Adieux: A Farewell to Sartre*, trans. Patrick O'Brian (Harmondsworth: Penguin, 1985), 201.

75. Alberto Giacometti, "Le Rêve, le sphinx et la mort de T.," *Labyrinthe* (Geneva), nos. 22–23 (December 15, 1946): 12–13. A reprint of this key text can be found in *Alberto Giacometti: Sculptures, peintures, dessins* (Paris: Musée d'Art Moderne de la Ville de Paris, 1991), 412–414. For a helpful intellectual overview see Frances Morris, ed., *Paris Postwar: Art and Existentialism, 1945–1955* (London: Tate Gallery, 1993).

76. For an incisive discussion of fear of the void see Vidler, *Warped Space*, 17–24.

77. Hohl, *Alberto Giacometti*, 205, 207.

78. Maurice Merleau-Ponty, *Phenomenology of Perception*, trans. Colin Smith (London: Routledge and Kegan Paul, 1962), 256, quoted in Hohl, *Alberto*

Giacometti, 206. I have utilized Smith's translation of the passage rather than the slightly different rendering present in Hohl's text.

79. "In the matter of scale we have two opposites to be avoided. One is claustrophobia, the fear of space which is too small, which too oppressively encloses us; the other is agoraphobia, the dread of large open space"; Walter Gropius, "The Human Scale," in Tyrwhitt, Sert, and Rogers, *CIAM 8*, 54.

80. See Carol Herselle Krinsky, *Gordon Bunshaft of Skidmore, Owings & Merrill* (New York and Cambridge, Mass.: Architectural History Foundation and MIT Press, 1988), 72–77.

81. Hohl, *Alberto Giacometti*, 143.

82. Jerrold Lanes, "Alberto Giacometti," *Paris/New York Arts Yearbook* 3 (1959): 154.

83. Edoardo Weiss, "Agoraphobia and Its Relation to Hysterical Attacks and Traumas," *International Journal of Psycho-Analysis* 16 (1960): 67. For a more recent discussion of agoraphobia see Paul Carter, *Repressed Spaces: The Poetics of Agoraphobia* (London: Reaktion Books, 2002).

84. For a detailed analysis of this scene in *Scarlet Street* see my "Down These Seen Streets a Man Must Go: Siegfried Kracauer, 'Hollywood's Terror Films,' and the Spatiality of Film Noir," *New German Critique*, 89 (spring/summer 2003): 113–114.

85. Krinsky, *Gordon Bunshaft*, 76.

3. WALKING CURES

1. Kenneth Burke, "The Four Master Tropes," in *A Grammar of Motives* (1945; reprint, Berkeley: University of California Press, 1969), 503–517, esp. 506–511.

2. Walter Benjamin, *Charles Baudelaire: A Lyric Poet in the Era of High Capitalism*, trans. Harry Zohn (London: NLB, 1973), 86–87.

3. For a discussion of the increasingly suburbanized context of film exhibition see Douglas Gomery, *Shared Pleasures: A History of Movie Presentation in the United States* (Madison: University of Wisconsin Press, 1992), esp. 83–102. One might note the description by film critic Manny Farber of the often-decrepit cinemas, soon to be overshadowed by their suburban counterparts, in which films noir often were exhibited. See Manny Farber, "Underground Films" (1957), in *Negative Space: Many Farber on the Movies* (1971; reprint, New York: Da Capo, 1998), 12–24.

4. The most significant articulations of the discourse of the flaneur remain Charles Baudelaire, "The Painter of Modern Life" (1863), in *Selected Writings on Art and Artists*, trans. P. E. Charvet (Cambridge: Cambridge University Press, 1981), 390–435; and Walter Benjamin, "The Flaneur," in *The Arcades Project*, trans. Howard Eiland and Kevin McLaughlin (Cambridge, Mass.: Belknap Press of Harvard University Press, 1999), 416–455; and idem, "The Return of the Flaneur," in *Selected Writings*, vol. 2: *1927–1934*, trans. Rodney Livingstone et al., ed. Michael W. Jennings, Howard Eiland, and Gary Smith (Cambridge, Mass: Belknap Press of Harvard University Press, 1999), 262–267. Secondary discussions of these and

other instances of *flânerie* can be found in Dana Brand, *The Spectator and the City in Nineteenth-Century American Literature* (Cambridge: Cambridge University Press, 1991); Keith Tester, ed., *The Flaneur* (London: Routledge, 1994); Anke Gleber, *The Art of Taking a Walk: Flanerie, Literature, and Film in Weimar Culture* (Princeton: Princeton University Press, 1999); Deborah L. Parsons, *Streetwalking the Metropolis: Women, the City, and Modernity* (Oxford: Oxford University Press, 2000); and Francesco Careri, *Walkscapes: Walking as an Aesthetic Practice*, trans. Steven Piccolo and Paul Hammond (Barcelona: Gustavo Gili, 2002). Specifically cinematic explorations of *flânerie* include Anne Friedberg, *Window Shopping: Cinema and the Postmodern* (Berkeley: University of California Press, 1993); and Giuliana Bruno, *Streetwalking on a Ruined Map: Cultural Theory and the City Films of Elvira Notari* (Princeton: Princeton University Press, 1993). More general discussions of walking through the city can be found in Michel de Certeau, "Walking in the City," in *The Practice of Everyday Life*, trans. Stephen F. Rendall (Berkeley: University of California Press, 1984), 91–110; and Romedi Passini, *Wayfinding in Architecture* (New York: Van Nostrand Reinhold, 1984).

5. For an insightful analysis of the film in relation to the pulp fiction of Cornell Woolrich see David Reid and Jayne L. Walker, "Strange Pursuit: Cornell Woolrich and the Abandoned City of the Forties," in *Shades of Noir: A Reader*, ed. Joan Copjec (London: Verso, 1993), 57–96.

6. See Ellen Wiley Todd, *The "New Woman" Revised: Painting and Gender Politics on Fourteenth Street* (Berkeley: University of California Press, 1993), 84–136.

7. Cornell Woolrich, *The Black Curtain* (New York: Simon and Schuster, 1941), 17.

8. Ibid., 19.

9. See Wayne Attoe and Donn Logan, *American Urban Architecture: Catalysts in the Design of Cities* (Berkeley: University of California Press, 1989), 133.

10. Edward S. Casey, *Remembering: A Phenomenological Study*, 2d ed. (Bloomington: Indiana University Press, 2000), 186, 195.

11. Woolrich, *The Black Curtain*, 177.

12. One need only mention *The Trial* (Orson Welles, 1963) and *Alphaville* (Jean-Luc Godard, 1965).

13. Woolrich, *The Black Curtain*, 82. One might also cite the scene in *The Best Years of Our Lives* (William Wyler, 1946), in which the newly reopened postwar chain drugstore is equipped with an overhead window through which the store manager can spy upon his employees.

14. Dr. E. Minkowski, "Bergson's Conceptions as Applied to Psychopathology," trans. Fredric J. Farnell, M.D., *Journal of Nervous and Mental Disease* 63 (June 1926): 561.

15. Ibid., 558.

16. Woolrich, *The Black Curtain*, 7. I first proposed the notion of the "walking cure" in my 1992 doctoral dissertation, "Film Noir and Urban Space" (University of California at Santa Cruz).

17. See Walter Benjamin, "On Some Motifs in Baudelaire" (1939), in *Illuminations*, trans. Harry Zohn, ed. Hannah Arendt (New York: Schocken, 1969), 155–

200, esp. 157; and idem, "Experience and Poverty," in Jennings, Eiland, and Smith, *Selected Writings,* 2: 731–738.

18. Benjamin, "On Some Motifs in Baudelaire," 160.

19. See Max Page, *The Creative Destruction of Manhattan, 1900–1940* (Chicago: University of Chicago Press, 1999), esp. 69–110; and Richard Plunz, *A History of Public Housing in New York City* (New York: Columbia University Press, 1990), 207–246.

20. See Bernard J. Frieden, *The Future of Old Neighborhoods: Rebuilding for a Changing Population* (Cambridge, Mass.: Joint Center for Urban Studies of the Massachusetts Institute of Technology and Harvard University, 1964); Arthur Simon, *Stuyvesant Town: Pattern for Two Americas* (New York: New York University Press, 1970); and M. Christine Boyer, *Dreaming the Rational City: The Myth of American City Planning* (Cambridge, Mass.: MIT Press, 1983).

21. John Ruskin, *The Seven Lamps of Architecture* (1849; reprint, New York: A. L. Burt, n.d.), 169.

22. Richard Terdiman, *Present Past: Modernity and the Memory Crisis* (Ithaca: Cornell University Press, 1993), 27.

23. Miriam Bratu Hansen, "Introduction," in Siegfried Kracauer, *Theory of Film: The Redemption of Physical Reality* (1960; reprint, Princeton: Princeton University Press, 1997), x.

24. Robert Beauregard, "Between Modernity and Postmodernity: The Ambiguous Position of U.S. Planning," *Environment and Planning D: Society and Space* 7 (1989): 381–395.

25. See Jean-François Lyotard, *The Postmodern Condition: A Report on Knowledge* (1979), trans. Geoff Bennington and Brian Massumi (Minneapolis: University of Minnesota Press, 1984).

26. Colin Rowe and Fred Koetter, *Collage City* (Cambridge, Mass.: MIT Press, 1978), 4.

27. Kracauer, *Theory of Film,* 68.

28. This "psychic permeation" of objects recalls Benjamin's famous discussion of the "optical unconscious" in his essay "The Work of Art in the Age of Technological Reproducibility," in *Selected Writings,* vol. 3: *1935–1938,* trans. Edmund Jephcott et al., ed. Howard Eiland and Michael W. Jennings (Cambridge, Mass.: Belknap Press of Harvard University Press, 2002), 101–133.

29. Hansen, "Introduction," xxi.

30. Kracauer, *Theory of Film,* 300.

31. Kristin Thompson, "The Concept of Cinematic Excess," *Cine-Tracts* 1 (summer 1977): 55–56. This article also appears in idem, *Eisenstein's Ivan the Terrible: A Neoformalist Analysis* (Princeton: Princeton University Press, 1981), 287–302.

32. See Bertolt Brecht, "Alienation Effects in Chinese Acting" (1935), in *Brecht on Theater,* trans. John Willett (New York: Hill and Wang, 1964), 91–99; and Victor Shklovsky, "Art as Technique" (1917), in *Russian Formalist Criticism: Four Essays,* trans. Lee T. Lemon and Marion J. Reis (Lincoln: University of Nebraska Press, 1965), 3–24.

33. Kracauer, *Theory of Film,* 170.

34. See Edmund Husserl, "Philosophy as Rigorous Science" (1911), trans. Quentin Lauer, in *Husserl: Shorter Works*, ed. Peter McCormick and Frederick Elliston (Notre Dame: University of Notre Dame Press, 1981), 166–197, esp. 176.

35. Ian Aitken claims that *Theory of Film* strongly reflects the influence of Husserl and his concept of the *Lebenswelt*, although neither this notion nor any direct reference to Husserl appears in Kracauer's book. See Ian Aitken, "Distraction and Redemption: Kracauer, Surrealism, and Phenomenology," *Screen* 39 (summer 1998): 124–140.

36. Kracauer, *Theory of Film*, 291.

37. "Fatalism pervades film noir. Not only is destiny unfavorable, not only do characters fall into impossible situations or meet with death, but these declines and demises are presented not simply as mere outrageous circumstances, but as fated. The aura of inevitability bathes the action"; Maureen Turim, *Flashbacks in Film: Memory and History* (New York: Routledge, 1989), 170. See chap. 5 in Turim's book for an admirable discussion of the flashback in film noir.

38. For a similar insight with respect to the work of Raymond Chandler see Fredric Jameson, "On Raymond Chandler," in *The Poetics of Murder*, ed. Glenn W. Most and William Stowe (San Diego: Harcourt Brace Jovanovich, 1983), 122–148.

39. For a discussion of film noir in relation to Surrealism see James Naremore, *More than Night: Film Noir in Its Contexts* (Berkeley: University of California Press, 1998), 17–19. The similarities and differences between Kracauer's film theory and Surrealist understandings of cinema are discussed by Aitken in "Distraction and Redemption," esp. 130–140. One might also note Kracauer's citation of the following quote from a figure close to the French Surrealists, Roger Caillois: "The cinema emphasizes . . . the contingency of human relationships. The tragic heroes slay each other only among themselves; one locks them up like wild animals in the arena so that they may tear themselves to pieces. On the screen, as in the street, the passer-by is killed by the gangster because he happens to be there, for this world has no order, it is a place of movement and collision"; Roger Caillois, "Le cinéma, le meurte et la tragédie," *Revue Internationale de Filmologie* 2, no. 5, 91; quoted in Kracauer, *Theory of Film*, 267.

40. For an excellent discussion of the architectural inspiration for the main waiting room, the tepidarium of the Roman baths of Caracalla, see Lorraine B. Diehl, *The Late, Great Pennsylvania Station* (New York and Boston: American Heritage Press/Houghton Mifflin, 1985), 16.

41. For a discussion of the architecture of Pennsylvania Station, see Nathan Silver, *Lost New York* (New York: American Legacy Press, 1967), 32–38; and Robert A. M. Stern, Gregory Gilmartin, and John Massengale, *New York 1900: Metropolitan Architecture and Urbanism, 1890–1915* (New York: Rizzoli, 1983), 40–43; and Lewis Mumford, "Is New York Expendable?" (1955), in *From the Ground Up* (San Diego: Harcourt Brace Jovanovich, n.d.), 201–209.

42. Kracauer, *Theory of Film*, 72–73.

43. Wolfgang Schivelbusch, *The Railway Journey: Trains and Travel in the Nineteenth Century*, trans. Anselm Hollo (New York: Urizen, 1977), 162.

44. See Robert A. M. Stern, Thomas Mellins, and David Fishman, *New York*

1960: Architecture and Urbanism between the Second World War and the Bicentennial (New York: Monacelli, 1995), 1114. This discussion of Pennsylvania Station also contains an excellent bibliography.

45. Phil Donnelly, a train dispatcher in Pennsylvania Station, recalled the station's final years: "The station was grimy on the outside, and there was a certain monotony about the exterior along the sides. Perhaps this building that now resembled a mausoleum reminded people on some level that the age of railroad was gone and it made them nervous to have this relic here, reminding them of something that no longer lived"; quoted in Diehl, *The Late, Great Pennsylvania Station*, 145.

46. Georg Simmel, "The Metropolis and Mental Life," trans. Hans Gerth, in *Simmel on Culture*, ed. David Frisby and Mike Featherstone (London: Sage, 1997), 415.

47. Christine Buci-Glucksmann, "Catastrophic Utopia: The Feminine as Allegory of the Modern," trans. Katharine Streip, in *The Making of the Modern Body: Sexuality and Society in the Nineteenth Century*, ed. Catherine Gallagher and Thomas Laqueur (Berkeley: University of California Press, 1987), 221.

48. See Walter Benjamin, *The Origin of German Tragic Drama*, trans. John Osborne (London: New Left, 1977), esp. 159–195.

49. Siegfried Kracauer, "Photography," in *The Mass Ornament: Weimar Essays*, trans. Thomas Levin (Cambridge, Mass.: Harvard University Press, 1995), 63.

50. As when Davey is introduced in his apartment surrounded by photographs of his family.

51. William Klein, *Life Is Good and Good for You in New York: Trance Witness Revels* (Paris: Editions du Seuil, 1956). A new edition of this book appeared under the title *New York 1954–55* (Manchester: Dewi Lewis, 1995), 4.

52. Henri Lefebvre, *The Production of Space*, trans. Donald Nicholson-Smith (Cambridge, Mass.: Basil Blackwell, 1991), 309–310.

53. For the significance of the mannequin in Benjamin, see Angelika Rauch, "The *Trauerspiel* of the Prostituted Body, or Woman as Allegory of Modernity," *Cultural Critique* 10 (fall 1988): 77–88, esp. 84.

54. Grady Clay, "Shapely Women and Cities: An Editorial: What's the Urban Equivalent of '38–24–34'?" *Landscape Architecture* 49 (autumn 1958): 7.

55. See Guy Debord, "Theory of the Dérive" (1956) and "Two Accounts of the Dérive" (1956), in *Theory of the Dérive and Other Situationist Writings on the City*, ed. Libero Andreotti and Xavier Costa (Barcelona: Museum of Contemporary Art, 1996), 22–32.

56. For an account of the legacy of the Situationists, see Simon Sadler, *The Situationist City* (Cambridge, Mass.: MIT Press, 1998); and *Guy Debord and the Situationist International: Texts and Documents*, ed. Thomas McDonough (Cambridge, Mass.: MIT Press, 2002).

57. See [Guy Debord?], "The Destruction of Rue Sauvage," in Andreotti and Costa, *Theory of the Dérive*, 45. For broader historical overviews see Norma Evenson, "The Assassination of Les Halles," *Journal of the Society of Architectural Historians* 32 (December 1973): 308–315; and Louis Chevalier, *The Assassination of Paris*, trans. David P. Jordan (Chicago: University of Chicago Press, 1994).

58. For a detailed exegesis of the notion of the "insolite" contemporaneous with the French discussion of film noir and the discourse of the Situationists, see Michel Guiomar, "L'insolite," *Revue d'Esthétique*, April–June 1957, 113–145.

59. Kevin Lynch, *The Image of the City* (Cambridge, Mass.: MIT Press, 1960).

60. Lynch later noted that "mature self-confident people can cope with drab or confused surroundings, but such places are crucial difficulties for those internally disoriented, or for those at some critical stage of their development." See Kevin Lynch, "Reconsidering *The Image of the City*" (1984), in *City Sense and City Design: Writings and Projects of Kevin Lynch*, ed. Tridib Banerjee and Michael Southworth (Cambridge, Mass.: MIT Press, 1990), 250.

61. We later learn that the murderer is from the East Coast, a fact that suggests his lack of familiarity with Los Angeles geography.

62. Lynch offers the following summary of his respondents' views of Los Angeles: "In Los Angeles, there is an impression that the fluidity of the environment and the absence of physical elements which anchor to the past are exciting and disturbing. Many descriptions of the scene by established residents, young or old, were accompanied by the ghosts of what used to be there. Changes, such as those wrought by the freeway system, have left scars on the mental image. The interviewer remarked: 'There seems to be a bitterness or nostalgia among natives which could be resentment at the many changes, or just inability to reorient fast enough to keep up with them'"; *The Image of the City*, 45. This characterization of Los Angeles as a city lacking historical reference points has become increasingly prevalent since Lynch wrote his book. I would suggest that it needs to be rethought and perhaps supplanted by different strategies of cognitive mapping. For one preliminary effort in this direction see Philip J. Ethington, "Los Angeles and the Problem of Historical Knowledge," http://www.usc.edu/LAS/history/historylab/Text/Essay_full.htm.

63. Raymond Chandler, *The High Window*, in *Four Complete Philip Marlowe Novels* (New York: Avenel, 1986), 395–396. The spot where Hammer parks his car in *Kiss Me Deadly* is identical with that described as the parking space of Marlowe in the novel. For a helpful discussion of this novel and another classic treatment of Bunker Hill, John Fante's *Ask the Dust* (1939), see Norman Klein, "The Sunshine Strategy: Buying and Selling the Fantasy of Los Angeles," in *20th Century Los Angeles: Power, Promotion and Social Conflict*, ed. Klein and Martin J. Schiesl (Claremont, Calif.: Regina, 1990), 1–38.

64. Despite the continuing growth of interest in the history of Los Angeles, there still exists no comprehensive history of the Bunker Hill area and its urban redevelopment. Four of the more useful studies that address it are Donald Craig Parson, "Urban Politics during the Cold War: Public Housing, Urban Renewal, and Suburbanization in Los Angeles" (Ph.D. diss., University of California at Los Angeles, 1985); Anastasia Loukaitou-Sideris and Gail Sainsbury, "Lost Streets of Bunker Hill," *California History* 74 (winter 1995–96): 394–407; Mike Davis, *City of Quartz: Excavating the Future in Los Angeles* (London: Verso, 1990), esp. 72–74 and 230–232; Dana Cuff, *The Provisional City: Los Angeles Stories of Architecture and Urbanism* (Cambridge, Mass.: MIT Press, 2000). For the general history and prehistory of urban renewal see S. E. Sanders and A. J. Rabuck, *New City Patterns: The*

Technique of and a Technique for Urban Reintegration (New York: Reinhold, 1946); Martin Anderson, *The Federal Bulldozer: A Critical Analysis of Urban Renewal, 1949–1962* (Cambridge, Mass.: MIT Press, 1964); Boyer, *Dreaming the Rational City;* and Robert M. Fogelson, *Downtown: Its Rise and Fall, 1880–1950* (New Haven: Yale University Press, 2001).

65. Lynch, *The Image of the City*, 42.

66. Kenneth Burke, "The Four Master Tropes," 506.

67. *Southwestern Contractor,* December 7, 1912, 1.

68. Wm. H. Babcock & Sons, "Report on the Economic and Engineering Feasibility of Regrading the Bunker Hill Area Los Angeles," 1931, 10.

69. Timothy G. Turner, "Angels Flight Leads to World of Yesterday," *Los Angeles Times*, February 1, 1951.

70. Ibid.

71. "Let's Cure Eyesore on Bunker Hill," *Los Angeles Mirror,* March 9, 1951.

72. Editorial, ibid., September 7, 1956.

73. Oran W. Asa, "Architects' Dream and Taxpayer's Nightmare," *Highland Park News-Herald and Journal,* September 15, 1960, 28.

74. Bob Lawrence, "Fight Looms on Bunker Hill Redevelopment Program," *Inglewood News-Advertiser,* December 2, 1954.

75. Herbert D. Wilhoit in *Covina Daily Tribune,* December 14, 1955.

76. Community Redevelopment Agency of the City of Los Angeles, California, Bunker Hill Urban Renewal Project, "Final Argument," January 7, 1959, 2–3.

77. Mrs W., "Disturbed," *Los Angeles Herald and Express,* March 23, 1951.

78. "Bunker Hearing Continued," *Los Angeles Examiner,* August 31, 1956.

79. "4 Bunker Hill Plans Offered," ibid., July 11, 1956.

80. "'Hill' Deal Moves On," *Morningside News Advertiser,* February 22, 1956.

81. Mike Davis, "Bunker Hill: Hollywood's Dark Shadow," in *Cinema and the City: Film and Urban Society in Global Context*, ed. Mark Shiel and Tony Fitzmaurice (Oxford: Blackwell, 2001), 33–45. Davis convincingly relates Bunker Hill to an older discourse of middle-class fascination with the nocturnal slum that he discerns in the work of Dickens, Sue, and O. Henry.

82. See Cornell Woolrich (writing as George Hopley), *Night Has a Thousand Eyes* (1945; reprint, New York: Paperback Library, 1967).

83. Fred Zinnemann, *An Autobiography* (London: Bloomsbury, 1992), 74. See *Act of Violence* screenplay (August 12, 1947), MGM Collection, Special Collections, University of Southern California Library. Revealingly, the earliest treatments of the story are set in San Francisco.

84. The film was photographed in downtown Los Angeles near Commercial Street, the Santa Fe freight yards, Bunker Hill, and the Glendale railroad depot. Santa Monica was the location of Santa Lisa. For an account by the film's cinematographer see Robert Surtees, "The Story of Filming *Act of Violence*," *American Cinematographer* 29 (August 1948): 268, 282–284.

85. For the director's analysis of this scene see Arthur Nolletti Jr., "Conversation with Fred Zinnemann," in *The Films of Fred Zinnemann: Critical Perspectives*, ed. Nolletti (Albany: SUNY Press, 1999), 18.

86. Around this same time a group of painters also began to depict Bunker Hill. See William Pugsley, *Bunker Hill: Last of the Lofty Mansions* (Corona del Mar, Calif.: Trans-Anglo, 1977), 29.

87. See Walt Wheelock, *Angels Flight* (Los Angeles: Borden, 1993); and Virginia L. Comer, *Angels Flight: A History of Bunker Hill's Incline Railway* (Los Angeles: Historical Society of Southern California, 1996).

88. See Davis, *City of Quartz*, 230.

89. See Larry Gordon, "Groundbreaking Ceremony at Bunker Hill Celebrates the Planned Restoration of Angels Flight, 'the Shortest Railway in the World,' Which Has Been Closed since 1969," *Los Angeles Times*, March 10, 1995, B1.

90. As Joseph T. Bill, executive director of the CRA, noted, "Over a period of years a number of sites to which the funicular could be removed have been suggested. These include Disneyland, Knotts Berry Farm, Travel Town in Griffith Park, the proposed zoo in Elysian Park, the Hollywood Bowl and the amphitheater used for the Pilgrimage Play. In addition, a rancher near Newhall would like to acquire it, and a developer would like to use Angels Flight to hoist diners to a restaurant atop a 500-foot mountain there"; quoted in Walt Wheelock, *Angels Flight* (Glendale, Calif.: La Siesta, 1961), 32.

91. Community Redevelopment Agency of Los Angeles, "Progress Report: Five Year Implementation Plan Bunker Hill Urban Renewal Project," December 19, 1996, 4. The future of Angels Flight remains uncertain after an accident on February 1, 2001, in which the two cars of the funicular railway collided, injuring eight passengers, one of them fatally.

92. James Dao, "Looking at a Post Office, Amtrak Sees a Home," *New York Times*, May 13, 1992, A16.

93. See David W. Dunlap, "Amtrak Unveils Design for Making New York Post Office into a Terminal," *New York Times*, May 2, 1993, 22; Ada Louise Huxtable, "On the Right Track," *New York Times*, November 28, 1994, A15; Herbert Muschamp, "Preserving the Shrines of an Age, Not the Spirit," *New York Times*, April 30, 1995, 40; idem, "Style and Symbolism Meet in Design for Penn Station," *New York Times*, May 16, 1999, 1, 33; and "Penn Station Expansion Plan to Proceed," *New York Times*, October 13, 2001, A11.

94. For discussions of this tendency in urban design see Nan Ellin, *Postmodern Urbanism*, rev. ed. (New York: Princeton Architectural Press, 1999); and Michael Sorkin, ed., *Variations on a Theme Park* (New York: Hill and Wang, 1992).

95. Sigmund Freud, "The Uncanny," in *The Standard Edition of the Complete Psychological Works of Sigmund Freud*, trans. and ed. James Strachey in collaboration with Anna Freud, vol. 17 (London: Hogarth Press, 1955), 243. See also Paul Tillich, "Die technische Stadt als Symbol" (1928), in *Auf der Grenze. Eine Auswahl aus dem Lebenswerk* (Munich: Piper, 1987), 220-225; and Anthony Vidler, *The Architectural Uncanny: Essays in the Modern Unhomely* (Cambridge, Mass.: MIT Press, 1992).

96. Quoted in Diehl, *The Late, Great Pennsylvania Station*, 29.

97. See Svetlana Boym, *The Future of Nostalgia* (New York: Basic Books, 2001), 49-55.

4. CENTRIFUGAL SPACE

1. Four novels by Chandler (*The Big Sleep, Farewell My Lovely, The High Window,* and *The Lady in the Lake*) were adapted for the screen during the 1940s. In addition, Chandler wrote the screenplay for *The Blue Dahlia* and collaborated with Billy Wilder on the screenplay of *Double Indemnity.* For a complete account of his Hollywood career see William Luhr, *Raymond Chandler and Film* (New York: Frederick Ungar, 1982).

2. Raymond Chandler, "Blackmailers Don't Shoot" (1933), in *Stories and Early Novels* (New York: Library of America, 1995), 13; idem, "Pick-Up on Noon Street" (1936), ibid., 299.

3. Fredric Jameson, "The Synoptic Chandler," in *Shades of Noir: A Reader,* ed. Joan Copjec (London: Verso, 1993), 33–34. Valuable contributions to understanding the work of Chandler remain Dorothy Gardiner and Kathrine Sorley Walker, eds., *Raymond Chandler Speaking* (Boston: Houghton Mifflin, 1977); Frank MacShane, *The Life of Raymond Chandler* (Harmondsworth: Penguin, 1976); Miriam Gross, ed., *The World of Raymond Chandler* (New York: A & W, 1978); and *Selected Letters of Raymond Chandler,* ed. Frank MacShane (New York: Columbia University Press, 1981). For a discussion of the relation between the writings of Zola and visuality see Leo Braudy, "Zola on Film: The Ambiguities of Naturalism," in *Native Informant: Essays on Film, Fiction, and Popular Culture* (New York: Oxford University Press, 1991), 95–106.

4. For a thoughtful discussion of roads and automobility in Chandler see William Alexander McClung, *Landscapes of Desire: Anglo Mythologies of Los Angeles* (Berkeley: University of California Press, 2000), esp. 185–197.

5. For the prehistory of freeways in Los Angeles see Matthew W. Roth, "Mullholland Highway and the Engineering Culture of Los Angles in the 1920s," *Technology and Culture* 40 (July 1999): 545–575. The future of highways in the region is discussed in the key document *A Comprehensive Report on the Master Plan of Highways for the Los Angeles County Regional Planning District,* vol. 1: *The Plan and Its Preparation* (Los Angeles: Regional Planning Commission, Los Angeles County Regional Planning District, 1941). A general discussion of the freeway in American literature is found in Kris Lackey, *Road Frames: The American Highway Narrative* (Lincoln: University of Nebraska Press, 1997).

6. For discussions of the vitality of Central Avenue during the 1940s see Clora Bryant et al., eds., *Central Avenue Sounds: Jazz in Los Angeles* (Berkeley: University of California Press, 1998).

7. Many examples of urban decentralization and the expansion of the city beyond its traditional boundaries can be supplied for the period before 1929. Perhaps the most famous case remains the metropolitan area of Paris, which grew from seven communes beyond the city boundaries in 1851 to twenty-nine in 1872. Between 1861 and 1872 its ten eccentric arrondissements gained 200,000 inhabitants. For a discussion of the history of Paris, see David H. Pinckney, *Napoleon III and the Rebuilding of Paris* (Princeton: Princeton University Press, 1958), esp. 165–171. The standard text on the garden city movement is Ebenezer Howard, *Garden Cities of To-Morrow* (1902; reprint, Cambridge, Mass.: MIT Press, 1965).

8. Chandler, *The High Window*, in *Stories and Early Novels*, 1055.

9. Idem, "Blackmailers Don't Shoot," ibid., 15.

10. See in this regard Reyner Banham, *Los Angeles: The Architecture of Four Ecologies* (Harmondsworth: Penguin, 1971).

11. For one attempt to resolve the assertion that "it is Chandler's pre-1914 Los Angeles that Marlowe is regretting," see David Smith, "The Public Eye of Raymond Chandler," *American Studies* 14 (1980): 423–442, esp. 430.

12. Chandler, *The Little Sister* (1949), in *Later Novels and Other Writings* (New York: Library of America, 1995), 268, 358.

13. Letter to James Sandoe, June 16, 1949, in Gardiner and Walker, *Raymond Chandler Speaking*, 58.

14. Letter to Michael Gilbert, December 19, 1957, quoted in MacShane, *The Life of Raymond Chandler*, 252.

15. Fredric Jameson, "On Raymond Chandler," in *The Poetics of Murder*, ed. Glenn W. Most and William W. Stowe (San Diego: Harcourt Brace Jovanovich, 1983), 122–148.

16. There is no reference to the streetcar track repair in the film's original screenplay. See Billy Wilder, *Double Indemnity* (Berkeley: University of California Press, 2000), 7.

17. For a discussion of the declining fortunes of the Los Angeles electric trolley system see Spencer Crump, *Ride the Big Red Cars: How the Trolleys Helped Build Southern California* (Los Angeles: Crest, 1962), esp. 200–209; and Martin Wachs, "The Evolution of Transportation in Los Angeles: Images of Past Policies and Future Prospects," in *The City: Los Angeles and Urban Theory at the End of the Twentieth Century*, ed. Allen J. Scott and Edward W. Soja (Berkeley: University of California Press, 1996), 106–159. Both authors demonstrate conclusively that the decline of the trolleys was a consequence of decreasing quality of service and the growing popularity of express buses. They thereby refute the allegation that General Motors sabotaged public transportation in Los Angeles.

18. For the history of automobility in southern California see Scott Bottles, *Los Angeles and the Automobile* (Berkeley: University of California Press, 1987); and Ashleigh Brilliant, *The Great Car Craze: How Southern California Collided with the Automobile in the 1920s* (Santa Barbara: Woodbridge, 1989). For more general studies of automobility see James J. Flink, *The Automobile Age* (Cambridge, Mass.: MIT Press, 1988); and Joel Wachs and Margaret Crawford, eds., *The Car and the City* (Ann Arbor: University of Michigan Press, 1992).

19. Herbert Marcuse, "Some Social Implications of Modern Technology" (1941), in *Collected Papers of Herbert Marcuse*, vol. 1: *Technology, War, and Fascism* (London: Routledge, 1998), 46.

20. Ibid.

21. Michel Foucault, "Space, Knowledge, and Power," interview by Paul Rabinow, trans. Christian Hubert, in *The Foucault Reader*, ed. Rabinow (New York: Pantheon, 1984), 244.

22. Descriptions of the spatial environment as exhibiting centrifugal and centripetal tendencies are frequent in the literature of twentieth-century American urban geography and planning. The characterization of the modern city as centripe-

tal appears throughout Frank Lloyd Wright, *The Disappearing City* (New York: William Farquhar Payson, 1932). An early attempt to define the conceptual opposition is Charles C. Colby, "Centrifugal and Centripetal Forces in Urban Geography," *Annals of the Association of American Geographers* 23 (March 1933): 1–20. A later example is José Luis Sert, *Can Our Cities Survive? An ABC of Urban Problems, Their Analysis, Their Solutions* (Cambridge, Mass.: Harvard University Press, 1947), 156.

23. John Lewis, *Music from "Odds against Tomorrow,"* The Modern Jazz Quartet, Blue Note compact disc 7934152, 1990.

24. As one historian notes, "between 1950 and 1960 urban population grew by about 45 percent, but it occupied twice as much land: 12,804 square miles in 1950 compared with 25,554 miles in 1960. The reason, quite simply, is that the outward shift of urban population is also predominantly a shift from multiple- to single-family dwellings"; John B. Rae, *The Road and the Car in American Life* (Cambridge, Mass.: MIT Press, 1971), 226–227.

25. For an overview of this development see David Lyon, *The Electronic Eye: The Rise of Surveillance Society* (Minneapolis: University of Minnesota Press, 1994).

26. See Jean Gottmann, *Megalopolis: The Urbanized Northeastern Seaboard of the United States* (Cambridge, Mass.: MIT Press, 1961); Rob Kling, Spencer Olin, and Mark Poster, eds., *Postsuburban California: The Transformation of Orange County since World War II* (Berkeley: University of California Press, 1990); and Joel Garreau, *Edge City: Life on the New Frontier* (New York: Doubleday, 1991).

27. "And even today the notion of a structure lacking any center represents the unthinkable itself"; Jacques Derrida, "Structure, Sign, and Play in Discourse of the Human Sciences," in *The Structuralist Controversy: The Languages of Criticism and the Sciences of Man*, ed. Richard Macksey and Eugenio Donato (Baltimore: Johns Hopkins University Press, 1970), 248.

28. For discussions of the shopping center as a hybrid spatial form see Richard Longstreth, *City Center to Regional Mall: Architecture, the Automobile, and Retailing in Los Angeles, 1920–1950* (Cambridge, Mass.: MIT Press, 1997).

29. For studies of these transportation technologies see Sam Bass Warner Jr., *Streetcar Suburbs: The Process of Growth in Boston (1870–1900)*, 2d ed. (Cambridge, Mass.: Harvard University Press, 1978); and George W. Hilton and John F. Due, *The Electric Interurban Railway in America* (Stanford: Stanford University Press, 1960).

30. Thomas V. Czarnowski, "The Street as a Communications Artifact," in *On Streets*, ed. Stanford Anderson (Cambridge, Mass.: MIT Press, 1986), 210.

31. Frank Lloyd Wright, *The Living City* (New York: Horizon, 1958), 31.

32. Ibid., 134.

33. See Lewis Mumford, "Megalopolis as Anti-City" (1962–63), in Mumford, *Architecture as a Home for Man: Essays for Architectural Record*, ed. Jeanne M. Davern (New York: Architectural Record Books, 1975), 121.

34. Le Corbusier, *The City of Tomorrow*, trans. Frederick Etchells (Cambridge, Mass.: MIT Press, 1971), 165.

35. Le Corbusier, *The Radiant City* (1933), trans. Pamela Knight, Eleanor Levieux, and Derek Coltman (London: Faber and Faber, 1967), 196–197.

36. Tracy B. Augur, "The Dispersal of Cities as a Defense Measure," *Journal of the American Institute of Planners* 14 (summer 1948): 31. Augur worked as a planner at the Tennessee Valley Authority and was president of the American Institute of Planners. This article contributes to the discussion of urban dispersal as a civil defense strategy that was conducted in American planning journals at the end of the 1940s. See also Jacob Marschak, Edward Teller, and Lawrence R. Klein, "Dispersal of Cities and Industries," *Bulletin of Atomic Scientists* 1, no. 9 (April 15, 1946): 13–16; and Elmer T. Peterson, ed., *Cities Are Abnormal* (Norman: University of Oklahoma Press, 1946).

37. The "postcity" literature is enormous. For a technological and economic view of the city's demise, see Kenneth Boulding, "The Death of the City: A Frightened Look at Postcivilization," in *The Historian and the City*, ed. Oscar Handlin and John Burchard (Cambridge, Mass.: MIT Press, 1963). A negative analysis of the social consequences of decentralization is found in Mumford, "Megalopolis as Anti-City," 121–128.

38. Although they seldom (if ever) actually built highways, the principal modernist architects of the early twentieth century frequently wrote about them. Examples of these analyses include Mies van der Rohe, "Expressways as an Artistic Problem" (1932), in *The Artless Word: Mies van der Rohe on the Building Art*, trans. Mark Jarzombek, ed. Fritz Neumeyer (Cambridge, Mass.: MIT Press, 1991); Le Corbusier, *The Radiant City* (1933), 196–197; and Wright, *The Living City*, 116.

39. For discussions of relations among the railroad and cinema, see Museum of Modern Art, *Junction and Journey: Trains and Film* (New York, 1991); and Lynne Kirby, *Parallel Tracks: The Railroad and Silent Cinema* (Durham, N.C.: Duke University Press, 1997).

40. The concept of the freeway, a route free of side-entry access roads, originates around this time with the Norris Freeway built in 1933 by the TVA. See Norman T. Newton, *Design on the Land: The Development of Landscape Architecture* (Cambridge, Mass.: Harvard University Press, 1971), 617.

41. Richard Guy Wilson, "The Machine in the Landscape," in Richard Guy Wilson, Dianne H. Pilgrim, and Dickran Tashjian, *The Machine Age in America, 1918–1941* (New York: Brooklyn Museum in association with Harry N. Abrams, 1986), 91. This article, published in an exhibition catalog, contains a very useful summary of highway development up to 1941, as well as an excellent bibliography.

42. Between 1935 and 1945 the profession of planning witnessed extraordinary growth. Examples include the founding in 1935 of the *Journal of the American Institute of Planners*, the creation of the National Resources Planning Board in 1940, the establishment in 1941 of the first graduate programs in city planning at the University of Michigan, the University of Washington, and the Illinois Institute of Technology, and the rise of local planning boards and commissions.

43. Benton Mackaye and Lewis Mumford, "Townless Highways for the Motorist: A Proposal for the Automobile Age," *Harper's Monthly*, August 1931, 349.

44. For a discussion of the history of the Bureau of Public Roads see Tom Lewis, *Divided Highways: Building the Interstate Highways, Transforming American Life* (New York: Viking, 1997); and Bruce E. Seely, *Building the American Highway System: Engineers as Policy Makers* (Philadelphia: Temple University Press, 1987).

45. See Thomas H. MacDonald, "Federal Highway Progress," *American Civic Annual*, 1934, 165–168.

46. Bureau of Public Roads, *Toll Roads and Free Roads: Message from the President of the United States* . . . , 76th Cong., 1st sess., 1939, H. Doc. 272, 93, quoted in Seely, *Building the American Highway System*, 171.

47. Seely, *Building the American Highway System*, 181. For a later statement of similar themes see Buford M. Hayden, "The Planning Challenge of the Federal Highway Program," *American City*, September 1956, 130–132.

48. A serious intellectual biography of Bel Geddes remains to be written. For general overviews of his life and career, see the three-part article by Geoffrey T. Hellman that appeared in the *New Yorker*, February 8, 15, 22, 1941; Jeffrey L. Meikle, *Twentieth Century Limited: Industrial Design in America, 1925–1939* (Philadelphia: Temple University Press, 1975); and Arthur J. Pulos, *American Design Ethic: A History of Industrial Design* (Cambridge, Mass.: MIT Press, 1983). The span of his interests and activities can also be discerned in the outdated, sometimes inaccurate but nonetheless useful volume, Frederick J. Hunter, ed., *Catalog of the Norman Bel Geddes Theatre Collection: Humanities Research Center, University of Texas at Austin* (Boston: G. K. Hall, 1973). For recent discussions of his design work see the special thematic issue of *Rassegna* 16, no. 60 (1994).

49. Bel Geddes was an accomplished theatrical designer who worked on a plan for an auditorium for the performance of Dante's *Divine Comedy* and numerous stage sets. For a discussion of this phase of his career, see Norman Bel Geddes, *A Project for Theatrical Presentation of the Divine Comedy of Dante Alighieri* (New York: Theatre Arts, 1924); and the chapter "Industrializing the Theater," in his *Horizons* (1932; reprint, New York: Dover, 1977), 140–158. The discussion of Soviet film on 158 is especially suggestive and hints at the influence of Sergei Eisenstein, whom he describes meeting in his autobiography, *Miracle in the Evening* (Garden City, N.Y.: Doubleday, 1960), 326–328. Expressing his admiration for Eisenstein's *The Film Sense*, Bel Geddes goes so far as to claim that the technique for marking up a script that he developed in his work on the Dante play influenced the Soviet director. Early in his career Bel Geddes designed movie theaters and worked as an art director for D. W. Griffith and Cecil B. De Mille. His single directorial credit, a poorly received 1917 historical drama produced by Universal, *Nathan Hale*, does not appear to have led him to direct other films. Though deeply knowledgeable about the European silent-film tradition and sometimes active in producing short promotional films for his clients, cinematic production remained secondary to his work in theater, as Bel Geddes makes clear in *Miracle in the Evening*, 313–322.

50. Quoted in Roland Marchand, "The Designers Go to the Fair II: Norman Bel Geddes, The General Motors 'Futurama,' and the Visit to the Factory Transformed," *Design Issues* 8 (spring 1992): 38. This essay remains the most sophisticated study of Bel Geddes yet completed, and I am greatly indebted to it. See also Marchand's masterful study of corporate visual imagery, *Creating the Corporate Soul: The Rise of Public Relations and Corporate Imagery in American Big Business* (Berkeley: University of California Press, 1998). A detailed discussion of the architectural and design components of the Futurama can be found in Robert Coombs, "Norman Bel Geddes: Highways and Horizons," *Perspecta* 13–14 (1971): 11–27.

51. The model of the City of 1960 was actually completed in 1937 as part of an advertising campaign for Shell Oil. It occupied 35,738 square feet and contained two million individual buildings. The dramatic *sfumato* effect that seemed to bathe the buildings in *Magic Motorways* in hazy sunshine was attained by burning smoke pots in the photography studio. For a discussion of its history, see Marchand, ibid.; and Jeffrey L. Meikle, *The City of Tomorrow: Model 1937* (London: Pentagram Design, 1984).

52. The City of 1960 proposed by Bel Geddes must be understood within a long history of planned urban communities that includes Claude-Nicolas Ledoux's 1780 plan for Chaux, the phalansteries of Charles Fourier, and the modernist experimentations of Le Corbusier's City of Three Million and Frank Lloyd Wright's Broadacre City. For an account of Ledoux, see Anthony Vidler, *Claude-Nicolas Ledoux: Architecture and Social Reform at the End of the Ancien Regime* (Cambridge, Mass.: MIT Press, 1990). Relevant developments in the nineteenth century are treated by Vidler in "The New World: The Reconstruction of Urban Utopias in Late Nineteenth Century France," *Perspecta* 13–14 (1971): 244–256. A useful summary of twentieth-century plans can be found in Robert Fishman, *Urban Utopias in the Twentieth Century: Ebenezer Howard, Frank Lloyd Wright, Le Corbusier* (Cambridge, Mass.: MIT Press, 1982). For a discussion of Bel Geddes' appropriation of the Plan Voisin (1925) and Radiant City (1930) of Le Corbusier, see Folke T. Kihlstedt, "Utopia Realized: The World's Fairs of the 1930s," in *Imagining Tomorrow: History, Technology, and the American Future*, ed. Joseph J. Corn (Cambridge, Mass.: MIT Press, 1986), 106.

53. For a discussion of the contact between Bel Geddes and Mendelsohn and the actual design of the Futurama by Albert Kahn and Eero Saarinen, see Meikle, *Twentieth Century Limited*, 49, 201.

54. Clearly indebted to the nineteenth-century mass-cultural forms of the panorama and the diorama, the Futurama also significantly differs from them. As with the panorama, its spectators are mobile and must advance through the exhibition space to follow a narrative. This feature distinguishes it from the diorama, in which the viewer remains stationary before an array of changing painted views. Yet unlike both the panorama and diorama, the exhibit of Bel Geddes displayed not a transparent painting, but a large-scale model in which carefully sculpted beams of light orchestrated the scene beneath the spectator's gaze. Here the influence of Bel Geddes' career in the theater, especially his work with Max Reinhardt, can be seen. Strictly speaking, the Futurama was neither panorama nor diorama, but a hybrid form in which spectators moved past a model city and highway. The flow of traffic through the model was carefully animated, and the presence of movement within the scene differentiates it from earlier mass-cultural genres. Yet the strategy of transporting fairgoers through the spectacle in rubber-tired vehicles also recalls the 1832 Berlin pleorama, in which an audience viewed painted images while seated in a ship, as well as the 1904 Hale's Tour attraction, in which films were projected to spectators in simulated railroad cars. For discussions of these technologies, see Anne Friedberg, *Window Shopping: Cinema and the Postmodern* (Berkeley: University of California Press, 1993), 20–29; Helmut Gernsheim and Alison Gernsheim, *L. J. M. Daguerre: The History of the Diorama and the Daguerreotype*

(New York: Dover, 1968), 14–47; and Raymond Fielding, "Hale's Tour: Ultrarealism in the Pre-1910 Motion Picture," in *Film before Griffith*, ed. John L. Fell (Berkeley: University of California Press, 1983), 116–130.

55. Best known for its strident attack on the congested metropolis as a source of physical danger and moral decay, the film also praises highways and garden communities, albeit in a less hyperbolic fashion than Bel Geddes. For a discussion of the film see *The City Life* 6 (June 5, 1939): 64–65.

56. Eugene Raskin, "Fairer than Fair," *Pencil Points* 18 (February 1937): 92.

57. The fair contained numerous exhibitions that suggested the modalities of centrifugal space, including a model "Democracity" of the decentralized future, a display of suburban homes of the "Town of Tomorrow," and a "Roads of the World" feature in which visitors could experience driving over replicas of notable highways of the past and present. A complete listing of exhibits is found in *Official Guide Book of the New York World's Fair 1939* (New York: Exposition Publications, 1939).

58. Douglas Haskell, "To-morrow and the World's Fair," *Architectural Record* 88 (August 1940): 68, quoted in Meikle, *Twentieth Century Limited*, 198.

59. Marchand, "The Designers Go to the Fair II," 32. Although Bel Geddes frequently describes the effect of the Futurama as panoramic, he also appropriated cinematic metaphors, as in his description of the glass frame placed before the spectators that limited their vision to a rectangle. See "Proposal to General Motors," job file 381, box 9, folder 1–2, 5, Norman Bel Geddes Collection, Harry Ransom Humanities Research Center, University of Texas, Austin.

60. Though ostensibly providing an encounter with the highway and the city of the future, the presentational mode of the Futurama reminded many observers of the experience of airplane travel. This effect was scarcely coincidental, for Bel Geddes relied heavily on aerial photographs in designing the model. See his "Memo to Tavarez of 8/11/38," job file 381, box 19d, file 42, 1, Norman Bel Geddes Collection.

61. Quoted in Marchand, "The Designers Go to the Fair II," 34.

62. Norman Bel Geddes, *Magic Motorways* (New York: Random House, 1940). This book has been curiously overlooked in studies of the career of the designer, despite what seems to have been its considerable impact on popular awareness of highway planning at the time. Among the correspondence in the Bel Geddes Collection from appreciative recipients of the book are letters from the White House, Arthur Hays Sulzberger, David Sarnoff, Thomas E. Dewey, and top executives at General Motors and Shell Oil.

63. Ibid., 277–278.

64. Quoted in Marchand, "The Designers Go to the Fair II," 37.

65. See David Nye, *American Technological Sublime* (Cambridge, Mass.: MIT Press, 1994).

66. Sigfried Giedion, *Space, Time and Architecture: The Growth of a New Tradition* (Cambridge, Mass.: Harvard University Press, 1941), 732.

67. Ibid., 733. Anyone who has ever been stuck in traffic en route to New York's Kennedy Airport will find highly amusing Giedion's description of one of the worst highway bottlenecks as a facilitator of movement.

68. Ibid., 729–730.

69. Ibid., 431–432.

70. One wonders whether Giedion actually visited the Futurama.

71. Bel Geddes, *Magic Motorways*, 272–273.

72. The earliest discussions of regional planning—a blanket term covering diverse political and ideological projects—took place during the mid-1920s but became more widespread after the Depression. A useful collection of initial statements can be found in Carl Sussman, ed., *Planning the Fourth Migration: The Neglected Vision of the Regional Planning Association of America* (Cambridge, Mass.: MIT Press, 1976). See also Mark Luccarelli, *Lewis Mumford and the Ecological Region: The Politics of Planning* (New York: Guilford, 1995).

73. For an account of the hostility of General Motors management toward the New Deal and their goals for the Futurama, see Marchand, "The Designers Go to the Fair II," 29. Critiques of the Futurama and of Bel Geddes' highway concept written by observers at the time include Bruce Bliven Jr., "Metropolis: 1960 Style," *New Republic*, September 29, 1937, 211–212; and Rexford G. Tugwell, "Parts of a New Civilization," *Saturday Review of Literature* 21, April 13, 1940, 3–4.

74. See Seely, *Building the American Highway System*, 210.

75. Quoted in Marchand, "The Designers Go to the Fair II," 40.

76. Tom Lewis suggests that the chief of the Bureau of Public Roads, Thomas H. MacDonald, understood highway construction in relation to "four different but integrated components of American life, each of which contributed to the welfare of the nation." These included agriculture, recreation, commerce, and defense. For a recent discussion of the value of highways to specific military objectives see Lewis, *Divided Highways*, esp. 12, 66, 90, 107–108, 152.

77. See Thomas H. MacDonald, "The New Federal Highway Program," *American Planning and Civic Annual*, 1942, 51–55.

78. Bel Geddes, *Magic Motorways*, 295–296.

79. George E. Mowry and Blaine A. Brownell, *The Urban Nation, 1920–1980* (New York: Hill and Wang, 1981), 166. "By the fall of 1941 the defense program had been under way less than a year and a half, yet in that brief time the number of Americans who had left their homes in search of new jobs or had been displaced by defense activities was greater than the entire migration from the Old World to American shores from the time of the voyage of the Mayflower to the outbreak of the Revolution"; Mel Scott, *American City Planning since 1890: A History Commemorating the Fiftieth Anniversary of the American Institute of Planners* (Berkeley: University of California Press, 1969), 386.

80. Scott, *American City Planning*, 378, 394.

81. "Having thought in terms of rural roads for so many years, the inclination of the State and Federal engineers on first approaching city problems was to regard urban congestion as a hindrance to the flow of intercity and interstate traffic and to try to expedite travel by the construction of routes skirting the edge of urban areas. In many cases such bypasses have been justified, but early studies showed that most of the traffic approaching a city wants to go into it and that a bypass solves only a small part of the problem"; John T. Lynch, "Traffic Planning in American Cities," *Public Roads* 24 (October–November–December 1945): 161. The rural-urban an-

tagonisms suggested by this statement, as well as the palpable anxiety attached to the urban center, is fascinating. See also Thomas H. MacDonald, "The City's Place in Post-War Highway Planning," *American City*, February 1943, 42–44; idem, "The Interstate System in Urban Areas," *American Planning and Civic Annual*, 1950, 114–119; and Charles M. Nelson, "Expressways and the Planning of Tomorrow's Cities," *Planning*, 1950, 116–125.

82. "In Chicago, Ill. the movement of vehicles throughout the city on a typical weekday was determined by observing license numbers as the vehicles passed different survey stations. Several thousand Boy Scouts were used to man the stations and several hundred supervisors were required to direct the work"; Lynch, "Traffic Planning," 167.

83. See "Travel Patterns in 50 Cities," *Public Roads* 30, no. 5 (December 1958), for a particularly thorough example of this type of research.

84. Francis Bello, "The Car and the City," in Editors of Fortune, *The Exploding Metropolis* (Garden City, N.Y.: Doubleday, 1958), 53.

85. Ibid., 58–59.

86. On March 22, 1939, President Franklin Roosevelt hosted a dinner for Bel Geddes at the White House. Included in the evening's festivities was a viewing of his model highways exhibit set up in the West Hall. Although the assembled guests discussed the creation of a Federal Land Authority to acquire rights-of-way for highway construction, it does not appear that the ideas of the designer exerted any direct influence upon the president or the highway policy of his administration. See Mark H. Rose, *Interstate: Express Highway Politics, 1941–1956* (Lawrence: Regents Press of Kansas, 1979), 11. Nor did Robert Moses react with any more enthusiasm to the Futurama, which he termed "bunk." See the editorial "Super-Highways," *New York Times*, January 28, 1940, sec. 4, p. 8; and Meikle, *Twentieth Century Limited*, 208, for a discussion of contact between Moses and Bel Geddes. Yet despite the prevailing skepticism toward an interstate highway system, which the *New York Times* termed "a needless and expensive luxury," his motorway scheme did capture the attention and evident admiration of the planning profession, as evidenced by the depiction of the Futurama on the cover of the July 1939 issue of *American City*. See the enthusiastic report in "The Magic City of Progress," 40–41. In the postwar period Bel Geddes continued his work as a planner and apostle of decentralization and is perhaps best known for his "Toledo Tomorrow" model of 1945. See "Toledo: A Model of Proposed Changes in the Transportation Pattern Arouses Citizen Interest in the City's Future," *Architectural Record*, August 1945, 119–123.

87. Statistics taken from "Mileage and Cost of Federal Aid Highway Improvements: 1917 to 1957," chart in U.S. Bureau of the Census, *Historical Statistics of the United States, Colonial Times to 1957* (Washington, D.C., 1960), 458.

88. U.S. Congress, House, *Hearings on H.R. 2426*, 956, quoted in Seely, *Building the Highway System*, 191.

89. John R. Griffith, "The Complete Highway: Modern Transportation in the Light of Ancient Philosophy," *Landscape Architecture* 47 (January 1957): 352.

90. The convergence between the mission of highway engineers to construct

roads and the possibilities offered by cinema to shape vision did not escape notice during the 1950s. As one landscape architect observed in 1957, "The science of optics has made great advances in recent years, but little has been written about just how speed affects vision. How is seeing modified by increasing speed? Most artists today are concerned with this problem. How can we apply what is known and is being discovered to this field of highway design? The complexity of the problem indicates, as in so many planning problems, that the job can be accomplished only by teams of talented technicians working together. Techniques from the movie industry, such as cinemascope, cinerama, animation, et cetera, may become useful tools in this study, just as aerial surveys and photogrammetric methods have already proven their value"; Geraldine Knight Scott, "Highway Aesthetics," *Landscape Architecture* 47 (October 1957): 32. See also Carl Goldschmidt, "Windshield Vistas—Who Cares?" *Journal of the American Institute of Planners* 24, no. 3 (1958): 158–166. One might note the publication by László Moholy-Nagy of *Vision in Motion* (Chicago: Paul Theobald, 1947) a decade earlier as the most conspicuous research by an artist into the problem of speed and vision. The work during the late 1950s of Kevin Lynch and his Bauhaus-trained teacher Gyorgy Kepes on problems of visual and urban perception also suggests the influx of European modernist understandings of movement and vision into postwar theories of planning and city form.

91. Bill Severn and Sue Severn, *Highways to Tomorrow* (Englewood Cliffs, N.J.: Prentice-Hall, 1959), 1–2.

92. For discussions of the relation of the interstate highway system to the metropolis contemporaneous with its planning see "The National Highway Program: A Challenge to Cities," *American City*, August 1956, 11; and "The Urban Framework to the State Highway Plan," *American City*, October 1956, 136–139. General overviews can be found in Seely, *Building the American Highway System*, 193–195; and Lewis, *Divided Highways*, 179–210.

93. Lewis Mumford, *The Highway and the City* (New York: New American Library, 1963), 247.

94. *They Drive by Night* was adapted from *Long Haul* (New York: Carrick and Evans, 1938). *Thieves' Highway* was adapted from *Thieves' Market* (1949; reprint, Berkeley: University of California Press, 1997). For an overview of the career of Bezzerides see the foreword by Garrett White.

95. Harry Brand (director of publicity, 20th Century–Fox Studio), "Vital Statistics on *Hard Bargain*," 5, undated press release in *Thieves' Highway* file in collection of University of Southern California Film and Television Archive. (The original working titles of the film were *Collision* and *Hard Bargain*.)

96. Here one might also mention the extensive location scouting and photography on the outskirts of Phoenix and in California's central valley employed by Alfred Hitchcock in *Psycho* (1960). See Janet Leigh with Christopher Nickens, *Behind the Scenes of Psycho: The Classic Thriller* (New York: Harmony, 1995), 24–26.

97. "Don't get many trucks nowadays since the new highway is in," a gas station attendant mentions to the gang in the film's clearest acknowledgment of the interstate system.

98. Suggestive here is the painting from the 1950s by Roger Kuntz, *Santa Ana Arrows*, which takes the flatness and graphic directness of the freeway sign as its subject.

99. Paul Virilio, *The Aesthetics of Disappearance*, trans. Philip Beitchman (New York: Semiotext(e), 1991), 58.

100. Apart from the opening sequence during which the train robbery is committed and one nocturnal driving sequence, there are no night scenes in the film. Nor are there scenes of recognizable Los Angeles landmarks, except for a small sign identifying the city and the concluding sequence on the Harbor Freeway.

101. The use of radio throughout *Plunder Road* is of the greatest interest as a telling example of the communication and surveillance practices of centrifugal space. News bulletins audible in the trucks of the gang members and in roadside restaurants provide the only information on their actual spatial locations. Especially significant is this "simultaneity" of communication, which allows the characters to monitor their own pursuit on police radios. The classic film noir trope of the nightclub with its jazz orchestra is reproduced during the scene in which music is heard on a radio in a truck stop.

102. Henri Lefebvre, *The Production of Space*, trans. Donald Nicholson-Smith (Cambridge, Mass.: Basil Blackwell, 1991), 313.

103. Scott, *American City Planning*, 539.

104. See the remarks on the Harbor Freeway by Albert C. Martin, designer of such buildings in the redeveloped Los Angeles downtown as the Arco and Bank of America towers, in Henry Sutherland, "New 'Main Street' Changing L.A.," *Los Angeles Times*, February 19, 1967, sec. J, p. 1.

105. "The essential point here is . . . a fight to the death between an individual and a network that threatens fundamental freedoms (among which that of commerce is not, in this system, the least important) . . . On a small or a grand scale, the idea is that of the 'combo' dominating and exerting its influence, it being understood that the combo is undemocratic and (it is the same thing) un-American. It can, then, be seen that paranoia is not an American malediction consequent upon some unspecified spell cast over the whole country, that would then allow a magical explanation of *film noir*: on the contrary, it is a matter of a contradiction inherent in the economic and political system of the United States, in which the citizen must constantly be reassured of his rights in the face of economic concentrations and federal power, the inhabitant of the small town in the face of the big city, the wage-earner in the face of the rich"; Marc Vernet, "*Film Noir* on the Edge of Doom," trans. J. Swenson, in Copjec, *Shades of Noir*, 19–20.

106. As an ideal visual trope for the inchoate spatial order of capitalism, the freeway would come to fascinate many filmmakers, and it pleases me to imagine a twenty-seven-year-old Jean-Luc Godard watching the ending of *Plunder Road* and filing it away for reappropriation a decade later in *Weekend*. The attraction of many post-1960 directors (Antonioni, Wenders, Tanner) to the highway is common knowledge, but needs to be understood, as I have tried to suggest, in relation to historical events and changes in the spatial environment already evident in the 1930s.

107. The work of M. Christine Boyer remains among the very few notable attempts to treat these issues. See her "Mobility and Modernism in the American City," *Center* 5 (1989): 86–104.

108. The most significant difference between the German and American construction of highways during the 1930s remains the centralization of the Deutsches Strassenwesen, which contrasts markedly with the federalist emphasis on cooperation between state transportation departments and Washington advocated by the Bureau of Public Roads. For a discussion of this, see Seely, *Building the American Highway System*, 72–73. On the construction of the German Autobahn see Edward Dimendberg, "The Will to Motorization: Cinema, Highways, and Modernity," *October* 73 (1995): 97–137. For the history of roads more generally see M. G. Lay, *Ways of the World: A History of the World's Roads and of the Vehicles That Used Them* (New Brunswick, N.J.: Rutgers University Press, 1992). Although the federal government would play a more prominent role in highway construction after the war, the most celebrated prewar projects were planned and executed by local officials such as Robert Moses. These include the Southern State Parkway and Jones Beach (1929), Grand Central Parkway, and the Triboro Bridge (1936). Despite the notorious megalomania of Moses, his building feats (unlike the German Autobahn) garnered popular acclaim without generating nationalist rhetoric. The standard study of Moses remains Robert Caro, *The Power Broker: Robert Moses and the Fall of New York* (New York: Alfred A. Knopf, 1974). For two more nuanced recent revisionist assessments see Marshall Berman, *All That Is Solid Melts into Air: The Experience of Modernity* (New York: Simon and Schuster, 1982), 290–312; and Phillip Lopate, "Rethinking Robert Moses: What If New York's Notorious Master Builder Wasn't Such a Bad Guy after All?" *Metropolis* 22 (August–September 2002): 42, 44, 46, 48.

5. SIMULTANEITY, THE MEDIA ENVIRONMENT, AND THE END OF FILM NOIR

1. My source for these statistics is Spencer Selby, *Dark City: The Film Noir* (Jefferson, N.C.: McFarland, 1984), 204–210. Selby lists 490 titles produced between 1940 and 1959 as belonging to the film noir cycle. Given the conflicting definitions of film noir, any such compilation remains debatable. Yet the overall decline in the production of films noir after 1949 suggested by Selby's filmography is echoed by that of Silver and Ward, who list 34 titles in 1950, 12 in 1955, and a mere 3 in 1958 and 1959; Alain Silver and Elizabeth Ward, eds., *Film Noir: An Encyclopedic Reference to the American Style* (Woodstock, N.Y.: Overlook, 1979).

2. The creator of *Dragnet*, Jack Webb, drew inspiration from the police procedural *He Walked by Night* (Alfred Werker, 1949). It began as a radio show and was transformed into a television series that ran from 1952 to 1959. *The Naked City* was aired on the ABC television network from 1958 to 1963 and closed each episode with the same voice-over narration that concluded the original film.

3. Typical is Robert Kolker's observation: "The suggestion has been made that the decline of black-and-white cinematography contributed to the decline of

noir, but more likely the viability of its conventions had worn down, and further shifts in ideology demanded a change in the films that embodied it. Rather than the bourgeois man undone, a favorite theme of forties *noir*, the fifties were fond of portraying the bourgeois man at bay, threatened but triumphant. The anxieties of the fifties needed a different expression than those of the forties; reassurance and affirmation became more important than reinforcement of fears and uncertainties"; *A Cinema of Loneliness: Penn, Kubrick, Scorsese, Spielberg, Altman*, 2d ed. (New York: Oxford University Press, 1988), 24. For the demise of the system of B movie production and its impact upon film noir see James Naremore, *More than Night: Film Noir in Its Contexts* (Berkeley: University of California Press, 1998), 136–166.

4. Raymond Borde and Etienne Chaumeton, *A Panorama of American Film Noir, 1941–1953*, trans. Paul Hammond (San Francisco: City Lights Books, 2002), 83.

5. See Lynn Spigel, *Make Room for TV: Television and the Family Ideal* (Chicago: University of Chicago Press, 1992), esp. 1, 32–33.

6. Statistics cited in Steven Lubar, *Info Culture: The Smithsonian Book of the Information Age* (Boston: Houghton Mifflin, 1993), 248.

7. The transition from San Francisco to Los Angeles in *This Gun for Hire* (1942) is one example.

8. Anthony Vidler, "The Scenes of the Street: Transformations in Ideal and Reality, 1750–1871," in *On Streets*, ed. Stanford Anderson (Cambridge, Mass.: MIT Press, 1986), 87.

9. For a discussion of these issues see Erik Barnouw, *A History of Broadcasting in the United States: A Tower in Babel*, vol. 1: *To 1933* (New York: Oxford University Press, 1968).

10. David Sarnoff, "Memo" to his superior while working for American Marconi (1916), quoted in Morgan E. McMahon, *A Flick of the Switch, 1930–1950* (Palos Verdes Peninsula, Calif.: Vintage Radio, 1975), 5.

11. See Alice Kaplan, *Reproductions of Banality: Fascism, Literature, and French Intellectual Life* (Minneapolis: University of Minnesota Press, 1986), esp. 133–136, for an insightful discussion of radio simultaneity and political mobilization in Vichy France. The significance of radio during the Third Reich is treated by Horst J. P. Bergmeier and Rainer E. Lotz in *Hitler's Airwaves: The Inside Story of Nazi Radio Broadcasting and Propaganda Swing* (New Haven: Yale University Press, 1997). For a discussion of radio in relation to American militarization see Erik Barnouw, *The Golden Web: A History of Broadcasting in the United States*, vol. 2: *1933 to 1953* (New York: Oxford University Press, 1968).

12. Frank Stanton, "The Critical Necessity for an Informed Public," *Journal of Broadcasting* 2 (summer 1958): 203.

13. Ibid., 195. This article, published in 1958, anticipates many themes developed by Marshall McLuhan in his *Understanding Media* of 1965.

14. See Michael Brian Schiffer, *The Portable Radio in American Life* (Phoenix: University of Arizona Press, 1991).

15. Marshall McLuhan, *Understanding Media: The Extensions of Man* (New York: McGraw Hill, 1965), 298.

16. Today, of course, the entire system of radio and television programming and ratings is segmented by time and space (morning programs for automobile commuters, afternoon soap operas for housewives) to deliver the proper target audience to advertisers.

17. Melvin M. Webber, "The Urban Place and the Nonplace Realm," in *Explorations into Urban Structure*, ed. Webber et al. (Philadelphia: University of Pennsylvania Press, 1964), 79–153.

18. Herbert Marshall McLuhan, *The Mechanical Bride: Folklore of Industrial Man* (New York: Vanguard, 1951), 4.

19. Mary Ann Doane, "Information, Crisis, Catastrophe," in *Logics of Television: Essays in Cultural Criticism*, ed. Patricia Mellencamp (Bloomington: Indiana University Press, 1990), 225.

20. Marshall McLuhan to Ezra Pound, January 5, 1951, in *Letters of Marshall McLuhan*, ed. Matie Molinaro, Corinne McLuhan, and William Toye (Toronto: Oxford University Press, 1987), 217.

21. See Blaise Cendrars, *Complete Poems*, trans. Ron Padgett (Berkeley: University of California Press, 1992); idem, "The Modern, a New Art, the Cinema" (1919), in *French Film Theory and Criticism: A History/Anthology*, ed. Richard Abel (Princeton: Princeton University Press, 1988), 182–183. See also Stephen Kern, *The Culture of Time and Space: 1880–1918* (Cambridge, Mass.: Harvard University Press, 1983), 70–75.

22. Joseph Frank, "Spatial Form in Modern Literature," in *The Idea of Spatial Form* (New Brunswick, N.J.: Rutgers University Press, 1991), 15.

23. Ezra Pound, "A Retrospect" (1918), in *The English Modernist Reader, 1910–1930*, ed. Peter Faulkner (Iowa City: University of Iowa Press, 1986), 60.

24. Marshall McLuhan to Ezra Pound, January 5, 1951, in Molinaro, McLuhan, and Toye, *Letters of Marshall McLuhan*, 218. See also Sergei Eisenstein, "The Cinematographic Principle and the Ideogram" (1929), in *Film Form*, trans. Jay Leyda (New York: Harcourt, Brace, 1949), 28–44.

25. McLuhan, *The Mechanical Bride*, 3, 5. The notion that the globe "becomes a very small village-like affair" in the electronic age appears in a letter from McLuhan to Edward S. Morgan, May 16, 1959, in Molinaro, McLuhan, and Toye, *Letters of Marshall McLuhan*, 253.

26. See McLuhan, *Understanding Media*, 305.

27. Ibid., 306n.

28. Tom Milne, *Joseph Losey* (Garden City, N.Y.: Doubleday, 1968), 85.

29. For a discussion of early television consumption in public see Anna McCarthy, *Ambient Television: Visual Culture and Public Space* (Durham, N.C.: Duke University Press, 2001), esp. 29–62.

30. See Mark J. Williams, *Remote Possibilities: A History of Early Television in Los Angeles, 1930–1952* (Durham: Duke University Press, forthcoming).

31. This point is expressed more directly in the screenplay of the Losey film. Consider the following exchange between J. W. Colt, publisher of the *Morning Herald*, and Marshall, head of the criminal underworld. Marshall says to Colt, "Let's be honest, John, we're not too far apart in our thinking about the police de-

partment. I've been enjoying the series you've been running . . . We want you to have an exclusive story." Colt responds to Marshall's invitation to be present when the child murderer is turned over to the police by blackmailing Carney, the chief of police: "Look, Carney, I have a proposition . . . How would you like your picture in the paper arresting the big boy himself . . . Marshall, of course. And wait—with the baby killer. What do I want? Only a transcript of your secret testimony in front of the grand jury . . . Now, don't take that tone. I feel the public is entitled to all the facts, and if you don't . . ."; *M* screenplay by Waldo Salt, 99-A, Script Collection, Margaret Herrick Library of the Academy of Motion Picture Arts and Sciences, Beverly Hills, Calif. This exchange intimates that the newspaper publisher is the most powerful of the three men. A similarly cynical view of the power of the print media is evident in Billy Wilder's 1951 film *The Big Carnival*.

32. At this same time the motion picture industry was discovering how television could be used to produce greater results at the box office by reaching residents across Los Angeles. An advertisement for the 1950 Columbia release *711 Ocean Drive* noted: "44% of those from homes with television sets volunteered they had heard about *711 Ocean Drive* on television. 76% when asked said they had heard about the picture on television. Television added 25% to attendance. The best buy in Los Angeles is television"; *Daily Variety*, October 20, 1950, 9.

33. *Variety*, June 28, 1950, p. 6, notes that "Director Joseph Losey winds Seymour Nebenzal's production of *M* tomorrow four days under schedule."

34. For a good presentation of these trends see Greg Hise, *Magnetic Los Angeles: Planning the Twentieth-Century Metropolis* (Baltimore: Johns Hopkins University Press, 1997).

35. Anastasia Loukaitou-Sideris and Gail Sainsbury, "Lost Streets of Bunker Hill," *California History* 74 (winter 1995–96): 394.

36. For a helpful contemporary survey of the mixed opinions on the redevelopment of Bunker Hill see Les Wagner, "Rejuvenation of Bunker Hill to Start Oct. 1," *Los Angeles Mirror News*, June 22, 1960, 8.

37. For an incisive analysis of the legacy of the downtown core and its relevance to future developments in the region see Robert Fishman, "Re-Imagining Los Angeles," in *Rethinking Los Angeles*, ed. Michael J. Dear, H. Eric Schockman, and Greg Hise (Thousand Oaks and Los Angeles: Sage Publications in association with Southern California Studies Center of the University of Southern California, 1996), 251–261.

38. Jean-Paul Sartre, "American Cities" (1945), in *Literary and Philosophical Essays*, trans. Annette Michelson (New York: Collier, 1962), 120–122.

39. For a discussion of the notion of the mobilized gaze see Anne Friedberg, *Window Shopping: Cinema and the Postmodern* (Berkeley: University of California Press, 1993).

40. Mel Scott, *Metropolitan Los Angeles: One Community* (Los Angeles: Haynes Foundation, 1949), 94.

41. Indeed, the murderer Harrow is presented to the underworld jury in a garage where he is imprisoned in a convertible, the top of which is unrolled to introduce him to the arbiters of justice.

42. Although it shares many architectural elements with the arcade, the Bradbury Building is an enclosed space rather than a passageway between streets or blocks. For an exhaustive study of the architectural type see Johann Friedrich Geist, *Arcades: The History of a Building Type*, trans. Jane O. Newman and John H. Smith (Cambridge, Mass.: MIT Press, 1983).

43. For a discussion of the glass architecture of the arcade as a phantasmagoric space see Walter Benjamin, *The Arcades Project*, trans. Howard Eiland and Kevin McLaughlin (Cambridge, Mass.: Belknap Press of Harvard University Press, 1999), 31–61; and Philippe Hamon, *Expositions: Literature and Architecture in Nineteenth-Century France*, trans. Katia Sainson-Frank and Lisa Maguire (Berkeley: University of California Press, 1992), esp. 71–73.

44. Esther McCoy and Raymond Girvigian, "Bradbury Building," in *Data Book Report: Historic American Buildings Survey* (Los Angeles: American Institute of Architects Preservation Committee, September 1963). For a discussion of the recent renovation of the Bradbury Building see Aaron Betsky, "Full Circle," *Architectural Record*, January 1993, 108–110.

45. For Losey's notes on the characters of the child murderer and the lawyer see Joseph Losey, *L'Oeil du maître*, ed. Michel Ciment (Arles: Institut Lumière/ Acts Sud), 95–108.

46. Consider the following lines from the screenplay of *M*, spoken by a marine sergeant: "An outfit like ours is what they need. The boys down in the legion post got an idea how to handle this guy! This gets any worse we'll form a vigilante committee." These lines, which do not appear in the film, suggest the activities of the House Committee. *M* script, scene 53A, Script Collection, Margaret Herrick Library of the Academy of Motion Picture Arts and Sciences.

47. There exists a striking parallel between the two versions of *M* and the manner in which each manifested a change in the relation of its director to his respective national cinema. After directing *M* in 1931, Lang made *The Testament of Dr. Mabuse* in 1932. In July 1933 he left Germany and began his career abroad, first in Paris, then in Hollywood. After directing *M* in 1950 (released in March 1951), Losey made *The Big Night* in 1951. In order to avoid a subpoena from the House Un-American Activities Committee, Losey left Los Angeles for Paris in July 1951 and began a period of work in Europe. Two years and one film after directing their versions of *M*, both men had left the cultures and cinema industries in which they formerly had prospered.

48. Quoted in column by Ezra Goodman, *Los Angeles Daily News*, June, 28, 1950.

49. *Variety*, August 2, 1950, 2.

50. Larry Ceplair and Steven Englund, *The Inquisition in Hollywood: Politics in the Film Community, 1930–1960* (Berkeley: University of California Press, 1983), 387.

51. Lowell E. Redlings, "*M* Remake Genuine Thriller: David Wayne Impressive as Psychopathic Killer," *Citizen News*, October 26, 1951; clipping in film file collection of the Margaret Herrick Library of the Academy of Motion Picture Arts and Sciences.

52. The scapegoat theme is particularly evident in the final zoom shot of the film's opening credit sequence, in which the director's name appears against the frightening silhouette of the child murderer standing on the beach, his craggy physique bearing a strong physical resemblance to the film director. The comparison between Langley, sacrificial victim of the bar, and Losey, victim of the blacklist, is also suggested by the similarity between their names and the fact that Langley is an amalgam of Lang and Losey. For a stimulating treatment of the scapegoat motif see Rene Girard, *Violence and the Sacred*, trans. Patrick Gregory (Baltimore: Johns Hopkins University Press, 1977).

53. Roland Barthes, "Introduction to the Structural Analysis of Narratives," in *Image/Music/Text*, trans. Stephen Heath (New York: Hill and Wang, 1977), 96.

54. The crucial exception to this is the apprehension and murder of Rollie after he carelessly leaves on the police radio in his truck.

55. Perfect simultaneity is, of course, semantically redundant, giving this moment in the film a deeply ironic twist.

56. One cannot view this scene without thinking of the famous traffic-jam sequence in Jean-Luc Godard's *Weekend* (1967). As a transitional film between the noir cycle of the 1940s and the work of a later filmmaker such as Godard, the value of a film such as *Plunder Road* becomes clear.

57. Henri Lefebvre, *The Production of Space*, trans. Donald Nicholson-Smith (Cambridge, Mass.: Basil Blackwell, 1991), 393.

58. According to articles published in *Daily Variety* in October 1949, these scenes were filmed in the Kentucky cities of Lexington and Keenland, and in Cincinnati, Ohio.

59. See David Harvey, *The Condition of Postmodernity* (Oxford: Basil Blackwell, 1989), esp. 284–307. I am grateful to Daniel Herwitz for making this connection.

60. Lefebvre, *The Production of Space*, 206.

61. W. R. Burnett, *The Asphalt Jungle* (London: White Lion, 1950), 15.

62. Lefebvre, *The Production of Space*, 35.

63. For a thoughtful analysis of Tatum's wielding of discourse see J. P. Telotte, *Voices in the Dark: The Narrative Patterns of Film Noir* (Urbana: University of Illinois Press, 1989), 183–186.

64. Jean Baudrillard, *The Ecstasy of Communication*, trans. Bernard and Caroline Schutze, ed. Sylvère Lotringer (New York: Semiotext(e), 1988), 19–20.

65. The opposition between live news coverage and preplanned and scripted media events is usefully sketched by Daniel Dayan and Elihu Katz in *Media Events: The Live Broadcasting of History* (Cambridge, Mass.: Harvard University Press, 1992), 9. Although the television coverage of the Minosa rescue is live, its musical accompaniment and increasingly formulaic character edge toward the scripted character of the media event noted by Dayan and Katz.

66. See Cameron Crowe, *Conversations with Wilder* (New York: Knopf, 1999), esp. 142–144.

67. Max Picard, *Hitler in Our Selves*, trans. Heinrich Hauser, ed. Robert S. Hartmann (Hinsdale, Ill.: Henry Regnery, 1947), 57–58.

68. Gilles Deleuze, *Cinema 1: The Movement Image*, trans. Hugh Tomlinson

and Barbara Habberjam (Minneapolis: University of Minnesota Press, 1986), 209–210.

69. For the relation between the statistical foundations of the insurance business and detective fiction see Joan Copjec, *Read My Desire: Lacan against the Historicists* (Cambridge, Mass.: MIT Press, 1994), 163–200.

70. The appearance of Wilder's film at the very beginning of the television age seems prescient. As Porfirio notes, "Though the sensational entrapment of Floyd Collins in 1925 has been mentioned as a possible source for this film, Billy Wilder admitted to me in an interview that its immediate inspiration was the tragedy of Kathy Fiscus, a little girl who fell into an abandoned well in the Los Angeles area and remained there for twenty-seven hours before workers retrieved her lifeless body, the first such calamity to be covered live by television (Los Angeles station KTLA, April 8–10, 1949)"; Robert Gerald Porfirio, "The Dark Age of Film Noir: A Study of the American *Film Noir* (1940–1960)," 2 vols. (Ph.D. diss., Yale University, 1979), 2: 105. As perhaps the earliest example of the "media spectacle" film later made familiar by *Nashville* (Robert Altman, 1975), *The Big Carnival* confirms McLuhan's thesis that earlier communication media become the content of their successors: the film explores the effects of print journalism and radio broadcasting that would become even more hyperbolic with television.

71. Fredric Jameson, *Postmodernism, or the Cultural Logic of Late Capitalism* (Durham, N.C.: Duke University Press, 1991), 280–281.

72. Lefebvre, *Production of Space*, 93.

73. For a comprehensive collection of writings on melodrama see Marcia Landy, ed., *Imitations of Life: A Reader on Film and Television Melodrama* (Detroit: Wayne State University Press, 1991).

74. Laura Mulvey, "Pandora: Topographies of the Mask and Curiosity," in *Sexuality and Space*, ed. Beatriz Colomina (New York: Princeton Architectural Press, 1992), 60.

75. Victor Burgin, *In/Different Spaces: Place and Memory and Visual Culture* (Berkeley: University of California Press, 1996), 157.

76. See Lynn Spigel, *Welcome to the Dreamhouse: Popular Media and Postwar Suburbs* (Durham and London: Duke University Press, 2001).

77. For examples of the critique of suburbia see A. C. Spectorsky, *The Exurbanites* (Philadelphia: J. B. Lippincott, 1955); John Keats, *The Crack in the Picture Window* (Boston: Houghton Mifflin, 1957); David Riesman, "The Suburban Dislocation" (1957) and "Flight and Search in the New Suburbs" (1959,) in *Abundance for What? And Other Essays* (Garden City, N.Y.: Doubleday, 1964), 226–269.

78. Apart from an early appreciation by Martin Scorsese, Irving Lerner's career as a director of films noir has received little attention. Trained as an anthropologist in the Columbia University class of 1929, he came to cinema in the 1930s after assisting his mentor, Ruth Benedict, on the production of an ethnographic documentary about a Bahamian dance troupe. He was a founding member in 1930 of the Workers Film and Photo League; worked with Paul Strand, Henri Cartier-Bresson, and Joris Ivens on political documentaries about labor strikes; and later became an assistant to Ralph Steiner. In 1938 Lerner accompanied Fritz Lang to

Hollywood and wrote the songs and script for his musical *You and Me* (1938). From 1941 to 1945 he worked for the Office of War Information, producing civilian propaganda films with Frank Capra screenwriter Robert Riskin and Maya Deren's husband, Alexander Hamid. These films were designed "to prove that we were not a land of gangsters who chewed gum, who were drinking cola, and would kill other gangsters." Autobiographical sketch by Irving Lerner, 3, Irving Lerner Papers, Special Collections, UCLA Research Library, box 11, file 13. By 1939 Lerner had become established as a leading editor of documentary films. He directed a 1941 documentary for the Philadelphia Housing Authority, written by Muriel Rukeyser (*A Place to Live*), befriended Sergei Eisenstein, and collaborated in 1947 with Bertolt Brecht and Joseph Losey on a screen treatment for *Galileo*. Despite this roster of distinguished collaborators and the good notices received by *Murder by Contract*, Lerner never became a fixture of Hollywood. As he notes in his unpublished autobiography, "I did not follow the Hollywood game, and did not move in the circle one had to be in . . . I was always an outsider, on the extreme outer edge . . . Indeed I could have made for sure many more films than I produced, in fact, but surely not the way I liked to make [them]"; ibid., 7. For additional information on Lerner see William Alexander, *Film on the Left: American Documentary Film from 1931 to 1942* (Princeton: Princeton University Press, 1981), 13.

79. See Edith Wyschogrod, *Spirit in Ashes: Hegel, Heidegger, and Man-Made Mass Death* (New Haven: Yale University Press, 1985).

80. "The Atomic Bomb and the Future City," *American City*, August 1946, 5.

81. See Paul Boyer, *By the Bomb's Early Light: American Thought and Culture at the Dawn of the Atomic Age* (New York: Pantheon, 1985), esp. chap. 26; and Spencer Weart, *Nuclear Fear: A History of Images* (Cambridge, Mass.: Harvard University Press, 1988), chap. 7, for discussions of civil defense measures in the 1950s. For more recent assessments see Laura McEnaney, *Civil Defense Begins at Home: Militarization Meets Everyday Life in the Fifties* (Princeton: Princeton University Press, 2000); and Andrew D. Grossman, *Neither Dead nor Red: Civilian Defense and American Political Development during the Early Cold War* (New York: Routledge, 2001).

82. Howard Earl, "Dispersal Is Bridge to Survival in Present Civil Defense Approach," *Western City*, May 1955, 33.

83. Jacob Marshak, Edward Teller, and Lawrence R. Klein, "Dispersal of Cities and Industries," *Bulletin of Atomic Scientists* 1, no. 9 (April 15, 1946): 13.

84. Ernest Oppenheimer, "The Challenge of Our Time," *Bulletin of Atomic Scientists* 3, no. 12 (1947): 372.

85. Tracy Augur, "The Dispersal of Cities as a Defense Measure," *Journal of the American Institute of Planners* 14 (summer 1948): 30.

86. Paul Windels, "How Should Our Cities Grow?" *Journal of the American Institute of Architects* 14 (November 1950): 225.

87. Ludwig Hilberseimer, "Cities and Defense" (1945), in Richard Pommer, David Spaeth, and Kevin Harrington, *In the Shadow of Mies: Ludwig Hilberseimer, Architect, Educator, and Urban Planner* (New York: Art Institute of Chicago and Rizzoli International Publications, 1988), 93. See also Ludwig Hilberseimer, *The*

New Regional Pattern (Chicago: Paul Theobald, 1949) and *The Nature of Cities* (Chicago: Paul Theobald, 1955).

88. Albert Mayer, "A New-Town Program," *Journal of the American Institute of Architects* 15 (January 1951): 8. For a discussion of Mayer's career as an architect of the Fort Greene Houses and Manhattan House projects see Robert A. M. Stern, Thomas Mellins, and David Fishman, *New York 1960* (New York: Monacelli, 1960), esp. 901, 840.

89. Marshak, "Dispersal of Cities and Industries," 14.

90. Augur, "Dispersal of Cities as Defense Measure," 32.

91. Wiener's proposal is discussed in "How U.S. Cities Can Prepare for Atomic War," *Life*, December 18, 1950, 77, 79.

92. Dale O. Smith, "Evacuation: The Wall of the Modern City," *Air Force Magazine*, February 1955, quoted in Earl, "Dispersal Is the Bridge to Survival," 33. Paul Virilio, "The Overexposed City," trans. Astrid Hustvedt, *Zone* 1–2, 14–31. See also James D. Tracy, ed., *City Walls: The Urban Enceinte in Global Perspective* (Cambridge: Cambridge University Press, 2001).

93. Mark Osteen, "The Big Secret: Film Noir and Nuclear Fear," *Journal of Popular Film and Television* 22 (summer 1994): 80. For an overview of the genre of the nuclear film see Jerome F. Shapiro, *Atomic Bomb Cinema: The Apocalyptic Imagination on Film* (New York: Routledge, 2001).

94. Al Horwits (director of publicity, Columbia Studios), Synopsis of *City of Fear*, June 18, 1958, 1, Script Collection, Margaret Herrick Library of the Academy of Motion Picture Arts and Sciences. The pressbook for the film suggests the strong cultural cachet of radioactivity: "'City of Fear' offers Showmanship. Excitement for Millions! A Strong Title! Grand New Star Talent! A Desperate Manhunt! A Terrified Community! 72 Suspenseful Hours! A Package of Panic! and, of course, RADIOACTIVITY!" Among its suggestions for promoting the film, it proposes that theater owners borrow a Geiger counter to utilize in their own "treasure-type hunt" and that they "simulate radioactivity with staccato taps over p.a. system."

95. *City of Fear* screenplay, March 14, 1958, 15, Irving Lerner Collection, Special Collections, UCLA Research Library.

96. Jacques Derrida, *Dissemination*, trans. Barbara Johnson (Chicago: University of Chicago Press, 1981), 95–116.

97. The best discussion of the technical and industrial preconditions of film noir remains Paul Kerr, "Out of What Past? Notes on the B Film Noir," *Screen Education* 32–33 (autumn–winter 1979–1980): 45–65.

98. For discussions of *City of Fear* in relation to the B movie see Irving Lerner, "Breaking Down the Conventional Barriers," *Films and Filming*, April 1961, 18–19; and Arthur Knight, "Sleeping Beauties," *Saturday Review of Literature*, January 3, 1959.

99. Augur, "Dispersal of Cities as Defense Measure," 35.

100. Treatments of urban renewal are found in Martin Anderson, *The Federal Bulldozer: A Critical Analysis of Urban Renewal, 1949–1962* (Cambridge, Mass.: MIT

Press, 1964); and Robert Beauregard, *Voices of Decline: The Postwar Fate of U.S. Cities* (Cambridge, Mass.: Basil Blackwell, 1993).

101. Rosamond G. Roberts, *3000 Families Move to Make Way for Stuyvesant Town: A Story of Tenant Relocation Bureau, Inc.* (New York: James Felt and Company/Tenant Relocation Bureau, 1947), 15.

102. Georges Bataille, "Concerning the Accounts Given by the Residents of Hiroshima" (1947), trans. Alan Keenan, *American Imago* 48, no. 4 (1991): 497–514. This is a translation of the essay "A propos de récit d'habitants d'Hiroshima," which appears in Bataille's *Oeuvres complètes*, vol. 2 (Paris: Gallimard, 1988), 172–187.

103. See Frank Krutnik, *In a Lonely Street: Film Noir, Genre, and Masculinity* (London: Routledge, 1991).

104. Jack Moffitt, review of *City of Fear, Variety*, November 16, 1959.

105. Autobiographical sketch by Irving Lerner, 7, box 11, file 13, Irving Lerner Papers, Department of Special Collections, UCLA Young Research Library.

106. Weart, *Nuclear Fear*, 130.

107. Reyner Banham, *Los Angeles: The Architecture of Four Ecologies* (London: Penguin, 1971), 172.

INDEX